BREAK O UT !

Books By James Schevill

Poetry
  Tensions
  The American Fantasies
  The Right To Greet
  Selected Poems: 1945-1959
  Private Dooms and Public Destinations: Poems 1945-1962
  The Stalingrad Elegies
  Violence and Glory: Poems 1962-1968
  The Buddhist Car and Other Characters

Biography and Criticism
  Sherwood Anderson: His Life and Work
  The Roaring Market and The Silent Tomb
  Breakout! In Search of New Theatrical Environments

Plays
  High Sinners, Low Angels
  The Bloody Tenet
  Voices of Mass and Capital A
  The Black President and Other Plays
  Lovecraft's Follies

Translation
  The Cid (a translation of Corneille's *Le Cid*)

BREAK OUT!

in search of New Theatrical Environments

written and edited by JAMES SCHEVILL

THE **SWALLOW PRESS** INC.

CHICAGO

First Edition

Published by
The Swallow Press Incorporated
1139 South Wabash Avenue
Chicago, Illinois 60605

This book is printed on 100% recycled paper

ISBN (paperbound edition) 0-8040-0640-7
ISBN (clothbound edition) 0-8040-0574-5
LIBRARY OF CONGRESS CATALOG CARD NUMBER 77-189192

Note: Requests for permission to reprint any of the previously published articles or to perform any of the plays included in this book should be referred to the authors, their publishers, or agents as indicated in the Acknowledgements at the end of the book.

If American theatre is to endure, it must search for new visions and spaces, new audiences, and a new unity of the arts and sciences. This book is dedicated to that search.

Contents

Illustrations

INTRODUCTION

In Hesse's novel, *Steppenwolf*, the protagonist, Harry Haller, writes of an encounter in an alley with a man carrying a signboard. The signboard reads:

ANARCHIST EVENING ENTERTAINMENT

MAGIC THEATRE

ENTRANCE NOT FOR EVERYONE

The Magic Theatre of the mind, of the imagination, is the first vision that enchants us. It presents us with an infinite variety of characters, situations, and places with no technical hindrances. No real theatre can surpass these inner visions. No real theatre can afford to forget them. The Magic Theatre measures our visions against the restrictions and confinements of our everyday lives. It compels us to see the exciting possibility of theatre in different spaces, different environments, rather than theatre confined by conventional demands.

Theatre to me is the physical word, the ability to center the word in a physical context, to root the word, the concept, in astonishing visual, musical, and physical actions. Without the action of language, theatre becomes, mime and dance. With a language that springs mainly from literary expression, theatre becomes separated from its legendary qualities of communion. Those who call for a theatre that is anti-language, or separated from language, do not understand the physical nature of language.

When Artaud writes, "It is essential to put an end to the subju-

xiii

gation of the theatre to the text, and to recover the notion of a kind of unique language half-way between gesture and thought," what does he mean? Certainly, one can agree with the first part of his statement. A theatre that enthrones language to the exclusion of other sensibilities suffers from the characteristic American problem of overspecialized personality. But Artaud's "unique language half-way between gesture and thought" remains a mystery, the search for the physical word in which modern theatre is involved.

If playwright, designer, composer, and director are involved in the search for the physical word, what about their relationship to the audience? Too much time is wasted in tiresome discussions of the stage that we need—flexible, proscenium, round, open. Partisanship for a particular kind of stage is usually beside the point. The important principle is the flexible, intimate relationship between audience and actors. Theatre today must be intimate so that the most subtle as well as the broadest effects can be used. Otherwise theatre cannot hope to compete with films. The film audience is the most powerful today; if we do not begin with that premise we do theatre an injustice.

The luxurious power of the motion picture industry shines from a full-page advertisement in the *New York Times* called, "THE BIG SQUEEZE":

> . . . The movies get you out of yourself, out of your house, away from all the many, the little, the pressing things that apply The Big Squeeze.
>
> You sit in the dark. In the wide dark. In the wide cool dark. You look—and you relax. You're in a different world. The world, as you once saw it, is re-born. . . .
>
> Suddenly you realize you've escaped the neighborhood theatre. You're living again. You're in love with your wife—as you always were, but you forgot. You get home and the kids are asleep. The house is quiet. Something you saw in the movie queen, you realize, is what you once saw in your wife—and now see again. The day hasn't been so bad after all. THE BIG SQUEEZE IS GONE!

All we need to do for audiences is to go into the wide, cool dark of entertainment. But what happens after we leave the wide, cool dark? The Big Squeeze again. The term entertainment can be highly frustrating unless we understand its real meaning.

This collection of creative and critical pieces is a record of my search over a period of many years for new theatrical visions and spaces. I have tried to put this book together with a particular suspicion of two over-used words, environment and anthology. Environment I take to be, as simply as possible, the space, the conditions, and surroundings in which we live and work. In theatre, for my purposes, I would like to define environment as the space in which we live and act out the realities and fantasies of our beings. My aim is to investigate the breakout from conventional theatres of entertainment, particularly from the proscenium arch (although I believe fine proscenium arch productions are still possible under certain circumstances described in this book). I am particularly interested in the escape from large, wealthy theatres into more intimate dramatic encounters indoors and outdoors. Not that these breakouts are new; only the social conditions are new. Fortunately, theatre is always breaking out of the conventions that seek to control it. The central, vital paradox of theatre is that it is both the most social and the most rebellious of the arts.

Anthology is a word that implies too often an expedient class-work opportunism for anthologist, reader, and publisher alike, an easy catch-all in which to simplify everything. I have tried to avoid the framework of a conventional anthology by presenting my selections in the context of actual dramatic practice, dialogue, and confrontation with the major theatrical questions of our time. (Obviously, in such a book as this, there are economic restrictions that prevent me from publishing certain material that I would have liked to include.) I hope this book will help to unify playwright, director, designer, composer, and audience rather than confine them in their familiar, specialized compartments. My own reflections and commentary are scattered deliberately throughout the text. Any text not identified by the author's name is mine.

J.S.

Visions of Theatre:
From Epidaurus to
City Streets

If theatre begins in visions, dreams, it becomes immediately clear how restricted we are if confined indoors. Something about the vitality of life in the streets, in the country, in the open, demands that we perform there. One of the most extraordinary experiences I have ever had was in the ancient Greek theatre at Epidaurus. Suddenly you remember Epidaurus was a center of healing, body and soul. Sitting high in the enormous theatre, looking out over the valley and jagged hills, it seems a magical paradox that the dry, hard, desert soil responds with such grace. Water in Greece has a blessed meaning. Mycenae, the fountainhead of myth, the legendary source of ancestral curses, is nearby. At Epidaurus healing and physical torment are forever linked in this haunted land where myth cannot die. No wonder it is a birthplace and still a searching place for Greek drama.

The sun is setting late in the evening as the large audience, some twelve thousand people, settles down. Sophocle's *Philoctetes* is the appropriate play to be performed. The summation of a long life of tragic vision, it is the story of the healing of a demonic wound. A snake, often a symbol to the Greeks of divine power, has bitten Philoctetes, and his wound will not heal. Exiled by his comrades because of the stench of his wound and his disturbing cries of agony, Philoctetes exists bitterly on a remote island. Here the action of the play takes place, where supreme isolation and torment must yield finally to social necessity and redemptive cure.

Originally Greek plays were performed at sunrise, Apollo as divine healer. In the 1960s I am waiting for a play to begin at sunset. Everything seems turned around, going into the dark. Yet this is a mythical place, still appropriate to the curses and cures of *Philoctetes.* Theatre here seems incredibly far away from the closed, indoor stages of my distant country.

Suddenly, far down the road toward the museum and the hotel, a disturbance takes place. People are standing up, peering. A strange procession is coming up the road, moving out of the growing shadows of the sinking sun. They seem to be emerging from time, out of history. They surge into view, marching proudly together, the company of the National Theatre in their costumes. Far more than the beginning of a play, this is a ceremony I will never forget: actors marching out of their legendary past into their ancient theatre of healing, their eternal present time. Into the theatre they march and the audience is on its feet, applauding, smiles of radiant welcome everywhere. This is what the theatre of vision has been and can be. Dionysius and Apollo still live no matter how their names and images have been altered by the invasions of conquering civilizations.

Jan Kott, the critic and director, presents a moving vision of the effect of dream on theatre in his short piece, "At Night":

> For the last two days one could feel the approaching storm. Even at night the air was stuffy. I was invited to the theatre. The stage was situated high up, in a narrow passage between the house and a wall. The street came down steeply, paved with smooth stones. I was seated below. High up, on the stage, three women were trying to persuade a young boy to do something. One of the women was very beautiful. The performance was in a language I did not know. I could not even remotely guess what language they were speaking. Then only the women were left on the stage, among them the beautiful one. Later there was a crowd of men, shouting and throwing their arms about. Everything ended with a love scene, gro-

tesque and obscene at first, then heartrendingly sad. From above, stones were thrown, slowly at first, then with violent speed, like an avalanche. The sidewalk on the right, along the wall, began to move. I could not understand how this was done. After all, the sidewalk and the house were real. The music was just percussion, very shrill, full of rising, broken syncopations.

Then the director appeared. He said that the first part of the performance was not important, but the second was an adaptation of *Doctor Faustus;* and this cannot be done in any other way, except by having the falling stones and the sidewalk moving alongside the wall, and the music of broken syncopations.

I was moved. It occurred to me that this was the true theatre I had always dreamed about; that once or twice before I had been to that theatre. But I could not remember what performance I had seen. Even when I woke up, I tried to recall for quite a while what the previous program of that theatre had been.

In Kott's dream, it is astonishing how the classical and the modern elements merge. His ideal theatre is outdoors, yet in the city. The sidewalk moves as in a Piscator belt, the music is percussive, syncopated, yet the play is *Doctor Faustus.* Perhaps more than we have recognized, theatre too is trapped between its natural, outdoor origins and its contemporary indoor functions. To clarify this confusion, it is worthwhile to look closely at the possibilities of theatre outdoors.

Let us begin with the Black Revolution. Black theatre is growing rapidly in two fundamental directions. Naturalistic theatre is still powerful in black drama because black communities and playwrights still feel a great need for confronting real characters in real situations. Their problems are too real and immediate for the ironic fantasies of isolation that characterize much white avant-garde theatre. Other black playwrights like LeRoi Jones and Ed Bullins, who have written naturalistically, now extend their work into more fantastic dimensions. In his *State Office Building Curse,* Bullins presents an angry ritualistic curse as an "OPEN HOUSE"

urban vision. The curse as magical reality, not a mere performance. Beware of black magic. Such a curse is inconceivable shut
away indoors. Here we are at some strange black Epidaurus again,
this time in the streets of Harlem, waiting to be healed:

State Office Building Curse:
A Scenario to Ultimate Action

Site of the New York State Office Building at 125th Street
and Seventh Avenue in Harlem.

First day of public opening—OPEN HOUSE.

Out front, on the sidewalks: politicians, American flags,
Harlem crowds, Black National flags, numerous cops and
plainclothesmen.

Speechmaking by Rockefeller, Lindsay, Javits, Chisholm,
Rangle and Sutton. Maybe Powell.

Ribbon cutting. Crowds pour into building for look-see.
Black crowds to see the false marble madness. Brothers in
Afros and clean heads and just heads. Sisters with the brothers. Children. Some older Black people, unattached to the
artificial integration political machine.

Black folks checking out the cement tomb, Black folks on
pig-guided tours, wandering alone around the tunnels and
caves of the twentieth-century crypt, examining the files, getting lost in the basement, in the rest rooms.

Closing. All out. Black people ushered out by guards and
cops. American flags lowered as night sets on Harlem.

Later: hours later. Way into the black night. Exterior of the
State Office Building. Quiet Seventh Avenue at that hour.
Almost deserted 125th Street at 3 A.M.

Explosion rips the whole State Office Building apart. Fire.
Torn-out windows. Total destruction through explosives.

Fire engines. TV cameramen. Photographers. Silent brothers and sisters standing on far side of the street looking know-
ingly at each other.

And the Black crowd senses the moment in Revolutionary
Black History and begins a festival to celebrate the emerging

Black nation of Harlem.
Blackness.

Lawrence Ferlinghetti's, *The Jig Is Up,* reveals another kind of outdoors vision. The bucolic atmosphere of a city park in the South turns into a comic, exultant vision of racial purgation. The rhythm is slow, quiet, nostalgic, gently suited to the setting—the death of a false, genteel tradition. If this were staged in a theatre, what would happen to the ritualistic effect of a formal promenade in a park and the strange, calm mission of the scavengers?

The Jig Is Up

The scene: a public park in Charlotte, North Carolina. A crowd of very well-dressed Whites is strolling about under the trees, very sedately, very calmly, arm in arm.

Suddenly they fall screaming to the ground and start to crawl around and roll in great heaps of autumn leaves, roaring like animals.

Now a big empty garbage truck appears and a strange exultant wailing rises from the people as they throw themselves in front of the truck. The Negro driver blows his horn but the wailing grows louder & wilder.

The Negro scavengers descend from the truck and proceed gently to throw all the people into big burlap bags, two in each bag. Some couples, wrongly paired, scream, break and run to other partners. Finally all the Whites are loaded into bags on the truck.

The scavengers climb to their places up front, light cigars, stretch, and relax. One stretches out on the hood, smoking, eyes closed.

In the back there is a great thrashing about in the burlap bags, and the strange exultant wailing continues. It reaches a climax and suddenly dies out. In the silence the thrashing ceases. The Negro on the hood takes out a harmonica and, eyes closed, begins softly to play "Swing Low, Sweet Chariot." After a long time he stops playing. The scavengers all continue smoking silently, eyes closed, motionless.

After a long time, the driver starts his motor up very quietly. He lets it idle very quietly. Then he guns it, and the truck roars off.

In the middle 1960's, when I was directing the Poetry Center and teaching drama and poetry in the writing program at San Francisco State College, I began to realize more and more the theatrical significance of what was happening in the streets. One talked about dramatic theory and practice in the classroom only to look up, startled, and watch that theory happen outside of your window. An example, one spontaneous action, the kind of action that happened throughout the country . . .

1967—The Marine Corps has come on campus to recruit again. After their last visit, when anti-war student groups surprised and besieged them with pickets and protests, they are prepared. . . . They send in four marines in full-dress uniforms, medals gleaming from spic and span jackets, hands encased in white gloves. Rigid, perfect postures, pride of the corps, racial equality and military justice represented by one Negro in dark glasses closely linked to his Marine pals . . . *We enforce equality! . . . Join us and be free! . . . Freedom is the discipline of formality! . . .*

Triumph of the Marines claiming their formal power over the territory . . . Students gaping out the windows, alive suddenly to their audience role . . . Where is the Public New-Sense, the rituals of release? . . . Here they come . . . Here *It* comes . . .

It is a monstrous head of poodle hair eliminating a forehead, almost covering fervent, deep-set animal eyes. . . . *It* is dressed in an immensely over-sized mock uniform topped with motorcycle crash helmet. . . . The mock uniform has fantastic purple-striped pants, golden jacket with enormous sergeant stripes decorated with tinsel stars, high priest-like collar covered with skull and bones insignia, paper medals cut out of cartoons covering the chest down to gut level . . . .

It begins to recruit, wailing, chanting, mumbling: "Fellow

id-i-ots ... En-lissst in sal-vaaa-tion war! ... Grrrrrowwwl
with meee for freeeeeee-dumb! ... Kill Kong! Kill Kong! ...
Grab your frontier gun! Be your own Kit, Kit, Kitty Carson!
... Learn how to bloooow up yellow, pink, black peeeepuls in
ten eeeeasy lessons ... Sound out the Ala-mo Hello, the Ala-
mo Hellll-low ... LBJaybird says Vietnumb is just an Ala-
mow Hello-low ... Join your Tex-ass Rangers ... Get down
in the gritty of the nitty-gritty ... Groooove with ol' Charlie
Cong ... Prove your right to a tweested man-hood by volun-
teering for your nearest Air Delivery ... Play tick-tack-toe
with hell-i-cop-ter clouds ... Throw gren-ade toys with gleee-
ful fingerings ... Learn how to fuck native girls in luscious
jungle bushes ... Get your free, shit-proof pants ... *Kill
Kong! ... Kill Kong! ... Kill Kong! ...*"
    End of inside class ... Beginning of outside class ... *It*
wails on, joined soon by other fantastic mock-uniforms confronting the immobile formalists ... Dramatic warfare over
the public territory ...

Much of this spontaneous activity during the 1960's was influenced by such companies as The San Francisco Mime Troupe, The
Bread and Puppet Theatre, and El Teatro Campesino. These three
groups, in particular, established national reputations for their
performances in the streets, in parks, and in all kinds of buildings
from cafeterias to gymnasiums. The following discussion between
the founding heads of the three theatres, R. G. Davis, Peter Schumann, and Luis Valdez, took place at San Francisco State College
in September, 1968. The moderator of the discussion was Juris
Svendsen, the actor, teacher, and critic.

from A Panel Discussion

    R. G. DAVIS: What is the base of this Radical Theatre Festi-
val? It seems to me when you establish one, you can establish two
and then you can get three. One, two, three Vietnams. One, two,
three, many radical theatres, hopefully. The life of one theatre is
really dependent on the life of other theatres.
    Harold Clurman once said that the Group Theatre (probably the

most significant theatre in the U. S. for many, many years) died because they were the only group around. They were 20 people involved in radical or political theatre, but they had nowhere to go, no one to talk to, and they died.

Well, it's been my conception of the life of the Mime Troupe, as well as the life of everybody else, that the only way we can survive is to support other people. That is, we become part of the movement and the movement becomes a part of us—but we also support the other radical theatres.

A long time ago I suggested that anybody who left the Mime Troupe should work with the other radical theatres and, in the same way, anybody who leaves the other radical theatres, because of personality problems, or tired or such, should come work with us, so there's an interchange and not the competition that goes, "Well, we don't like your work because so and so said. . . ." We have differences about what we do, but I don't think we have any differences about what we want to see happen: the personalities are radical, the activity is radical, and the content is radical. I think we are all in one way or another opposed to the plastic world of the U. S., the whole middle class monstrosity.

By bringing these three groups together, we establish the existence of a movement, we make a statement, a kind of camaraderie as well as a kind of conversation. But we should not be like superduper friends who do not see differences and do not criticize each other in some very appropriate ways.

When the Mime Troupe shows "Patelin" for instance, we do a "cranky" which we have taken lock, stock, and barrel—not the design, but the basic idea—from Peter Schumann's theater. And I think the Teatro Campesino's "actos" have come from a knowledge of commedia, in part.

That kind of exchange is very beautiful. When the Mime Troupe gets into a situation where we need to do something very quick and agitational, we certainly can do it in an "acto" style.

I don't think you will find the images Peter Schumann brings to the theatre anyplace in the U. S. What he brings is Brechtian, very European, medieval images, very strong, beautiful, sculptured images. Nobody makes masks for the stage as well as he does, very strong, very powerful; he knows what to do with the face.

But he's a sculptor, not necessarily a director. After last night's performance, he said it was an anti-show; the Mime Troupe does a show-show. We do trip, trip, trip, and they do an anti-show. In other words, he doesn't perform at all. You can do that if you are Peter Schumann. If you are not Peter Schumann, you have to learn how.

No matter what you do in any one of the three companies, you have to find out who you are. There's no bullshit about it. You cannot get up on stage and perform commedia in a real way unless you know who you are first. You cannot get up in Teatro and play Mexican-American farmworker: either you are or you aren't. It's obvious to everyone. Either you are for the Chicano operation or for La Raza or whatever, and you know it—or it shows. And so too with Bread and Puppet—you can see that the people who are not there are not there.

Let's say I decided to buy a puppet show from Mr. Schumann. I give him $200, that means $50 a week for his family for a month. We do it. We buy the whole image. Could we do it? Could the Mime Troupe do it? I think we could, but we'd have to learn to do exactly as he's done: present people on the stage in a very real out-front way. And they must believe in it or they can't do it. The technique involves a philosophical-psychological examination of the political and emotional content of what's going on; an intimate emotional response; Stanislavsky is not enough.

The technique of the radical theatre is in your commitment and your understanding of the political nature of reality. With Schumann, I see very heavy pacifist, very religious-mystical stuff. Some of it I don't agree with. I don't believe I'm a pacifist anymore. I don't know if I ever was. Last night's performance [of *Reiteration*—which Schumann describes as "a longish production based on *A Man Says Good-bye To His Mother*"] which is a street play, was not pacifist. It was much stronger, but I don't know if Schumann believes in the Viet Cong defense of their own country as an absolute necessity.

I think where we'd have to deal, sometime, is do you believe war is bad per se? Or do you understand that national liberation wars are absolutely necessary—that revolutions in countries dominated by American imperialism are the only way to get free of American imperialism? Pacifism does not work in Vietnam, it's been tried by the Buddhists, and it's a wonderful thing, but it doesn't stop American bombers, and it doesn't stop American guns, and it doesn't stop American defoliation. The Vietnamese have no way of talking to the American G.I. or the American government and saying: "Look, it's our country, we're good people, why don't you leave us alone?" They haven't, they won't, and they are not going to.

Schumann's beautiful, strong images, his very deep commitment, seem a religious commitment—which is something I don't have and Mime Troupe people do not tangibly know of—or know of but haven't faced. We talk about television, and rock bands and the plastic world—we deal with it. We're middle class people, Mime Troupe middle class people. We have to get it out of our systems, but it's very hard because we've all lived with it. Schumann brings just a whole different beautiful thing. The time is much different. People don't like to go through that time. I'm committed to that time because I know something about him and about the people. I like that torture, if it's torture. Bread and Puppet's time space is very different, it's sculptured time; quite different from commercial theater, from the Mime Troupe or Teatro or most people's theater.

In Teatro Campesino, there's a social time difference—very immediate, very now, emotional Mexican-American time. The songs are rapid. The language rapid. Closer to the American disease, which is speed, speed, speed, speed (and will kill and does.) But we're in it and I don't think you can avoid it when you deal with American stuff.

Americans are so fucking hip. Middle class kids understand everything quick, but nothing below that. The hip generation (and I'm part of it), everybody understands, like, Dig that! Absolutely! Yeah! But ask them about what's really going on underneath and they have no knowledge. Everybody's so freaking television hip, so fast, that they're impatient with Schumann's time, which is absolutely necessary. Because sometime or other, you have to sit down and say where you are. And I don't mean Zen, and I don't mean Buddhism, and I don't necessarily mean religion. Maybe religion is the only place where you can stop and think, but sooner or later everybody has to do that.

Teatro's time is more like our time, and Luis is more theatrical than sculptural. Luis himself, as a performer, is fantastic. You watch him closely, he's really a great mime and that's why we're going to offer him a job, get him to give up this other stuff!!

JURIS SVENDSEN: Let me ask Luis Valdez to speak of both troupes.

LUIS VALDEZ: A starting point, perhaps. Four years ago I was in San Jose shortly after my first play was produced—*The Shrunken Head of Pancho Villa*. I walked out in the street and there was the San Francisco Mime Troupe. I'd been searching for something with the play, with my whole life as a Chicano, farmworker, city boy also, and never caught up with it. I couldn't find it in academic theatre. Professional theatre was just totally out of range because you can't find that in the Valley or in the colleges. I knew it was there, but I'd never found it. So I walked out into that street that afternoon and there was the S. F. Mime Troupe and it was fantastic: the light, the color, the sound.

The sound is very important. He talked about our speed. I think the most important thing is noise, our noise; we like to make noise. That's because this society doesn't allow Mexicans to make noise. We're supposed to get off the streets, and stay at *la cantina* and keep our mouths shut. You know, it's not like Mexico; you don't have guys hawking tacos and tamales and even pepsi cola on the corners. You don't do that, not in this country. There are laws, there are streets, there are sidewalks. SHUT UP, learn English. You can't serenade or they'll come and bust you. You can't come out with a *corrida*. You can't go "Ay, yai, yai, YAI!" You can't.

So that's what our theatre is doing. There are no "Ay, yai, yai's" in academic theatre. I ran into a few Mexicans—Tennessee Williams' racist stereotypes; Eugene O'Neill is worse, you know. There ain't anybody, nobody. I was looking for a theatre that expressed something. And what came the closest to my feeling was commedia, and that was the Mime Troupe.

So I came to San Francisco and joined the Mime Troupe. There was obviously something happening, a fantastic difference from all that bullshit in the academic theatre about scenery and lighting. You have to be surrounded by a blockhouse to do conventional theatre, that little thing in space, to say your lines, if it won't work out right. And it doesn't get across the seats to the audience anyway. Who responds to Tennessee Williams or Arthur Miller picking his liver apart? You can't respond to that shit. The Mime Troupe is outside, in the park. They're out, they're alive. They draw your attention in spite of all those urban distractions—pedestrians, traffic, etc. They say "Fuck the distractions, I've got something to say and you pay attention to it because it's said well."

I sometimes think the best propaganda comes through and is merged with the best art. In the theatre, art is communication and propaganda; but organizing and politics and teaching are nothing but that, communication. So the more artful you are, not arty, artful, the more propagandistic you are.

I think the Mime Troupe is trying to reach a different group than we're trying to reach. They have a much more sophisticated approach. They intellectualize and sometimes it goes over the heads of people. As Ron [Davis] was saying, the hip people say, "Yeah, we understand." But they don't really. So the question is how to really communicate these ideas. Our bag in Teatro isn't nearly as sophisticated. We stick to one, two, three, that equals six.

Bread and Puppet: that too, is a cultural shock. It works with reality on two levels, neither of which is even vaguely like the "realistic" theatre. I first saw them at the Newport Folk Festival. The puppets to begin with—those huge, fantastic puppets. The production was *Chicken Little*. Peter took theatrical realism and blew it apart and said, "People have different visions; people are something else; people can be fifty feet high." There are other forces working in the universe besides this realistic shit. Life goes beyond that; it's much more mystical; it's much more magical; it's more acid-like. And these huge figures come in at the beginning and the Mother Earth figure started creating all these creatures; they come out from under her skirt. She laid an egg and out came a creature with a bill and a funny looking face. All different forms of creation. Beautiful image. Yes, and the kid, six years old, I think, with a papier maché head. He was a cop. A cop running around with a club hitting everybody. Three feet high, a cop. What really got to me in *A Man Says Goodbye To His Mother* was the use of the airplane and the little paper house. Again, that took the realistic perspective and blew it all to hell. From the infinite to the infinitesimal, you see. It was a little wooden airplane, but it got the point across so strongly because the little kid that plays becomes the pilot that's dropping all those bombs. And there's tremendous truth in that.

The Mime troupe does it by using the body in beautiful contortions. That's mime: body movement, a tremendous sense of timing. They fill the stage with action and human forms in constant motion—or frozen, when it's necessary.

I don't think they know what the fuck they're doing in academic theatre or in professional theatre, really. And that's because nobody knows what the fuck they're doing in this country.

All of a sudden, you see with clarity, and you say, you don't need all that shit! You don't need a hundred thousand dollars to start a theatre group. You can do it with nothing, nothing. Do a play about naked people. That's it. The theatre is in you. It's your soul, it's your heart, it's the constant reaffirmation of what life is all about.

The society strays away from all this. It seems to reach peaks. Where the society is expressive of life, it really bustles. I suppose capitalism was expressive of the utmost of life at one historical point. It's no longer that way. Now perhaps socialism can be the most expressive form of what life is all about. And after that it will be some other *ism,* perhaps. I don't know, man will invent a name. There are dead things in this society. They're dying all around us all the time. Shells from the past, bits and pieces that just cling.

Some people still live in 1920. They still think Eugene O'Neill's *Emperor Jones* is a really fantastic play. But it isn't, it's a racist play.

I can't name plays about Mexicans, because there aren't any. But we dig what the Bread and Puppet Theatre is doing. We dig what the Mime Troupe is doing. In our own work, we're utilizing everything that theatre has given us, everything we've got. We are working with a certain reality, but it's always tempered by a need to say something. The Mime Troupe has a need to say something, and this shapes what they do. And there's obviously something that matters very much to the Bread and Puppet Theatre; and this, ultimately, shapes what they do.

That's the most important thing. You've got to have something to say or get off the fucking stage.

SVENDSEN: How about you Peter? If you could comment on how you see the other groups, then we could go on to the next thing: how you want to be seen and what you want to do.

PETER SCHUMANN: The best way for me to start talking about the Mime Troupe or Campesino is by responding to the things they've said or contrasting what we do to the Mime Troupe or Campesino.

What Ronny said is true: our play is an anti-play, a performance which is not really a performance. The Mime Troupe and Campesino have a lot of theatricality, and this is their work. In that is their message, and in that is their love. With us, it is certainly not so. The play usually grows out of a workshop: after working with people for a time you get to the point where you put it together and you put it in front of people. Like our play *Reiteration* was a response to a task; it is based on a play we were asked to do on a street corner in East Harlem. They needed this play within two days. We didn't have anything. We did a rehearsal and there happened to be this little airplane and a baby doll in the studio, and I think that is how the play came together. It was very accidental and it was also because of the task: we were forced to do something in two days that could be done with four players on the street corner and could be carried very easily, and they didn't have money for it either.

But, then, for us that's the whole difference. We don't have this big interest in theatre, like Ronny has and like Luis has. Most of the people in the company are not actors or mimes. Most come for political reasons. We actually have a hard time with actors, when we do get actors into plays.

But it's valid for an actor to learn these things to a degree. What Ronny calls a-theatrical or anti-theatrical stuff, like standing on stage and trying to get beyond what you act. To try to stay there and say something like you would to Uncle Joe.

What do I feel unifies different theatres like ours? (By the way, I don't particularly like the term radical theatre. I feel it's a quantitative term which doesn't apply to us, too much.) But we all feel theatre has to have something as simple as a purpose, you see. It shouldn't just be because somebody likes to do it, or because they were sent to acting school. Compare this with a painter who feels he doesn't have to sit and paint what he wants, but paints for the purpose of bringing it somewhere. And this means he also decides where to carry it and whom he shows it to. This is what the three companies here are very much concerned with. And we want our show to serve that simple purpose: to speak about an issue to somebody, to an audience.

DAVIS: Why do you talk about "story"? You once said you didn't like *L'Amant Militaire* because it drove message in a heavy-handed way and you like stories laid out, like *Rinaldini*—that's an example of the "cranky" you've done which is a story. It's different from a play.

SCHUMANN: Yeah, that's right.

SVENDSEN: Why do you call it story?

SCHUMANN: Because it is nothing but that.

DAVIS: Where does it go? What do we do with it?

SCHUMANN: That's a good question. I don't know.

SVENDSEN: How do you see your way of bringing the story across that is different from the Mime Troupe's way?

SCHUMANN: The Mime Troupe obviously has the stress on

play. It brings the story across by doing a lot of things with it. And we do it the other way around: take everything out and leave just this little bit which is the story.

DAVIS: Do you think this story communicates enough without the play?

SCHUMANN: Yes, I guess so. But, that's our limitation. We are just not enough of the theatre to feel we could do more than the story itself and a few lines. In *Reiteration,* at first we had other lines in, like we had her spilling the soup, and the airplane bombing the soup, and stuff like that. The play had a little too much sidetrack. And we had to cut it out. It didn't work any more; it was getting phony, it was getting picturesque. All the work was constantly trying to get away from the story. So we threw it all out again and ended with just these particular lines.

DAVIS: Do you think you could come in with another group and teach them to do that play?

SCHUMANN: Yes. We did it just a little while ago with high school kids. We gave the play to them and just gave them instructions and they directed it. They made a funny play. But it was beautiful. The kids really wanted to say this thing. They played it for their fellow students. The narrator was a girl and she was very emotional on every line: "AND THE MAN NEEDED A GUN" she said, "AND HE NEEDED A GAS MASK." But it was terrific.

SVENDSEN: I think Ronny is pressing about the story to find out if it is a limitation or an end result. I think the question comes from the situation—in the theatre particularly—of not knowing what stories to tell. Going further: when you don't know what stories to tell, you also don't know what to do outside of the theatre.

SCHUMANN: That's true. I think the trouble with legitimate theatre or academic theatre and so on, is that they don't have a story. Basically that's it. If you look at a good American puppet show, with all its fancy puppets and all that, there's only one thing missing. It has nothing to tell. The puppets do all kinds of tricky things, but there's no story that's worth telling. And most of the modern theatre I have seen doesn't have a story, a legend, a story.

You know, that's what makes a picture good, it makes a piece of music good. The purpose, the fullness of the story, the thing that tells it to the other guy. You call it fable. The history of our country consists of digging old fables out, dressing them up again. Most of the stories in the world usually are very similar. There's a constant flow of a few basic stories going through the drama departments at all times. But there's always something new coming into these old stories.

VALDEZ: Are you consciously trying for an intellectual or an emotional response in *Reiteration*?

SCHUMANN: It would be unfair of me to answer that because we didn't think that way. We didn't think, "What do we want to achieve in this story?"—except at first when we wanted to be on an East Harlem street corner and say to these mothers, some of whom we knew had received that little letter: "Here. Hear this. Here's your letter." That was the reality of this play. The letter is the first sign you get when they kill your son. Our message was to put that letter into a context that was well-known to them, to say it in a way which they probably were not used to themselves.

SVENDSEN: I was particularly impressed with your way of doing theatre with silence. Would you comment on the Teatro Campesino and its noise, particularly in respect to your kind of silence, your kind of time—and could you also comment on the social aspects of that?

SCHUMANN: I actually agree 100% with what both Ronny and Luis said about noise. They cannot drop out of this noise that is already here, in this civilization and in our cities. Instead of deserting it, we should use it, do something with it; respond to it by making more noise or by loving it and finding that in it which is pure noise.

DAVIS: But we're talking about a different noise. Luis is talking about *gritos,* which is a human noise; you're talking about a band, man-made instruments making noise. We're talking about singing songs. That's different from machinery or air things. It's become mechanical and electronic. And I think that the unity of that is human sound, human-created sound, guitar sound.

SCHUMANN: But the response, that is the same thing still. Because the guy who wants to talk with all this noise has to scream. In the street, if you want to be heard, you have to use this loud shouting.

VALDEZ: Well, I think your images scream. They don't make any noise, but they scream, sometimes.

SCHUMANN: No, I wanted to say about this . . . take rock and roll, isn't that . . .

SVENDSEN: That's noise. . . .

SCHUMANN: That's noise.

DAVIS: Don't put it down or we'll get wiped out . . .

SVENDSEN: Ah, but why do you go to silence?

SCHUMANN: I don't know. Probably partly because . . . I'm a sculptor and it's just my personal gear to do it that way. But I also feel this is a great means to work with—to not use noise. Also it's not quite fair to judge all our things by that criticism because we do have very jumpy and loud and noisy stuff.

DAVIS: But your timing is much different than ours.

SVENDSEN: In a way, you're sculptural to the extent that your means are sculptural—people and objects. But your method is musical, and that then becomes still more contradictory. Why do you use silence when you're a musician as well? I suspect that you are an alchemist and a magician, not a revolutionary; a Paracelsus. So why the silence too when your method is musical, baroque?

SCHUMANN: That's true. The first play is a piece of baroque music, a concerto. Its message is partly to be a piece of music like that, if you would just listen to it and not look at it. I guess you would get as much of the message as when you look at it. Because it is a musical composition with these few musical means, a tiny little tune; the silences and a few lines.

DAVIS: One problem about your stuff when it goes into the theatre and commercial critics look at it is that they can't understand it because their eyes and their ears are in tune to bang, bang, bang. And they can't stop. Even the guys from the *Village Voice*.

The complaint is that your time is too long. Your time is too long indoors, because they are used to superficial time. It should be imperative that your shows not be done in a theatre, because it's anti-theatre. It's sort of hard to be anti-theatre in a theatre. It becomes sort of pretentious, avant-garde—and you're not avant-garde. In a gym, like last night, it seemed to be appropriate. It was essential that it be there. You create the space. Time can be allowed to take its course, if the surroundings will allow that. Like, if there's a building behind you that's been up for two hundred years, it's evident that you can take a little time. But if the building was just put up yesterday, and it's got pre-fabricated plastic all over it, you've got to speed up.

SVENDSEN: In what social space do you think you should be performing ideally?

SCHUMANN: In gyms. I agree.

SVENDSEN: You admit everything and deny nothing, right? Silence, silence is big.

SCHUMANN: The gym is a good spot. We don't really like to play in theatres. For one thing, I really feel a theatre is a misconstruction in itself. To have a place that's there and all the things are set already; the whole big machinery! If I would go into a theatre, I would love to do a light show. All the lights are there and all these technicians. If we would . . . take over Broadway, then I think we would have to do light shows and shows with garbage and paper. All those people are to clean the floors and it would be a great show just to work with them, cleaning up the floors. It is all unused material. It's all there for nothing. And so to create these things, you see, that's theatre. To do something to the space and not just assume, "I'm here" . . . these are the means, and then we do something with them.

VALDEZ: I'd like to add that you have to touch them where they are. Our way of working is to incite people, to say "Go on, do it, it's easy. Go on, everyone, let's go!" And before you know it, everybody's getting up, "What, what?" And you're all out the door. We put a flag up there and you follow the flag, right? That kind of thing—in fact, set up a whirlwind . . .

SCHUMANN: That's exactly how I would describe what you do.

VALDEZ: But you have to engage people and say, "Okay, this is what we want to do." Our whole thing is that we want to do something after this thing is through in the theatre. It's not the theatre; it's on the flatbed truck, the hall, the street, wherever. After, something has to happen. What now?

SCHUMANN: But isn't that the same hang-up we have in giving messages through theatre? Instead of going a step further and getting the election booth turned around or whatever, we go out and do another message; do another play or play it again, instead of taking action. I mean, we have the same trouble as the audience we might blame for not picking up the axe or the shovel or whatever after the show . . .

VALDEZ: We never blame the audience.

SCHUMANN: I mean, these are two very similar hang-ups.

DAVIS: I think inciting has to be looked at in many different ways. It seems to me you are working with three levels in radical theatre. One, you play in a commercial way. They like you because you are a bunch of freaks or you're ethnic, or you're dirty, or you're religious, or you're different. They like you that way. That's the superficial way. An audience which appreciates you sees some difference between you and the commercial theatre, that's one kind of audience. There's another kind of audience. They are very much like you and really want to do what you're doing and live as you do. That's the movement or the people who are not plastic. But the most difficult area is in our own companies. Radicalizing, intelligently training our own members so the companies themselves do what we call great theatre and are dedicated to the same kinds of images.

You can incite people in many different ways. Certainly, people are incited by the way Teatro does it. And, certainly, in another way, people are moved by the way Peter does it. One night people would be incited to go and smash windows. Another night they should come back and see Peter's thing and figure out why they smashed the windows, and why we are living here, and why we are. There is too much pointless radical behavior. SDS on campus:

"Let's run out there, let's do it! Registration lines—we got to destroy registration lines! We go do it!" And people say, "Well, why are you doing it?" "Well, we're doing it, because we've got to do it. Let's go out there! Get the flags!" Boom! You get there and you don't know why you're there. This is a problem of radical behavior. There's a lot of sound and not enough reasonable alternative.

I think we react too automatically. We're essentially talking about an affirmative life. We want to make a lot of noise of our own. And we don't want to be told, "You're not making it well, you're not doing it well." Although we should do it well, we want to make our own noise.

VALDEZ: You know the two noises that we have in *Pancho Villa?* We have two very loud farts.

DAVIS: How do you train to do a fart?

VALDEZ: You know, it's an art.

SVENDSEN: One thing that has impressed me about the radical theatres is that radicalization begins in the troupes themselves. There should be no difficulty in defining radical theatre: it's less what it says than what it does, above all what it does in its own group.

DAVIS: More often than not, when we come to a problem we deal with it in an intellectual way. The people in the shows are more radicalized than the people watching. Individuals ask, "Why do you play for people who agree with you?" and I say, "They don't, because, hopefully, we're ahead of the audiences that think we're radical or liberal."

The job of the artist in politics is to take leaps the politicos never take.

The Bread & Puppet Theatre at Cate Farm

One of the most astonishing "total experiences" at Goddard College in Vermont is the presence of the Bread & Puppet Theatre, which moved to the college's Cate Farm in June, 1970. In the college Calendar, Peter Schumann describes the theatre's subsequent activities at Goddard:

> A very full summer, working six to seven days a week, eight to twelve hours a day, with 11 Goddard students, lots of construction and puppet building, banner & poster-printing, beer-brewing, bread-baking, and gardening; old and new puppets marched in two local parades & short shows played at barbecues; a new show, *The Grey Lady Cantata,* was created and performed by the whole group at the annual puppeteers festival at the University of Connecticut in August. More shows, old & new, were given during September, in our circus tent, in the beautifully fixed-up barn (thank you, John Kruse and crew), and in the meadow (thank you alfalfa, clover, and sunny weather): *Fire King Story, Grey Lady Cantata, and Domestic Resurrection.* Then most puppeteers left on a 3-month cross-country tour. Later in the fall we showed eternal Punch & Judy and paper-cranky movies to small groups from local schools and Goddard's Headstart Program. In the waning rays of the autumn sun, scores of plaster casts spewed forth hundreds of paper-maché figures for the first paper-maché cathedral of Vermont, with the help of many students, sometimes to readings of poetry, Doyle and Twain, sometimes with hot wine.
>
> A week before Thanksgiving, rehearsals began on *Eating and Drinking in the Year of Our Lord,* with twelve to fifteen students, first in the freezing barn, then in Paul Vela's studio. This pilgrims-meet-Indians happening was performed twice in the Library Well, once at the Putney School.
>
> For the last seven years, we've done *The Christmas Story* and wanted to do it again in 1970, so we efficiently sent out a large mailing to local schools, libraries and churches. Results: two negative replies to about fifty letters and flyers. But we ended up playing over twenty times between December 6 and January 29. . . . Most of these performances were done for free. . . .
>
> In the newly-heated workshop in the Cate Farm barn, plastering, pasting, and painting continued, plus a new project—the building of many large musical instruments, horns of

garden hose and fiddles of gallon tins. All this work came together to produce, in late January, Vermont's First Paper-Maché Cathedral Exhibit in the Library Well. A week in the mounting, it culminated in a midnight event titled: *Genghis Khan and the Women.*

February began with two demonstrations in Montpelier protesting the invastion of Laos, the second one with a large contingent in masks depicting the faces of war: death, prisoners, business-as-usual . . . .

Until mid-April the Bread & Puppet Threatre will be mostly on the road. . . .

At Cate Farm, after April 15, we want to continue rehearsing and constructing (dreaming of a white snow-show before it all melts) big outdoor events of winter and spring, plus work on a children's theatre to play in nearby schools.

Then there will be several day-long events: a) Second National Paper-Maché Festival (expanding the first Vermont Paper-Maché Cathedral and mounting it to the barn); b) Combined Tin-can Fiddle and Washing-machine-agitator horn Convention (both building and playing new instruments); c) Masonite-rubbing and banner-printing Conspiracy (politics, daisies, beasts, angels to be printed and mounted on flagpoles).

And the regular, at least once-weekly, baking of sourdough rye bread. Anyone interested in learning, watching, call 8509 for next baking.

We need performers, helpers and musicians for most of this. Response from the college and the community has been fine, and the participation, assistance, and cooperation of Goddard and its members, and others, have resulted in good things. We hope they continue.

Specific days and times of events, rehearsals, and workshops will be posted and properly announced on campus.

It is unnecessary to comment on the profound educational and community implications in these astonishing activities. Members of the Bread & Puppet Theatre commune take vows of poverty and their dedication is apparent. Their concept of theatre has not only high aesthetic standards, but also a way of life that unites theatre and society in a way that few other theatre companies have managed to achieve. In many ways, it seems to me that Peter Schumann's vision is the purest and strongest in theatre today. With his incredible, infectious energy watching and transforming everything, he is a rare combination of leader and youthful participant. First and foremost a sculptor with an inbred Germanic, expressionist vision, he has adapted this vision to an infinite number of American and Oriental variations. When I visited Cate Farm in June, 1971, he showed me a powerful, enormous head of the God of Hell that he had designed for a Japanese Kyogen, the farcical part of a Noh drama that he was adapting to fit with elements of the Calley trial.

Beginning to cover walls of the barn at Cate Farm were a variety of masks and sculptures, mostly made of wallpaper paste and the *New York Times,* which are eventually designed to become The Paper Maché Cathedral. "Like Kurt Schwitters," I said instinctively to Schumann, thinking of Schwitter's famous Merzbau in Germany which the Nazis destroyed. "Yes, like Schwitters," Schumann nodded, smiling. But Schumann's sculptural vision is basically theatrical, variations of timeless heads and faces, as opposed to Schwitters' collage-effects of assembling into abstract forms an infinite variety of commonplace objects. The Paper Maché Cathedral is both an extraordinary religious and social commentary on the confusions and discoveries of our time. It has a massive, powerful scale that somehow retains a compassionate view of humanity.

Compassion, in fact, is the keynote of Schumann's Bread & Puppet Theatre. It is the remarkable way in which he varies his work according to the environment in which he is performing. A strong ethical, religious feeling is the basis of this compassion. It underlines the company's parades, which combine fun and gaiety with pointed social questions. The Pointer, for example, (see photo) is a remarkable Schumann parade figure who poses in front of monuments, statues, banks—wherever he pleases—and points an enormous, questioning finger and thumb at these public places in a way that makes you re-consider their functions. If the effect were merely one of accusation, the gesture would only be satirical and quickly forgotten. The effect is much deeper because of the large, haunting mask of The Pointer and the dramatic scale on which he is conceived. In the May, 1971 demonstrations in Washington against the war in Indochina, Schumann used other figures from *Fire* (see photo) and The Feeder, a figure who presents wine and bread, and The Apostles, all in front of the Capitol.

Playing on the streets, in front of public buildings, in parks, in fields, the Bread & Puppet Theatre uses open-air environments well. *Fire*, a tremendously moving, wordless, ritualistic elegy performed in memory of those who immolated themselves in protest against the Viet Nam War, is played to small, intimate audiences of only 100. Other works such as *The Domestic Resurrection Circus* are performed in large halls, gymnasiums, or similar spaces, that can seat hundreds of spectators. In the latter work, which the Bread & Puppet Theatre performed in Sayles Hall at Brown University during the Rhode Island Theatre Festival '71, Schumann uses huge, ritualistic figures in a processional and stationary groupings to indicate the menacing commercial and militaristic forces that govern our lives. A Hell-Mouth suspended from the ceiling and a gargoyle-plane figure, suggestive of air warfare, spread their destruction from above. On the floor, through the audience, human-scale figures move in comic circus acts, in sexual mystery, in supplication and prayer, to their destinies. At the end of *Domestic Resurrection Circus*, the cast begins to sing "The storm is coming," forms an Ark, invites the audience aboard, and leaves the building to continue the voyage of the Ark outside. Theoretically, depending on weather and the success of the merger between actors and audience, the voyage is capable of indefinite extension. When I saw it in Providence, it seemed clear that many of the actors would be taken home by members of the audience for further explorations and celebrations.

Celebration involves the establishment of a mysterious, unifying rhythm, and this is another of Schumann's unique contributions to theatre. Many of his works are presented in an incredibly slow, persistent, inevitable rhythm. Some members of his audiences, used to fast, pounding, aggressive rhythms, often find Bread & Puppet performances tedious. However, a new spirit is at work in society—particularly among young people—that is searching for more natural relationships, that scorns neat, tidy forms, and it is to this spirit that Schumann appeals. He combines the amateur and the professional in a way that to him is the rhythm of reality, a measure that permits constant pauses, awkward interruptions, even accidents, since such chance events are the course of life. Yet he always shapes the flow of events with his unique vision which remains intensely personal and dramatic in its plastic, sculptural power. At Cate Farm I remarked to him about the slow rhythms in many of his pieces. He smiled, waved his hand at the green Vermont landscape, and said: "Here it is a really slow rhythm." In fact, the slowness of his rhythm is what enables him to perform in the way that he does—to use giant figures, to use ritualistic effects, such as the ceremonial lighting of candles, to use "pick-up," amateur performers who actually enhance the feeling of audience participation. The flow of his rhythm becomes, in the end, a reflection of his vision—to regain our sense of wonder, of laughter, we must pause to reflect; we must learn again a natural, patient rhythm that is part of the body's physical discovery, rather than let the machine conquer us with its inhuman mastery of speed.

A drizzling rain fell on Cate Farm during our visit. Beyond the barn, Schumann pointed out with respect the towering, brooding presence of a dead elm tree. He combines the joyous, infectious sensibility of a child, a gleeful participant in every activity, with the visionary, critical eye of visual master who knows and learns instinctively, by practice, where his theatre must go. Like every art, theatre requires discipline, and Schumann and his wife provide it. The structure is loose, the manner of living easy and free, but the dedication to work struck me as being like a medieval guild—the master craftsman and his disciples. Perhaps this is the way the arts can function best in our society, setting up situations in communities and colleges where artists can create and teach by example. Schumann has worked in city slums, at Coney Island, and now in the green, rolling Vermont countryside, with adjacent cemetery to remind him of eternal time. In Vermont he seems at home, his restless imagination planning, transforming, radiating out over the peaceful landscape. As I left the farm, the members of the theatre were taking a break and one puppeteer was strumming his guitar and singing a Mexican song while the others listened on the porch in the rain. A Mexican song in Vermont. As Schumann says,

> Puppeteers are carnival people, conceived at country fairs, born in garbage cans, married to dancing bears, and committed to a fullsize job of exaggerating up-to-date plights and catastrophes, celebrating glorious particles of dust in the evening sun, and demonstrating pain and great tender love which are at the heart of our world. In the year of our Lord 1971 we continue working on our circus, your domestic resurrection circus, where the whole unabridged universe will be brought to your attention, our monstrous human fate explained. Master Death exhumed, Lady World materialized. Little U.S.-man with his disqualified liver recommended to your neighborly compassion, and proposed for your latest urban renewal project.

Pros and Cons of Outdoor Theatre:
Or - Don't do it unless it's interesting!

R.G. DAVIS

The San Francisco Mime Troupe has worked in the parks of the Bay Area since 1962. Working in the parks means dealing with the public in the parks, the politics of the public parks, and making the parks public!! In 1962 we did 2 shows and in 1969 we did 125. In the space of some years we have performed commedia del 'arte, puppets, and this year, a Chinese opera and Brecht's *Congress of the Whitewashers*. The Gorilla Marching Band, a creation out of a VDC march sometime in 1966, has been on the streets in parades, demonstrations around the country: Madison, Harvard, Presidio

21, and even a Saint Patrick's Day Parade. Attracting attention on the street or in parks demands a breaking with realistic forms of theatre and creating odd shapes, or outrageous character types, and loud noises. We first used commedia dell'arte, a popular outdoor theatre form performed in Italy from 1500 to 1700. It is large-gestured, loud, and raucous. The stereotypes are masked and the plots are fast and complicated.

The important ingredient was making the "old style" relevant and "modern." So we added American accents—Italian, Jewish, Spanish, French—strong movement, and made sure the content of the stories was "modern" i.e. money, sex, capitalism, war, anti-pacifism. (You know, the regular subjects.) The puppet shows were first on street corners. We tried to sell newspapers as a front for the performance. It is illegal to block the sidewalk, but if you're doing "business" that's o.k.; so we began by selling papers. Later, we moved into the parks—with permits—and presented thirty to thirty-five minute shows. The material for the puppet shows, surrounded by that now famous Gorilla Marching Band (regular marching band paraphernalia in mummers' [rag] costume) is relevant and useful—in fact so useful it might be illegal.

Guerrilla theatre (agit-prop), designed to awake political consciousness, may not draw attention to itself from the start, but may sneak into an area, pull its trick off and split—often in ordinary or realistic costumes. If one wants to blast off the casing of alienation, then ordinary street clothes are important. Surprise is the key, and, when smashing a pie at Clark Kerr or at the Marine Recruiting Officer, one needs "get-away-clothes." But radical street or park theatre that is designed to persuade, educate, and challenge ideas is better in non-naturalistic, masked, or highly costumed styles.

For us, working outdoors includes a great sense of improvisation in that anything that the audience hears the actors also hear. No fourth or third wall, not even earplugs—all is open. We perform a little "game" on our stage, and the audience accepts that "game"— unless, of course, bells, dogs, or drunks break in, then all, both performers and audience, deal with the intrusion. The heart and guts of the Mime Troupe's activities are based upon its explorations in the parks. There is the risk, the unknown audience: poor, upper class, white, black, brown, uninformed, pedants; the price: "sit on the grass." Our job is to entertain them long enough so they listen to instructions on how to change our country, and to donate some cash so we can survive.

Theatre in the Streets

Bertolt Brecht: Epic Theatre and Life in the Streets

A theatrical style becomes dangerously artificial when it is too divorced from everyday life in the streets. That is the unique value of open-air visions of theatre. At the beginning of his essay, "The Street Scene," Bertolt Brecht quotes as an example of "natural, epic theatre" an eyewitness "demonstrating to a collection of people how a traffic accident took place."

The example is a reflection of Brecht's curious, intense personality. Early in 1946, when I met Brecht, he was living in a spacious studio apartment in New York. I had to walk up several flights of stairs to reach the apartment on the top floor. Through the door, as I waited, raged the squabble of pontifical radio voices. A short, wiry man in his shirtsleeves, with close-cropped hair, opened the door. Grinning broadly, he pointed to the radio and said: "That's the best theatre in America. Marvelous, the way they stutter around, go forward a little, go back then forward, then back some more." Confused for a moment, I began slowly to make out that the radio voices were representatives of an UNRRA conference at the United Nations. Listening intensely, Brecht gesticulated and acted out with his body the invisible UNRRA delegates "stuttering" and "going forwards and backwards," as he repeated with glee. More than any of his articles, this was a revelation of what Brecht meant by epic theatre, the close relationship with social problems, the emphasis on the tragi-comic connections of political forces. Far from seeming emotionless and didactic, Brecht's theatre derives its excitement, wit, and tension from its author's shrewd, colorful personality.

His face was thin, bony, marked with a singular force of will that made him seem much younger than his forty-eight years. After he had turned off the radio, he fiddled constantly with his glasses, removing them, placing them on a shelf, or dangling them from a finger while he talked with a flow of nervous energy. His eyes sparkled continuously with his characteristically wry sense of humor. The mouth which grinned easily could also set firmly and stubbornly as he stressed a point. A stubble of beard, a wrinkled workshirt open at the neck, revealed a man who at first sight seemed little aware of the conceits of dress, but who was said to be extremely conscious of his proletarian appearance. When he opened the door, a cigar was clenched in his hand. As he stood listening to the radio, gesturing with the cigar in delight, puffing out clouds of smoke, the cigar assumed a new importance. Here was a constant cigar smoker, like the great modern architect, Mies Van Der Rohe. Mies Van Der Rohe once said: "For true greatness, you have to go through the clouds." This statement was accompanied by a photograph of the architect staring into space through clouds of cigar smoke. Ironically, I thought the real meaning of this grandiose vision was that for Mies Van Der Rohe and Brecht the structures of the imagination were reached through clouds generated by cigars. Brecht has said, in a famous statement, that a spectator should view the action of a play in the relaxed, yet critical attitude a man has when he is smoking. When you saw Brecht smoking, you realized immediately the qualities of pleasure and stimulation which he derived from cigars. He smoked each one down to the stub. Then, clutched between his second and third fingers, the stub made an emphatic punctuation mark as he gesticulated in supporting clarification of his words. More and more I understood his belief that the gesture in drama is an inseparable part of the word, and that the word has to be realized through the gesture.

Books were piled around the room, books of all kinds and nations. A small model of a theatre stood on a shelf in one room. The only decoration on the walls was a signed drawing of George Grosz. Here was the Grosz of his great pre-Hitler period—the Berlin of *The Threepenny Opera*—depicting the savage lines of a decayed city and a desperate, poverty-stricken people preyed on by sadistic generals and power-hungry industrialists. Years later, in January, 1956, when I saw the American premiere of *Mother Courage* at the Actor's Workshop in San Francisco, I began to understand how much *Mother Courage* and other later works of Brecht stemmed from the atmosphere of Berlin in the 1920s. However, exile from Germany created one important development in Brecht's work. It gave him a deeper and more complex sense of humanity than Grosz' sinister puppets. He turned from such characters as the bitterly cynical Macheath of *The Threepenny Opera*, influenced by the decaying agonies of the Weimar Republic, to Shen Te in *The Good Woman of Setzuan*, who can still affirm at the end of the play:

> Yet pity pained me so, I was an angry wolf at the sight of misery.
> Then I felt how I was changing and kind words changed to ashes in my mouth.

> And yet I wished to be an Angel to the Suburbs.
> To give was a delight. A happy face and I walked on clouds.
> Condemn me: everything I did to help my neighbor,
> To love my lover, and to save my little son from want.
> For your great plans, O gods, I was too poor and small.
> (Bentley and Apelbaum translation)

During his exile from Germany, the change in his work was reflected in his growing interest in the painter, Pieter Bruegel. Like Bruegel's canvas, Brecht's is vast; neither isolates individual, psychological problems. Bruegel paints allegories earthbound in human reality that often contrast the force and beauty of human nature with man's confusions and limitations. In Bruegel's *The Carrying of the Cross*, Christ is a small figure almost lost in the eager sightseers swarming up the hill to the crucifixion as to a fair, but the figure of Christ is in the exact center of the canvas. Aldous Huxley observed of this painting: "Other artists have pretended to be angels, painting the scene with a knowledge of its significance. But Bruegel resolutely remains a human onlooker." The description fits Brecht perfectly. Mother Courage is a great figure; she exists at the exact center of the play, giving it meaning and warmth. But she is a lonely figure, surrounded by people she cannot understand, lost in the terrible forces of war. Bruegel was known as "Pieter the Droll," a painter absorbed in the coarse, peasant's view of life, with a peculiar interest in the grotesque. This again fits Brecht, who in *Mother Courage* and his later plays, attempts to depict, with a grotesque mixture of humor and pathos, the isolated struggle of individuals caught and shaped in the crucible of social forces.

The drollness of Brecht came out as we began to talk about the possibilities of theatre in post-war Germany. Brecht began: "The German theatre like everything else in the country is completely destroyed. But it can be built up by starting over again." He was referring not only to the destruction and death caused by the war, but also to his belief that the Nazis destroyed German theatre by their grandiose, cluttered productions and their mannered, rhetorical style of acting. "All Germans have the mystical tendency," Brecht continued with a smile. "This may make it difficult for them to rebuild properly. It is their great fault. Perhaps now that they have to make material things they will improve. Certainly, all Germans have been completely conquered now, including myself." He laughed, which I remembered when I read in a German newspaper of one of the last pronouncements of his life in the 1950's, an Open Letter to the Bundestag, West Germany's parliament. In this letter he implored the members to veto compulsory military service in the new armed forces of Western Germany and pleaded for a plebescite to be held in both parts of Germany.

I asked Brecht if there were any directors or actors in the German theatre in whom he had confidence for the future. "Very few, very few," he said, shaking his head. "The Nazis saw to that.

It will take a long time to create a new German theatre, although theatre can be played anywhere, in the ruins, even in a subway station. All you need are lights and the right kind of spirit. The difficulty is that German actors and directors have all been trained in this exaggerated, twisted style. Of course there may be people I don't know of who may have grown and survived despite Hitler. One man, who has survived somehow, is a very good Regisseur. That is Erich Engel." In 1949, Engel co-directed with Brecht the Berlin premiere of Brecht's *Mr. Puntila and His Servant Matti* with the Berliner Ensemble. After Brecht's death, Engel became the chief director of the company. "The only trouble with Engel," Brecht continued, his lips wrinkling into a grin, "is that he drinks too much black coffee and he has a little too much Kantian sensibility. Nevertheless, he is very good. Maybe he'll improve now that there is no more black coffee. Black coffee makes a man too edgy and sharp." Brecht emphasized the word, *scharf,* giving it an untranslatable tone as he laughed and gestured with his hand and the stub of his cigar.

Brecht feared the sentimental basis of American theatre, its tendency to drown the stage in scenery and language with little relationship to reality. "American theatre is back in the 1890s," he said with a frown (meaning the 1890s in Germany, not in the United States). "You have never heard of the new effects, or if you do use them, you use them briefly as tricks. Even though Piscator teaches here in New York, you have never really experimented with the treadmill, or projections, or films, or any of the other devices that we used in Germany in the 1920s." He was referring to the famous treadmill which Piscator had used in his Berlin production of *The Good Soldier Schweik,* and to the many German productions of the late 1920s that had used projections and films for scenic and narrative effects.

"Even the way you Americans use costumes is all wrong," Brecht continued. "All you need to portray *all* religious tradition is three costumes, if the costumes are correct. In America you use ten costumes and none are correct." Brecht did not imply that all religious tradition *should be* portrayed by three costumes. He himself used many costumes, beautifully and expensively designed, for his Berliner Ensemble productions. What he objected to on Broadway and in Hollywood was the sentimental elaboration of effect, the belief in overpowering the mind by a visual swamp of sentiment. Against this kind of easy, banal, emotional mood, he opposed his misunderstood "alienation" of the action, his *Verfremdungseffekt,* as he called it. This "alienation" of the action was not intended to drum emotion out of the theatre, as many critics interpreted it, but to bring about a combination of reason and emotion. Hollywood, in particular, Brecht said, was a fantasy of juvenile emotions, a confusion of commercialism and misguided talents. "The theatre," he continued, "particularly the musical stage which often has a fresh, theatrical quality, is better, but it will never be the force it can be until it learns the everyday language, how to live in reality. As for Hollywood, I'm afraid there is no hope there."

The image of America in Brecht's work is a puzzling one— fantastic, brutal, chaotic, materialistic, romantic, daring, primitive—a strange mixture of attraction and repulsion, the same attitudes that Brecht revealed in conversation about the United States. Reading Brecht's work and talking to him was a lesson in what the United States meant to Europeans in the 1920s, and a warning why the United States is still regarded by Europeans as a puzzling mixture of materialism and openheartedness. Although the frontier is gone, many Europeans still long for its sense of opportunity, its primitive equality, and Brecht was a primary example of this yearning. Because he spoke English poorly, he was never close to many Americans. His image of the United States was largely a reflection from books, from radio, press, television, and films. Harried by the Un-American Activities Committee after the end of World War II, he was called to Washington to testify and denied that he had ever been a member of the Communist Party. To the Committee, which had no idea of the importance of his work or his relationship to Communism, he put on a characteristically ironic performance. When the Committee read one of his didactic, Communist marching songs and asked, "Did you write that, Mr.

Brecht?" he replied, "No, I wrote a German poem, but that is very different from this." The poor German translator at the hearings had a thicker accent than Brecht's and the hearing dissolved in laughter and ridicule. At the end, the chairman actually congratulated Brecht on his testimony. In a statement that he was not permitted to read before the Committee, but which was published later, Brecht said:

> Being called before the Un-American Activities Committee, however, I feel free for the first time to say a few words about American matters: looking back on my experiences as a playwright and poet in the Europe of the last two decades, I wish to say that the great American people would lose much and risk much if they allowed anybody to restrict free competition of ideas in cultural fields, or to interfere with art which must be free in order to be art. We are living in a dangerous world. Our state of civilization is such that mankind already is capable of becoming enormously wealthy but, as a whole, is still poverty-ridden. Great wars have been suffered, greater ones are imminent, we are told. One of them might well wipe out mankind as a whole. We might be the last generation of the specimen, man, on this earth. The ideas about how to make use of the new capabilities of production have not been developed much since the days when the horse had to do what man could not do. Do you not think that, in such a predicament, every new idea should be examined carefully and freely? Art can present clearly and even make nobler such ideas.

During my brief visits with Brecht, I showed him a translation I had made of one of his poems. He worked over the first part of it carefully with me and, as a result, I think it has more than ordinary interest. Technically, the poem illustrates the irregular speech rhythms which interested Brecht and which he used so masterfully. He was particularly careful about details, about rhythms, about the precise accent, or gesture, that a word should receive in a sentence if spoken properly. He was interested mainly in the spoken quality of the poem. Here one sensed the unity in his mind between his poetry and his plays.

One of the greatest and least-appreciated achievements of Brecht in the theatre was to restore a sense of poetry to a naturalistic, prose-ridden stage. Because of his sardonic sense of reality, Brecht did not make the mistake of thinking that a high-flown, rhetorical poetry could again rule the stage. He knew that the twentieth century was an era of transition in theatre as well as society. He sensed that poetry of the stage had to be colloquial, direct, not sentimental. Consequently, he tended in his later plays to shape his language on three levels: conversational, earthy prose for conventional scenes, poetic prose for scenes that required a greater variety of ideas and imagery, and poetry for scenes that required a formal beauty of statement.

One side of Brecht was stern and uncompromising. "Truth is concrete," was the slogan he liked to keep on his study wall. The scholarly, didactic side of his character was easy to see. As a friend of his once told me, Brecht looked like "a papal legate, and just escaped being one." When I left him after the last visit, he had been talking about the great changes in society and the theatre brought about by the machine. He gestured wryly with the stub of his cigar, smiled, and said: "One day we may all live in planes, all the time." Brecht was saved from his inherent didactic nature by his wit, his wide range of interests, and his eagerness for change and new experiences—characteristics that were so strong in him that his individuality could not be suppressed by the political pressures to which he was exposed. These qualities of Brecht's nature, his ability to shape the life of the streets into theatre, are particularly evident in the concluding lines of Galileo's first speech when he says to the boy, Andrea:

> GALILEO: I tell you that still in our lifetime astronomy will be discussed in the streets. Even the fishwife's sons will run to school. The people of our cities eager for fresh ideas will be eager for a new astronomy which allows the earth to move as well. Always the stars were supposed to be fastened inside a crystal vault, so that they couldn't fall down. Today we've found enough courage to let them float freely, without any support; and they're off on great

journeys like our ships, vast journeys without support of any kind.

And the earth rolls joyously around the sun, and the fishwives, merchants, princes and cardinals roll with it, and even the Pope.

But overnight the world has lost its center, and in the morning has woken to find more centers than can be counted. So that now anyone can be seen as the center or no one at all. Suddenly, there is a lot of room.

Our ships travel far across the seas, our stars soar far out through space; even the rooks in chess have begun to sweep up and down board.

What does the poet say?

ANDREA: Oh early morning of beginnings!
Oh breath of winds, which
Comes from new shores!

Brecht was a master of contradictions, of opposites. This is the source and power of his work, as it was of his personality. Humor and tragedy, exile and rootedness, the Bible and Existentialism, material and spiritual power, Communism and Democracy, peace and violence, science and art—he broke through the specialized forces of our time, ignoring the fact that these forces could not often be unified. It was no accident that he chose to be buried in the old huguenot cemetery in Berlin, near the grave of Hegel, the master philosopher of the dialectical method.

The Street Scene
A Basic Model for an Epic Theatre

BERTOLT BRECHT

In the decade and a half that followed the World War a comparatively new way of acting was tried out in a number of German theatres. Its qualities of clear description and reporting and its use of choruses and projections as a means of commentary earned it the name of "epic." The actor used a somewhat complex technique to detach himself from the character portrayed; he forced the spectator to look at the play's situations from such an angle that they necessarily became subject to his criticism. Supporters of this epic theatre argued that the new subject-matter, the highly involved incidents of the class war in its acutest and most terrible stage, would be mastered more easily by such a method, since it would thereby become possible to portray social processes as seen in their causal relationships. But the result of these experiments was that aesthetics found itself up against a whole series of substantial difficulties.

It is comparatively easy to set up a basic model for epic theatre. For practical experiments I usually picked as my example of completely simple, "natural" epic theatre an incident such as can be seen at any street corner: an eyewitness demonstrating to a collection of people how a traffic accident took place. The bystanders may not have observed what happened, or they may simply not agree with him, may "see things a different way"; the point is that the demonstrator acts the behavior of driver or victim or both in such a way that the bystanders are able to form an opinion about the accident.

Such an example of the most primitive type of epic theatre seems easy to understand. Yet experience has shown that it presents astounding difficulties to the reader or listener as soon as he is asked to see the implications of treating this kind of street corner demonstration as a basic form of major theatre, theatre for a scientific age. What this means of course is that the epic theatre may appear richer, more intricate and complex in every particular, yet to be major theatre it need at bottom only contain the same elements as a street-corner demonstration of this sort; nor could it any longer be termed epic theatre if any of the main elements of the street-corner demonstration were lacking. Until this is understood it is impossible really to understand what follows. Until one understands the novelty, unfamiliarity, and direct challenge to the critical faculties of the suggestion that street-corner demonstration of this sort can serve as a satisfactory basic model of major theatre one cannot really understand what follows.

Consider: the incident is clearly very far from what we mean by an artistic one. The demonstrator need not be an artist. The capacities he needs to achieve his aim are in effect universal. Suppose he cannot carry out some particular movement as quickly as the victim he is imitating; all he need do is to explain that *he* moves three times as fast, and the demonstration neither suffers in essentials nor loses its point. On the contrary it is important that he should not be too perfect. His demonstration would be spoilt if the bystanders' attention were drawn to his powers of transformation. He has to avoid presenting himself in such a way that someone calls out "What a lifelike portrayal of a chauffeur!" He must not "cast a spell" over anyone. He should not transport people from normality to "higher realms." He need not dispose of any special powers of suggestion.

It is most important that one of the main features of the ordinary theatre should be excluded from our street scene: the engendering of illusion. The street demonstrator's performance is essentially repetitive. The event has taken place; what you are seeing now is a repeat. If the scene in the theatre follows the street scene in this respect, then the theatre will stop pretending not to be theatre, just as the street-corner demonstration admits it is a demonstration (and does not pretend to be the actual event). The element of rehearsal in the acting and of learning by heart in the text, the whole machinery and the whole process of preparation: it all becomes plainly apparent. What room is left for experience? Is the reality portrayed still experienced in any sense?

The street scene determines what kind of experience is to be prepared for the spectator. There is no question but that the street-corner demonstrator has been through an "experience," but he is not out to make his demonstration serve as an "experience" for the audience. Even the experience of the driver and the victim is only partially communicated by him, and he by no means tries to turn it into an enjoyable experience for the spectator, however lifelike he may make his demonstration. The demonstration would become no less valid if he did not reproduce the fear caused by the accident; on the contrary, it would lose validity if he did. He is not interested in creating pure emotions. It is important to understand that a theatre which follows his lead in this respect undergoes a positive change of function.

One essential element of the street scene must also be present in the theatrical scene if this is to qualify as epic, namely that the demonstration should have a socially practical significance. Whether our street demonstrator is out to show that one attitude on the part of driver or pedestrian makes an accident inevitable where another would not, or whether he is demonstrating with a view to fixing the responsibility, his demonstration has a practical purpose, intervenes socially.

The demonstrator's purpose determines how thoroughly he has to imitate. Our demonstrator need not imitate every aspect of his characters' behavior, but only so much as gives a picture. Generally the theatre scene will give much fuller pictures, corresponding to its more extensive range of interest. How do street scene and theatre scene link up here? To take a point of detail, the victim's voice may have played no immediate part in the accident. Eye-witnesses may disagree as to whether a cry they heard ("Look out!") came from the victim or from someone else, and this may give our demonstrator a motive for imitating the voice. The question can be settled by demonstrating whether the voice was an old man's or a woman's, or merely whether it was high or low. Again, the answer may depend on whether it was that of an educated person or not. Loud or soft may play a great part, as the driver could be correspondingly more or less guilty. A whole series of characteristics of the victim ask to be portrayed. Was he absent-minded? Was his attention distracted? If so, by what? What, on the evidence of his behavior, could have made him liable to be distracted by just that circumstance and no other? Etc., etc. It can be seen that our street-corner demonstration provides opportunities for a pretty rich and varied portrayal of human types. Yet a theatre which tries to restrict its essential elements to those provided by our street scene will have to acknowledge certain limits to imitation. It must be able to justify any outlay in terms of its purpose.[1]

The demonstration may for instance be dominated by the question of compensation for the victim, etc. The driver risks being sacked from his job, losing his license, going to prison; the victim risks a heavy hospital bill, loss of job, permanent disfigurement, possibly unfitness for work. This is the area within which the demonstrator builds up his characters. The victim may have had a

---

[1] We often come across demonstrations of an everyday sort which are more thorough imitations than our street-corner accident demands. Generally they are comic ones. Our next-door neighbor may decide to "take off" the rapacious behavior of our common landlord. Such an imitation is often rich and full of variety. Closer examination will show however that even so apparently complex an imitation concentrates on one specific side of the landlord's behavior. The imitation is summary or selective, deliberately leaving out those occasions where the landlord strikes our neighbor as "perfectly sensible," though such occasions of course occur. He is far from giving a rounded picture; for that would have no comic impact at all. The street scene, perforce adopting a wider angle of vision, at this point lands in difficulties which must not be underestimated. It has to be just as successful in promoting criticism, but the incidents in question are far more complex. It must promote positive as well as negative criticism, and as part of a single process. You have to understand what is involved in winning the audience's approval by means of a critical approach. Here again we have a precedent in our street scene, i.e. in any demonstration of an everyday sort. Next-door neighbor and street demonstrator can reproduce their subject's "sensible" or his "senseless" behavior alike, by submitting it for an opinion. When it crops up in the course of events, however (when a man switches from being sensible to being senseless, or the other way round), then they usually need some form of commentary in order to change the angle of their portrayal. Hence, as already mentioned, certain difficulties for the theatre scene. These cannot be dealt with here.

companion; the driver may have had his girl sitting alongside him. That would bring out the social element better and allow the characters to be more fully drawn.

Another essential element in the street scene is that the demonstrator should derive his characters entirely from their actions. He imitates their actions and so allows conclusions to be drawn about them. A theatre that follows him in this will be largely breaking with the orthodox theatre's habit of basing the actions on the characters and having the former exempted from criticism by presenting them as an unavoidable consequence deriving by natural law from the characters who perform them. To the street demonstrator, the character of the man being demonstrated remains a quantity that need not be completely defined. Within certain limits, he may be like this or like that; it doesn't matter. What the demonstrator is concerned with are his accident-prone and accident-proof qualities.[2] The theatrical scene may show more fully-defined individuals. But it must then be in a position to treat their individuality as a special case and outline the field within which, once more, its most socially relevant effects are produced. Our street demonstrator's possibilities of demonstration are narrowly restricted (indeed, we chose this model so that the limits should be as narrow as possible). If the essential elements of the theatrical scene are limited to those of the street scene, then its greater richness must be an enrichment only. The question of border-line cases becomes acute.

Let us take a specific detail. Can our street demonstrator, say, ever become entitled to use an excited tone of voice in repeating the driver's statement that he has been exhausted by too long a spell of work? (In theory this is no more possible than for a returning messenger to start telling his fellow-countrymen of his talk with the king with the words "I saw the bearded king.") It can only be possible, let alone unavoidable, if one imagines a street-corner situation where such excitement, specifically about this

---

[2] The same situation will be produced by all those people whose characters fulfil the conditions laid down by him and show the features that he imitates.

aspect of the affair, plays a particular part. (In the instance above this would be so if the king had sworn never to cut his beard off until . . . etc.) We have to find a point of view for our demonstrator that allows him to submit this excitement to criticism. Only if he adopts a quite definite point of view can he be entitled to imitate the driver's excited voice; e.g., if he blames drivers as such for doing too little to reduce their hours of work. ("Look at him. Doesn't even belong to a union, but gets worked up soon enough when an accident happens. 'Ten hours I've been at the wheel.' ")

Before it can get as far as this, i.e., be able to suggest a point of view to the actor, the theatre needs to take a number of steps. By widening its field of vision and showing the driver in other situations besides that of the accident, the theatre in no way exceeds its model; it merely creates a further situation on the same pattern. One can imagine a scene of the same kind as the street scene which provides a well-argued demonstration showing how such emotions as the driver's develop, or another which involves making comparisons between tones of voice. In order not to exceed the model scene, the theatre only has to develop a technique for submitting emotions to the spectator's criticism. Of course this does not mean that the spectator must be barred on principle from sharing certain emotions that are put before him; nonetheless, to communicate emotions is only one particular form (phase, consequence) of criticism. The theatre's demonstrator, the actor, must apply a technique which will let him reproduce the tone of the subject demonstrated with a certain reserve, with detachment (so that the spectator can say: "He's getting excited—in vain, too late, at last . . ." etc.). In short, the actor must remain a demonstrator; he must present the person demonstrated as a stranger, he must not suppress the "*he* did that, *he* said that" element in his performance. He must not go so far as to be wholly transformed into the person demonstrated.

One essential element of the street scene lies in the natural attitude adopted by the demonstrator, which is two-fold; he is always taking two situations into account. He behaves naturally as a demonstrator, and he lets the subject of the demonstration behave naturally too. He never forgets, nor does he allow it to be forgotten, that he is not the subject but the demonstrator. That is to say, what the audience sees is not a fusion between demonstrator and subject, not some third, independent, uncontradictory entity with isolated features of (a) demonstrator and (b) subject, such as the orthodox theatre puts before us in its productions.[3] The feelings and opinions of demonstrator and demonstrated are not merged into one.

We now come to one of those elements that are peculiar to the epic theatre, the so-called A-effect (alienation effect): What is involved here is, briefly, a technique of taking the human social incidents to be portrayed and labelling them as something striking, something that calls for explanation, is not to be taken for granted, not just natural. The object of this "effect" is to allow the spectator to criticize constructively from a social point of view. Can we show that this A-effect is significant for our street demonstrator?

We can picture what happens if he fails to make use of it. The following situation could occur. One of the spectators might say: "But if the victim stepped off the curb with his right foot, as you showed him doing. . . ." The demonstrator might interrupt saying: "I showed him stepping off with his left foot." By arguing which foot he really stepped off with in his demonstration, and, even more, how the victim himself acted, the demonstration can be so transformed that the A-effect occurs. The demonstrator achieves it by paying exact attention this time to his movements, executing them carefully, probably in slow motion; in this way he alienates the little subincident, emphasizes its importance, makes it worthy of notice. And so the epic theatre's alienation effect proves to have its uses for our street demonstrator too; in other words it is also to be found in this small everyday scene of natural street-corner theatre, which has little to do with art. The direct changeover from representation to commentary that is so characteristic of the epic theatre is still more easily recognized as one element of any street demonstration. Wherever he feels he can, the demonstrator breaks

[3] Most clearly worked out by Stanislavsky.

off his imitation in order to give explanations. The epic theatre's choruses and documentary projections, the direct addressing of the audience by its actors, are at bottom just this.

It will have been observed, not without astonishment I hope, that I have not named any strictly artistic elements as characterizing our street scene and, with it, that of the epic theatre. The street demonstrator can carry out a successful demonstration with no greater abilities than, in effect, anybody has. What about the epic theatre's value as art?

The epic theatre wants to establish its basic model at the street corner, i.e. to return to the very simplest "natural" theatre, a social enterprise whose origins, means and ends are practical and earthly. The model works without any need or programmatic theatrical phrases like "the urge to self-expression," "making a part one's own," "spiritual experience," "the play instinct," "the story-teller's art," etc. Does that mean that the epic theatre isn't concerned with art?

It might be as well to begin by putting the question differently, thus: can we make use of artistic abilities for the purposes of our street scene? Obviously yes. Even the street-corner demonstration includes artistic elements. Artistic abilities in some small degree are to be found in any man. It does no harm to remember this when one is confronted with great art. Undoubtedly what we call artistic abilities can be exercised at any time within the limits imposed by our street scene model. They will function as artistic abilities even though they do not exceed these limits (for instance; when there is meant to be no complete transformation of demonstrator into subject). And true enough, the epic theatre is an extremely artistic affair, hardly thinkable without artists and virtuosity, imagination, humor and fellow-feeling; it cannot be practised without all these and much else too. It has got to be entertaining, it has got to be instructive. How then can art be developed out of the elements of the street scene, without adding any or leaving any out? How does it evolve into the theatrical scene with its fabricated story, its trained actors, its lofty style of speaking, its make-up, its team performance by a number of players? Do we need to add to our elements in order to move on from the "natural" demonstration to the "artificial"?

Is it not true that the additions which we must make to our model in order to arrive at epic theatre are of a fundamental kind? A brief examination will show that they are not. Take the *story*. There was nothing fabricated about our street accident. Nor does the orthodox theatre deal only in fabrications; think for instance of the historical play. Nonetheless less a story can be performed at the street corner too. Our demonstrator may at any time be in a position to say: "The driver was guilty, because it all happened the way I showed you. He wouldn't be guilty if it had happened the way I'm going to show you now." And he can fabricate an incident and demonstrate it. Or take the fact that the text is learnt by heart. As a witness in a court case, the demonstrator may have written down the subject's exact words, learnt them by heart and rehearsed them; in that case he too is performing a text he has learned. Or take a rehearsed program by several players: it doesn't always have to be artistic purposes that bring about a demonstration of this sort; one need only think of the French police technique of making the chief figures in any criminal case re-enact certain crucial situations before a police audience. Or take making-up. Minor changes in appearance—ruffling one's hair, for instance—can occur at any time within the framework of the non-artistic type of demonstration. Nor is make-up itself used solely for theatrical purposes. In the street scene the driver's moustache may be particularly significant. It may have influenced the testimony of the possible girl companion suggested earlier. This can be represented by our demonstrator making the driver stroke an imaginary moustache when prompting his companion's evidence. In this way the demonstrator can do a good deal to discredit her as a witness. Moving on to the use of a real moustache in the theatre, however, is not an entirely easy transition, and the same difficulty occurs with respect to *costume*. Our demonstrator may under given circumstances put on the driver's cap—for instance if he wants to show that he was drunk (he had it on crooked)—but he can only do so conditionally, under these circumstances (see what was said about borderline cases earlier). However, where there is a demonstration by several demonstrators of the kind referred to above we can have costume so that the various characters can be distinguished. This again is only a limited use of costume. There must be no question of creating an illusion that the demonstrators really are these characters. (The epic theatre can counteract this illusion by especially exaggerated costume or by garments that are somehow marked out as objects for display.) Moreover we can suggest another model as a substitute for ours on this point: the kind of street demonstration given by hawkers. To sell their neckties these people will portray a badly-dressed and a well-dressed man; with a few props and technical tricks they can perform significant little scenes where they submit essentially to the same restrictions as apply to the demonstrator in our street scene: they will pick up tie, hat, stick, gloves and give certain significant imitations of a man of the world, and the whole time they will refer to him as "*he*"! With hawkers we also find *verse* being used within the same framework as that of our basic model. They use firm irregular rhythms to sell braces and newspapers alike.

Reflecting along these lines we see that our basic model will work. The elements of natural and of artificial epic theatre are the same. Our street-corner theatre is primitive; origins, aims, and methods of its performance are close to home. But there is no doubt that it is a meaningful phenomenon with a clear social function that dominates all its elements. The performance's origins lie in an incident that can be judged one way or another, that may repeat itself in different forms and is not finished but is bound to have consequences, so that this judgment has some significance. The object of the performance is to make it easier to give an opinion on the incident. Its means correspond to that. The epic theatre is a highly skilled theatre with complex contents and far-reaching social objectives. In setting up the street scene as a basic model for it we pass on the clear social function and give the epic theatre criteria by which to decide whether an incident is meaningful or not. The basic model has a practical significance. As producer and actors work to build up a performance involving many difficult questions—technical problems, social ones—it allows them to check whether the social function of the whole apparatus is still clearly intact.

Theatre in Streets and Open Spaces

Theatre in the streets and open spaces has developed several characteristics:

1) Almost exclusively it is performed by young people who can cope with difficult, impromptu conditions. This makes for fervor, zeal, exultant rhythms, and frequently, awkward, inexperienced conceptions and performances.

2) It is politically radical or mystical-anarchistic in nature. Often, the particular group may be communal in its life-style and these beliefs are reflected in performance.

3) The style varies from documentary naturalism to grotesque surrealism. A wide range of improvisatory and experimental approaches are found.

4) The radical changes on college and university campuses have contributed greatly to street drama.

There follow several examples of recent street and open air drama in France and the United States. In the traditional sense of character and action, these are not plays; they have an energy and purpose of their own. They seek to use theatre to change society, to create new images that will challenge the bureaucratic status quo and the expanding military technology. They burst out of theatres into open space.

As Gilles Sandier wrote about J.P. Bisson's play, *The Red Morning,* in *La Quinzaine Littéraire* in 1969: "This is a good example of a new type of theatre, *red* theatre, red because it is authentically revolutionary—both in the subversive nature of its content and the manner in which its structure breaks away from all past theatrical tradition. The *play* has been replaced by dramatic images connected in a chain, like the words of a poem. The characters have been replaced by actors, young people twenty to twenty-five years old, who are simultaneously and successively all the characters which the poem calls on them to be. The audience has become the faithful attending a new Mass. ... J.P. Bisson's play is not a political play. But it is revolutionary, inasmuch as revolution is implied in the realization that we can no longer go on living as we have in the past. It is a machine of images which function as a continual call to revolt and protest, whether by representing actual scenes of contemporary life or by using "cultural" references to theatrical, pictorial art, or religious stereotypes: flagellation, burial, cult of the Virgin. The content of these odds and ends is turned against the culture that has transmitted them.

"It is obvious since May 1968 that the expression 'popular theatre' can have no other meaning but one implying total cultural revolution. This revolution is the only thing that can make the theatre acceptable (because anything else is becoming increasingly unbearable). In the theatre, the sign of this revolution is the breaking away from an enclosed setting (and even the Brechtian setting). The conflict is no longer between "participation" of a bourgeois type and didactic and critical 'distance,' but between the play in its totality and its new function of calling and communicating. A play like *The Red Morning* seems capable of inaugurating this, especially because its language and themes are immediately comprehensible to a popular public, a public of laborers and young people, and because it breaks with the traditional strictures of theatrical form."

The Red Morning
a play for two metal barrels, twelve barefeet,
a board, and a "prominence."
JEAN-PIERRE BISSON
TRANSLATED BY THEODORE DUBOIS

A Note by the Translator

In the little theatres of the Monge and Montparnasse sec-
tors of the Paris Latin Quarter, significant experiments in
French and world theatre are taking place. The actors are
sometimes amateurs—students or struggling artists, friends or
acquaintances of a young and talented director, members of
the international diaspora that gathers in Paris and forms that
city's unique and colorful artistic sub-culture. The plays in
these little theatres often have to be geared to very low production budgets—so low that in a city like New York they
would be prohibitive. The length of their runs are predetermined and generally rather short. They often operate under
conditions requiring a simplicity of means not far from that
demanded by street theatre. (In fact, it is easy to imagine
many of these plays, and especially those of a political or
guerrilla nature like *Le Matin Rouge,* being performed outdoors and being still more effective there.) The result is an
atmosphere of unencumbered originality and genuineness.

Jean-Pierre Bisson's *Le Matin Rouge* was written shortly
before the revolution which took place in France in May 1968.
After being introduced to an international audience at the
theater festival of Nancy the following summer, it had a three-
month run, from the beginning of March to the end of April
1969, at the Theatre de Plaisance in the Montparnasse district
of Paris, under its author's direction.

Le Matin Rouge or, as I have translated it, *The Red Morning,* is immediately distinguished from conventional theatre by
its explicitly revolutionary character, both as regards form and
message. It does not have a plot in the usual sense; rather, the

play consists of a series of actions. Its only unifying thread is a broadly defined situation of street gang versus police, a situation in which the actors are youths and the youths are actors, creating their own play of loosely related episodes within the play in which they find themselves. The actors play people who are acting. They are six young persons miming the society around them while it destroys them.

The public authorities in Paris certainly recognized the political implications of *The Red Morning,* and as a result they harassed the production continually. The first time I attended the play, the audience had to wait almost an hour before the performance began. City fire inspectors had chosen show time to make their appearance and to insist that steps at one end of the staging were too close to the theatre entrance and therefore a fire hazard. The show could not go on until carpenters had removed the steps and the inspectors had been appeased in a half dozen other long-nosed, bureaucratic ways. Their purpose, of course, was to stall the performance long enough for the audience to become impatient and leave. But they did not count on the stubbornness of their countrymen. Everyone simply waited. The show went on. And the audience had all the more sympathy for the six "repressed" players.

The Théâtre de Plaisance is a small rectangular room. The stage-area is at one end, elevated above the audience, but without a proscenium. The entire theatre was painted dull black. A ramp led from the stage up to a scaffold-like platform which extended the stage-area along the entire right wall of the theatre. Behind this were the steps which the fire inspectors insisted be removed. As a result, the actors had to jump to pull themselves up onto the platform during performances; and, at the frantic pace the play was performed, they did so at the cost of bruises and the danger of falling.

The script cannot give an adequate idea of the experience an audience received at an actual performance of *The Red Morning,* because it is essentially a play of action and mime. The intervals between the various episodes in the script were sometimes ten minutes long, a frantic, rapid choreography of visual impressions. Words were always secondary to action. Sequences of a ritualistic nature were interspersed between more realistic acting.

As a prelude to the performance, the six actors began a game of tag which they played until they were heated and perspiring. They retained this feverish pitch throughout the performance. For an hour and a half they wove in and out of the various roles in the play, never remaining in any fixed characterization. Their only props were two metal barrels, a few lengths of chain, their clothes in some cases, and white chalk with which to draw sexual and political graffiti on the stage walls.

The Red Morning is a re-enactment of real situations in which the actors' society and their individual lives are immersed. It is the portrayal of the dark night of society's soul. It is morning, because the situation is seen with the lucidity, disillusionment, and despair which the clear light of a hoped for dawn can bring. The morning is red, red for revolution.

Theodore DuBois

Notice

The actors should appear while the audience is coming in, but without giving any indication of what is going to take place.

The play should be preceded by a long build-up which two actors begin and the others all join successively. It can be a game of tag or some other kind of physical exercise. Its pace should increase until the actors are in a sweat and free from the physical and mental inhibitions they picked up during the day.

Motionless—concentration. The play begins in sharp mockery: ". . . that faggot!" Perhaps in the manner of J. Bosch.

Although the first episodes are rather slow, the general rhythm of the play should increase rapidly. The scene with the heroes of Vietnam and other Algerias is supposed to be grotesque and absolutely wild. The act-ors should be reckless, and not worry about hurting themselves.

We can express ourselves adequately only if our bodies are capable of carrying us where we'd never have thought we could go.

The text concerning the Indochinese War should be divided up according to the personalities of the actors. The fast rhythm of this text requires that their voices be quite different from each other. Throughout the play, whether the characters be the father, the fiancée, the National Guardsmen, or even Hamlet, they should all be interpreted in the spirit of the play and not by identifying with what are meant to be only outlines.

The spirit of the play is hatred, the normal consequence of my suffering, from having had to blush for twenty years at people obsessed with the human ass—who've forgotten the pleasure they had in begetting me, turned it into something obscene, and made me their sewer.

A funeral is a rather sickening ceremony where a group of people come together like a family and think they've the right and duty to orchestrate their grievances. Each person that arrives is supposed to set off a new barrage of sobbing howls. But ever with an open eye. No one but the wormy old priest has enough imagination to look at the dead girl with appetite.

Wouldn't it be more natural to take leave of the dead by making love with them for a last time—everyone—forgetting about love scenes with oceans in them. An ocean is no more necessary for love than a lake is in the midst of factories. If everyone is supposed to waste time dreaming about his banal summer vacation, why don't we just blow in our hands so that the wind and sea. . . . It's enough to make you want to blow your brains out, a laborer-friend told me.

The people we hate and will caricature are part of everyday life. There are the fat, stupid butchers in the city market. (They've moved to the suburbs now, but their stench is as bad as ever.) And we'll shed similar tears for the club-swinging cops who stand over us and make us do push-ups while they hold their balls and laugh. But then I feel a wonderful moment brush nearer me in the streets everyday: we'll come up from behind, from behind if you please, and strangle everyone who supported Vichy or gloriously en-

throned the Fifth Republic. And then we'll chop the police con-
voys to little pieces. And then, quickly, after the radio has announced that three deaths took place accidentally between the 1st
and 30th of May, 1968, we'll run like hell, in our barefeet. To the
cellar. And for a long while, we'll just shit. Then we'll beat on the
floor, walls, the garbage barrels, then see if our voices carry
through the screens, find out if we can make a hell of a noise or
quietly caress ... and slowly, bang, bang, ha, ha, raise a roaring
ruckus of arms, legs, hands, heads, and feet in the common shit?
Beginning the eternal Mass that always needs a brandished crucifix
or cock—an altar or a garbage barrel—a whore open to anybody's
fingers or a Virgin holding a foetus. When the great fart is heard,
the leader strips and makes like a cross. And every night he forces
us to spit on him, whip him, and run him through carrying olive
branches and never a single night forget to take him, lay him out
flat and impale Mary on her sweet Jesus who pushes through her
famous blue and white, comes, and we do too, of course—or do
you expect resurrection. ... Our Mass will contain Croisille Bar-
rouh's ode. Completely disfigure it.

To regain your composure: Take a cigarette and don't put
anything in it ... Smoke ... passing it around like a lost woman
... mother ... stop it, it's been years since.... Drop father take
your car and spend six months in San Francisco. It lasts. You've
got too much make-up on ... excuse us for snickering.... Everything's rushing by. Corinne the raped mini-skirt. I love you. I'm
crying and my tears and sperm'll become a Molotov cocktail. It all
quickly passes even for St. Mary the school-teacher who loved me
and, not finding a cellar, was polished to death by Mauriac the
friend of Butterfly who's selling his book about years in the pen so
preciously. It keeps passing faster, but there's always an idiot at the
thee-aw-tah who's too snobbish to get the point and says, "There
was a bit of beauty in it." Nothing can stop them now because
they're the majority and had to choose between the extreme left of
the Rothschilds and the extreme right of the St. Gobain chemical
works. We're really proud and happy because a candidate who
claimed to be one of us managed to win one percent of the vote

between those two cheeks, and there he goes covered with shit. Even the barricade of girls we threw up to protect us from all that and we can't tip the scales for how can you make love when there are blue uniforms everywhere. Suffocation suicide is all we're headed for and anyone who says different is going to catch my cobblestone in the head.

J.-P.B.

The Paris Market District (Les Halles)

1ST BUTCHER: Well, here comes that faggot again on his way ta the toilets.

2ND BUTCHER: What pretty curls he has!

1ST BUTCHER: Takin' his girl friend. Isn' that nice!

2ND BUTCHER: With his queer littul ass swingin' in his queer littul pants.

1ST BUTCHER: *approaching Denis:* Hullo, dear.

2ND BUTCHER: *approaching Denis:* C'n we shake yer littul hand, dear?

1ST BUTCHER: What'sa matter? Ain't we yer type?

2ND BUTCHER: How 'bout a little kiss, right here? *(He puckers.)*

1ST BUTCHER: Like you give your brother.

2ND BUTCHER, *mockingly:* C'n we stroke you gently?

DENIS, *sharply:* Leave us alone!

1ST BUTCHER: Now the fairy's gone and got 'is gander up.

2ND BUTCHER, *walking right up to Denis and glaring at him:* How 'bout loanin' us yer friend? . . . *(loudly)* She can't do you much good.
> *(They laugh.)*

1ST BUTCHER: Give 'm a few taps, Pierre.
> *(The girl screams, while the 2nd Butcher beats up Denis. Denis yells out at each blow.)*

2ND BUTCHER: And now, young lady, yer gonna git yer miniskirt wrinkled.
> *(The girl screams, The 2nd Butcher rapes Corinne by*

*throwing her down on the back of the 1st Butcher who is
kneeling on all fours. The 2nd Butcher stands between
Corinne's legs, pumps away, breathing in gasps in rhythm
with his pumping. Then he throws her to the ground.)*

2ND BUTCHER, *getting up:* Now, she really got somethin' that
time, didn' she? *(They both laugh.)* I can't stand them guys
wit long hair ... Nothin' but sissies ... When I was that age, I
already had a trade ... an' I had guts, too, but nowadays
they're all good fer nothin'. Hey, let's go 'ave dinner. How
'bout some onion soup ta git our strength back after all that
exertin'. O.K.?

(The two butchers laugh and leave.)

CORINNE: Denis! ...

(Silence. Denis turns away and gets up.)

CORINNE: Denis.

*(She gets up and goes to join the rest of the group with
Denis. Denis leaves the group and, making the noise of
machine-gun fire vocally, he pretends he is gunning people
down.)*

DENIS, *changing his voice:* Captain, take immediate command of
the squadron.

—Right, Sir.

—Annihilate the column coming up to the west of Desdatt, the
Abruzzi capital. Franco is at the head of it. Give them everything you've got.

—Yes, Sir.

—On the double.

Anyone but my father would now realize—this mission is going to
succeed or fail—it's a matter of life or death—I've thought of
everything—carefully planned every string in my net—Doug-
lousky—to the east is country I've pacified—to the west, desert and sand. The mass executions I ordered and everyday
bombings should have them prostrate by now. I've buried
them in their trenches, ha, ha—Damned rice-paddies—To the
south, the Indians have been herded into the demilitarized
zone—dirtying up the war like cows—and they need a change

of bedding—The north's alright—tourism is flourishing
there—a mass concentration of German Jews—I'm here—
with the strong support of my artillery—Behind—*(He makes
the noise of gunfire.)*
—What's the matter, Captain?
—It's the rebels, sir.
—What about them?
—Waves of 'em pourin' over us, sir; the army's bein' submerged!
We have to retreat, sir!
—Run away?—Run away?—Never!—You're no true Spaniard,
Gomez, if you can say, Run away. Running away isn't Span-
ish, Gomez.
Changing his voice. And, of course, he killed him with one shot
right through the head.
Oh, here come those rebels—3rd column, bare sabres!—Take them
from behind—remember, remember that your country is
watching you and it's so that Spain and Castile may live.
(Sadly) Olè-è-è—Go ahead, men, olè, beautiful piece of butch-
ery, olè—Up ahead—They died stoically on their horses—
And then, then I took command of the 3rd regiment of Hus-
sards and I sabered my way through—and it wasn't long
before there wasn't a rebel left—1914—1914—Pontau.
Changing his voice Oh! magnificent, magnificent.
Since then, the country has rested in the cup of my hands and it's
marching—to its destiny of progress and triumph. Thank you.
THE FATHER *(acted by a fellow in the group):* What were you
doing on your bed, you filthy piss-head?
    The clichés are distributed.
DENIS: On my bed? Nothing, nothing at all, really! . . . Why?
What do you think? I can't stand it . . . Why are you always
insinuating? . . . On the bed? Nothing, I'm telling you, nothing! Why?
THE FATHER: Don't get all excited. What's coming over you?
(He whines.) When I was your age, you know, I suffered—I
really had it bad—It's not the same anymore; you kids've got
everything—But when I was your age, believe me, it wasn't

like it is now—I was working for my bread and butter when I was just twelve years old, and my mother made me hand over everything I earned—You see what I mean, what I'm trying to tell you, son—We didn't have things like movies or television to enjoy ourselves—I wish I'd had a chance to get an education like you have—You're really lucky and you don't know it—But you just better before it's too late—Get it into your head—When I was your age, my parents didn't give me the chances I've given you—But maybe that's why you don't know what life's all about—Oh, it's your mother's fault, alright, the way she coddles you—But she'll reap what she sows—Like everything else—You know what I mean, he who laughs last laughs best—You'll make your bed and lie in it—A rolling stone—You know I've always tried hard to be good to you; but give you an inch and you take a yard—You can tell what a man is by what he knows—You have to push your own way up in this world; nobody gives a damn for the next guy—Earn your bed and board first, then worry about the rest—Not everybody can be president; the world needs plumbers, too—If you don't learn a trade, you'll always be at the bottom of the pile—There's more to happiness than money, but it helps—It's none of my business, you do what you want—I've got a roof over my head and I know how to earn my living; you make your decisions; I wash my hands of it—I don't give a damn.

The group falls to the ground.

The following text is distributed.

—Fire, damn it!—Fire on the bastards!—Oh! I'm hit—Keep firing, Jesus, cover me—Sweet Jesus, what a way to die—in this God-forsaken place *(He imitates the sound of a crow and looks up at the vultures.)* Waiting for me to die! Oh! Oh!—I'm pissing blood—My God, I'm holding my guts—The flies! Oh!—I can't let myself sleep, just don't sleep—I'm so thirsty—*(He imitates the sound of gun-fire.)* The bastard wants to finish me—the son of a bitch of a Jap! *(He gets up and imitates his father:)* Why don't you take some of your

brother's example? He's a man—He's got blood in his veins—
You want me to say it? He's got a man's balls—He's fighting
for his country—When he was just fifteen years old he was
already fighting at the dances—He wasn't afraid of anybody—I'm telling you—He'd always come home from school
with his clothes torn, sometimes with a black eye, but you
could tell he'd won, he'd always win. I can still see him
smiling at me with a tooth missing, and saying, "Don't worry,
Dad, I'm a man!"

THE FATHER: You'd never know you were brothers; you're a
real coward, afraid of your own shadow—and you want me to
buy you a guitar on top of it all? What do you intend to do
with it? Go play Beatnik? Your hair's long enough already—
All you need's the guitar and no bath for awhile—You know
what you are, what you really are? You're a fairy! Yes, a
fairy—Keep quiet, Yoyo, I'm just saying what I think. I have
a right to, haven't I?—I say my son's a queer fairy.

DENIS, *imitating the fiancée's voice:* Don't be too hard on your
son, Mr. Brochon. Think instead of Néné who's over there
covering himself with glory, fighting like a hero.

THE FIANCEE: And I'm waiting for him here with you, his
family, looking at the photographs of when he was just a little
baby without any clothes on. There's one I like especially,
where he's, hee, hee, doing his peepee, holding his little dingle.
Let's sit down around the table now; Mrs. Brochon's got such
a lovely roast rabbit in sauce and mushrooms with buttered
carrots ready for us, with a good bottle of Beaujolais from
your wine-cellar, Mr. Brochon. Let's drink to your son's and
my engagement; let's drink till we feel good—and happy.

THE FATHER: Yes, I know you love our son a lot—and we think
very much of you, too. Come here, you're our daughter now,
our girl, our little girl. Come on, don't be afraid; I'm not a big
bad wolf—Ay! come here now; you don't mind if I call you
my little girl, do you? Sit down; we'll have a good meal, till we
bust, ha! Give me your hand. Can I give you a little kiss?
Hou! hou! hou! Oh! you've got a cute little hand *(He kisses*

her with a loud smack.) Yes, you're our little girl now. Hee, hee.

    The entire text that follows is to be distributed among the actors.

The actor begins by trying to sing the French national anthem: Allons z'enfants de la Patrie le jour de ... ah, ah ... contre nous de la tyrannie l'étendard sanglant ... oh, oh ... the sun's going down. *(He imitates the death toll of a bell.)* I've got to keep walking, as far as I can ... Mimi. Mimi. I'm thinking of you. I love you ... with all my heart ... you and France and my parents. Dad, take care of Mimi for me; she's alone in the world. Take good care of her. Tell her what I was like when I was little, and how I liked to fight. Please forgive me, everyone I ever punched because you laughed at me or forgot ... Oh my God, it hurts ... so bad. A year in Vietnam. My share. The fellows liked me ... respected me, I think.

Imitating a number of soldiers: Brochon is the man to go, sir; he's the best man for the job, there's no doubt about it, sir. Everyone thinks the world of him, sir, he's a hero. As soon as he comes back from his mission, let him do it, sir. Damn it, Brochon's a man that doesn't give a damn about danger. He's a swell guy, a real man, that Brochon!

Changing voice: In testimony to the enthusiastic homage rendered by his fellow soldiers to this man who served above and beyond the call of duty, it gives me great pleasure to award Brochon the Purple Heart, here on this battlefield, now pacified, where he distinguished himself so magnificently. Brochon!

Another voice: Excuse me, sir, but Brochon isn't here ... , sir. He's been away on a mission for the last five days, sir.

The preceding voice: What a man! always on mission. ... He's got fire in his ass, Brichon has!

Other voice: Brōchon, sir.

The officer's voice: Eh? Oh, excuse me. Brōchon. Hmm. Brochon 863-1000.

Denis' natural voice: I'm getting close to camp. I can see the lights.

I've got to make it. Standing. My guts in my hand, but standing. *(He imitates vocally a bell ringing a death toll.)*
Everyone's voice: Hey! It's Brochon! It's Brochon. Brochon's back
... can I give you a hand, Brochon?
Denis' voice: No, I'm alright! I've carried 'em four hundred miles
through the rice paddies under enemy fire; I can go three
hundred feet to make my report!
Clicking his heels: Present and accounted for, sir. Sgt. Brochon
reporting.
The officer's voice: Brochon! What a man! Everyone's proud of
you here. Are you wounded?
Denis' voice: It's nothing, sir, just a scratch ... Mission's accom-
plished, sir!
Good work. You're to leave on another in fifteen minutes.
Yes, sir.
Dismissed! ... Oh, Brochon! I almost forgot your Purple
Heart. *(He tosses it to him.)*
Thank you, sir. *(He salutes like a fanatic, and hums a military
march.)*
Imitating the father's voice: Mimi, little chicken, look at your man!
Our son, our son's been decorated with the ...
The real father speaks: The Purple Heart. I've got to admit I'm
real proud of him. *(He sniffles.)* I don't go for crying and
sentimentalizing, but I'm telling you it does something to a
man to see his boy's name in big letters in the Pentagon
Dispatch and to know that everybody's reading: Brochon rec.
purp. heart.
> *Two boys imitate reporters' voices and relay back and
> forth very quickly:*
I saw Jean-Paul Brochon—I met—Jean-Paul Brochon during a
night of intense fighting, heavy combat—Jean-Paul distinguished himself yet again—The Viet-Minh were swarming
around Hill 713, and Jean-Paul Brochon, yes Jean-Paul Brochon, charged at them alone, yes, that's right, alone, without
regard for leg or limb, and captured the enemy quarter-mas-
ter, which completely confused the enemy and precipitated

their retreat—Jean-Paul Brochon is an everyday fellow like
you and me. Although Jean-Paul Brochon doesn't say much,
he consented to give us a few words. Jean-Paul Brochon
doesn't say much because his mind's on the job he's got to
do—Jean-Paul, what do you think of this war?
—*(Silence.)* I don't think. I fight.
—Do you think France will ultimately win?
—That's what I'm here for.
—People at home are following you every day on television.
You're a sensation. *(Silence.)* Jean-Paul Brochon, can you tell
us what you intend to do tomorrow?
—Tomorrow I'm going to kill fifteen Viet-Minh in front of the
television cameras, for the folks at home.
—Thank you, Jean-Paul Brochon . . . That's the man he is: Tomorrow he'll kill fifteen Viet-Minh for the folks at home. Courageous, lucid, intelligent, sensitive, and profound, a hero . . . A
French hero, in a tradition of heroes. Yes, tonight, all of you
who are listening, all of you who are watching, you can feel
secure, secure so long as France produces men like that. There
isn't another nation in the world that can look on such sons
with such pride. The war has been a long one—since June 15,
1958, when the first military adviser was shot. And now it's
May 2, 1975. Perhaps some of us have lost sons, husbands,
fiancés, fathers. And maybe some of you feel that drafting
fourteen year-olds like we have to this year is hard, too hard,
and perhaps we'll mention, once again, the seventy thousand
thirty-seven dead, who've given up their lives gloriously. But is
that what's really important? Isn't what's really important the
fact that our country is showing the world how truly great it
is, how magnificent, extraordinary, and absolutely unique the
spirit of the French people is? If it hadn't been for this Vietnamese War, would we have ever known such a superb soldier
as Jean-Paul Brochon? And so, I ask you, doesn't every one of
us say, as he overlooks his little private griefs, doesn't every
one of us say: Thank you, Jean-Paul Brochon. Thank you,
Brochon. Thank you, Jean-Paul, you are France and we're

behind you. Thank you, ladies and gentlemen, for your attention.

> *Denis gets up, inspired. He strikes a number of poses. He
> recites Hamlet's monologue, pronouncing the best-known
> parts very affectedly:*

—Nymph, in thy orisons be all my sins remembered.

> *Ophelia appears. The others applaud enthusiastically.*

SOMEONE ELSE: Tonight was a triumph!

HER: Yes, you gave an extraordinary performance.

HIM: No, it isn't perfect enough yet. I can do better. But you were
ravishing ... yes, yes ... beautiful, deeply troubling. It's because of you I played so well—for the first time tonight, my
despicable "me" didn't gnaw at me. Every daily banal thought
left me, and I was filled instead with the love of Hamlet for
Ophelia, and Hamlet's soul-rending sorrow; it filled me ...
deliciously. *(He drops to one knee.)* I love you, Marianne, I
have since the first day I saw you. It sounds crazy, but what's
crazier than love? The first time I set eyes on you, your
fragility and purity pierced through me. I can never more be
anything but a puppet that responds to the tiniest breeze
through your hair, to the tiniest motion of your tiniest finger,
or the beating of your eyelashes ... and the language of your
eyes when you look at me.

DENIS AND ONE OF THE OTHERS, *back and forth:* Love me;
we will be Ophelia and Hamlet, Marianne and Octavius, Juliet
and Romeo, Iseult and Tristan, Ondine and the Knight. Our
life will be a wonderful dream, and we will ever live as these
great lovers—

HER: I love you.

THE FATHER: A whore's nipple, it's cold this morning. Well, I'd
better move my ass if I don' wanta be late fo' work—I'm
takin' two dollars fo' lunch—Well, I gotta eat, don't I?—It's
not my fault if there's inflatin'. I can't work all night too. Just
git yer son ta go ta work. All he does is goof off like a damned
poet. Let 'im git a job drivin' a taxi or somethin'; he's got 'is

drivin' license. There's nothin' disgraceful 'bout workin'—The
gentleman lets us house 'im an' feed 'im—Shit! when I was 'is
age, I earned my bread an' butter. Why can't he do the same,
is he the president's son or somethin'? Keep talkin', keep
talkin', it's really interestin'. All 'is ol' man's gotta do is work
fo' 'is twenty year ol' boy who's still unskilled labor. You sure
haven' got any pride. All the gentleman has ta do is sleep an'
jerk off in the nice warm house, an' dream—An' I have ta go
out an' work till my ass drops off—Oh, don' worry, don'
worry one bit, you're always right.

> *The group begins to sob violently They place a board
> across the two metal barrels to make a table, and they lay
> the body of No. 4 on it. The group laments loudly.*

ALL: Oh, oh, oh, oh . . .

NO. 3: Oh! They beat him to death with their berets.

THE LEADER: Ooooh! Ooooh!

NO. 3: My dear brethren, we have gathered together tonight in
great sadness, and we shed our tears at having lost one of our
dear companions. But, my dear brethren, let us not permit our
minds to be clouded with impious despair. Our sister, Violaine
Leduc, present here in this earthly box, should rather inspire
us to overcome our excessive attachment to the things of this
world. Violaine Leduc is at rest here among us as she was on
the day of her birth; she has rediscovered her original purity.
Her life was a long road of suffering, of insatiable masturbation, of unacknowledged sleep-ins, of half-rapes, and finally of
hope in that future life outside the door of which she stands in
pregnant expectation today. As God's minister among you,
desirous always to seek out one of his lost sheep, I reached out
for her and lifted her up in my consecrated arms. I remember
the day I saw her slowly climb the hill to my rectory. It was a
fresh morning, and I had drunk nothing for two days but a bit
of hot chocolate. I watched this warm meal laboring steadily
up the rocky slope of my abstinence. She pushed gently on my
little gate—it never closes properly—and she clumped through
the weeds in my little garden. I spoke to her paternally and

welcomed her with my white hand clasping the Bible as it has
so often clasped soft, round, gentle souls for Christ's sake. . . .

NO. 2: You've found pea . . ea . . eace . . . You've found Jesus . . .
You're happy in the Kingdom . . . You are with Christ,
Go . . o . . od. . . .

NO. 3: She was afraid, for the forest was near; and it was filled
with satyrs and people. I reassured her humbly that, although
my abode was poor, it was safe, and that in this cottage
unknown to men, she had nothing to fear but her own conscience. And I, a poor, miserable hermit, would be able to
furnish her with that perfect nourishment that would befit her
while she remained in the bower of a poor servant of God. She
remained near me for six days, as I devoted myself to my
daily prayers and she searched for faith as she came and went,
so beautifully moved as I gazed on her. Then she approached
to consecrate herself to God; she was dressed in white transparent linen, revealing all she offered to God. I adored her
holy gifts, every little extremity; I treasured them as revela-
tions given me by the bountiful goodness of Our Lord Jesus
Christ. Little by little, praised be the divine glory, each night
became a Mass and my bed an altar; and the centurion's holy
lance drew near the holy holy water font. And after a while I
could no longer bear that the graces of God be hidden, and I
desired to worship Our Lord's seven joys. That linen gown . . .
I must admit I surprised her somewhat; but I told her that it
was the feast of St. John, and she accepted the honor. From
then on, every day was a happy one. . . . Everyday I offered
her my wine. . . . And she would tell you, if she could, that my
wine is white. . . . Everyday, she held her chalice to me, and it
was a deep one. Thus, in consummate sacrifice to the Lord, we
kissed the crucifix, outstretched arms, legs, feet nailed by the
desire to love, and the hollow where vinegar mixed with wine.
She was frightened and began to put all her weakened faith in
the creed I taught her. I became an apostle; I called eleven
others, and you came and made your way where I had gone

before you. On the road of olives ... she was not forgotten, but was honored, but was honored ... Aaaah Aaaah!

—You've all come together here, and I know why—but it's better not to mention such things. Well, I came as a friend, friends since we were kids, and when I hit her I thought ... Come on, Violaine, let's go have a little fun ... and now I find all of you here wheezing like mummies around her; and I wanted to take her dancing this afternoon. *(Sobs.)*

—*(Curious.)* Yes, indeed, so you didn't know what had happened! And if I hadn't been the first to meet you in the stairway, you'd have come in and yelled out, "Hey! where's my sweet little bitch, let's go fishing!" And then I would have seen you and I would have been the first to tell you, "Mr. Gaston, Violaine has passed away" ... On earth we weep for her ... and hope to see her eternally in heaven ... hope ... to see her eternally in heaven ...

NO. 3: Violaine Leduc, fuck you, Violaine. I want you, and your forehead is like ice and your lips are hard as rocks. She'd give in under me. You're stiff as a board; but I can still see you. Your face is sinking, just when, just when I'd like to wake you up and shove you a piece of purple. I'd like to see you get red. I'd like you to flesh-quiver. I'd like you to coffin-enjoy. I'd like you to embalmed-fornicate. I'd like you to miracle-move, to ice-laugh, to smiling-rot. Remember, maiden, maiden blushing in the olive trees, that you lay and spread for me the first time. You're my bottle of tea. And when we get drunk now, you'll always be with us, and vomit and we'll all jerk off on you rigolo, and eat you, a little piece for each of us, so as not to forget you.

THE JOURNALIST: We live in strange times. When our generation was young and making its place in the world, we were enthusiastic. We believed in things and were willing to defend them. But what do we see around us today? Non-conformists who worship screaming, self-styled poets. There is no longer respect for anything. We live in a world devoid of heroes, priests, or moralists. The birth of children is postponed as inopportune; marriage has become useless and old-fashioned; and even death is laughed at as a poor joke. I remember the day I met the Pope, and I remember the sublime day I attended church services with our present chief executive. Like myself, he fondly recalls the sweet Springtime of Old France. The precocious religious blossoming of our children carefully cultivated until they were twelve years old. The inconspicuous and often efficacious labor of the proud guild system. The thought that I will pass away as a member of the French Academy fills me with peaceful serenity. So, why should mischievous uncombed boys and girls disturb the celestial tranquility created by their parents who know better the lessons of experience? Young people, I implore you, do not play at being sorcerer's apprentices. I abjure you, all you rock bands, Stones, Doctors, Bay-tils, and others, think of your duty as members of society. Live for your neighbor. The road leading to the factories is a beautiful one, and you will be happy, worthy of your fathers who are watching you. This commentary has been brought to you by Hervy Pluchet.

NO. 4, *gets up:* Alright! I think you want to; and besides, it'll make them happy . . .

(Very dim lighting.)

NO. 4, *imitating a girl:* It's nice here. Who'd have thought we'd have found a sand dune in a place like this? At night it feels like the sea is all around us. But we shouldn't stick around until morning, because instead of the ocean, there's really nothing here but clusters of factories spewing black smoke. This must be the highest point in the town. Oh! I can feel the sea, you know, when I ride the La Rochelle ferry, I can smell the salt, oooh I inhale it like this, oooh and I get drunk on it everytime. *(He pants with joy.)* It's true, I wish I was there. You probably think I'm kinda crazy because I talk so much, don't you? I'm the kinda girl that gets on your nerves, aren't I, because I'm so complicated, eh? Can I have another drink of that cognac?

NO. 3: You're getting drunk.

NO. 4: Tastes good. Want some? I really mean it, I feel good with you. You're my little brother, aren't you, now? Oh, you taste good. *(Gasps of pleasure.)* You like me? Oh, I shouldn't ask you; I'm so crazy. You don't want me, do you? Because sometimes, you know, I just would like people to be a little nice to me, that's all. You think I'm crazy, don't you? But I need it; I really do. You may have the impression that I'm of easy virtue, but I'm nobody's whore. I like to feel you warm beside me. If it wasn't for you, you know, I'd commit suicide. Don't you think I could? ... Men are funny. Oooh, they're warm and hard ... You're strong ... I like it when you begin to want me; I get the vibrations right away ... First, you look kinda funny with your eyes getting a little big; and then you seem to be in a hurry, you get nervous, you rub my blouse with your shoulder, you open it and your hands touch in.... You take my tit, always the right one, and you paw it, then you touch the tip of it, and then ... you hurt me ... I like it. ... I know your hand ... it thinks for a minute; I know it is thinking about going farther in.... One finger, two fingers, the whole five of them reach in all over, and my tit pulsates, it breathes. Your hand dizzily slides over my belly that quivers-jumps.... You take hold of my sex.... You touch it, take it, and open me up.

NO. 3: Your big buns soft down.

NO. 4: You trace their outline and fill your hands.

NO. 3: I squeeze them out of shape.

NO. 4: You bite me.

NO. 3: I lick you with my puppy-dog tongue. You stand like a statue and I kneel in front of you, kissing you, taking your cherry in my mouth. Your ivory-black body trembles, like a rustling willow; you are tied to four wild horses that rip you apart.

NO. 4: Oh! you're rough. Oh! you're hurting me. Roooo ... You feel good ... There ... You're long.

NO. 3: Come! as far as I take you, but come quick! Oooh!

No. 4 gives a long cry. Silence ...

NO. 4: I love you. I'm your little sister flooded over with tears.

NO. 3: It's hot in here.

NO. 4: Your little sister is a long skinny stick; she doesn't please anybody except you, little brother. We can go walking the roads, both of us, and play a guitar and have a little monkey that'll dance in the snow. We'll call him Cappy. I don't know how to please you like some young girl that can only flirt, wiggle and connive. I'm your big boy with a hole.

NO. 3: It's hot in here.

NO. 4: O.K. I get the message. See you later.

> *The group gathers together again slowly. Denis stands to one side. The others advance towards him threateningly. A dim light on the group. Denis crosses the stage, so that his path and that of the group intersect.*

NO. 2: Hello there . . . *(Denis freezes in his tracks and is silent.)* Isn't even polite. Cat got your tongue? . . . Look, we say hello to you nice-like, and you make like you're deaf or something. That makes me mad.

DENIS: Leave me alone; I'm not bothering you.

NO. 2: Oh, you're not going to get off that easy, dearie. You insulted me; now you've got to fight me, fair and square-like, according to the rules.

DENIS, *weakly:* There are . . . there are rules for fighting?

NO. 2: You'll see. Us fellows, here, we're kinda special. In fact, very special.

> *No. 4 takes off his jacket and makes Denis put it on. No. 3 ties No. 2's right leg to Denis' left leg, and gives him an imaginary knife. They fight and roll on the ground.*

NO. 3: The cops!

> *All of the group runs off in every direction. Denis and No. 2, tied to each other, try to run away, but they keep falling over their tied legs. They stay on the ground, and two cops arrive.*

1st COP: Well, hello. You look good trussed up like that; all ready for us to toss you into the wagon. What're you doing here, freaks? *(Silence.)* Don't answer, eh? *(The cop gives one of*

them a kick. They both fall, dragging each other down.) O.K.,
girls, you don't want to be polite? Get on your stomachs!
O.K., push-ups. Move it. One, two, one, two . . . and say: I'm
too freaky to fuck Bridget Bardot, I'm too freaky to fuck
Bridget Bardot. Say it, say it. *(Denis and No. 2 say it weakly.)*
O.K., and now we're going to clip those locks of yours!

DENIS AND NO. 2: No, no!

1st COP: You'll see whether it's no or not. You'll see whether
you're going to prance around the city anymore like a couple
of queer good-for-nothings.

> *Shadows appear at the back of the stage. The shadows
> begin to run. It is the leader of the group. No. 3, and No. 4
> who take out their imaginary knives and cut the throats of
> the two policemen from behind. Only the two dead police-
> men are left on the stage.*

A RADIO ANNOUNCER'S VOICE, *imitated by one of the boys:*
Two guardians of the peace pursuing an organized gang
caught in the act were viciously murdered today. A represen-
tative of the President of the Republic accompanied the local
chief of police to pay honor to these courageous victims of
duty. Their sacrifice is not in vain for, in grateful recognition,
they have been decorated with the Police Medal, which is the
highest existing distinction given posthumously. Every effort is
being made to apprehend their murderers. Public opinion is
alarmed by such acts of violence on the part of remarkably
organized young outlaws. You are advised not to walk
through the poorer sections of the city after dark. Watch over
your daughters. In case of emergency, call us at 272-1111.

> *The fellows who played the cops rejoin the others who are
> standing against the wall.*

DENIS: There's no escape.

NO. 4: We can try to make it over the border.

NO. 2: There isn't anymore border or anything; there isn't anything but cops around now.

NO. 5: We shouldn't have killed 'em.

DENIS: Would you have rather had them cut our hair off?

NO. 5: Shut up. What we have to worry about now is getting out of here.

NO. 3: I know a cellar, or a hole really, that's under an abandoned foundation.

THE LEADER: Far from here?

NO. 3: Not too.

THE LEADER: Let's go.

> *The group runs off in every direction. They come back on together, in the imaginary cellar.*

—It's kind of eerie.

—I can't see anything.

—Wait a minute, I'll light a match.

—We'll be alright down in back. No one'll think of looking for us here.

DENIS: It's shit.

NO. 3: Should have found something else. The thing we've got to do is hide here just as long as we can until they've forgotten about us.

DENIS: Forget that we killed two cops? You'll see if they forget us!

NO. 3: I'm talking about the people with sense.

DENIS: What good's your sense going to do you in a hole?

THE LEADER: Shut up. We've got better things to do than piss on each other.

> *An improvisation of rhythm now follows, accomplished by beating fists, feet and chains on the barrels. It should begin slowly and rise in intensity, over a considerable amount of time, until it is a rapid roar. Meanwhile, Christ should stand with arms outstretched in a cross, be dragged, beaten, spit upon, wounded, and on him Corinne the Virgin should be lain as in intercourse—and anything else that can be thought up, such as a mad masturbation pantomime by one actor, using the loose end of his belt as his phallus. Finally, an American kiss between Christ and the Virgin. Alleluia! The group disperses.*
> *Denis and No. 3 stand to the side of the stage:*

DENIS: Excuse me, would you have a subway ticket you could let me have, please?

> *The rest of the group pretend they are offended bourgeois and they draw away from Denis.*
>
> *Denis and No. 3 pass a cigarette back and forth and smoke it with great enjoyment. Meanwhile, the trial takes place.*

The Trial:

NO. 2: You will betray your friends.

NO. 4: You will defile your girlfriend.

THE LEADER: You will suffer eternal boredom.

NO. 4: You will become hatred.

DENIS: You will become violence.

NO. 2: And you will always find someone more violent than you.

NO. 4: You will cast away gentleness.

NO. 2: In the face of kindness, your mournful spirit will cry out, "Deceit."

DENIS: You will loathe yourself.

NO. 2: At night, you will agonize when you think of your past and you will not be able to drive the memory of it out of your ever vigilant spirit.

> *The following text is distributed.*

NO. 4: You will find no rest. Demons will sit beside you and tap on your shoulder. They will laugh wildly; and you will laugh, too, for a long time, drinking bottles of universal scorn; and when the cellar is empty, boredom and nothingness will enter into you and you will be able neither to sleep nor to forget.

> *The following text is distributed.*

NO. 2: In the daytime, an angel will knock on the door. Then you will hide your horns and tail, and invite him to join you at the table; and you will paint your face with flour and smiles to hide your teeth blackened with vice. You will offer him something to drink, and then you will tear off his wings and throw them into a cauldron of pitch and all of you, one after the other, will defile him and then . . . you will be bored and you will be able neither to sleep nor to forget.

> *At the end of the trial, the group joins Denis and No. 3 who are sprawled at the side of the stage, and everyone joins in the smoking. Then the 'lost woman' appears, played by Corinne. In general, in this play, all the feminine roles should be played by the same actress.*

THE LOST WOMAN: Squash them! Can't you see that you have to squash them with your heel like toads. *(She approaches.)*

NO. 3: Who are you?

THE WOMAN: The Lost Woman.

NO. 3, *getting on his knees comically:* Squash me, vamp. *(Silence.)*
> *During the Lost Woman's monologue, the group smokes without listening.*

THE WOMAN: If you had known me when ... you would have respected me, mold-face. Back when I was a wife and an exemplary mother ... I was pure as snow when I married, a fragile reed for the appetite of a husband who was base from the first day ... (softly) from the first night. I had to let him spread me and soil me every night for twelve years. He'd run his hands over me and make my body wilt and then that putrid, detestable flow in all my body-canal, a grimace of disgust, purse my lips to spit out the atrocious infusion ... I got two children I wanted to love with all my sullied flesh, but their faces resembled their father's bloodshot face, and I couldn't help but see him ... and suffer from it ... I hated them. Since then, I've been walking these underground alleys and I feel pure. I'm a young girl, a virgin and I'm looking for a young white and black man who will court me, court me for the first time. Every night, I come down here and I walk ... meeting rats and vampires ... and tonight, I've met you. *(To No. 3)* You, you don't attract me. The nights you offer must be the same as those with my husband, and he's nothing but a laborer. He's rough as a butcher, as crass and sickening ... but you, you've actually made an effort to attain with your knowledge the crass ignorance of my husband. You think you're refined in evil, when in fact you do no better than the basest instincts of the most primitive animal. Get away from

me, you're afraid of women, I know. *(To Denis:)* You, you
attract me ... Yes, I can see that you're brand new, like me,
that's what I want and what I like in you. Come with me, we'll
learn everything and discover everything together. Why are
you laughing? *(Silence.)* It's true, we're timid, we blush at
anything, and of course our hands tremble a little, we're going
to invent child's games, and pretend to really be playing them.
And we'll laugh loud, too loud, and speak high and in falsetto
and not think for an instant where our hands are touching ...
and then ... who can laugh at such graceful awkwardness,
such pink pleasure to anticipate?

THE WOMAN: Eh? What's he saying? He's really crazy ... Hee,
hee, hee ... *(She exits.)*

DENIS: Corinne.

NO. 3: This place is turning into a real low-rent district.

DENIS: What are you doing here?

CORRINNE: I don't know. I walked and walked and walked, I
fell into this hole ... I wanted to sleep, I'm tired ...

DENIS: But it's dangerous here; we killed two cops.

CORINNE: It doesn't matter ...

NO. 3: It matters to us. The cops may have followed you ...

CORINNE: No, nobody follows me anymore.

NO. 3: Hear that? Nobody follows her anymore. Then you can
serve up the grub ...

DENIS: What did you say?

NO. 3: I said that if the girl stays, she has to do her share. She
belongs to everyone, that's all.

DENIS: But we're engaged.

NO. 3: That's what I said; it's time to marry her.

CORINNE: Let him be. What does it matter ... anymore.

THE LEADER: I'm telling you for the last time to get back into
your basket. I'll de-ball the first one of you that touches her.
(To Corinne:) What's your name?

CORINNE: Corinne.

THE LEADER: You will be called Mary; you will be the Virgin, and we will adore you. *(He points to No. 3.)* He will be your slave.

NO. 3: The man's flipped his lid. *(The Leader hits him across the head.)*

The Mass of St. Mary:

> *The Virgin stands on a promontory, either a raised area of the floor or one of the metal barrels, with a bunch of rags, or one of the boys' shirts, wrapped up like a baby in her arms. No. 3 claps stones in his hands. All lie prostrate.*

THE LEADER: Virgin Mary, full of grace, the Lord is with you.

ALL: And we're with you.

NO. 2: You are beauty.

ALL, *chant:* You're so pure, so pure so pu . . u . . ure. You're so pu . . u . . ure.

NO. 2: Holy Mary, I like girls. But as soon as any girl goes out on the street, the fellows dirty her for me right away. They look at her breasts; they touch them worse with their eyes than with their hands. Their eyes dart between her legs and run over her hips that I'd kissed just that morning with all my love and with all my foolish purity erect. Then they look at her face and wilt it. But you've stayed so pure and nobody's look can ever dirty you. Be our mother, our first wife.

> *The leader slowly undresses and reverently lays his clothes at the Virgin's feet. The others follow his example.*

THE LEADER, *to No. 3:* You there, you belong to the Virgin; say what you have to say.

> *(No. 3 approaches, as the others repeat in a panting manner:)*

ALL: Say what you have to say, say what you have to say, say what you have to say . . .

NO. 3: When I was born, everyone said I was a beautiful baby. But I quickly realized that everything around me was ugly. Unfortunately, I had parents. A father and a mother. They didn't have much left even then, except poor worn-out memories. My mother spent her time not listening to my father, and my father spent all his time trying to get through to her. When they touched me, I lost my beauty and I began to resemble them. I had my father's eyes and my mother's chin. Everyone thought it was nice except me. When I was seven years old, I realized that my life was finished because I resembled those two. I tried to become a little cultivated. I began to read a lot. ... My parents never read anything except the almanac and the evening paper, so everything I read in my books churned around in me and couldn't get out. I became closed in on myself; I became a liar, a poet, a good-for-nothing, and deep down, my blood changed to venom. I became a reptile, and I really began to suffer, which, I guess, is a good thing. I crawled up and down the highways and country roads, the ones with white and yellow lines painted on them, dying from the heat. People threw stones at me like they do at any homeless, penniless beggar walking around in rags. And everyday those stones ripped my belly open a little more. Sometimes, I had the pleasure of biting someone weaker than me, like some lost Little Red Riding Hood, and letting my venom flow into her ... and then, of course, I was hungry and you can't steal an apple in this damned country where construction workers think they run the place and they lynch you up kicking you in the stomach till the work whistle blows.

THE LEADER: Do you love our Virgin?

NO. 3: She looks to me more virgin than most fourteen year olds.

THE LEADER: She's our mother.

NO. 3: A person has only one mother. And whatever she was, there's not much I could do about the one I got. She was an amateur, but she was my mother.

THE LEADER: Your mother was neither beautiful nor pure. Mary is. Your mother is in Mary, but purified and beautified.

NO. 3: Every mother is soiled. That was my first heartbreak. She was a whore; she kept sleeping with my father all the time.

THE LEADER: Shut up. Get on your knees, and adore her. (*He throws No. 3 down on the ground.*)

NO. 2: Say mommy, say mommy.

ALL, *very softly:* Mom ... mo..o..om ... mom ...
mo..o..om *(Very loudly:)* Mom ... mo..o..om ...

> *They all pant and gasp, saying Mom. The leader gets down behind No. 3, takes him in his arms, rocks him slowly, and talks to him in baby-talk.*

THE LEADER: Hi, Mommy *(Silence.)*

Did you sleep well?

Mommy, I'm hungry.

Mommy, I love you.

Mommy, I want a cowboy pistol.

Mommy, you're pretty.

I want to sleep in your bed.

Instead of Daddy.

What does Daddy do?

You want me to tell him to go away?

No you don't have white hair; you don't look tired at all.

ALL, *in a suffering tone:* Mom ... mo..o..om ... mo..o..om
...mo..o..om ... mo..o..om ...

THE LEADER: Did Mommy's little man sleep well?

NO. 3: No.

THE LEADER: Tell me what was the matter.

NO. 3: I masturbated all night.

> *The boys in the gang laugh and yell as they goose each other.*

CORINNE-ST. MARY: It is not a sin, my son.

ALL, *amazed:* She spoke, she spoke. The Blessed Virgin spoke. Holy Married Mother, a miracle, a miracle, pray for us, a miracle.

> *Then follows a tableau representing the miracles at Lourdes. They imitate the crippled, the blind, etc.*

ALL, *repeating continuously and ever more loudly:* Mo..o..om, Mary, Mommy, Mo..o..om, Mary, Mommy ... *(Organ music.)*

> *Suddenly, they all stop and raise their eyes as they listen.*

THE VOICE, *spoken by one of the boys upstage:* Hey down there, what's all the racket?! We can't hear ourselves think up here.

Quiet down or we'll call the cops. Go take your orgies some-
place else.

NO. 3: Who are you?

THE VOICE: The tenant upstairs.

NO. 3: But there isn't any house above us.

THE VOICE: This is a seven story tenement building, and everyone's at their windows wondering who's making all the noise
in the middle of the night. They have to be up at six in the
morning; and now they can look forward to going to work
tired and falling asleep at their desks and work benches and
the foremen making nasty remarks and some may be fired and
their wives and children will go hungry and they'll find themselves in the street and all come to a bad end.

NO. 3: No, Holy Mary, holy Mary holy . . . holy . . .

NO. 2: Save us, don't let it be true, tell us it isn't true that there's
anyone up there. Tell us we're alone . . . that there really isn't
anything up there.

ALL, *crying out:* Save us, save us.

THE LEADER: Quiet! Listen to me. We'll get out of here. We'll
take our Virgin with us and leave and go far away. Then we'll
find . . .

DENIS: But we'll run into the cops the minute we show our noses
out of here. You know they'll beat the hell out of us till we
belch our guts like dogs' vomit.

NO. 2: We have to save *her.* All you're doing is thinking of
yourselves, but she's the one we've got to save. We've got to
do anything to save her, so she at least will survive. Only the
Blessed Virgin can filter love down into every mole hole in the
world.

DENIS: We're all going to croak. How can we save anyone, when
we can't even save ourselves?

NO. 3, *approaching Denis:* I think you loved her a long time ago.
You loved her the way a young man often loves a young girl
. . . for her body and its secrets. You loved her, adolescent, as
a remedy for your ceaseless masturbation. And when you
spoke love to her, you were thinking of her milky skin, the

strange weight of her breasts in your hand, a remarkable
caress and then ripping brutality . . . and now you want to run
away as fast as your legs will carry you. You don't even
remember her belly . . . disappear if you want, we don't need
you. *(Denis stays.)*
THE LEADER: We'll spend the night here. Let's get some sleep.
Who'll keep watch?
NO. 3: I will.
DENIS: We're hungry.
THE LEADER: Dig up some roots, then. Eat dirt. And if you find
enough of it, put a little pile of it beside each one of us. That
can be your job. You don't have to sleep tonight; you be our
provider. *(To all.)* Good night, moles. Maybe it's our last night
in this hole, so let's warm each other one last time.
 *All press around the leader who lies down on a rise in the
cellar floor, the promontory. No. 3 paces back and forth
across the stage, while Denis draws into the background,
gazing downwards.*
NO. 3: It's not at all easy. *(To the Virgin.)* You think I'm a saint,
your saint or your high priest? Well, I'm not. Say something.
There're just the two of us, the others are sleeping. You're not
going to make me believe that you're a statue and can't talk.
Come on, this is all fallacious follishness. The only thing that's
true is the terrible ideas I'm getting . . . you hear me? No? I'm
an erect animal, and I can fuck you up good. All I think about
are panties and hair; I can feel my little finger in your touch-
hole, you hear?, then spit, spit in my face! I haven't changed;
I'm horny, and boney, and bored—hornily trudging the prim-
rose path of bored perdition . . . I'm going to jump on you and
soil you up for good. You'll never forget how dirty my body
felt, or my hairy cock that's soaked itself in every vice until it's
oozing, pustulating, shitty and dripping slime. You'll already
have started to rot when you get up, you'll limp, crushed,
spread wide open, bleeding . . . You think I've become your
angel? Well, I'm still a toad. Does it bother me? I can never
strip off this infested skin of mine. I'd shed it like a rattlesnake

if I could, rip it off, with my mouth gaping open ... feel my
skin slide off, torn off ... and fall. What am I doing here? In
this cellar with a bunch of crazy kids? I had a dozen little
vices to satisfy, tasty little sins to commit, little crimes to
perpetrate. I haven't shopped around for basic impurities yet
today. I'm losing my time here. A muscled hustler romping
around with pre-puberty babies. Come on, come on, Virgin
Mary, full of grace, I must say you've got curves they don't
give you in the churches. Come on now, let's interpenetrate in
profound communion; you'll see, I'll make like a big candle,
the one you pay fifteen francs for in chapel. Spread your
mummy buns, bummy nun, and I'll sleep with a church statue.
Glory to God who provides such sins on earth as it is in
heaven. Aren't you coming? *(He sits down.)* Once upon a
time, I was sleeping on a sidewalk of amazingly cold cement
with a dozen or more friends all covered with mud and vice.
We spent our days begging for pieces of bread and sausage,
and our nights eating them ... and washing them down with a
bit of red wine in a cafe that accommodated our style of
living. At night we'd give ourselves over to all the poor pleasures you can imagine. Each time it'd go hard on one of us or
on some poor girl who didn't have anything better to hope for
anyway. But there was one girl in our gang, a really very
pretty girl, that we never touched. No one thought of doing it
except me; it seemed stupid for poor people to give up the
chance for real pleasure they had. But everytime I suggested
it, the others all got mad. So I waited for the right moment ...
She didn't suspect a thing. She was smiling up at the sun, the
rain, the trees, the cops, and us. She was like a butterfly
gorged with warmth and orange waves that lives happily,
which is a thing I found rather extraordinary ... She was
raped by fifteen cops in a square where the kids had left their
sand-cakes, shovels and little lost pails. Apparently, she was a
virgin until then. They hurt her so badly that she hemor-
rhaged. All the blood got them excited and they filled her up
with sand to stop the bleeding. *(Silence.)*

CORINNE THE VIRGIN: You loved her, didn't you?

NO. 3: Yes, I loved her. You can tell, can't you, statue? Not bad. I
still love her. That's love ... But how can I look at her again
or touch her without killing those fifteen cops first. I have to
get them one by one. If I don't, I won't ever be able to look at
her without getting sick. Yes ... perhaps ... BETTER ...
perhaps ... not to do anything ... just gently, gently make
love to her ... with ... love ... and let those fifteen pigs laugh
in their sperm. I can't forgive them ... but the best thing ... is
Peace. *(He gets up, sits down, looks, calmly places his hands
on his knees, breathes ... stretches out his arms and legs,
remains motionless, all his body relaxes, as warmth enters
him, he becomes soft and peaceful.)* Oh .. .. my God ... I can
feel Oh I can feel that I love, that I love with all my body
that's changing oh oh *(He cries out in pain.)* I'm losing my old
rags, my old skin, all the filth in me is leaving me ... It hurts.
(He cries out, like a woman in childbirth.) Mother.

> *He holds himself, gasping, at the Virgin's feet; he turns
> towards her and, getting up, reaches for the bundle of rags
> she is holding.*

Would you like me to hold him for a little while?. He must get
heavy. I'll keep him warm in my arms. I'll hold him close ... I
won't sleep, I'll look at the moon, the ink-black sky and the
stars, and I will love ... I'll love to feel little again, like a tiny
baby, with my bundle in my arms like two lovers hugging
each other tightly to protect each other from the universe ...
and then they're not afraid of anything. Nothing can hurt
them, because nothing more matters. Nothing can separate
them ... They are love. My lips aren't used to talking about
love yet ... I feel stiff or that I'm making a funny face. I'm
still tempted sometimes by vicious thoughts. They say: Come
on, come on, here under the tent, you'll find three naked
women, and each one has different colored hair. One a red-
head, one brunette, and one platinum-blond ... Come on, you
can come in free; you can touch them and can ... but I put
them out of my mind ... although it's still hard. But I suc-

ceed, and I see you here in my arms and rock you gently and never get tired . . . I just feel a little awkward because I never did it before . . .

A VOICE: Come out with your hands up, down there. The whole police force has you surrounded.

EVERYONE: Capital punishment! Capital punishment!

THE LEADER: Don't move, don't answer. Who's got something to fight with?

NO. 2: A knife.

NO. 4: A club.

DENIS: A stone.

NO. 3: A stone.

THE LEADER: Surround our Virgin. Protect her to the end.
    They build a barricade of barrels, boards, and chains, and arm themselves with chains.

NO. 4: What about the child?

NO. 3: I'll take care of him.

DENIS: What if they get a hold of her?

NO. 3. I said I'd take care of it.

DENIS: If we left our Virgin to them, maybe they'd change, maybe they'd get better?

THE LEADER: A saint doesn't mean anything to them. All they think about is their pot roast . . .

NO. 2: Maybe we could all run out in different directions and then meet somewhere?

THE LEADER: We're not leaving.

DENIS: But . . . what if they ask us who killed the two cops?

THE LEADER: We all killed them.
    Two of the boys approach, playing the role of two National Guardsmen.

THE GANG: Stop where you are, don't come any closer.

1ST NATIONAL GUARDSMAN: We're goin' ta wipe ya out, ya bastards, we're goin' ta pour over ya.

DENIS: My goodness, it's the two butchers.

2ND NATIONAL GUARDSMAN: Yah, we're butchers at night and National Guard in the daytime.

They approach.

THE GANG: Ah ah!

    A combat reporter, played by one of the National Guardsmen, arises.

THE REPORTER: ... Reporting to you from Republican Radio. I've just arrived on the scene and the battle has begun. Some have fallen, but everyone's marching with guns ready. The bandits are remarkably well-armed; they have army-model, automatic rifles and, oh, I just had to duck a volley of fire; that was a close one! took my hat! ... What's happening now? The National Guard has been called up and they're showering the enemy position with offensive fire. It's a hard, hard battle.

THE LEADER, *jumping forward:* Shut up, you bastard! *(He pushes the reporter down, but the latter keeps speaking into his imaginary microphone.)*

NO. 2: Wait a minute, it's not true, we're only ... *(Someone makes the noise of machine-gun fire, and he falls.)*

DENIS, *jumping forward:* You damned butchers ... Corinne ...

NO. 3: Lay off them, or there'll be no end to it.

    Denis turns back towards No. 3, and he collapses as someone makes the noise of machine-gun fire. No. 3 remains alone, facing the two National Guardsmen.

NO. 3: Come on, come on, kill me! Just leave her alone, I beg you, not her, she's the Blessed Virgin, she's Holy Love ... understand?

    The National Guardsmen laugh and shower him with kicks.

1ST NATIONAL GUARDSMAN: The Blessed Virgin, an' I'm a fuckin' priest. Look. *(He makes an obscene gesture.)* O.K., freak, you killed the policemen?

NO. 3: I know, I know, it's wrong to kill, I know.

1ST NATIONAL GUARDSMAN: You bastard, yer goin' ta see yer littul mouth fly in the air in pieces. It's goin' ta explode away an' you'll sound like a fuckin' fairy, an' you'll say, 'Thank you, Sir, once again, please, Sir ...'

NO. 3: But you don't have a right to. I want to speak; and if I'm
accused of a crime, I have a right to be heard. I want to speak
... to say what I've learned ... to help you, to help you love.
... *(The National Guardsmen laugh.)* Only love can save us.

2ND NATIONAL GUARDSMAN: Bah! Any love you make
you'll 'ave ta do with yer foot. *(He emasculates him with a
kick. No. 3 gives a piercing scream.)*

THE HOMOSEXUAL, *(played by one of the gang who had gone
to the back of the theatre to die, and now returns in this role):*
When I was very young, I loved my brother. He was fifteen
and I was thirteen. We used to go into the garden behind our
house and softly touch each other's bodies. We were built
nicely then; I was still a little fat, pink, and solid too ... We
used to spend hours looking at each other ... And sometimes
things would happen when we'd touch each other that surprised us. But they were beautiful surprises, they felt like
nature itself, and made us warm afterwards. We planted a
mulberry-tree on the spot where we used to go; and it grew so
quickly that we had fruit from it the year after. The berries
had a strangely wonderful taste, bitter and savage like love.
When we ate them, we reached such pleasure, such extraordinary pleasure, that all we could do is lie quietly, holding
hands, feeling like we were riding through heaven ... One day
a policeman surprised us there, and he brought us to juvenile
court. They separated us, isolated us, and beat us. I tried to
escape, and got an extra sentence ... I couldn't see my
brother anymore, and this made me indescribably miserable.
When I grew up, they drafted me into the army; it would have
been alright if my brother could have been with me. When I
asked if he could, they laughed and said that I'd find thousands of brothers in the army. I answered that I'd never love
anyone but my brother. They punched me until I was dizzy.
Since then, they take me on all their military missions. And
when we stop for the night, they tie me around a tree, facing
it, and they hurt me a lot, torture me. They say they're making
love to me, but I don't believe it because it hurts too much

and they don't seem to really love me ... I understand your
sorrow; I loved my brother as you love this woman.

> *By means of gestures, they begin to caress each other very
> chastely.*

THE NATIONAL GUARDSMEN, *laughing:* Fire on the freaky
queers! *(They fire.)*

1ST NATIONAL GUARDSMAN: An' now the Holy Cunt.
(Laughing, they approach the Virgin.)

1ST NATIONAL GUARDSMAN: What's she doin' up there? I
wanna ask 'er 'bout the weather.

CORINNE THE VIRGIN: Don't come near me, or you'll be
damned. Don't look at me. Prostrate yourselves, you excrement, you are dust because hate is in you and you love no
one, you're going where your desires and your personal pleasure are leading you,
you love money
you're violent
you're impure
you're vile
you don't know what beauty is
you think you've nothing to learn from anyone else
you're ignorant and you were going to touch me,
I would have blasted you with lightning.

1ST NATIONAL GUARDSMAN: What's she talkin' about? I
hope she doesn't think yappin's gonna impress us. You'll see,
you littul bitch.

> *They approach her. They are suddenly petrified. The Vir-
> gin descends from her promontory, goes to No. 3, lifts his
> head, brushes the dirt from his wounds and weeps softly.
> The National Guardsmen have fallen to the ground in
> terror like the centurions at Easter. The music rises and
> continues in* DARKNESS.

Scenes from *Exorcism for Now: a ritual*

THEODORE DUBOIS

Playwright's Note

This play was written and performed at Brown University, Providence, Rhode Island, in conjunction with the Student Strike for Peace which followed in the wake of the Kent and Jackson State murders. With the encouragement of John Emigh (professor in theatre arts) and James Schevill (playwright and professor of drama at Brown), militant students formed a guerrilla theatre to speak to the people of Providence. Most of the plays by this group were very short, designed for performance in the city business districts, shopping centers, etc. But the desirability of having, in addition, a longer play for announced performance on the campuses of neighboring colleges and in city parks was also suggested. This is the script for that play; I had the task of writing it, but it arose from ideas by Robert Bailey (head of Sock 'n Buskin Theatre at Brown) and Andrew Arnault (head of Production Workshop at Brown), as well as myself, and evolved to a large extent from a group effort while it was already in rehearsal. It was performed for the first time on May 29, 1970, under Robert Bailey's direction. Due to limitations of time and means, this and subsequent performances were in an abbreviated form and contained a number of divergencies from the present script.

CAST

Twenty people who represent:
  Characters who watch the ritual:

$$4 \begin{cases} \text{Nixon} \\ \text{Agnew} \\ \text{the old lady} \\ \text{the businessman} \end{cases}$$

The Military Chorus:(MC's)

$$6 \begin{cases} \text{4 soldiers (including Pete and Mike)} \\ \text{2 policemen} \\ \text{(double as Viet Cong, generals, construction-} \\ \text{workers, and preacher)} \end{cases}$$

The People's Chorus:(PC's)

$$10 \begin{cases} \text{Jim} \\ \text{Joan} \\ \text{Paul} \\ \text{Sheila} \\ \text{Cinthy} \\ \text{and 5 others} \\ \text{(double as Mr. and Mrs. average American,} \\ \text{the Vietnamese man and woman, and Jeremiah)} \end{cases}$$

Music: 2 guitars and 2 percussion.

The actors should bear in mind, as they develop their interpretations, that we seek to convince the audience and not to alienate them.

Everything is done in *absolute silence,* except for the continual rock beat (guitars and percussion; perhaps flutes at times) and except for the sounds, recitations and songs explicitly called for in the script.

Microphones, megaphones, or even bullhorns are to be used for the speeches when necessary. There should be no attempt to conceal them; they will, rather, contribute to the effect.

A pole which can double as a stake and as a flagpole, as well as the rallying-point of the ritual, must be set up in the rear-center of the stage-area.

All the members of the cast are present in the stage-area in couples. The members of each couple show each other affection and love by such obvious signs as chaste touches, etc. This action continues for several minutes, in absolute silence. The unity of this action makes evident to the audience that the dividing of the group into opposite choruses or sides during the rest of the play is purely ritual representation. The young people will be playing roles. They will be acting out events above and beyond their control as their means of possessing these events, rather than of being possessed by them as they are in real life. By means of ritually possessing the events, they can control them, even if only by wishful thinking. This ritual is an act of hope, until its people are destroyed.

A transition into the beginning of the ritual is provided as percussion and guitars begin a strong rock beat which will be maintained, with variations, throughout the ceremony. In full view of the audience: Two fellows take up the poles which support the Nixon and Agnew masks. Another fellow puts on a coat and tie to represent the businessman. A girl dons contemporary old, old lady clothes and applies heavy rouge and lipstick to her face to represent the old lady. Four fellows strip down to khaki shorts, combat boots, and soldier helmets, and carry rifles; two other fellows strip down to blue shirts, blue shorts, black shoes and police caps, and wear pistol holsters. These six together from the Military Chorus (MC's). The remaining persons, dressed in their hippyish clothes for the most part, form a People's Chorus (PC's) representing themselves.

Part I. Introduction

Nixon & Agnew are to one side of the stage-area. (They are represented by large masks at the tops of poles supported by actors and will remain present in this position throughout the ritual, overseeing all that happens.) They recite in unison, Keep the World Safe:

"Keep the world safe.
Keep the Communists out.
Police the world.
Kill the Communists.
Law and order. Law and order.
American law and order for everybody.

Keep the world safe.
Keep the world safe."
   *The old lady stands to the opposite side of the stage-area
   from Nixon & Agnew. With a rather bewildered expression on her face, she appears to have simply wandered in
   from somewhere. After a few moments, one of the PC's
   brings chairs for her and for the businessman who has
   appeared beside her. They gratefully accept them. (The
   old lady and the businessman will remain present in this
   position throughout the play, watching all that happens.)*
[Editor's Note: Following the completion of "Part I. Introduction," there follows:
   Part II. The Situation at Home
   Part III. The Induction
   Part IV. The War and finally:]

            Part V. Protest and Repression at Home
   *Jeremiah appears on the opposite side of the stage-area
   from Nixon & Agnew. (He is an old man who has the
   general appearance of having just been plugged into an
   electric socket. His only garment is a loose shirt of sackcloth, reaching to just below his knees. He is barefoot and
   bareheaded, and his hair is disheveled.) He looks down at
   the Vietnamese woman for a moment; then he begins an
   intertwining of monologues with Nixon & Agnew and the
   two soldiers who still guard the dead Vietnamese prisoner.
   (Each person is addressing his own imaginary audience
   and not the other members of the "dialogue."*
   *Jeremiah's voice tends to be high and hysterical; Nixon
   tries to be reassuring and conciliating; Agnew is forceful,
   Hitlerian in tone.*
   The rock beat remains rapid, but soft, throughout.)
JEREMIAH: Thus says the Lord through his servant Jeremiah: I
   am now going to summon all the kingdoms of the North, and
   they will pour disaster over the inhabitants of this land.
   Vanity you have pursued,

vanity you have become.

Your hands are covered with the blood of innocent men.

Yes, for all these you will have to answer.

(Jer. 1: 1, 14, 15; 2: 5, 34)

NIXON: I ask for support of our brave men fighting tonight halfway around the world. We live in an age of anarchy both abroad and at home. We see mindless attacks on all the great institutions which have been created by free civilizations in the last five hundred years . . .

AGNEW: . . . the most precipitous decline in respect for law of any decade in our history. Some of those who call each other "intellectuals" helped to sow the wind. America reaped the whirlwind . . .

JEREMIAH: . . . Those for the plague, to the plague;

those for the sword, to the sword;

those for famine, to famine;

those for captivity, into captivity! . . . (Jer. 15: 2)

NIXON: . . . Here in the United States, great universities are being systematically destroyed . . .

AGNEW: . . . an effete corps of impudent snobs who characterize themselves as intellectuals . . .

NIXON: *informally:* . . . You know, you see these bums blowing up the campuses. Listen, get rid of the war and there'll be another one.

(*formally*) Small nations all over the world find themselves under attack from within and from without . . .

AGNEW: . . . hard core dissidents and professional anarchists . . .

There is again the sound of gunfire, and the Vietnamese woman, to one side, pantomimes having been shot in the stomach. She slowly dies.

NIXON: . . . The American people are assailed by counsels of doubt and defeat from some of the most widely known opinion leaders of the nation . . .

AGNEW: . . . These arrogant ones and their admirers in the Congress of the United States are asking us to repudiate principles that have made this country great . . .

1ST SOLDIER: Our orders stressed the importance of the body count, for the reports back home.

2ND SOLDIER: Our policy was that once contact was made, we kept firing until everything in the kill-zone was killed. We did not take prisoners.

1ST SOLDIER: My policy was that a man does not surrender during a fire-fight. If a VC comes out of a fight to give himself up, that man is dead.

JEREMIAH: I am in anguish! I writhe with pain! Walls of my heart! My heart is throbbing! I cannot keep quiet, for I have heard the cry of war.

Ruin on ruin is the news: the whole land is laid waste; in one moment all that sheltered me is gone.

I looked to the earth, and saw a formless waste; to the heavens and their light had gone.

The wooded country had become a desert, and all its towns were in ruins.

I looked, and saw no man at all, the very birds of heaven had fled.

I hear screams . . . (Jer. 4: 19, 20, 23-26, 31)

NIXON: . . . If we failed to meet this challenge, all other nations will be on notice that, despite its overwhelming power, the United States, when a real crisis comes, will be found wanting . . .

AGNEW: . . . a masochistic compulsion to destroy their country's strength, whether or not it is constructive. And they rouse themselves to a continual emotional crescendo—substituting disruptive demonstration for reason and precipitate action for persuasion . . .

NIXON: . . . Does the richest and strongest nation in the history of the world have the character to meet a direct challenge by a group which rejects every effort to win a just peace, ignores our warning, tramples on solemn agreements, and so forth?

My fellow Americans: During my campaign I promised . . .

JEREMIAH: Weep bitterly for the man who has gone away, since

he will never come back,
never see his native land again. (Jer. 22: 10)

AGNEW: . . . Years of permissiveness and indulgence finally culminated in the days of disorder—in violence in our cities and
on our campuses . . .

NIXON: . . . Sure you came here to demonstrate and shout your
slogans on the Ellipse. That is all right. Just keep it peaceful.
Remember, I feel just as deeply as you do about this . . .

AGNEW: . . . And if you walked through Harlem, or Berkeley, or
Columbia or Watts at the height of the disorders, you could
hear—through the din of the battle between police and riot-
ers—the unmistakable sound of chickens coming home to
roost . . .

NIXON: . . . I feel just as deeply as you do about this . . .

AGNEW: . . . When I say "we," I don't mean the government. . . .

> *The MC's stack the four bodies (two soldiers and two
> Vietnamese) up-center so that they are sitting back to back
> in a circle.*
> *Half of the PC's goose-step about the stage-area, giving
> the fascist salute, in obvious caricature, and chanting:*

United States, Sieg Heil!

> *Three of the PC's (one on each side and Joan in the
> center,) while remaining in the stage-area, move about and
> cry out passionately to the audience:*

Do something. Don't just sit there. This is your problem. Don't let
this useless killing and dying go on. It's your problem.

200 more Americans dead in Cambodia. Stop it. Write your
Congressmen. Speak to your friends. It's your problem.

Can't you see it? The end doesn't justify the means. America
is making a desert of Indochina, and thousands and thousands are dying in the war. It's your problem. Do something.
It's your problem.

> *Three soldiers line up, drop to one knee, and pantomime
> firing into the crowd of PC's. There is the sound of a
> gunshot. The girl (Joan) falls.*
> *The PC's, thunder-struck, stop in their tracks and look at*

the dead girl. One or two bend over her. Kent Tableau. The PC's, slowly and softly, and then progressively more rapidly and more intensely, chant the word, Why?

The soldiers advance on the PC's with guns ready. The PC's fall prostrate in front of the soldiers and recite softly- submissively, while the MC's recite sternly, Keep America Safe:

Keep America safe.

Keep the Communists out.

Police America.

Kill the Communists.

Law and order. Law and order.

American law and order.

Keep America safe.

Keep America safe.

Jeremiah enters with a basket of ashes. He sits cosslegged facing the audience, dumps the ashes over his head, and exits.

The businessman rises from his chair and announces, on the part of the government, that permission is given to the PC's to have a memorial service for their dead:

"Recognizing the sincerity of these young people, despite their lack of experience, and grieved with all our fellow citizens that their rashness has ended so tragically, we have decided to allow them to conduct a short memorial service for their friends. We do this in the hope that it will make the tragic *uselessness* of such deaths all the more evident to everyone. We believe that it will at least show our young people that we understand. Furthermore, it will be a pleasure to send our personal representatives to the ceremony, trusting that all will be conducted in a spirit of nonviolence."

The 3 soldiers go to one side and, at ease, pantomime laughing and talking among themselves during what fol- lows.

The musical beat becomes dirge-like.

Sheila rises to her feet and begins to struggle with Joan's

*body, trying to lift her. The other PC's join Sheila. They
lift Joan to the height of their shoulders and carry her in
procession around the stage-area. They set her down with
the four other bodies. During all this, they say in unison*
The Litany of the Dead.
*The 2 policemen stand watch over the proceedings.
(The italicized portions of the Litany are repeated by each
PC individually, one immediately after the other, in such a
manner as to produce a wave-effect of sound, falling away
like echoes into silence.)*
45,000 American boys. *Why?*
182,000 alleged Viet Cong boys, girls, men, and women. *Why?*
Thousands of Vietnamese civilians counted or not in the body
count. *Why?*
The American protesters who have been shot. *Why?*

For the old men in leather chairs, *they died.*
For the folks back home, *they died.*
For abstract theories, *they died.*
For their farms and fields, *they died.*
For the ambitions of world powers, *they died.*
For a world police state, *they died.*
For the value of the dollar, *they died.*
For the sake of their consciences, *they died.*
  *The PC's kneel, sit, etc. in a circle around the bodies. A
  girl PC, accompanied by the musicians or accompanying
  herself on a guitar, sings* When the Dawn Comes:
When the dawn comes
Will men listen to each other
Instead of only to themselves?
Will they try to understand
The differences they see
Beyond their own horizons?
Will men respect their fellowmen
More than private creeds or beliefs?
Will men respect their fellowmen

Instead of using guns and death
To confirm the rules or ways of life
They think are best for everyone?
Will men turn from judging self-righteously,
And be compassionate instead?
Will they curb the selfish motives
Concealed beneath their high ideals?
Or is it just a foolish dream
That wars will someday cease,
Armies will evaporate,
And with them the police state,
And little men will live in peace?
The dawn will come someday, I hope,
The dawn will come someday.

> *The* Litany of the Dead *is continued, but this time an opposite effect, from softness to loudness, is produced on the italicized, final words:*

From the old men in leather chairs, *be free.*
From the folks back home, *be free.*
From abstract theories, *be free.*
From those who destroy farms and fields, *be free.*
From the ambitions of world powers, *be free.*
From a world police state, *be free.*
From the value of the dollar, *be free.*
From those who coerce our consciences, *be free.*

> *Intensity increases during this last part of the* Litany *until the PC's are yelling out* "Be free!" *The rhythm of the rock beat also grows in intensity and rapidity. At the end of the* Litany, *several PC's jump up and dance to the music, shouting "Freedom! Freedom!" The other PC's join them, dancing and shouting "Freedom!"*
>
> *During the dance, the two PC's acting the roles of (dead) Vietnamese man & woman inconspicuously resume their roles of Mr. & Mrs. average American.*
>
> *Jeremiah prophesies (pantomimes), standing on his head. He prophesies to the old lady, although he may not be*

heard above the din.

*The old lady begins to apply heavy rouge and lipstick to
her face.*

JEREMIAH: You may dress yourself in scarlet
put on ornaments of gold,
enlarge your eyes with paint
but you make yourself pretty in vain. (Jer.4: 30)

*The MC's, alarmed by the dancers' shouts, line up again
at the side, drop to one knee and hold their rifles ready to
fire. The PC's notice them and freeze in their tracks.*

*Jeremiah pantomimes prophecying Hamlet-like to a head
of lettuce which he holds out like Yorick's skull.*

*During this short moment of arrested, frightened stillness
on the part of the PC's, the old lady, who has just finished
applying her rouge and lipstick, cries out:* Who'll make
love to me? Who'll make love to me? I am the Great
Whore . . .

The businessman begins to neck with the old lady.

*The PC's turn to flee. They take two steps and pantomime
being gunned down by the MC's. (This must be done
rapidly.)*

*A masculine voice over powerful sound equipment, a bull-
horn, or megaphone declares the beginning of martial law
in the U.S. (actually a military coup engineered by the
fascist forces within the government.) It should be spoken
rapidly, but also clearly and forcefully:*

This is an announcement from the General Staff of the Armed
Forces, in conjunction with the CIA and FBI, addressed to all
citizens and residents of the United States of America. In an
effort to annihilate once and for all the subversive elements
which have been hindering the smooth-functioning of our
society and in order to destroy once and for all the Communistic threat to our nation's interests both at home and abroad,
a state of emergency is hereby declared and martial law will
be in force throughout these United States until further notice.

Jeremiah returns with a gallon-can marked GASOLINE.

> *He sits cross-legged facing the audience and applies liquid
> from the can to himself, rubbing it onto his face, arms,
> and legs. He also pours an ignitable liquid in a semi-circle
> around in front of him. Towards the end of the announce-
> ment of martial law, he lights it so as to simulate a protes-
> ter's self-immolation that aborts.*
> *The Nixon mask is taken down. A Hitler-mustache is
> stuck onto the upper lip of the Agnew mask.*

In view of the president's hesitation to deal as firmly with the
problem as recent events require, his powers are hereby suspended indefinitely. Neither shall the Congress and the Supreme Court, the state legislatures and district or state courts,
reconvene until the loyalty of their members has been established.

A state of general mobilization is hereby declared. All military
personnel, National Guard units, and reserve units are to
report for active duty at once, under the immediate command
of the Pentagon.

All passports are declared revoked. No one is to leave or enter
the country without personal permission.

Radio transmissions on any frequency, whether commercial
or private, are forbidden. Official announcements and news
may be heard over this Civil Defense network. Telephone and
telegraph service is also discontinued for all unauthorized
persons until further notice. All rights of publication are
hereby suspended, and in the future will be accorded only
with the approval of a central censorship board.

All places of assembly, including churches and synagogues,
are declared temporarily closed. Any assembly of more than
three persons in any place whatsoever will be considered an
assembly to conspire and the assembled parties will be
charged with treason.

Justice, law, and order will be administered by the military
courts. We encourage you, fellow citizens, to cooperate with
these efforts to purge our democracy of the Red Communistic

ideas which threaten it. All violators of these prescriptions and of those forthcoming will be dealth with firmly and finally.

Mr. and Mrs. average American, the old lady and Jeremiah come forward cautiously and examine the bodies of the dead PC's. They look up in horror at the soldiers, who are still kneeling in firing position, and say in unison the Here and There Chant:

It could *not* happen here, only there.
> Here, there.
> There, here.

It could *not* happen here, it could *not* happen here,
> only there.
>> With Hitler in Germany
>> With Mussolini in Italy
>> With Franco in Spain
>> With the Generals in Greece
>> With Ky and Thieu in South Vietnam

It could *not* happen in the United States,
> but it *has*,
> it *has!*

The old lady screams. The MC's fire; and Mr. and Mrs. average American, the old lady and Jeremiah fall dead.

The MC's then move on the audience. They pull up any stakes and ropes that divide off the stage-area, take away any props, and, most importantly, force the audience to leave the area, as though they are breaking up an illegal assembly:

G'wan home. There ain't nothing to see.

Break it up. Move on. Move on.

You know you shouldn't be here. Move out.

Hurry it up. Get out of here if you know what's good for you.

There ain't nothing to see. There's no reason for you to be here. Everything's under control.

G'wan home. The show's over. Mind your own business.

The audience is cleared out, forcefully, by the MC's. The ritual is over . . . and over again.

from *The New Chautauqua*
Plays Without Playwright

FREDERICK GAINES

Playwright's Note

The New Chautauqua was written primarily for use by the AnyPlace Theatre of Minneapolis-St. Paul. It was written with the particular demands and assets of that company in mind. The company demanded plays that were both flexible and transportable into the streets of the Twin Cities. Its assets included a broad background of experience in dance, mime, theatre, and music. The playlets are intended as material for the actor, dancer, mime, and musician.

The normal performance of *The New Chautauqua* will include only a fraction of the total material printed here. The director and actors are to select each night the material that is most pertinent to the place and the occasion. The playlets fall into six broad categories: Prologue, Fairy Tales and Parables, Kings and Queens, Men and Man, Gods and Pretense, Epilogue and Admonition. There is no fixed order to the playlets. I have grouped them, but they are grouped for convenience, not for dictating the progress of an evening's performance. As here published, the playlets are grouped into four possible playing orders. The category of each playlet is indicated, along with an identifying "title."

Because the players are expected to do a great deal of shaping and rewriting, the playlets have been deliberately left as scenarios. I would expect that if different actors within the company were to perform the same dialogue on different nights, it would sound and look quite different to those in the audience. Also, I've made no attempt to provide music for any of the lyrics or for the transitions between plays. The company may fit the music to the occasion, judging itself which song would best bridge the distance between the scenes.

I have provided only one prologue for the entire piece. It's my belief that the material for the prologue should be largely musical and improvised with the audience. I have used the one name, Chautauqua, throughout. The name implies more than a particular actor: it is a function. The Chautauqua is the actor closest to the audience's sympathies. It is a function that passes from one actor to another. It is represented to the audience by a particular property, which therefore should be large and easily recognizable.

Prologue

The play will begin with a musical number. When it is done, the company selects the actor to play Chautauqua. He puts on the hat or necklace which is Chautauqua's, starts his walk across the stage, stops, listens, turns to the audience.

CHAUTAUQUA: Who? You? Nah. Not for you. For me. Sure. Me. For Chautauqua. That's me. *(An actor behind him whispers his real name.)* Whadda ya mean? Chautauqua! Nobody else: Chautauqua. Here, see this hat? This hat says I'm Chautauqua, the new Chautauqua, the new child. What's he know, huh? *(walking up to him)* What do you know, huh? *(The actor smiles, says nothing.)* There, you see. *(Starts away and again his name in life is whispered.)* What'd he say? *(Waits to see if the audience will tell him.)* Right: Chautauqua. The clown. The in-between, all-around, Mister Everything. But for you, the name is ... *(Whispers his real name and the entire cast calls out: "Chautauqua!")* Who? *(They repeat it; then he turns and points to each of them and they call out their names in turn.)* And when I wear this, I'm Chautauqua. People of this city *(the name of the city in which the play is being performed may be supplied here)*: the New Chautauqua comes to town.

GODS AND PRETENSE: MAN THE CREATOR

A scene for two actors. The scene begins with the puppet maker,

Gepetto, selecting his piece of wood from among the stock. All of the company are lined up along the back wall, stiff, wooden, the stock. He selects the piece he wants and moves it downstage. As soon as the others know that they are not in the scene, they drop out.

GEPETTO: Yes, you'll do. Fine. Good, straight grain, not too soft, not too hard. There now, stand there. What shall I make of you? A girl puppet or a boy puppet? A boy, I think. Yes. *(miming all of his tools)* Ah, Gepetto, you're getting old, talking to yourself now. What does the wood care? Nothing. What it knows from being a boy, girl is nothing. There. Where's my file and saw? Gepetto, you're getting old, can't remember where you put things from one day to the next. Ah, there. *(Goes to work filing the arms, completing it quickly, talking to himself as he does.)* You're going to be just fine, just fine. Just listen to Gepetto and all will come out. Good enough arm. *(testing it)* Seems to work. Maybe a little more off here. Yes, now the other. *(When he goes to the other side of the puppet, the completed arm experiments with itself unseen by Gepetto.)* Now, let's see if they match up. *(Stands back and judges them.)* Little too short this one. *(Pulls the shorter arm down a little.)* Two arms . . . what's next? Ah, yes, the legs. *(Bends down and quickly makes the legs, masking his action so that he can do it quickly. The arms meet each other, explore the body of the puppet.)* These two all right. As good a legs as any boy has. What did I do with my paint pots now? *(He searches for his paint and the puppet dances a little on its legs and ends up in a different spot from that where Gepetto had left him. Gepetto is puzzled.)* Can't even remember where you left him, Gepetto. Such a mind you have. What first? Eyes. Has to have eyes. *(As he paints, each eye opens; when they are complete, Gepetto goes behind the puppet and tests the eyes, making them open, close, cross.)* Need a little something for those lips, a little life, huh? *(Paints.)* Oh, that's a silly smile. This one's up to no good. Lazy boy, this one. But I always like mine smiling. I know they're happy. Well, clean up now. *(Gepetto goes to pick up his imaginary pots and put them away. The puppet opens his mouth, stretches it, sticks out his tongue, flips it around, says: "Gepetto." Gepetto stops, sees no one, continues. The puppet says: "Gepetto." Gepetto searches for the voice. Finally, Gepetto discovers the puppet.)*

GEPETTO: You!

PUPPET: Who else?

GEPETTO: But you can't talk!

PUPPET: If you say so.

GEPETTO: But it isn't possible. It's not natural. Wood doesn't talk. I know that. I learned it in school.

PUPPET: Wood doesn't talk?

GEPETTO: No. Who told you you could?

PUPPET: Me. I said, it's about time and I did it. Then I sang a little song and danced a little dance and did a little tap . . .

GEPETTO: Stop! Stop! *(The puppet stops dancing.)* You can't do that! You know that you can't do that. I know it. You are wood and I have made you. I have put strings and levers . . . *(Operates a string and something moves)* and when I move, they move. But without . . . you cannot do it. You do what I say, when I say.

PUPPET: Thanks a lot for making me, friend. I'll remember you. *(Starts to leave.)*

GEPETTO: Where do you think you're going?

PUPPET: Anywhere but here.

GEPETTO: You cannot go before I sell you. I did not make you to give you away.

PUPPET: Sell me?

GEPETTO: That's right.

PUPPET: What do I get to say about this?

GEPETTO: Nothing, that is quite clear in the contract.

PUPPET: I didn't sign anything.

GEPETTO: How could you? You need a name to sign. It was between me and your old owner.

PUPPET: I have a name.

GEPETTO: And what is it?

PUPPET: Puppet.

GEPETTO: That is a thing—no name. No, you've no name and will have none unless I give it to you.

PUPPET: Wait. I feel a name coming to me. Yes . . . yes. From a long time ago, long, long ago, before you made me, before you even saw the wood . . . Beech. No, no . . . Mahogany.

GEPETTO: Beech, mahogany. What kind of mumbo jumbo is that? Men do not talk like that. A name is something like mine: Gepetto. That's a name.

PUPPET: Doesn't do much for me.

GEPETTO: It does for you, if I give it to you. From here on, you'll be known as Booker T. Gepetto. A fine name.

PUPPET: I get to sign a contract now?

GEPETTO: Only people can do that.

PUPPET: Then . . . I won't be.

GEPETTO: What do you mean—won't be?

PUPPET: I'll be a tree again. Back to the forest for ol' Booker T. They understand names like mahogany there.

GEPETTO: They won't recognize you now. You've been gone too long. You're wearin' pants, talking right, you're half a man now.

PUPPET, *freezing:* I'm a tree.

GEPETTO: If you're a tree, I'll break you into firewood and burn you to warm my house.

PUPPET: That's it, huh: firewood or slave?

GEPETTO: That's it. Take your choice.

PUPPET: Firewood.

GEPETTO: You'll regret this. No one else gave you clothes, sent you to church, schools, gave you an occupation. Go ahead, you'll remember the good old times soon enough and come begging back. *(starting to set him on fire)*

PUPPET, *Uncle Tomin':* Oh, no, Massa 'petto, you knows I'se jist funnin'. Why hell, I'd shore nuf rather be your nigger than just 'bout anything else.

GEPETTO, *turning away:* I'm glad you've come to your senses.

PUPPET: Oh, yassa. De time to burn will come later. *(Winks at audience, follows Gepetto off.)*

EPILOGUE
AND ADMONITION: CONQUEST OF PAN

A scene for flutist and company.

MAYOR *(quieting the mob):* All right, all right. Quiet now. Quiet down there so we can discuss this thing calmly, rationally. Now. Who reported this disturbance?

WOMAN: I did, Mr. Mayor.

MAYOR: Speak up then. Don't waste our time. We need action.

WOMAN: About midnight, I think, I was just laying down after putting all the dishes up to dry and making sure that the door was locked—I keep a sober house, Mr. Mayor, none of that nighttime galavanting around inside my four walls—well, I was just laying myself down in my bed, and I heard this noise. Kids, I thought to myself, those fool kids out boozing and singing again, so I reached over on my nightstand for my pistol—always keep it there in case of prowlers—and I leaned out the window to get a shot at them—just to put a little righteousness in 'em, you see—and, then, I see him, just the one of 'em, and he was laughing and blowing on the pipe of his—crazy, I thought, so I squeezed off this shot, winged him, I thought, but he just laughed like it tickled and off he danced, playing on that pipe. Well, I hurried right over to the city hall and got you up outa bed.

MAYOR: Anybody else see this man? *(A man raises his hand.)* Get a good look?

MAN: Oh, an evil-looking thing he was. About this high and grinning all the time. I just hid my head right down under the covers. He wasn't going to get any power over me.

MAYOR: Did you hear his song?

MAN: Oh, he was playing it all the time. Went something like this. *(He mimes whistling and we hear the flutist piping.)*

OLD WOMAN: That's it, that's it.

MAYOR: And a strange sort of feelin' to the music, huh? *(All agree.)* Like it was the devil or something? *(All agree.)* Citizens, we're faced with one of Satan's ministers. It is up to us to rout this demon from our midst. I've had reports already from the neighboring towns—wreaked havoc there, all the children, some grown folks, running around, acting as if their businesses didn't matter, carrying on, singing songs, dancing—we must act. *(Loud assent from the crowd and the piping gets louder.)* I say burn him at the stake! I say erase once and for all this presence from among us! This is a plain, hard-working town. We want none of his tomfoolery. We must harden ourselves to the task. *(Throughout the harangue, the flutist's song grows louder and louder and we can see him dancing as he plays. Slowly the members of the audience drift from the mayor's speech over to the growing line behind the flutist until the mayor is talking to no one but the old woman.)* Now, we know that this devil has the power to draw us away from the ways of this town. We know that he works a subtle poison into our limbs, into our souls—guard against him. Old woman, bind my legs. *(The old woman continues throughout to do as he tells her.)* Meet this threat here and beat it down. Take out your crosses, polish them with gold, gild your icons, stay to your prayers. Cut yourself off from the pleasures of the body, of the vacant wanderings of the soul. Citizens, I appeal to you: become the bridegrooms of our way. Follow my example. Deprive yourselves. Old woman, my arms and hands. Stop up your noses with candlewax so that you cannot smell the lascivious perfumes of his cult, bind your arms and legs so that the insidious rhythms of his satanic pipe do not dictate pleasure to them. Do as I have done. Castrate yourselves, walk eunuchs, but walk citizens of this town. Do as I do now, fill your ears with clay so that his sour notes of lust may not penetrate to guide your mind. Stand as I do now, celibate, protected. *(He sees no one but the old woman.)* Where . . .? Where have they gone?

OLD WOMAN: With him.

MAYOR: What's that?

OLD WOMAN: With him!

MAYOR: All? All but you. We shall stand. Together we shall resist and conquer him. *(She nods and he sees that she is crying.)* Crying . . . ? But . . . then, why have you stayed behind?

OLD WOMAN: I was unable to go. Like you, my legs are bound, but mine with years. Like you my arms are frozen to my sides, but mine with labor. I can no longer sing or follow the mountain paths with them. This town has left me old, crippled, and frightened. *(Pause. Then the flutist and his band sweep in and by and pick her up and carry her off with them. The mayor, determined not to appear frightened, stands, frozen.)*

MEN AND MAN: THE WAR GAME

A scene for three actors. The scene begins with the sound of machine-gun-like drumming, then the whistle of an overhead shell; two men enter from opposite sides of the stage; both take cover in the same shell hole.

CAPTAIN: Comin' this way . . . !

SERGEANT: Hit it! *(They cover up, wait until after the explosion.)*

CAPTAIN: You hit?

SERGEANT: Okay. You?

CAPTAIN: Fine. Know where we are?

SERGEANT, *(Laughs.):* Exactly. A war.

CAPTAIN: Very amusing.

SERGEANT: I get my laughs.

CAPTAIN: Looks like no man's land.

SERGEANT: About it.

CAPTAIN: If you can give me a little light, I'm going to try and get a fix on this map.

SERGEANT: Why bother?

CAPTAIN: I want to get out of here.

SERGEANT: The line that was there when you left has been changed a dozen times in the last hour.

CAPTAIN: I doubt that.

SERGEANT: Fine, doubt it. I'm staying here.

CAPTAIN: What's that?

SERGEANT: I'm staying.

CAPTAIN: I wasn't aware you had the choice, sergeant.

SERGEANT: *(Laughs.)* You commanding me, are you?

CAPTAIN: Is that so humorous to you?

SERGEANT: Yeah, yeah, it is. Two of us out here, a hundred of them, and you're still remembering the West Point manual.

CAPTAIN: What has West Point to do with it?

SERGEANT: Nothing, nothing. Only find yourself another dummy. Me, I'm staying.

CAPTAIN: Do you think you'll enjoy the jerry company?

SERGEANT: About as much as they enjoy mine.

CAPTAIN: And how long do you think you can hold out with one rifle?

SERGEANT: No rifle.

CAPTAIN: What do you mean?

SERGEANT: There's nothing in here. Empty. When they walk in, the hands go up and I walk with them.

CAPTAIN: Their prison camps aren't a lark, you know.

SERGEANT: You think this is? I'm staying.

CAPTAIN: Why'd you bother to come?

SERGEANT: *(Laughs.)* Come? Hell, you think I volunteered?

CAPTAIN: Draftee. I might have known.

SERGEANT: That means you're not, I take it.

CAPTAIN: When Black Jack raised his arm and gave the call, I came. I didn't ask why or when or would I get home. I came.

SERGEANT: Black Jack who?

CAPTAIN: Pershing.

SERGEANT: Oh, baby.

CAPTAIN: There's the difference between us, sergeant: I know and honor the man I serve.

SERGEANT: Yeah, well, congratulations, cap'n. You been out

here too long, friend, too long ... *(A noise is heard; they tense.)* No ammo, no ammo.

CAPTAIN: Get back in here, sergeant.

SERGEANT: See you, loony. *(Starts to surrender, but a Green Beret tumbles in.)* What ... !

BERET: Move over, friend, they're thick.

CAPTAIN: Jerries?

BERET. *to sergeant:* What's with him? *(The sergeant grins, taps his head.)* VC, Cap'n, charley and getting close.

SERGEANT: Wait a minute.

BERET: What's with you guys?

SERGEANT. Who you with?

BERET: Special forces, Green Berets.

SERGEANT: Okay, but what war?

BERET, *to captain:* Battle fatigue, sir?

CAPTAIN: What war, "Green Beret"?

BERET: Vietnam.

CAPTAIN: Vietnam.

SERGEANT: China?

BERET: China? Hell, no! Vietnam. Oh, Christ, I'm gettin' outa here. *(Leaving.)* I'll send a corpsman back.

CAPTAIN: Don't bother.

SERGEANT: M-1, friend?

BERET: You guys been out here too long. *(Leaves.)*

CAPTAIN: A long time too long. *(Looks at the sergeant; they begin to laugh, get the giggles.)* Where did you get lost?

SERGEANT: Belleau Wood.

CAPTAIN: That one again.

SERGEANT: Yeah, guerrilla stuff, you suppose?

CAPTAIN: Who cares?

SERGEANT: Yeah, who cares. Staying?

CAPTAIN: What's to look forward to? but that Vietnam?

SERGEANT: Where is it?

CAPTAIN, *laughing:* I haven't got the faintest. You? *(They laugh again.)*

SERGEANT: What now? *(Silence.)*

CAPTAIN: I don't know. What now?

EPILOGUE AND ADMONITION: PROSPERO
IN THE DAYLIGHT

A scene for the Chautauqua.

CHAUTAUQUA: It's over. We've come here and done our thing, and it's over. Don't believe it. You don't have to. There's nothing to sign, no sides to take, only us, you, what we've done here for an hour, together. All pretend. Not living. That doesn't happen on a stage, not anymore, not ever maybe. An hour of forget, of songs. These, our actors, are all rehearsed, those lines weren't theirs, or mine, or anyone's; but they learned them, they came here, conned you, cajoled you, yelled and sang at you, because that's what it's all about: pretend, forget. Life is out there, where you are, or now, me speaking to you and even these words, these apologies, are written down, put to memory, rehearsed. The castles we've built here, the clowns we've shown you, will be gone in another hour's time, a word remembered, a song, then gone. Go back there, where you live, where the street swells in this summer's heat, where it's easy to live, hour to hour, anger to anger, love to love. We'll join you there, in time.

Meter Maid

THE SAN FRANCISCO MIME TROUPE

M: Oh, dear, Oh dear.

P: Whassa matter, toots?

M: Do you have change for a quarter?

P: I got something better'n that—you wanna step in the Box?

M: No, really, I need it for the meter—so I can run inside the Hall of Justice and pay my last parking fine.

P: Wait, hold on, you mean you want change so you can pay money to the city for paying money to the city?

M: I guess you could put it that way. But if you can't help me . . .

P: Toots, I believe I can help you, more than you think. May I be so bold as to inquire, what would happen if you didn't pay your meter?

M: Same as now, I'd have to pay a fine.

P: What if you didn't pay the fine?

M: I . . . I guess they'd arrest me . . .

P: They could bust you in any state of the union, lock you up, extradite you back here, and then send you to jail at the discretion of the court. And do you know how much discretion a court has?

M: No.

P: About as much as a turd at a teaparty. Does that strike you as a little heavy?

M: Which?

P: The metaphor.

M: I don't take drugs. Are you sure you can give me change. . . .

P: Like I said before, toots, I'll give you something better. An I'll tell ya what, if ya don't like it, I'll pay your fine myself.

M: Oh, well that's very nice of you. Are you serious?

P: Serious? I'm delirious! And because you're such a looker I'm
even gonna throw in some visual aids. (Get it?—looker—visual aids.) Now, see that little fella you got in your hand there?
That is Mr. Meter. And I'm gonna tell you a few facts about
him.
Fact Number 1:

(CHART 1)

Last year Mr. Meter earned a million and a half dollars for
the city of San Francisco.

M: A million and a half dollars? Just in little . . .

P: . . . dimes and nickels and pennies, exactly. Now I sort of
wonder where all that lettuce disappeared, don't you?

M: Yes—where did all that lettuce disappear?

P: I'm glad you asked me that. A *million* of it went . . .

(CHART 2)

just to keep the meters running and

(CHART 3)

to pay for the lovely meter maids. If you can dig that gorgeous
hunk of brutal femininity, num, num.

M: You're a little preoccupied, aren't you?

P: Well wouldn't you be preoccupied if you had a man's hand up
your skirt?

M: You know, all this is beginning to make me wonder.

P: As well you might. Because those are only the facts about Mr.
Meter, but what I'm really here to do is to explode a few of
the myths. Myth number one: They say that Mr. Meter keeps
the flow of traffic moving. Well I have with me a scientific
diagram showing how the traffic moved in a given area of San
Francisco before meters were installed:

(CHART 4)

Isn't that appalling?

M: Icky.

P: Atrocious?

M: Ugh.

P: Pernicious?

M: I hate it.

Street theatre in Providence, R.I., 1970. "The whole point was to grab attention and focus that attention on the forces at work in the nation, including the forces at work in our minds and in the minds of the audience members. When it worked people were sometimes surprised by their thoughts and arguments." (John Emigh, 264) Photo by Michael St. A. Boyer.

Bern Porter, Setting for street theatre, ancient.

The San Francisco Mime Troupe performing *Comedia dell' Arte* in the park. "Guerrilla theatre (agit-prop), designed to awaken political consciousness, may not draw attention to itself from the start, but may sneak into an area, pull its trick off and split—often in ordinary or realistic costumes. . . . But radical street or park theatre that is designed to persuade, educate, and challenge ideas is better in non-naturalistic, masked or highly costumed styles." (R. G. Davis, 28)
Photo by The San Francisco Mime Troupe.

"The Feeder and the Apostles," The Bread and Puppet Theatre at the 24th of May Parade in Washington, D.C., 1971. (The gunman, top left, is not a part of the company. *Ed.*)

"The Pointer," The Bread and Puppet Theatre at the 24th of May Parade in Washington, D.C., 1971. "The Pointer is a remarkable Schumann figure who poses in front of monuments, statues, banks —wherever he pleases—and points an enormous, questioning finger and thumb at these public places in a way that makes you reconsider their functions." (24)

Sheriff Bill in John Lion's *Sheriff Bill*, The Magic Theatre of Berkeley.
Photo by Ken Howard.

Sheriff Bill and Sheriff Diddle in John Lion's *Sheriff Bill*, The Magic Theatre of Berkeley. "No scene in *Sheriff Bill* lasts more than five minutes. Each scene was approached from the point of view of production similar to creating an effective pop music number. Changes in locale were indicated by slides Costuming and posturing tended toward the flat effect of the comic strip." (John Lion, 187)
Photo by Ken Howard.

P: Let's get rid of it. I have with me a second diagram even more scientific than the first, showing the exact same area after six months of saturation metering.

(CHART 5)

Notice the dramatic improvement.

M: Yes, the color's different.

P: That's about it, toots. Myth number two: They say Mr. Meter helps the small businessman by improving his turnover.

(CHART 6)

Turnover. Ha! Ask your local grocer how he likes being surrounded by meters when across the street is Safeway with a free parking lot, not to mention scab grapes. That is, if your local grocer's still in business.

M: You know, all this is beginning to make me have a few reservations.

P: As well you might, toots—because all of this leads us to the big question.

(CHART 7)

What can you and I as armed revolutionary socialists, do about it?

M: And the other big question: Do you have change for my parking meter?

P: And the other big question: What is the big surprise I have for you, toots? And the answer to all three questions is (hand produces tab-top)   DA-Dah! Mr. Tab-top!

M: Mr. Who?

P: Mr. Tab-top from a 12-ounce can of Lucky Lager, Diet-Pepsi, or Shasta Soda Pop. Otherwise known as the parking meter token.

M: You don't mean . . .

P: Ah, but I do . . .

M: You aren't suggesting . . .

P: Accept this token of my esteem.

M *(taking it)*: Oh, but this is . . .

P: Democratic self-defense, a blow against U. S. Imperialism, and litterbugging. Long live aluminum.

M: Do you mean I should put this in my slot?

P: Yes, and I'd like to have it back when you're through with it. However, being a professional agitator, I have to get back to the laundromat—And so, I kiss your Lily White and your Big Pink and your little brown and I bid you a fond a-doo-doo. Don't take any wooden nickels. *(Exit).*

M: Well, willya look at that. Forty minutes free time. This is just incredible. *Meter Maid appears.*

MM: Stick 'em up.

M: What?

MM: I said stick them up!

M: Who are you?

MM: I am Lovely Rita, and I saw you stuff that tabtop in the meter.

M: That's impossible, there was this little man . . .

MM: All right you chronic malefactor, I'm going to blow yer . . . But first, a little social work: (Sweetly.) Don't you realize you're only cheating yourself, you poor wayward thing? Why, the meters are here for your own good.

M: What good?

MM: Why, to keep the traffic moving . . .

M: But it doesn't.

MM: I mean, to keep up the upkeep.

M: It all goes to keep up the meters and pay you.

MM: You wanna know something? This is now an illegal assembly. I hereby order you to disperse.

M: How can I disperse? There's only one of me.

MM: Hippie backtalk. I must prevent anarchy at whatever cost to myself or the Public. Blam, Blam. That's what we call a warning shot. Crime does not pay, especially if you're not a cop. *(Exit.)*

M: Ooo. She got me. All for forty minutes of free time. Remember folks, tabtop from a 12-ounce can of Lucky Lager, Diet-Pepsi, or Shasta Soda Pop—And if you're not thirsty, there's millions of them lying all over the streets—Ooof—Parking is such sweet sorrow. Drink Beer tonight. Park free tomorrow.

"The Exorcism of the Pentagon"
from *The Armies of the Night*

NORMAN MAILER

Well, let us move on to hear the music. It was being played by
the Fugs, or rather—to be scrupulously phenomenological—
Mailer heard the music first, then noticed the musicians and their
costumes, then recognized two of them as Ed Sanders and Tuli
Kupferberg and knew it was the Fugs. Great joy! They were much
better than the last time he had heard them in a grind-it-out
theatre on Macdougal Street. Now they were dressed in orange
and yellow and rose-colored capes and looked at once like Hindu
gurus, French musketeers, and Southern cavalry captains, and the
girls watching them, indeed sharing the platform with them, were
wearing love beads and leather bells—sandals, blossoms, and little
steel-rimmed spectacles abounded, and the music, no rather the
play, had begun, almost Shakespearean in its sinister announcement of great pleasures to come. Now the Participant recognized
that this was the beginning of the exorcism of the Pentagon, yes
the papers had made much of the permit requested by a hippie
leader named Abbie Hoffman to encircle the Pentagon with twelve
hundred men in order to form a ring of exorcism sufficiently
powerful to raise the Pentagon three hundred feet. In the air the
Pentagon would then, went the presumption, turn orange and
vibrate until all evil emissions had fled this levitation. At that point
the war in Vietnam would end.

The General Services Administrator who ruled on the permit
consented to let an attempt be made to raise the building ten feet,
but he could not go so far as to allow the encirclement. Of course,
exorcism without encirclement was like culinary art without a
fire—no one could properly expect a meal. Nonetheless the exorcism would proceed, and the Fugs were to serve as a theatrical
medium and would play their music on the rear bed of the truck

they had driven in here at the end of the parking lot nearest to the Pentagon some hundreds of yards from the speaker's stand where the rally was to take place.

Now, while an Indian triangle was repeatedly struck, and a cymbal was clanged, a mimeographed paper was passed around to the Marchers watching. It had a legend which went something like this:

> October 21, 1967, Washington, D.C., U.S.A., Planet Earth
>
> We Freemen, of all colors of the spectrum, in the name of God, Ra, Jehovah, Anubis, Osiris, Tlaloc, Quetzalcoatl, Thoth, Ptah, Allah, Krishna, Chango, Chimeke, Chukwu, Olisa-Bulu-Uwa, Imales, Orisasu, Odudua, Kali, Shiva-Shakra, Great Spirit, Dionysus, Yahweh, Thor, Bacchus, Isis, Jesus Christ, Maitreya, Buddha, Rama do exorcise and cast out the EVIL which has walled and captured the pentacle of power and perverted its use to the need of the total machine and its child the hydrogen bomb and has suffered the people of the planet earth, the American people and creatures of the mountains, woods, streams, and oceans grievous mental and physical torture and the constant torment of the imminent threat of utter destruction.
>
> We are demanding that the pentacle of power once again be used to serve the interests of GOD manifest in the world as man. We are embarking on a motion which is millennial in scope. Let this day, October 21, 1967, mark the beginning of suprapolitics.
>
> By act of reading this paper you are engaged in the Holy Ritual of Exorcism. To further participate focus your thought on the casting out of evil through the grace of GOD which is all (ours). A billion stars in a billion galaxies of space and time is the form of your power, and limitless is your name.

Now while the Indian triangle and the cymbal sounded, while a trumpet offered a mournful subterranean wail, full of sobs, and mahogany shadows of sorrow, and all sour groans from hell's dungeon, while finger bells tinkled and drums beat, so did a solemn voice speak something approximate to this: "In the name of the amulets of touching, seeing, groping, hearing and loving, we call upon the powers of the cosmos to protect our ceremonies in the name of Zeus, in the name of Anubis, god of the dead, in the name of all those killed because they do not comprehend, in the name of the lives of the soldiers in Vietnam who were killed because of a bad karma, in the name of sea-born Aphrodite, in the name of Magna Mater, in the name of Dionysus, Zagreus, Jesus, Yahweh, the unnamable, the quintessent finality of the Zoroastrian fire, in the name of Hermes, in the name of the Beak of Sok, in the name of scarab, in the name, in the name, in the name of the Tyrone Power Pound Cake Society in the Sky, in the name of Rah, Osiris, Horus, Nepta, Isis, in the name of the flowing living universe, in the name of the mouth of the river, we call upon the spirit ... to raise the Pentagon from its destiny and preserve it."

Now spoke another voice. "In the name, and all the names, it is you."

Now the voice intoned a new chant, leaving the echo of the harsh invocation of all giants and thunders in the beat of cymbals, triangles, drums, leather bells, the sour anguish of a trumpet reaching for evil scurried through the tents of a medieval carnival.

Then all the musicians suddenly cried out: "Out, demons, out—back to darkness, ye servants of Satan—out, demons, out! Out, demons, out!"

Voices from the back cried: "Out! ... Out! ... Out! ... Out!" mournful as the wind of a cave. Now the music went up louder and louder, and voices chanting, "Out, demons, out! Out, demons, out! Out, demons, out!"

He detested community sing—an old violation of his childhood had been the bouncing ball on the movie screen; he had wanted to watch a movie, not sing—but the invocation delivered some message to his throat. "Out, demons, out," he whispered, "out, demons, out." And his foot—simple American foot—was, of course, tapping. "Out, demons, out." Were any of the experts in the Pentagon now shuddering, or glory of partial unringed exorcism—even vibrating? Vibrating experts? "Out, demons, out! Out, demons, out!" He could hear Ed Sanders' voice, Ed of the red-gold

head and red-gold beard, editor and publisher of a poetry magazine called *Fuck You,* renaissance conductor, composer, instru-
mentalist, and vocalist of the Fugs, old protégé of Allen Ginsberg,
what mighty protégés was Allen amassing. Sanders spoke: "For
the first time in the history of the Pentagon there will be a grope-in
within a hundred feet of this place, within two hundred feet.
Seminal culmination in the spirit of peace and brotherhood, a real
grope for peace. All of you who want to protect this rite of love
may form a circle of protection around the lovers."

"Circle of protection," intoned another voice.

"These are the magic eyes of victory." Sanders went on. "Victory, victory for peace. Money made the Pentagon—melt it.
Money made the Pentagon, melt it for love."

Now came other voices, "Burn the money, burn the money,
burn it, burn it."

Sanders: "In the name of the generative power of Priapus, in the
name of the totality, we call upon the demons of the Pentagon to
rid themselves of the cancerous tumors of the war generals, all the
secretaries and soldiers who don't know what they're doing, all the
intrigue bureaucracy and hatred, all the spewing, coupled with
prostate cancer in the deathbed. Every Pentagon general lying
alone at night with a tortured psyche and an image of death in his
brain, every general, every general lying alone, every general lying
alone."

Wild cries followed, chants: "Out, demons, out! Out, demons,
out! Out! out! out! Out, demons, out."

Sanders: "In the name of the most sacred of sacred names
Xabrax Phresxner."

He was accompanied now by chants of, "hari, hari, hari, hari,
rama, rama, rama, rama, Krishna, hari Krishna, hari, hari, rama,
Krishna."

"Out, demons, out."

They all chanted: "End the fire and war, and war, end the
plague of death. End the fire and war, and war, end the plague of
death." In the background was the sound of a long sustained
Ommmm.

On which acidic journeys had the hippies met the witches and
the devils and the cutting edge of all primitive awe, the savage's

sense of explosion—the fuse of blasphemy, the cap of taboo now struck, the answering roar of the Gods—for what was explosion but connections made at the rate of 10 to the 10th exponent of the average rate of a dialogue and its habitual answer—had all the TNT and nuclear transcendencies of TNT exploded some devil's cauldron from the past?—was the past being consumed by the present? by nuclear blasts, and blasts into the collective living brain by way of all exploding acids, opiums, whiskies, speeds, and dopes?—the past was palpable to him, a tissue living in the tangible mansions of death, and death was disappearing, death was wasting of some incurable ill. When death disappeared, there would be no life.

Morbid thoughts for the edge of battle, thoughts out alone without wings of whiskey to bring them back, but Mailer had made his lonely odyssey into the land of the witches, it had taken him through three divorces and four wives to decide that some female phenomena could be explained by no hypothesis less thoroughgoing than the absolute existence of witches. A lonely journey, taken without help from his old drugs, no, rather a distillate of his most difficult experience, and he had arrived at it in great secrecy, for quondam Marxist, nonactive editor of a Socialist magazine, where and how could he explain or justify a striking force of witches—difficult enough to force a Socialist eye to focus on what was existential. Now, here, after several years of the blandest reports from the religious explorers of LSD, vague Tibetan lama goody-goodness auras of religiosity being the only publicly announced or even rumored fruit from all trips back from the buried Atlantis of LSD, now suddenly an entire generation of acid-heads seemed to have said goodbye to easy visions of heaven, no, now the witches were here, and rites of exorcism, and black terrors of the night—hippies being murdered. Yes, the hippies had gone from Tibet to Christ to the Middle Ages, now they were Revolutionary Alchemists. Well, thought Mailer, that was all right, he was a Left Conservative himself. "Out, demons, out! Out, demons, out!"

"You know I like this," he said to Lowell.

Lowell shook his head. He looked not untroubled. "It was all right for a while," he said, "but it's so damn repetitious."

Intimate, Enclosed Spaces

The battle against dead spaces; the battle to achieve exciting space relationships. Every theatre must always solve these problems in its own way and solve them again with every new production. If a company is fortunate enough to own its own building, the danger of a complacent familiarity soon arises, particularly in a conventional, inflexible theatre. The director, the designers, and the actors must force themselves again and again to overcome the lethargy that often comes from the feverish haste of productions and too great a familiarity with the technical problems involved.

At one end of the scale in the United States, we have the vast civic auditoriums, the killing arenas for drama where touring companies strive vainly to project naturally to enormous audiences lured to see the few remaining "Broadway hits." Then there are a relatively small number of theatres, of approximately six hundred to fifteen hundred seats, an essential size if the large-scale classics are to retain some intimacy and not disappear into distant space. Although often too inflexible in construction, these theatres are absolutely essential for regional companies and university groups to present the range of classical and modern drama and, alas, under the present system, to provide adequate box office remuneration to finance the productions.

However, there is another kind of more intimate, enclosed space that must be explored if theatre is to survive and change the cultural development of the country. This kind of space does not necessarily have to be the small, converted garage or storefront that one usually imagines. It can be a campus coffee shop or a cabaret where political and satirical skits are staged. Theatre can play anywhere, but in the age of technology, the actor finds it increasingly hard to develop his art unless he has the opportunity to work in intimate as well as large-scale settings.

In this section, various plays and articles indicate how theatre might flourish if it pursues a new kind of intimacy. I am not upholding intimacy as the only or the ideal goal in theatre. If this were to happen, it would mean the end of many great theatrical traditions from Greek and Oriental drama through modern epic theatre. However, the importance of real intimacy as an antidote to the false illusion of intimate television must be considered anew. What are the advantages of small spaces? Can certain themes and subjects be better presented in an environment that permits close scrutiny and contact? Can certain kinds of actors better develop their talents in intimate settings? A greater freedom to experiment, both artistically and financially, is only one possibility of the intimate space. In a time when television dominates and restricts families more and more to their houses, it seems likely that theatre will find new playing areas in homes. Consequently, this section begins with a manifesto for a Living Room Theatre that I once hoped to start in San Francisco.

A Manifesto For A Living Room Theatre

1) The search for the right environment is a major force behind the arts today. Drama in the streets is everywhere—the happening, the political protest. As the suspicion of the literal word in ironic America has increased, the desire for the physical, imaginative act of release has grown. The New York theatre has become commercially impossible for new, experimental work. Television has confined us to a new silence in our homes. We must liberate these homes.

2) We seek a new environment, an intimate space where the physical word can again celebrate the unity of physical action and

vital language. Theatre is the mysterious movement of the physical word. While drama in the streets can present a unique kind
of color and excitement, it tends to reflect mass force, not
individual exploration. On the streets or in the cavernous public
auditoriums of our cities, the individual confrontation that is the
essence of drama rarely happens or happens haphazardly. This
confrontation may be achieved in new ways in certain kinds of
intimate spaces that can be rearranged to suit different productions.

3) The living room is the natural arena of our environment. What
better place exists to confront our American problems? We
intend to create The Living Room Theatre. This will not be
merely a Chamber Theatre devoted to miniature works, We will
explore every possibility that the environment of a living room
presents. Since a living room is often a setting for all of the arts,
we will bring together poetry, music, dance, film, mime, art,
sculpture. At times we may present them in one, unified theatre
piece; at other times we may include on one program a new
musical work, a poetry reading, a play, a dance, the presentation of a unique sculpture or painting. However, the purpose of
our programs will always be dramatic, theatrical.

4) The Living Room Theatre, as a non-profit foundation, will be
financed from grants, contributions, and donations from performances. Our rehearsal time will be unlimited since we will not
be burdened by administrative, real estate problems with the
financial necessity to fill up space at a given time. We intend a
theatre of leisure and contemplation because it is these forces
that create real action and the power of change.

5) Living rooms will permit audiences of an ideal size for intimate
dramatic experience. The living room environment will substitute for the stage. Familiar props and regular lighting equipment of the living room will be used in creative ways. Advantage will be taken of the excitement or the boredom of a natural
environment. However, we will also feel free to transform the
living room environment in many different ways—for example,
in lighting, by the use of flashlights and projectors; in decor, by
the use of commissioned props, sets, paintings, and sculpture.

6) Our programs will consist entirely of new work. The frequently heard cries of alarm about the absence of new playwrights are nonsense. The truth is that there are almost no new theatres that demand the work of new playwrights. We will commission playwrights, composers, choreographers, film-makers, artists to create work for our theatre. In your living room, where you display the taste and tone of your lives, you will be able to compare that taste and tone with an exciting variety of contemporary artistic insights.

Grace Notes on Beckett's Environments

RUBY COHN

If it works, it's theatrical invention. If it doesn't, it's a gimmick. If it works, it's meaningful for our time. If it doesn't, it's mere updating. Beckett's plays imply but do not demand a picture-frame stage, and they demand what Michael Kirby has called matrix acting. Beckett's plays demand familiarity with Western cultural traditions—the more, the merrier. But more than Brecht's plays, they beguile us with estrangements. Like classics and commercials, they have been prey to the ritual syndrome, the happening syndrome, the intermedia syndrome. But their rigor requires strict renunciation of the fashionable for the fundamental. As Beckett wrote director Alan Schneider: "My work is a matter of fundamental sounds (no jokes intended) made as fully as possible." Only by intensifying the play's own environment can the sounds be heard "as fully as possible."

Love versus Honor, Desire versus Duty, Illusion versus Reality—these tried and true conflicts are today untrue, and very trying. None of today's *dramas* is reducible to these pure and simple-minded oppositions. And least of all Beckett. The conflict is in the confrontation—man confronts himself in the closed system of theatre. Not Man but man, a concrete comedian who may spend the time of his life frugally or prodigally, but who has only his life to spend. Clocks and calendars we have always with us, and why shouldn't they sprout like weeds in the small theatres Beckett requires? For *Endgame* and *Happy Days* maybe an hourglass or two, in which the sand will be sifted with painful slowness. For *Play* and *Come and Go* maybe a preplay and/or postplay metronome. But for all the plays, time concretized in a room, a box of space in the void.

If the theatre, however makeshift, is to house several Beckett

plays, let the artists loose on hats and containers. The derbies of
Godot, the nightcaps of Nagg and Nell, Hamm's toque, Clov's
Panama, Winnie's small ornate hat with feather, Willie's boater
can be duplicated and displayed. Or they can be points of departure for more inventive brain-covers. Similarly, ashbins and urns
can give birth to other containers, to be deployed at strategic
points in the theatre. But the playing area should not be cluttered
with extraneous bric-à-brac. Only light and space can modulate
Beckett's scenic directions, increasingly precise for each successive
play.

Waiting for Godot

And one of the malefactors which were hanged railed on
him, saying, If thou be Christ, save thyself and us.

But the other answering rebuked him, saying, Dost not thou
fear God, seeing thou art in the same condemnation?

And we indeed justly; for we receive the due reward of our
deeds: but this man hath done nothing amiss.

And he said unto Jesus, Lord, remember me when thou
comest into thy kingdom.

And Jesus said unto him, Verily I say unto thee, To-day
shalt thou be with me in paradise. (Luke 23:39-43)

Do not despair; one of the thieves was saved. Do not
presume; one of the thieves was damned. (St. Augustine)

These words should be on the program, or on the ceiling, or
somewhere in the environment, for they are the kernel of *Godot.*
Didi expounds them to us, but our sympathy with his perplexity
depends upon the Gospels in our cultural environment, and the
director should see that they *are* part of our environment, even
through last-minute cramming.

On stage, *"A country road. A tree."* These too have been, can be
blended into our environment. Joyce Kilmer wrote: "I think that I
shall never see/ A poem lovely as a tree." And some of the same
banality must attach to Godot's tree, of which Didi says: "Decidedly this tree will not have been the slightest use to us." But the
future perfect is a dubious tense, and the tree is of great theatrical

use. In an Algerian production, it might be a fig tree. In Brazil, a rubber tree toward which the tramps stretch their rubber necks. In California, a cactus or an irrigated citrus. If the tree is regional, the road should match. Sunbaked sand for Algeria, cleared jungle for Brazil, frontage road or manicured lawn for suburbia. If, as in many productions, the tree is simply a cross, should the road be a crossroads? If the tree suggests a cage, should there be stripes on the road?

When the Actor's Workshop played *Godot* at San Quentin prison, no concessions were made to the physical or human environment. The play was not only understood; it gave rise to play—a sustained interest in theatre. But maybe the prison suggestions need special underlining for those who believe themselves free. The director must judge his metaphysical as well as his physical environment.

In the first Paris production, the tree had two slim twining trunks, frail and inseparable like Didi and Gogo. And there was no road, but simply the Board. The Babylon Theatre, now defunct, had little warmth and no rake in January, 1953. Huddling in my coat, I always saw the stage derbies through other hats. Rather than Babylon, this foreshadowed Grotowski's "poor theater." In the first London production, the tree was sturdy, ready to protect and even embrace. For the first Dublin production, there was a small true tree, not even as tall as a man, with trunk thinner than a man's arm. The first American production—in sunny Miami— used three thick branches springing from no trunk (though the tramps "do" the tree on one leg each.) In foggy San Francisco, the tree's trunk was shaped like a question mark, from which dangled branches with Rosicrucian crosses. When Blin revived *Godot* in Paris, Giacometti sculpted a tree as spare and tentative as his human figures, whittled by surrounding space and light. The treeness of the tree was distinctly not all.

Road and mound have shown little variation; the playing area is usually the road, and any elevation serves as mound. But the background has varied from Blin's original musty cloths, to a cyclorama in London, to cloud suggestions cut through by barbed wire in both Dublin and San Francisco, independently. In Blau's second production, the entire theatre was converted to underground cave with life slowly emerging from the holocaust. I have also seen directors work against a blackboard, a brick wall, and a wooden fence. Never mind how they got there, on a country road, so long as they were justified by the total environment. Now that *Godot* is a classic, staging symbolism is more permissible, but the uninitiated need realistic concreteness.

Godot is Beckett's one play that allows a few textual changes. Translating from French to English, Beckett himself changed Lucky's references from French to Anglo-Irish, and the local directors might follow suit. Feckham, Peckham, Fulham, Clapham might perhaps be replaced by Fraternicity, Integricity, Santicity, and Simplicity in America of the nitty-gritty days. Or by place names of comic regional reference. For the two friends, however, Beckett kept the sparse French background even in English—Eiffel Tour, Pyrenees, Rhone, and the Macon country which evokes Gogo's explosion that he has "puked [his] puke of a life away . . . in the [invented] Cackon country." This faintly exotic quality is reenforced by the formal black suits and derbies, which recall the movie-comics Chaplin, Laurel, Hardy.

Pozzo and Lucky can be blended more easily into the actual environment. Beckett does not specify their dress, but most directors have followed Blin's lead of the tweedy squire and his uniformed lackey. The Free Southern Theatre found that a white Pozzo and a black Lucky so focused the attention of their (mainly black) audience that the rest of the play was diluted. The Hegelian Master-Slave dialectic must be theatricalized delicately, so as not to disturb the play's proportions. A Grape baron and a Chicano grapepicker is possible; or a dude rancher and a ranch-hand. As Alan Simpson discovered on his twelve-square foot stage, food faking is impossible in a small theatre; you need real chicken, turnips, carrots, radishes, but grape-juice can pass for wine.

The actor has problems with the stage environment and with that of his particular theatre. Didi and Gogo are almost never absent from the stage; they are glaringly on display, playing.

Though Pozzo and Lucky play only interludes, their play is more arduous. Peter Bull has described the skin ailment that resulted from his wearing Pozzo's bald rubber wig; Donal Donnelly, Dublin's Lucky, developed abrasions of the neck where the rope had rubbed. Beckett's playing is not all fun and games, though it is that too.

A skilled actor can embrace his environment at two subtle levels of Beckett's dialogue—the theatrical and the ontological. An ironic inclusiveness can point such remarks as Didi's "Charming evening we're having." Or Gogo's "I find this really most extraordinarily interesting." Gogo and Didi both use the physical realities of the playing room; Gogo when he indicates a place for Didi to urinate: "End of corridor, on the left." And Didi when he discourages Gogo's exit into the backdrop: "Imbecile! There's no way out there." Then, ironically, Didi gestures toward the audience: "There! Not a soul in sight!" Earlier, Didi had designated the auditorium as "that bog."

A bog that is theatre and world. But specifically and inclusively, Gogo gestures "towards the universe" as he asks Didi: "This one is enough for you?" And a little later, he explodes: "Look at this muckheap!" More subtle, however, are Didi's reactions to the human condition: "Where are all these corpses from?" "There's no lack of void." "This is becoming really insignificant." And the somewhat pretentious but nonetheless poignant "But at his place, at this moment of time, all mankind is us, whether we like it or not." It is a challenge for the actor to include *us,* whether *we* like it or not.

Endgame

All in whose nostrils was the breath of life, of all that was in dry land, died.

And every living substance was destroyed which was upon the face of the ground, both man, and cattle, and the creeping things, and the fowl of the heaven; and they were destroyed from the earth: and Noah only remained alive, and they that were with him in the ark. *(Genesis* 7:22-23)

One grain of corn is not a heap. Add a grain and there is still no heap. When does a heap begin? (Eubulides of Miletus)

In an earlier version of *Endgame*, Hamm commands Clov to read him the story of the flood from the Pentateuch. But Beckett actually forgot the name of "the old Greek" to whom Hamm refers, and most commentators identify him as Zeno, whose paradoxes bear on the same subject—the impossibility that parts will add up to a whole. These moments that do not add up to a life—the ending process—and games are the constants of the stage environment, which reaches only gradually toward our own.

Though Blin's first production of *Endgame* used a curving background to suggest the interior of a skull, most directors have chosen a rectangular last shelter, and Beckett's own 1967 Berlin production confirmed the angles. In either case, *Endgame* is more claustrophobic than *Godot*. But as in *Godot,* the actors of *Endgame* can include two environments in their meaning—the theatrical and the universal. Though there is no reference to the physical theatre, *Endgame* mocks theatre conventions—dialogue, soliloquy, aside. Clov's penultimate line is: "This is what we call making an exit." But the dialogue that mocks theatre also mocks life: "This is slow work." "This is not much fun." "This is deadly." "All life long the same inanities." And the actor has to choose between an immediate laugh and a searching resonance.

In only one passage does Clov include us in his environment:
Things are livening up.
(He gets up on ladder, raises the telescope, lets it fall.)
I did it on purpose.
(He gets down, picks up the telescope, turns it on auditorium.)
I see . . . a multitude . . . in transports . . . of joy.
(Pause.)
That's what I call a magnifier.
More usually, Clov turns his back to us when he climbs the ladder to look out of the sea-window or the earth-window. Or he disappears off stage into his ten-by-ten-by-ten kitchen.

Blind Hamm is never explicitly aware of our presence; his soliloquies and asides follow theatre convention, and he needs an onstage audience for his chronicle, but his stylistic comments are notes to himself. The box-set defines Hamm's limits, and the limits bound a dying world.

The box should not be floored by a literal chessboard. However, I have seen enriching environments for this poor theatre. In London's large Aldwych, the stage was bounded and foreshortened, so that we seemed to be looking down into a square hole. Performance in a gym extended the gamesmanship by baskets at opposite ends of the room, by a floor marked off for different courts, by the tentative nature of our folding chairs. Similarly, the shelter quality was emphasized by performance in a bar, with bottles visible beyond the backdrop, our glasses clutched against the encroaching void. And I can imagine a small, low-ceilinged theatre converted into ark, where we parasitically live on the ebbing life of the play.

Now that we have a detailed account of Beckett's own 1967 production of *Endgame,* it might serve as a model book, though Beckett himself would never set his own production as a model. And unlike Brecht, he seems not to have thought of his potential audience.

In directing, Beckett was particularly strict about underlining the *repetition* of gesture and mime. Similarly crippled, Nagg and Nell make slight, symmetrical movements. Clov wheels Hamm around the room twice, in a counterclockwise direction both times. Unable to sit, the toy dog is propped in a position that resembles Clov at Hamm's side. Clov always uses the ladder in the same way, and he climbs up to each window with the same difficulty. Nagg lifts his hand identically to rap twice on Nell's ashbin lid. Identically, too, Hamm lifts his toque three times. But the most obvious and insistent repetition is, of course, verbal, which Beckett increased on what he called "the echo principle." And which demands extreme concentration from the actor. One wrong cue, and Hamm and Clov find themselves repeating a routine that they completed ten minutes ago.

Beckett said that the most important line of the play was Nell's "Nothing is funnier than unhappiness." And he directed to emphasize the fun of unhappiness, but he added no business to the text. Rather, he accented the comedy by creating deliberate disjunction between gesture and dialogue; he had his actors first assume an attitude, and only then speak the line. This demands exceptional skill of Nagg and Nell, almost immobile in their bins. Since Clov is the only mobile character, he has most comic scope; bent double, Beckett's Clov always passed in front of Hamm's chair, momentarily obscuring him from the audience. Clov's upper half virtually disappeared into the garbage-cans when he spoke to Nagg or Nell; then he slowly emerged, with a look of some surprise at being back in the world.

Beckett had the stage world painted gray "Light black. From pole to pole." Hamm and Clov wore different shades of gray in their gray shelter. Beckett abandoned the red and white faces of the published text, for a uniform gray-white makeup on all four faces. He eliminated the bloodstains on Hamm's handkerchief, making it gray-white, like the window-curtains and the shroud-sheets. The garbage-cans were gray-black, their color blending into the gray walls. The lighting was particularly irksome to Beckett, who kept demanding more gray. The actors agreed with Beckett that there would be no final bows after each performance, since they were only pausing—*un temps*—before they continued to play. Before us and for us, who are dying in the same shelter.

Happy Days

We are back outdoors, but the horizon is a trompe-l'oeil back-cloth. Time passes in two stages, but the actors' environment changes *between* the acts: *Godot's* tree sprouts leaves, but Winnie sinks from waist to neck in the earth. And our presence is not acknowledged. No one turns a telescope upon us, or even a seeing eye. Gone are the tacit admissions that we are all in the same theatre, participating in play.

Winnie is constantly before our eyes, but she is unaware of us. The soliloquy that was a theatrical convention for Hamm is a mode of existence for her; she talks to convince herself that she exists, but she needs corroboration from Willie. So rarely, however, is that corroboration forthcoming, that she drives her monologue on, with its few subjects—Willie, observation of her almost empty environment, enumeration of the contents of her sack, invention of stories, recollection of lines of verse. Unlike *Godot* and *Endgame*, however, where the relevant biblical passages should be absorbed into *our* environment, I don't think there is much point to inserting into the program the play's lines of Shakespeare, Milton, Herrick, Gray, Keats, Fitzgerald, Browning, Charles Wolfe. Relevant as the fragments are to Winnie's situation, they do not *define* the situation, as the biblical citations do that of *Godot* and *Endgame*.

Godot's characters are estranged by costume and country, those of *Endgame* by their claustrophobic shelter; Winnie is half-dead, or at least half-buried. But how vigorous is her living half, and how similar to all of me, a woman in the world of things, seeking occasional corroboration from a fellow human being.

The play virtually consumes Winnie, and even the great Winnies—Beatrice Manley, Madeleine Renaud, Ruth White—tend to save themselves and us from the play's relentlessness. They sit comfortably in their mounds, so that we do not quite believe that the earth is pressing them down. They bask comfortably in the beautiful weather, so that we do not quite believe that the sun is blazing down. We don't want Winnie blistered and peeling, but we *do* need to feel the irony of all those repetitions of "happy day."

Winnie is totally absorbed by the illusionistic immediacy of her environment, and her long monologue contains no reference to the theatre as theatre, to us as audience, or even to theatre techniques by which the play moves through time. And yet, she does comment on her monologue; in Willie's absence or non-response, she acts as her own audience, and an actress can—with immense subtlety and skill—use our presence to evoke her dialogue as response to us. As certain lines in *Godot* and *Endgame* referred to the environment of theatre *and* of universe, Winnie's commentary divides between her words and the eyes of others (us?).

After delivering a good many words, Winnie faces us and can include us when she voices one of her deepest fears: "Words fail, there are times when even they fail." But she keeps using them nonetheless, and by Act II they are all she has. But by Act II, she no longer mentions words as such, but only sounds, cries, and the need to keep talking. Even more pointedly, she feels our gaze upon her. In Act I: "Strange feeling that someone is looking at me." And in Act II, at the beginning of the second happy day: "Someone is looking at me still. *(Pause.)* Caring for me still." Though the "someone" is Willie by the end of the act, it is us above all.

The open space of *Godot* and *Happy Days* is not so environmentally convertible as *Endgame.* But Jan Kott has seen Winnie in a hospital, and her prayer-confession smacks of church, in either of which we can feel a sadistic sun, in a small theatre. And this is the final environmental note: in spite of prizes, keep the theater small. In spite of publicity, keep the audience at a decorous distance, to be measured by the actor in time.

Explosion
An Overpopulation Farce for
Two Actors and Percussion

DAN GEROULD

A city apartment on a hot summer night. Open window, noises from the street and other apartments: voices of children of all ages, crying, yelling, screaming, chirping, chattering, buzzing, humming—first at normal speed, then gradually faster and faster.

On stage, a complete set of percussion instruments: snare drum, tom-toms, bass drum, tympani, xylophone, triangle, castanets, rattle, whip, cowbell, rachet—arranged as in a symphony orchestra. Three musicians (two men and a woman) dressed in evening clothes sit on chairs in a row behind the instruments except when they are called upon to play.

METHUSELAH *(as a young man) sits at a table eating his supper of sausages and eggs and drinking beer from a quart bottle. Now and then he puts his thumb over the mouth of the bottle and shakes it up to give it a good head—it froths out of the bottle into his mouth. As he eats and drinks, he reads aloud birth announcements from a stack of newspapers from around the world* (The New York Times, Le Figaro, Pravda, The Bombay Daily News, Mainichi Shimbun, *etc.), dropping each paper in a pile on the floor when he has finished it. Methuselah is dressed in green knee-length short pants with a comical raised cod-piece in yellow with an orange stripe, a red T-shirt that fits tightly, and heavy blue sneakers without socks. As he reads, he chuckles and comments with pleasure on the birth announcements.*

M. and Mme. Jean-Pierre Castel and M. and Mme. René de Labretoigne de Lavalette have the pleasure of announcing the birth of their grandson Jean-Claude, son of Jean-Michel and Chantal Castel on June 19, 13 rue Simon-le-Franc, Paris. Jean-Claude—that's a good name for a boy. Jean-Claude, son of Jean-Michel, son of Jean-Pierre.

Masanobu and Toyohiko Fukuyama have the honor of announcing the birth of their fourth son, Kitagawa, on June 25, Tokyo. Four sons! That's great. First, there was Higashi, then Nobuyuki, followed by Tatsue, and now Kitagawa.

Comrades Nikolai Alexandrovich and Valentina Mikhailovna Prokopovich are proud to announce the birth of their daughter, Sophia Nikolaevna on June 12, Krasnoarmeiskii Prospekt 678, Moscow. Little Sophia Nikolaevna. Is she cute! (Talking to the baby and making appropriate sounds and gestures.) "Sopha. *Sóphooshka. Sóphochka. Sophka. Sophik. Sophiyooshka.*

Alan and Joanne (née Putnam) Lachowitz joyfully announce the birth of Jonathan Owen, June 20. The proud grandparents are Mr. and Mrs. Irving Lachowitz and Mrs. Tina Putnam and the late Joseph Putnam. I'll bet they're proud. I'd be proud too. Even the late Joseph Putnam's proud. Jonathan Owen Lachowitz.

> *Suddenly MALTHUSIA appears next to Methuselah, either through a trap in the floor, from behind a screen, or out of the shadows. She is an antiseptic vision of beauty, instantly killing all joy. Malthusia is dressed in a nurse's uniform and wears a high starched white cap with a sharply crenellated top edge. Her long hair is rolled into a very tight bun on the back of her head and stuck full of large pins with white heads. Her uniform is white and stiffly starched, with long tight sleeves buttoned from the cuff to the shoulder, a squared-off collar, and a tucked yoke which buttons all the way down the front and has a wide white fabric belt with a small spiked stud in the center. She wears a white apron with a deep pocket di-*

rectly over her pelvis, white nylon stockings, and white oxfords. She speaks in a precise, intense voice which she never raises above a carefully controlled limit. On her left breast she wears a demometer which indicates the world's population. Her legs are tied together at the knees with a black ribbon—a mourning band for the world. When she moves, she hops.

MALTHUSIA; *grabbing Methuselah's arm just as he is about to bite into a sausage:* Stop! *(First percussionist snaps the whip.)* 146 thousand more today. *(Adjusts the demometer pinned on her left breast.)* Total: 358 thousand million. They're predicting 147 thousand tomorrow. Where are we going to put them? How are we going to feed them? What are we going to eat?

METHUSELAH: In the refrigerator there's *(to the accompaniment of rim shots on the snare drum):*
baloney
spareribs
large curd cottage cheese
four pounds of ground steak
cole slaw
ham
hard-boiled eggs
cold roast turkey

MALTHUSIA: By 1975 there'll be a 277 million increase in India alone. In ten years, no more turkeys, no more pigs. Every acre for soy beans. Then good-bye soy beans. The algae farms.

METHUSELAH, *(with the sausage still poised on his fork):* You'll never get me to eat algae.

MALTHUSIA: Listen! *(Second percussionist hits a tom-tom lightly with a drumstick.)* Hear that?

METHUSELAH: Hear what?

MALTHUSIA: Do you realize seventeen hundred Chinese are born every hour?

METHUSELAH: I'd like to read the names.

MALTHUSIA: By the year 2000 there'll be 10 thousand million of them. It's too late already. The worst famine in history is just around the corner. China, India, Pakistan will be first—then Egypt, Iran, Turkey. Within ten years the famines will spread to Africa, then Latin America. There'll be mass starvation of billions of people.

METHUSELAH: Malthusia, honey, when are we going to have some children?

MALTHUSIA: Do you know what it's like to starve to death? *(Like a nurse giving a report on a patient's progress.)* At first hunger is accompanied by severe pain in the stomach and epigastric region generally. Thirst becomes intense, and sleeplessness sets in.

METHUSELAH: There's nothing like children . . .

MALTHUSIA: A characteristic feeling of sinking and weakness occurs in the epigastric region, the thirst still continuing to an agonizing degree.

METHUSELAH: They're such a comfort to you in your old age . . .

MALTHUSIA: The face assumes an anxious, pale expression; the eyes are wild and staring; and the whole countenance and body participate in rapid general emaciation.

METHUSELAH: I don't want us to be a childless couple . . .

MALTHUSIA: The body exhales a fetid odor . . .

METHUSELAH: . . . have nothing to look forward to but the long years all alone . . .

MALTHUSIA: . . . the breath and lung secretions become strong smelling . . .

METHUSELAH: I want to see kids playing there on the floor . . .

MALTHUSIA: . . . and the skin is covered with a brownish secretion from the decomposition and organic decay of the tissues.

METHUSELAH: . . . hear children's laughter in the house . . .

MALTHUSIA: The gait totters . . .

METHUSELAH: . . . at Christmas . . .

MALTHUSIA: . . . the mind becomes impaired . . .

METHUSELAH: . . . all back from college . . .

MALTHUSIA: . . . delirium and convulsions may ensue . . .

METHUSELAH: . . . with their friends . . .

MALTHUSIA: . . . death occurs . . .

METHUSELAH: . . . and then they'll get married . . .

MALTHUSIA: . . . with or without diarrhea . . .

METHUSELAH: . . . and have kids of their own . . .

MALTHUSIA: The dead body goes more rapidly to decay than after death from ordinary causes.

METHUSELAH: I want to be an ANCESTOR.

MALTHUSIA: The whole human race will die of suffocation on November 15, 2007.

METHUSELAH, *picks up a newspaper:* Listen to this.

The marchese and the marchesa Tommasso della Gambetta take great pleasure in announcing the birth of their 12th, 13th, and 14th grandchildren, Bartolommeo, Gabriella, and Vittorio on July 2. Fourteen grandchildren! That means hundreds of great-great-grandchildren. Grandfather is the most beautiful word in the language.

MALTHUSIA: Sterile is.

METHUSELAH: I want someone to call me Grandpa—Grandpa Methuselah.

MALTHUSIA: No one ever will.

METHUSELAH: I want to put an announcement in the paper. In all the papers.

MALTHUSIA: Your only announcement will be your obituary.

This is the end of your line.

You can make love to me

Anytime you want

Anyway you want

As long as it's STERILE

As long as it's STERILE

METHUSELAH: Malthusia, I'm tired of sex without fertilization. Let me be a man and procreate.

MALTHUSIA, *pushing him away:* You're scuffing my shoes. *(Reaches in the pocket of her apron and brings out a tube of liquid white shoe polish with a squirter nozzle which she uses to spray her shoes.)* You're stepping all over my white shoes and getting them dirty. *(Suddenly stops and listens again.)* Hear That? *(The three percussionists with their ears bent over their instruments hit their tympani lightly and tune them.)* Listen!

METHUSELAH: I don't hear anything.

MALTHUSIA: There. Listen. *(The three percussionists continue tuning their instruments. Throughout the rest of the play, the musicians, sometimes singly, sometimes together in groups of two or three, play their tympani gradually and imperceptibly louder until the final crescendo.)*

METHUSELAH: I still can't hear anything.

MALTHUSIA: Boom! Another. Boom! Louder and louder. Closer and closer. Boom! Boom! Boom! *(She speaks softly and slowly.)*

METHUSELAH: Well, maybe there is a boom—but you can hardly hear it. *(Shakes up the beer and lets it froth into his mouth.)* It's a long way off.

MALTHUSIA: It's only nine months off.
I have an ear for conception.
I can hear it every time a baby's conceived in Pakistan. *(Third percussionist hits the triangle gently.)*
It pushes me another step to the wall. *(Recoils towards the wall as if pushed, hopping like a frightened frog.)*
Space closing in
Millions of embryos
Growing up
Going to school
Looking for apartments

METHUSELAH: I never should have taken you to the World's Fair on our honeymoon and let you see those flashing lights.

MALTHUSIA: That showed every birth in the whole world as it was taking place. I couldn't keep my eyes off it. It's still flashing in my head.

METHUSELAH: Look at you now. Going around putting intrauterine rings under the windshields of parked cars.

MALTHUSIA: And you riding around on buses at rush hour and pushing against pregnant women's stomachs.

METHUSELAH: I like to feel a few kicks of life. I can't bear to put my ear against your belly and hear it roar like an empty seashell.

MALTHUSIA: When I walk by a tenement on a hot August night and look up at the drawn blinds in bedroom windows, I see hundreds of children playing in the streets five years later. *(Gasping)* I can't breathe. I'm suffocating. Air, give me air! *(Rushes towards the audience as if to the open window and takes several deep breaths.)* Look at them. They're all out there.

METHUSELAH: Who?

MALTHUSIA: *(Second percussionist hits the tympani.)* Boom!
In the fertile night
In the tubes and organs of darkness
Hundreds of millions of reproductive acts

METHUSELAH, *lyrical:* In Assyria.

MALTHUSIA, *tragical:* In Cameroon.

METHUSELAH: In the Khanate of Turan.

MALTHUSIA: In Paphlygonia.

METHUSELAH: In Oudh.

MALTHUSIA: In Rio de Oro.

METHUSELAH: In the Kingdom of Pergamum.

MALTHUSIA: The sperm and the ovum.

METHUSELAH, *ecstatically:* Life! Life! Life!

MALTHUSIA: Trillions of microscopic spermatozoa swimming up and up and up!

METHUSELAH, *bursts into song:*
"FERTILIZING THE EGG" (to xylophone accompaniment)
The tiny spermatozoon
Learns to swim
Simply by being thrown in
Thrown in
And then it's up, up, up
To get the prize

Reflected in his tiny eyes
Fertilizing the egg
Fertilizing the egg
The egg
The egg
The egg

MALTHUSIA: What are you singing for? *(She slaps him.)* Two-
thirds of humanity goes to sleep hungry every night.

METHUSELAH, *getting down on his knees and trying to pull her
knees apart:*
Open your knees
Conceive
Bring forth
Flat on your back
Deliver
And moan

MALTHUSIA: Watch out for my shoes. *(Sprays again.)* There's
no more room. People on top of people. Reproducing. *(Sprays
again.)* Stepping on my shoes. *(Picks up one of Methuselah's
newspapers.)* Listen to this: Standing room only, says population expert. In underdeveloped countries growth rates increase
to nearly three per cent.

METHUSELAH: That's less than we get at the savings bank.

MALTHUSIA, *continues reading:* If continued for thirty years,
such growth rates will increase the world's population to the
point where there will be standing room only on the face of
the earth. Each inhabitant of the globe will have only one
square yard to stand in.

METHUSELAH: Just try to keep me cooped up like that in one
square yard!

MALTHUSIA, *reaches in the pocket of her apron and pulls out a
large compass with a piece of chalk attached to its moving
foot:* Then we'll make it a circle. *(She jabs the point of the
compass towards him.)*

METHUSELAH: What are you pointing that compass at me for?

MALTHUSIA: *Takes out a collapsible steel tape measure from*

*her apron pocket and adjusts the compass to a three-foot arc,
then draws a circle three feet in diameter in the middle of the
floor—all the time keeping an eye on Methuselah and protecting herself against a surprise attack with the sharp point of the
compass.* A circle one yard in diameter. *(Sprays the circle
white with the shoe spray.)* Get in.

METHUSELAH: In where?

MALTHUSIA: In the circle. *(Gives him a hard shove into the
circle.)*

METHUSELAH: I haven't finished my dinner. *(Tries to get out;
she shoves him back in.)* I'm hungry. I want to eat my dinner
and read my papers. *(Desperately grabbing at a paper.)*
Ramkrishna and Dhanvanthi Ranjit Sengupta take pride in
announcing the birth of their ... *(Malthusia first punches
holes in the paper with the compass and then rips it apart
savagely.)* You've ripped up their son! *(Methuselah tries to
pick up the pieces from the floor and piece them together.)* I
didn't even see what his name was!

MALTHUSIA, *rubbing her compass back and forth on her belt to
sharpen it and then blowing on it.* Good. That's one less. Now
back in that circle.

METHUSELAH, *producing from nowhere a fishnet, with a long
handle; tries to catch her in it, as she jabs at him:*
I'm a gladiator
Fighting for life
Trying to catch you
In my net *(After several skirmishes, succeeds in dropping the
net over her head.)*
I'll deliver you myself
On the floor of the taxi
Watch your contractions
Hear your screams
Dip my hand in *(Lifts the net up off her head, reaches into it,
and pulls out an imaginary baby.)*
"Behold, a son is born."

MALTHUSIA: Get away! *(Sprays her shoes.)* Don't get me all

dirty!
You can have sex, but you can't reproduce
You can sting all you want
But without the juice
Without the juice.
METHUSELAH: I'm so alone
Can't I people the world?
MALTHUSIA: At the Clinic
The beautiful white Clinic
I stamped out thirty-nine babies today.
(Stamps out thirty-nine babies to a series of rapid percussive blows on the drums.)
Thirty-nine empty places
Thirty-nine extra seats
Thirty-nine babies
That will never cry
Or eat.
METHUSELAH: Conspiracy to commit homicide. First-degree murder of the human race.
MALTHUSIA, *jabbing at his middle with the point of the compass:*
Ever see a picture of the swollen belly
Of a starving eight-year-old beggar girl in New Delhi? (A vicious jab.)
We're out to deflate swollen bellies. *(A reverberating held note on the tympani.)*
METHUSELAH, *shaking his finger at her in passionate denunciation; puts on a miter and reads from a huge volume of weighty bulls placed on a lectern:* Who does not abhor the lustful cruelty or cruel lust of impious men, a lust which goes so far that they procure poisons to extinguish and destroy the conceived fetus within the womb, even attempting by a wicked crime to destroy their own offspring before it is born? *(Castenets.)* Who, then, would not condemn with the most severe punishments the crimes of those who by poisons, po-

tions, and *maleficia* induce sterility in women, or impede by cursed medicines their conceiving or bearing? *(Cowbells.)*

MALTHUSIA: I'd like to sterilize you myself.
Perform the perfect vasectomy *(Acts out the operation in the air with the compass as a knife.)*
Local anesthetic
Short incisions on the scrotum
Cut the sperm ducts
Tie up the ends *(Cymbals lightly struck.)*
Send you on your way again
A new man. *(Shakes his hand.)*

METHUSELAH: That's a felony: wounding with intent to do grievous bodily harm. And what's more, private individuals are not free to destroy or mutilate their own members, or in any other way render themselves unfit for their natural functions.
When your ankles are swollen
And all turned purple
We'll see who's put
What in whose circle.

MALTHUSIA: If you had your way,
I'd lay eggs every day.

METHUSELAH, *laughing in an ugly way:* I almost got you pregnant once! Were you scared! You saw thirty-nine abortionists!

MALTHUSIA, *looks at her watch:* Time for the ten o'clock pills. *(Picks up a large jar of large pills and holds it up.)* Oh, pills, great blessing on mankind! *(Rubs her cheek against the jar.)* Tell me, pills, is there anything sacred about my rhythmic cycle of fertility, my periodic possession of procreative potential?

THE PILLS, *spoken by Malthusia as a ventriloquist holding the jar:* No, we've changed all that. *(Cymbal crash.)*

MALTHUSIA, *shakes out a handful of pills and swallows them all at once:* Thanks, pills. I'm free. Free from the curse of fertility.

METHUSELAH: You're eating them like peanuts. They're changing your metabolism. You're not as soft and feminine as you used to be. *(She tries to jab him in the crotch with the point of the compass.)*

MALTHUSIA: We're going to show that man can be detached from his reproductive organs.
Man's highest goal is
TOTAL CONTROL.

METHUSELAH, *running around and around in his circle:*
You'll never regiment people that way.
It's the one way man's still free.
Make man's mind captive
But never his genitals.

MALTHUSIA, *issuing ukases to drum roll:*
Childbirth becomes a crime.
Instead of sending out announcements, you get a summons to appear in court.
Mothers go directly from the hospital to jail.

METHUSELAH: Be fruitful and multiply.

MALTHUSIA: Be sterile and survive.

METHUSELAH: What I do
In my own bedroom
Is my own business.

MALTHUSIA: Bedroom! You don't have a bedroom.

METHUSELAH: What do you mean I don't have a bedroom? I'd like to know who's going to take it away from me?

MALTHUSIA: Ten thousand million Chinese. *(Third percussionist hits a large Chinese gong.)*

METHUSELAH, *getting pugnacious:*
I'd like to see them try it.
It's private property.
Fascist!
With your castration camps
We'll riot
Rise up
Destroy your hateful . . .

MALTHUSIA, *blows a whistle:*
>Stop! You're breaking the law.
>Birth Control Police will come and work you over. *(Begins chanting, continued through the next four speeches.)*

METHUSELAH: With their tape and putty
>Their trowels and hoses
>And their long blue surgical noses

MALTHUSIA: They'll seal you off.
>They'll tie you up.

METHUSELAH: They keep their glue in a giant vat.

MALTHUSIA: Your tubes will be neatly tied like a sausage your organs packaged like processed meat.

METHUSELAH: Freedom!
>In the middle of the night
>We'll take out your mechanical barriers
>Stick pins in
>Life will come oozing through
>Bootleg conception
>Ha, ha, ha
>You'll never stop man from reproducing
>Even if we starve to death for it *Laughs uproariously.*
>That's the way it's always been
>That's the way it'll always be
>We'll starve to death
>We'll starve to death
>But we'll go on reproducing.

MALTHUSIA: Don't punch those holes
>You're starting World War III

METHUSELAH: I'm only doing what's proper to man's nature. *(Percussionists hit cow-bells and shake tambourines; Methuselah does a short fertility dance in his circle.)*

MALTHUSIA: I defend the rights of the living to suppress the unborn hordes waiting to be born.

METHUSELAH: And I defend the rights of the yet unborn to be born

They're the vast majority
Those who've lived and who live now
Are just
A speck in the sea
Of those waiting to be born
Hear them beating on the door? *(The three percussionists play snare drums, tom-tom, and tympani.)*

IMPATIENT EMBRYOS, *outside the door:*
We want to get in
We want to get in
Into this room—
Through your womb

MALTHUSIA, *leaning all her weight against an imaginary door and trying to hold it shut against the embryos pushing against it from the other side:* Don't let them in! Help me!

METHUSELAH: I'll hold the door
You draw the shade
I've been waiting
For thirty-five years
The fertile moment
The fecund time
When the earth will teem

MALTHUSIA, *pulls down the shade; on the inside of the shade there is a large, brightly colored demographic chart of Asia which resembles a diagram of the genital anatomy of the female:* Projected growth rates in Asia. *(Illustrates her lecture by pointing to the chart with a long wooden pointer.)*
Merely to maintain her present starvation level of subsistence, Asia would have to increase her aggregate product by seventy-five percent in the next ten years. And the population rate will triple in only five years.

METHUSELAH: I'll start your labor pains. *(Sounds of someone repeatedly trying to start a car.)*

MALTHUSIA, *weeping softly:* While the nations of Asia are attempting to improve their miserable urban living conditions, their city populations will continue to increase geometrically—perhaps to five times the present size in only one generation. *(Convulsed with quiet sobbing.)*

METHUSELAH, *rubbing her stomach:*
Wombs to be filled
Wombs to be filled

MALTHUSIA, *through her tears:*
May all the wombs in the world
Be forever empty
I'd like to spray the entire surface of the earth with SPERMI-CIDES *(Hisses noticably.)*

METHUSELAH: From your mouth!

MALTHUSIA: From my mouth!

METHUSELAH: Wicked means for preventing the SEED from reaching the VESSEL. *(To the accompaniment of rim shots on the snare drum.)*
Condoms
Diaphragms
Pessaries
Rings
Douches
Jellies
Creams
Powders
Suppositories
Foam tablets
Disgusting
Filthy
Obscene
You can't talk about these things in public
You can't show them on stage or to children
You have to hide them
I've a better way
Decent
Wholesome
Clean

For the whole family
Hand me that box
MALTHUSIA, *hands him an olive drab box a foot long and six inches wide:* What's that?
METHUSELAH: Here's my baby. *(Opens the box and takes out the pieces.)* The F-14 Antipersonnel Mine.
MALTHUSIA: So that's what they make at your factory. I thought it was dynamite for blowing up rocks.
METHUSELAH: No, people.

Twelve pieces. *(Holding up the pieces.)*
Total cost: 89 cents
So simple even a child can assemble it
(Takes out a large color chart which resembles the male genitals.) ASSEMBLING THE F-14 ANTIPERSONNEL MINE. *(Hands Malthusia the chart and has her put it up alongside the population chart on the window shade; takes the pointer and, as he holds up each part, shows it on the chart.)*
Three-pronged head
Positive safety pin
Locking safety pin
Striker
Pull ring
Striker spring
—Notice all the safety divices—
Put the fuse in the firing case
The pressure of a man's foot triggers the fuse
The fuse produces flames which set off the detonator
The concussion produced by the detonator sets off the main charge

Imagine a whole field full of mines in spring
A birch forest planted with mines
Beautiful, eh?
Out in the open
Under the stars
With frost and dew
Makes what you're doing seem sordid, doesn't it?

So delicate
The pressure of a man's foot
A bare toe
Against one of these little prongs
Boom *(The first percussionist plays the tympani.)* There he
goes *(Looks up in the air.)*
MALTHUSIA: Murderer.
METHUSELAH: And your filthy discards muddying river banks?
There's embryo all over your hands
Innocent children's placenta on your apron *(Pointing)*
We give them a chance
Let them start the race
Live at least until they're old enough to go in the army
MALTHUSIA: Better never to exist at all
Think of your own son blown up
As he stepped down
On a patch of wet grass
In the heat of July
On a dusty field
In a field of rye
METHUSELAH: I was in the army
Navy
Marines
Fathered a few
In the Near East
And the Far East too
The invasion of Canaan
War of the Spanish succession
Siege of Constantinople
I wouldn't be a bit surprised
If one of my sons hasn't already stepped
On one of these babies *(Pats the F-14 Antipersonnel Mine,
whistles, and makes a head-over-heels gesture with his hand.)*
We ship them all over the world
Wherever there's a war going on
Millions of them like seeds in the earth

Waiting for the right foot
That's the way it's always been
That's the way it'll always be
Create people and kill them off
The way God does
Man doesn't want to exercise control
Not any kind of control:
Birth control
Arms control
Self control! *(Beats with the pointer on the floor; the three percussionists play their various instruments.)*
Boom
To father and to kill
Why do old ladies smile at pregnant women and soldiers
going off to war?
It's simple human nature
Birth and death
Each soldier has two professions:
Killing the enemy and fathering bastards
Wherever armies go
They leave behind
Corpses and babies
Corpses and babies
MALTHUSIA: Life's a horrible accident. Do away with it.
METHUSELAH: A beautiful accident
Get pregnant, get born, step on a mine
Invade, impregnate, kill
Only preventing life is evil, not its destruction
Even the church knows that
MALTHUSIA: No artificial contraception
But artificial ways of blowing people up!
METHUSELAH, *stroking the F-14 Antipersonnel Mine:*
Made by decent family men
Show the F-14 on the stage, give it to the kids to play with.
But you never heard of a toy contraceptive for children, did
you?

All little children hate birth control
The life prevented might be their own
(Reaches in his pocket and pulls out a toy land mine.) Here's the toy model F-14 Antipersonnel Mine. Put it under the tree at Christmas. It'll blow up the tin soldiers—it'll blow up the tree.

MALTHUSIA, *with clipboard and questionnaire:* What right did you have to be born? That's the question I'd like to put to every newborn baby.

METHUSELAH: Speaking for all babies, past, present, and future, I'd say *(speaks like a little boy in an advertisement):*
Everyone has a right to be born. Every egg in the whole world deserves to be fertilized.

MALTHUSIA: Everyone has a right not to be born. Mankind has the inalienable right not to exist.

METHUSELAH: You know what Pius XII told the Union of Italian Midwives in *Casti Conubii?*

VOICE: Reproductio est propositium solum conubii.

SIMULTANEOUS TRANSLATION: Procreation is the sold purpose of marriage. *(Thunderous applause by the midwives.)*

METHUSELAH: What would you do if I said I was going to fertilize you forcibly?

MALTHUSIA: Even the Pope said that a nun who is about to be raped has the right to practice birth control. (Terrified.) Get away from me.
A single emission contains
Three hundred million spermatozoa
Enough to populate
The whole of Europe

METHUSELAH: We'll populate it
Then destroy it
Over and over again
That's the way it's always been
That's the way it'll always be
(Holding up the F-14 Antipersonnel Mine.)

The F-14 Antipersonnel Mine
Guardian of the Future
MALTHUSIA, *holding up an extra-large intrauterine loop:*
The Intrauterine Loop
Guardian of the Future
METHUSELAH: Bury it in the ground. *(Gets out his tool set and with hammer, chisel, and saw, cuts a hole in the middle of his circle.)*
MALTHUSIA: Bury it in the womb. *(Drops the loop in her apron pocket.)*
METHUSELAH: Plant your mine. Pull your safety ring.
Fuse in its firing case.
Striker spring
Waiting, waiting.
MALTHUSIA, *rubbing her pocket:*
Stainless steel spiral
Coiled in the uterus
Waiting, waiting.
METHUSELAH: Lights out. *(Goes about the room and puts out each of the lights by smashing the bulb with his hammer.)*
MALTHUSIA, *her nurse's hat flies up off her head:*
My hat's come off
My hair's come down
I'm going out of control. *(Very slowly removes the long pins from her head and lets her long hair down, sticking each pin into Methuselah's codpiece like a pincushion.*
METHUSELAH: Time to deflower. *(Equally slowly, he peels down the top of her uniform in long strips which are painted purple on the inside and hang down like petals. Her body is painted orange and lavender, so that she resembles a flower.)*
MALTHUSIA, *in a little girl's voice, as though hypnotized or drugged:* Plants have flowers, each of which has eggs hidden within it. The eggs are in a part called the ovary. In most flowers, the ovary is just above where the petals join the stem. The egg cannot grow into a flower seed without a helper. This helper is called pollen. The pollen is often brought into an-

other flower by bees as they fly from flower to flower gathering nectar to make honey. Some of the pollen brushes off the bee onto a part of the flower just above the ovary. Each grain of pollen that the bee has brought forms a long tube that grows down toward the eggs. Each tube enters one egg. *(They mime and dance the story of the egg.) Your pollen's getting all over my pistil. (She takes a thermometer out of her pocket and puts it in her mouth, in a daze.)*

METHUSELAH: What are you doing with that thermometer?

MALTHUSIA: Taking my temperature. I'm afraid. I may be ovulating. Oh! You made me bite the thermometer in half. I've swallowed part of it.

METHUSELAH: Spit it out! It'll keep you from conceiving.

MALTHUSIA, *trying to read the remaining half of thermometer:* Oh, my God! I can't read it. The mercury's run all over my hand.

METHUSELAH: The sin of Onan.

MALTHUSIA, *eating the whole jar of pills:* I'm afraid. I'm on fire. I'm on fire. *(Flames shoot out from her body.)*

METHUSELAH: Thickened gasoline
Incendiary flames

MALTHUSIA: Foam jelly

METHUSELAH, *grabbing a portable fire extinguisher, reading the instructions, and spraying the foam all over her:*
To operate—hold upright.
1. Pull pin.
2. Raise handle.
3. Press lever.
4. Direct discharge at base of flame.

MALTHUSIA, *wiping the foam off her eyes and lips in huge hunks, like shaving cream:* I don't ever want to have children. I'm afraid of them. I don't know what to say to them. I hate them.

METHUSELAH, *on his knees before her, with chisel and hammer breaking the black band that holds her legs together:*
Ovulate

Open your knees
Conceive
Bring forth. *(He breaks the black band with his chisel; her legs open; a new-born baby's cry is heard; on the screen made by the window-shade, projected over the population chart and diagram of how to assemble the F-14 Antipersonnel Mine, there appears a large color slide of a smiling Oriental baby in rags.)*

MALTHUSIA: The enemy! Cause of all the world's problems. Prevent him. *(The slide changes to the baby grown-up as a young soldier.)*

METHUSELAH: Destroy him. *(Slide changes back to the baby.)*

MALTHUSIA: Wipe him out of his mother's womb. *(Slide changes back to soldier.)*

METHUSELAH: Blow him off the face of the earth. *(Slide changes back to baby.)*

MALTHUSIA: Together we'll exterminate him. *(Slide changes back to soldier.)*

METHUSELAH: Down. *(Pulls Malthusia down beside him on the floor and puts tin soldiers' hats on their heads.)*
He's dangerous. *(Slide changes back to baby.)*

MALTHUSIA: He's hungry.

METHUSELAH and MALTHUSIA, *infuriated:* He's smiling!

METHUSELAH: Creep. We're in a minefield. We could be blown up at any minute.

MALTHUSIA: My god, I think I'm pregnant. I feel something kicking in my stomach.

METHUSELAH: That's my foot.

MALTHUSIA: It's here, it's here. Waiting to go off. I can hear it. *(Ear to the ground.)* Like horses' hooves.

METHUSELAH: Give me the compass. We'll start probing. (Reciting from the manual.) WHEN THE SOLDIER BECOMES AWARE OF THE FACT THAT HE HAS ACCIDENTALLY ENTERED A MINEFIELD, THE FIRST RULE FOR SELF-PRESERVATION IS TO REMAIN IN PLACE. THE SOLDIER SHOULD EXAMINE THE AREA

AROUND HIS FEET IF HE IS STANDING OR IN HIS IMMEDIATE VICINITY IF KNEELING, PRONE OR SITTING. THIS EXAMINATION SHOULD BE MADE WITH A MINIMUM OF MOVEMENT, CAREFULLY AVOIDING SHIFTING OF WEIGHT. THE SOLDIER THEN MAKES A STEP-BY-STEP ESCAPE FROM THE FIELD, CAREFULLY PLACING EACH FOOT EX-ACTLY WHERE HE STEPPED IN ENTERING THE FIELD. IN THE MOST USUAL CASE, WHERE THE SOLDIER CANNOT BE SURE JUST WHERE HE HAS STEPPED, HE SHOULD CRAWL BACK OVER HIS ROUTE AS HE REMEMBERS IT. THE SOLDIER MUST MOVE SLOWLY, A FEW INCHES AT A TIME, GOING THROUGH AN EXACT ROUTINE: LOOK, FEEL WITH THE HANDS, PROBE WITH ANYTHING AVAILABLE, SUCH AS BAYONET, KNIFE, EVEN A PENCIL.

MALTHUSIA, *moaning constantly:* Oh, oh, oh. I'm fertile, I know I'm fertile.

METHUSELAH: THE SOLDIER CRAWLS FORWARD LOOKING, FEELING WITH HIS HANDS, AND PROB-ING. THE HANDS ARE USED PARTICULARLY TO LOCATE PRONGS STICKING UP FROM THE GROUND. THE SLEEVES ARE ROLLED UP TO IN-CREASE SENSITIVITY. THE SOLDIER FEELS BOTH UPWARD AND AHEAD BEFORE INCHING FOR-WARD. AFTER LOOKING AND FEELING WITH HIS HANDS, THE SOLDIER PROBES EVERY ONE AND A HALF TO SIX INCHES. THE PROBE IS PUSHED GENTLY, NOT STABBED, INTO THE GROUND AT AN ANGLE OF FORTY-FIVE DEGREES. IF PUSHED STRAIGHT DOWN, THE TIP OF THE PROBE MAY DETONATE A PRESSURE MINE. PROBING IS HARD, MONOTONOUS WORK. THE SOLDIER MUST RESIST THE NATURAL TENDENCY TO HURRY.

MALTHUSIA, *in agony:* Boom.

METHUSELAH, *in ecstasy:* Boom.

(The three percussionists reach a crescendo, playing the tympani and other drums.)

MALTHUSIA and METHUSELAH: Boom.

(There is a gigantic explosion that engulfs the entire stage. When the smoke lifts, the smiling Oriental baby in rags is still smiling. Malthusia, Methuselah, and the three percussionists are all corpses.)

The Pilots

The play takes place in a narrow, long aisle between the audience that is seated on both sides of the aisle. The aisle is perhaps the rail of an ocean liner on a ship outside of the Golden Gate, preparing to sail into San Francisco Bay. Two aged people, a determined Mr. and Mrs. who have been on a Grand Tour, are staring into the fog, listening tensely. They wear white wigs and grand, elderly clothes. Since they are experienced, pragmatic Americans, they are journeying *through* the fog, not *into* it. Above and behind them, throughout the play the audience sees a series of projected images. The projections are of ships sailing into the Golden Gate—sailboats, fishing boats, motorboats, a Chinese junk, ferryboats, counterpointed with naval vessels: destroyers, aircraft carriers, nuclear submarines, battleships, etc. Interspersed between these images of enigmatic voyages are many shots of western heroes, gunmen, and Indians. The heroes are both real and cinematic, legendary. Sometimes the faces of the heroes are meditative, serene; sometimes they explode in violent action. The violent actions are entirely silent and do *not* necessarily coincide with what is happening onstage. The actor or composer who plays the Pilot is at the end of the aisle beside his instruments and electronic equipment. In addition to being an electronic composer, he is also a one-man band creating sound and music. He is dressed in a coat and hat with a mask.

MR: The moaning . . . Can't you hear it?

MRS: Only fog . . . It's so thick . . .

MR, *annoyed:* I said *hear.* Listening is a lost art.

MRS, *stubbornly:* Listen yourself!

MR, *sharply:* I am listening to myself.

MRS, *charmed:* Seagulls . . .

MR: Foghorns . . . *(A foghorn is heard.)*

MRS, *delighted:* Warning blast . . . *(A warning blast is heard.)*

MR, *excited:* Warning blast is more like it. Open your ears for a change!

MRS, *looks at him, then resigns herself to listen:* I hear it . . .

MR, *intently peering:* The pilot ship . . .

MRS, *alarmed:* It's too close!

MR, *annoyed:* The pilot ship has to come close. Don't you know anything about crossing the bar?

MRS, *reflecting, then reciting emotionally:*
Sunset and evening star
And one clear call for me!
And may there be no moaning of the bar
When I put out to sea.

MR, *annoyed:* That's not funny. Tennyson's bar is not funny. It's heroic!

MRS, *shrugging:* How should I know what kind of bar he means? I hear moaning though . . . *(She listens intently.)*

MR: Heroic moaning . . . The bar is usually a sand bank lying menacingly a few fathoms below the deceptively clear surface of a harbor that seems safe but isn't.

MRS, *looking at him:* Do you love me?

MR: Of course I love you. Do you want to know about the bar or don't you?

MRS: I want to know, but I want a heroic teacher.

MR, *shrugging:* Listen and you'll find one maybe . . .

MRS, *listening:* I'm worried about the pilot ship. What'll he do?

MR, *annoyed:* He'll guide us through. You don't have to worry. A pilot knows everything. The pilot takes care of the bar. On the navigation charts it's called the Great Bar.

MRS: The Great Bar . . .

MR: It's about nine miles outside the Golden Gate and is eight hundred years wide.

MRS: That's a lot of years.

MR, *annoyed:* Eight hundred yards wide, not years.

MRS, *intent on the heroic moaning:* Such an old man, the pilot must be very deep.

MR: He doesn't have to be old, but he can't be young either. He has to have experience.

MRS: What does he look like?

MR: A hero.

MRS: You mean an athlete?

MR: Yes, not three hundred pounds like a tackle in football, not seven feet tall like a basketball star, but about six feet four inches and two hundred and twenty pounds of muscle.

MRS: That is a hero. Good-looking too. He could be on television.

MR, *nodding:* Yes, a defender, a gunman with brains.

MRS, *nodding:* An intellectual.

MR: No, his brains and body are united, a single man of unity, a physical and mental presence like a great tree over the world.

MRS, *delighted:* Like a tree of mystery . . .

MR: Like a tree of mystery. He knows what grows under the sea.

MRS: What grows?

MR: At its most shallow depth, the Great Bar is only twenty-two feet deep at mean low tide in an area known as the potato patch.

MRS, *puzzled:* How do they grow potatoes in the sea?

MR, *annoyed:* They don't grow potatoes in the sea. The sea grows its own things.

MRS, *resentful and nostalgic:* You don't love me anymore. We haven't had a very good vacation.

MR: I love you. We've never had a real vacation since our retirement.

MRS: Why didn't you enjoy the trip? It cost us enough.

MR: Retirement is very expensive. You have to find so many things to do.

MRS: Don't blame me. It wasn't my fault. You never stopped me. You could have helped me.

MR: I helped you. I threw him out!

MRS, *resentfully:* Well, you shouldn't have thrown him out. You shouldn't have called the police.

MR: One must defend his home.

MRS: How was I to know he was a fairy?

MR, *scornfully:* He was a twenty-eight-year old fairy and he was after your money.

MRS: But he had such good taste. I spent so much money.

MR, *sharply:* The house looks like a rainbow if you call that good taste.

MRS: How do you know what the house looks like? You're never there. You're always out doing something in the craft shop. What do you make there anyway?

MR: At least I make things! I don't just sit around. I use my retirement constructively.

MRS, *resentfully:* You could have retired with me instead of your craft shop. We could do some active things together.

MR, *angrily:* What do you think we've been doing on this trip?

MRS: I didn't like all the demonstrations against us. Those demonstrators should be arrested.

MR: Forget about the demonstrators.

MRS: I'm tired of apologizing for the Negroes and the wars. I'm not responsible for the Negroes and the wars.

MR: On this ship, there aren't any Negroes or wars. Are you interested or not in why it's called the potato patch?

MRS: Of course I'm interested. I'm intrigued about the pilot. He sounds so mysterious . . .

MR, *sharply:* Not the pilot, the potato patch! It's called the potato patch because, in the old days schooners loaded with potatoes lost their cargoes while crossing it.

MRS: The Great Bar or the potato patch?

MR, *annoyed:* Don't you listen? They're the same thing! The U.S. Army Engineers have to keep the main channel dredged to a depth of fifty feet.

MRS: The U.S. Army? Why not the Navy? Aren't they guarding the main channels too?

MR: I guess the Navy doesn't have that kind of equipment.

MRS: Do you have to have equipment to be a hero?

MR: Sometimes I suppose. Times change. You don't have to have much equipment if you're a pilot.

MRS: Does a pilot dredge in the potato patch?

MR: No, no. The pilot ships are operated by the San Francisco Bar Pilots. They're California's oldest established business.

MRS: You really admire pilots ... Why didn't you ever become one?

MR: I was too young. You have to think and act, combine discipline and freedom.

MRS: You never told me you admired their business so much.

MR: There have to be some secrets. Heroes are for secret admirations.

MRS: You never told me that you really disliked your own business.

MR, *reflecting:* Well, I liked it at times, when I could run with it.

MRS: It made you a lot of money.

MR, *shortly:* That's what a business is for. But you have to sit at a desk too much.

MRS: What's the matter with a desk? I like my desk.

MR: It's too heavy. It shrinks your legs beneath it. You want the desk to fly.

MRS: We haven't talked like this for a long time.

MR: That's not true. We talk, we snore at night.

MRS: Not to each other. You have your dreams.

MR, *doggedly:* We snore about lots of things.

MRS: Name lots of things.

MR: Our children ...

MRS: They've grown up. They all live in the suburbs. We don't see them much. Do you love our children?

MR: Of course I love our children.

MRS: Which one do you love the most?

MR: All of them.

MRS: Sometimes I think you don't even know how many there are ... How many children do we have?

MR, *annoyed:* Don't try to be funny about our children. Listen for the pilot ...

MRS: I am listening ... You never really spent much time with them. You never really learned how to love them. That's why they grew all that long hair.

MR: They cut if off as soon as they grew up to the suburbs. I did the best I could.

MRS: You should have been a pilot. You were too busy trying to fly your desk.

MR: There were too many children. You were always wanting to be filled up with children instead of me. It's a damn good thing we've got the pill now.

MRS: Maybe if we'd had the pill sooner you'd have loved me more.

MR: Are you accusing me of being a sexual failure?

MRS: No, but we never had much variety.

MR: At your age you're telling me you want variety?

MRS: Don't you want it too? *(A warning blast is heard, loud and intense.)*

MR, *peering over the rail:* There comes the pilot ship! That man on board is one of only twenty-five pilots who have between them eight hundred years of collective seamanship and knowledge of the Great Bar.

MRS: Eight hundred years ... That's a lot of tradition.

MR: We have all the power now. The only trouble is when a country gets so powerful, you're always on the defensive.

MRS: I get tired of the defensive, I'll tell you what. I don't like all those Europeans and Asians who are so jealous.

MR: Well, they've got plenty of reasons to be jealous. Take these pilots ... They get paid very high salaries, much more than European or Asian pilots. And they never have to sit at a desk. They're always standing or climbing. These pilots form a very small, exclusive body of men. They're the guardians each year of millions of dollars worth of shipping.

MRS, *excited:* The guardians ... That's why we have an eagle on our flag.

MR, *as the rhythm of excitement grows:* Right, and a bear on the California flag. These pilots guide all kinds of ships over the

Great Bar, giant ocean liners, freighters, yachts, battleships, aircraft carriers, supertankers!

MRS: They must have penetrating eyes!

MR: Twelve miles outside of the Golden Gate, a lightship with a bright red hull is anchored in the fog . . .

MRS, *peering eagerly:* A bright red hull—that's nice! Are we near it?

MR: An old, two-master schooner called the *California* cruises back and forth, back and forth, in sight of the lightship. The *California* was once a millionaire's Atlantic racer.

MRS: I bet you would have liked to buy an Atlantic racer. I'm sorry we spent so much money on the house.

MR: I was in the wrong business.

MRS: It's never too late to change.

MR: The country would have to change. You'd have to change too.

MRS: I might try.

MR: Or else I'd have to find another wife.

MRS: I don't know whether I could change. I'm too old.

MR: You're only sixty-four. *(Pause.)* Anyway, the *California* is one of San Francisco's two ocean pilot stations. The other is a converted U.S. Navy ocean minesweeper, *Golden Gate.*

MRS: You said the Navy didn't have anything to do with it.

MR, *annoyed:* It's not the Navy. It's converted to pilots. It's a real business. A pilot is always on duty. Even when he's home or out to a friend's house. He's always on duty like a doctor dedicated to his profession. When he's called, he takes a twelve-mile launch ride out to the lonely pilot station in the fog and boards the pilot boat. He waits in a snug cabin . . .

MRS: How do you mean a snug cabin?

MR: Luxurious, because he has to wait a long time. *Nothing gaudy* you understand. Simple luxury.

MRS: I don't think that's possible.

MR: You haven't seen the cabin of a pilot boat. The pilot has to have great patience. Sometimes he waits all day or all night or all day *and* all night.

MRS: That is a long time.

MR: While waiting on the pilot boat, he has to control himself. He can't blow up the way people do all the time. Even though he's in a very snug cabin, it's difficult. Every time he looks through the porthole, all he can see is the white fog swirling around. He eats, sleeps, reads, watches television . . .

MRS, *musing:* Television in the fog . . .

MR: If there's another pilot on board, then he can have a real conversation.

MRS: But usually he's alone.

MR: Alone until he hears four whistle blasts. That's the international signal calling for a pilot. When he hears that signal, the pilot boat works up into the lee of the incoming ship and the crewmen of the pilot boat lower a small yawl over the side. The pilot is taken to his waiting ship in the yawl.

MRS, *staring at him:* I never heard you talk like this before.

MR, *excitedly:* Then his moment arrives. The pilot ladder is dropped down.

MRS: Every pilot has his own ladder?

MR: Only for pilots! He waits for the down roll of the ship, grabs his pilot ladder, and climbs upward as fast as he can before the hull can roll back again and dunk him!

MRS: What happens if he gets dunked?

MR: If he gets dunked badly, that's the end. If there's a rolling sea in the fog, that's rough. He has to have courage. It's a dangerous business.

MRS: But it's exciting. You make it sound mysterious. Maybe I could change.

MR, *dubiously:* You may be too old.

MRS: I'm ten years younger than you. You're seventy-four!

MR: Seventy-four is not so old nowadays.

MRS: You could have an operation!

MR: Once he's on the bridge he takes over the ship. He's in complete charge of crossing the Great Bar. Even in clear weather he proceeds very slowly. He watches for buoys that mark the channel. He has very good eyes, but it takes more than eyesight. It takes experience.

MRS: You have time to get lots of experience!

MR: He has perception. He knows every moment of the way how deep the water is. Since it's foggy most of the time, he looks with his ears. He navigates by sounds. He listens to the bells and the diaphones and the birds. It's so lovely . . .

MRS, *eagerly:* I believe!

> *Mr. and Mrs. sing and dance the SONG OF THE PILOT.*
> *The Pilot dances too in his own area as composer.*

SONG OF THE PILOT

Listen to the birds
In their soundless flight.
They fly so high
Out of the sky . . .
Only the Pilot hears them.
He navigates by sounds.
He knows how deep the water
And how high
To fly out of the sky . . .
Listen to the birds
In their soundless flight . . .
Only the Pilot hears them
As they fly so high
Out of the sky . . .

MR: Of course he has radar too, but it's his sixth sense, his instinct about the sea and the Great Bar that pulls him through.

MRS: It must be hard to meet a pilot and get to know him.

MR: It's not easy. They're a special group of people. They keep to themselves. You can't call a pilot by his first name.

MRS: But they have families, they have children. They talk to their wives and children.

MR: When they have time.

MRS: They make time to talk to their wives and children. You know they do.

MR: Of course they do. They're pilots.

MRS: They've been to sea a lot. They make love with variety. They're very experienced men.

MR: It's hard to be a pilot. You can't expect too much of them.

MRS, *peering over the side:* Look, here comes the boat!

MR: The yawl you mean.

MRS, *excitedly:* Which one is the pilot?

MR: Can't you tell?

MRS: He looks so different.

MR: The others are bringing him. He's the biggest one sitting alone!

MRS: He looks so mysterious in his hat and overcoat. Doesn't he ever wear a uniform?

MR: Never. The uniform confines, restricts, designates. He remains only the pilot.

MRS, *intensely:* He's coming on board now. Why he scrambles up the ladder like King Kong. He's so strong.

MR: Pilots have the strength of giants.

MRS, *suddenly:* Why don't you go and meet him? You could make an appointment. It would only take a minute of his time.

MR: Don't be silly. You can't just go up and meet him. He's a very distant person. It's a bad fog . . .

MRS: It's worth a try. Are you afraid of him? Must he always be invisible?

MR: Why don't you try?

MRS, *afraid:* He may not like women.

MR: A pilot always likes women. Of course he has to be alone a lot . . . But when he comes ashore, when he's completed his task, then he can have as many women as he wants. Go on and try!

MRS, *hesitating:* Why don't we try it together?

MR: Three might make a triangle.

MRS: Still, we've married forty years. Wouldn't we be stronger together if anything happened?

MR: What could happen?

MRS: There's something mysterious about him. You know how treacherous mystery can be.

MR: He could never be guilty of betrayal.

MRS: I don't mean that. But he's so powerful.

MR: You think he might not lead us?

MRS: In a time of violence, you can't tell what a pilot will do.

MR: Here he comes! Pick up your courage! Get ready!

> *(Slowly, the enormous figure of the anonymous pilot appears over the rail. The fog swirls around him. He is a massive, impressive hulk in a dark overcoat with a dark hat pulled down over his forehead. He remains stationary at the rail, as if looking back silently at the sea. A long pause. Afraid, Mr. and Mrs. stare at him without moving.)*

MRS, *whispering:* Why is he so quiet?

MR: He doesn't need language. He looks, he perceives.

MRS: Then we can't talk to him. He doesn't speak a word.

MR: A pilot doesn't need to speak.

MRS: I don't like the idea of his not speaking. That's not friendly.

MR: It's the fog. Whom would he speak to?

MRS: You're right. He can't speak to the ship or the gulls.

MR: It's no use trying to meet him. What should we do?

MRS: We can't escape. We must face him.

MR: What if he's dangerous?

MRS: You assured me he wouldn't betray us.

MR: Danger is not betrayal. He looks as though he would do anything to reach his destiny.

MRS: If he attacks us, then we defend ourselves. We kill him.

MR: We're too old to kill anybody.

MRS: We're not too old for opportunity ... We're younger than we think.

MR: How young are we?

MRS: We don't have to die with these transplants.

MR, *beginning to undress, to grow younger:* We can live forever.

MRS' *undressing, growing younger:* We can be young forever.

MR: What if he kills us?

MRS: He might be carrying a pistol.

MR: Or a knife under his coat.

MRS: You can't even tell what race he is. He's very dark-skinned.

MR: We're young and strong again. We can't let foreigners triumph.

MRS: You're not even safe on deck these days. We'll make the decks safe again!

MR: Look, he doesn't even move!

MRS: He's acting very suspicious. He's too aloof. He's too old.

MR: How do we know what he might do? He might steer us against a reef.

MRS: He might find the wrong channel. We can't swim.

MR: He might ignore a buoy!

MRS: Or a foghorn!

MR: Or a warning blast! *(An immense warning blast is heard. The pilot still doesn't move.)*

MRS: Look! He didn't even jump a little.

MR: He belongs to the warning blast.

MRS: How can we defend ourselves?

MR: We'll hit him from behind.

MRS: You'll need a club.

MR: There's no time to break up a deck chair.

MRS, *pointing:* Hit him with a fire extinguisher then.

MR, *grabbing a fire extinguisher:* Help me!
(They tug at the fire extinguisher together.)

MRS: Don't let him turn around. Quickly!
(The pilot turns. He is wearing an old mask. They hammer the pilot down from behind. He falls.)

MR, *breathing hard:* We've won!

MRS, *breathing hard:* I can't believe it. I always thought victory was impossible for the old.

MR: Not when we can be young again. We'd better examine him, take a look at his papers.

MRS: He must have special papers.

MR: Top secret papers probably. Look!

MRS: What is it?

MR: Can't you see his face?

MRS: Is that what a hero looks like?

MR, *tugging at him:* He's as heavy as marble.

MRS: He's got a Roman look to him. Did you ever see such a long nose?

MR: And his hair . . . What do think of his hair?

MRS: It's all in curls . . . Would a pilot curl his hair nowadays?

MR: You think they sent up an imposter?

MRS: Where are his papers?

MR, *searching frantically:* He doesn't have any.

MRS: You mean they sent up a dummy?

MR: A sacrifice, a goat, an animal, a beast! *(He kicks and tears at the figure.)* I don't think he's even human!

MRS, *crying out:* They have no pity! Why do they do such things!

MR: They don't have to reason. For security I suppose.

MRS: But I don't feel safe. Shouldn't we feel safer than him?

MR, *savagely, giving the figure a last kick:* We won't feel safe as long as we wait.

MRS: What do we do?

MR, *looking up slowly into the fog:* We climb. Don't you understand? We're young. We climb . . .

MRS, *looking up slowly:* You mean we don't wait anymore . . .

MR, *savagely:* Damn right. We're not stupid Europeans or Orientals.

MRS: You're right. We can't wait for them to trick us again.

MR: We climb up, we change, we progress!

MRS, *joining in:* We become, we pursue!

MR, *putting his arm around her:* My ambition is flowing again. Can you feel it, my love?

MRS, *happily:* I can feel it. I'm so happy you're flowing again. *(She breaks away from him suddenly and looks up.)* It's so high up there . . .

MR: That's only because of the fog.

MRS: If we climb up there, what do we become?

MR, *staring at her:* Don't you understand, my dear? We'll be the pilot.

MRS: Together? Co-pilots?

MR: Put on the clothes.

> (*They struggle to put on the overcoat and hat which they tear off the figure. The overcoat is so large that he squeezes into one arm and she squeezes into the other arm. The hat is so large that it fits over both of their heads.*)

MR: Come on . . .

MRS: What do we do after we climb?

MR: We steer into the Golden Gate. We join the gold rush.

MRS: It will be our country? The maps are up there?

MR: Every direction is clearly drawn.

MRS, *looking up with a shudder:* Do we have to climb up there? It's so white.

MR: If you want to sit in a snug cabin . . .

MRS: Can we sleep, read, watch television? Will there be servants again?

MR: Yes, things will be free again.

MRS: Will our children be co-pilots too?

MR: Yes, they will inherit.

MRS, *fearfully:* How many children do we have?

> (*The lights black out slowly as they start to climb. Fragments of the SONG OF THE PILOT are heard on tape from the machine. Perhaps the pilot rises again, in another mask of power, and does his little dance again by the electronic equipment.*)

Love Reconciled To War

BY ROBERT HIVNOR

Downstage: a lounge (as in a college dorm) with three low chairs around a coffee table. Upstage: dark, to be revealed at the end. Two young women sit talking around the table. On the table, books, notebooks, and reading glasses.

DORA: The point seems to be—is it worth it?

BELLA: Um.

DORA: Values.

BELLA: Um.

DORA: But he deals with only one side of the equation.

BELLA: Oh?

DORA: Of course I admire the book immensely: startling, not to say alarming, insights into the whole nature of sexual life.

BELLA: Yes.

DORA: But it is oddly a book to end all books, for if the thesis is true, that sublimation, that culture, as we know it in the West, with all its richness, technical attainments et cetera is distorted by the tyranny of the genitals then so is the book. What I think I am saying is that when we pursue our studies—

BELLA, *nodding:* Pursue!

DORA: And learn to make judgements.

BELLA, *Doubt:* Oh?

DORA: And the boldest of us create.

BELLA, *Pause:* What?

DORA: Well—occasions. And a sense of style. Well there should be a sense of triumph there.

BELLA: So.

DORA: Well I mean to say. If there's no transformation going on here. If we're not changing anything. If in educating ourselves we are simply reasserting the tyranny of sex, why not say to hell with it and take off our clothes and hop to it?

BELLA: You always get depressed before an examination.

Another pretty girl, slinking with melancholy, enters.

DORA: What's the matter with *you?*

BELLA: Been to your own execution, dear?

Flora casts down a notebook and falls limply into a chair.

FLORA: I had the most depressing, debilitating, discouraging, disenchanting afternoon, and the worst of it is, I don't know why.

BELLA: You and Dora both.

FLORA: He was lecturing on, you know, Botticelli. And I like him, but instead of looking at the slides, I looked out the window. On Elm Street. On the top of Elm Street. The elms.

DORA: *(Impatience.)* Yes, yes.

FLORA: A bird was building a nest.

BELLA: Why not?

FLORA: Shots of Venus on the screen conquering Mars. And parked on this branch outside would be this bird with an old hair in its beak.

BELLA: What kind of a bird was it?

FLORA: I—don't-know-what-kind-of-a-bird-it-was. Kept coming and going. Twitchy. Bark brownish. And hours of this broken English about sacred and profane fat ladies, about how Heaven governs in threes, and then there was this joke about the three graces.

DORA: Joke?

FLORA: About Amor always being the middle term. *(Sighs.)* There was this pitiful yak yak of young people being tortured by an old joke they couldn't understand. Yes we were being *tortured!* Tortured by treasures from the Italian Renaissance!

BELLA, *pensively:* This twitchy little bird building a nest.

FLORA: It was some kind of *tyranny!*

DORA: That's what I was saying.

FLORA: I can't take it anymore.

DORA: We pursue—

FLORA: We stretch out our hands for truth and beauty, but it's guarded and policed by tyrants. I'm thinking of giving the whole thing up.

BELLA: *(Laughs.)*

DORA: Me too.

FLORA: I'm forsaken by every noble theme, every gracious idea, every charity.

BELLA: *(Scorn.)* You'd rather be in town scraping doo-doo from dirty diapers.

FLORA: What about *you?*

DORA: You're drooping too.

FLORA: You're drooping most of all.

BELLA: This is the way I sit when I'm thinking. *(They laugh.) (To Flora.)* You say Venus always conquered Mars in these paintings?

FLORA: Every time.

BELLA: If it were only possible! If beauty—female beauty—did actually civilize! Of course we know that there is a connection between eros and agression.

FLORA: There's no doubt about it. *(They all nod.)*

BELLA: But is Love stronger than War? I think they are painting a wish. I mean it was a beautiful dream but in real life I think love helps aggression.

DORA: Helps?

BELLA: Men fight. They shoot each other down. They can't fight all the time. They come home. The fleet's in. Amour. Next day. Men fight. They shoot each other down. There's something wrong with those masterpieces.

DORA: But don't you think that the fact that those apes love—I mean get in the state of mind to—to be gentle—don't you think—

FLORA: Yes I think the admiration of cultivated, beautiful women ameliorates the roughness of the fighter.

BELLA: But who is influencing whom? Tail does not wag dog. We are had. In some way our beauty is a necessary part—even a cause—of his wars.

FLORA: That would mean the more beautiful you are the more guilty.

DORA: But I've always been proud of— *(Pause while they look at her.)*

FLORA: Well there's no getting around it, you're beautiful, Dora.

BELLA: And you too, Flora.

DORA: And you too, Bella.

They droop.

Enter the House Mother, Madame Waters, a stately, commanding presence in her forties or fifties.

MADAME: Well now! What's this? What postures! In every line of your three young bodies I see despair.

BELLA: You are right there.

MADAME: You're not tired ...

DORA: Not *physically.*

FLORA: It's just—*(Sighs.)*

DORA: We—*(Sighs.)*

BELLA: The blues.

FLORA: The whole thing—*(She closes her eyes.)*

DORA: *(A moan.)*

MADAME: Well let me tell you three, it would be wrong not to face up to the discouragements of the life you have chosen. Vocational despair is a very real thing.

BELLA: Have *you* ever felt it?

MADAME: 'Course I have. Certainly when I was as young as you are. Professional studies are harder for a woman.

BELLA: Do you think it is because we are less aggressive than men?

MADAME: No, Bella, I think social factors obtain here. And that absurd sexual identity of the female as captive, as prize, the concept of the happy house arrest. *(They chuckle.)* Now perhaps one or all of you will marry.

FLORA, DORA, BELLA: No, No, No.

MADAME: But only after this chosen discipline has given you a glimpse of what human beings are capable of. After years with the philosophers, you can better judge what your husbands are. *(Dutiful laughter.)* Anyway, at moments like this when a black cloud comes into the room one just has to remember how much you mean to the rest of the world which is too benighted to feel despair. In Matthew Five we read—

BELLA: If the salt has lost its savor . . .

MADAME: Good girl. Less blasphemous, our Renaissance friend Pico. Or old Seneca.

BELLA: On the higher dignity of those who give?

FLORA: *(To Dora.)* And give and give!

MADAME: Yes! Giving! Giving what is precious—what is hard to give—a part of oneself. It is an—overflowing. You must overflow. If there is no magnaminity, it is not gracious. Not well favored.

> *The girls stand up, shoulders back, chins up.*

BELLA: Madame Waters, the black cloud is gone.

MADAME: *(Smiles.)* You know girls, if you could only see yourself grow. This burden you have chosen—this liberal art—is not just heavy. It transforms you day by day. Is it sacrifice? Or is it self-fulfillment? It is both! *(They laugh with agreement.)*

MADAME: Oh look what time it is!

> *They hastily pick up books and notebooks and scurry off stage right. The door bell rings, or rather sings, for what follows is quarter of a minute composition for (door) bells. Enters a handsome Captain of the Marines, hardened by war.*

CAPTAIN: Madame Waters?

MADAME: Yes?

CAPTAIN: Captain Bragg.

MADAME: How nice to meet you. *(They shake hands.)*

CAPTAIN: You know—*(He lowers his voice.)*

MADAME: Oh yes. I even voted for him. Captain, we were expecting you. Welcome back to the States and congratulations. That ribbon, rare though it is, is known to us.

CAPTAIN: You don't object to war?

MADAME: We teach "all things are born of strife and adversity" and he who opposes conflict blasphemes against the nature of the world. Beauty itself is a harmony of contending qualities.

CAPTAIN: Oh yes, beauty. Madame, for two years I have been hard, loud, sudden, mobile, mechanical, alert, extreme, linear, and Manichean. I have outflanked, probed, pinched, surprised, thrust, flashed, jetted, blinded, terminated. I wish to reconcile these things with Beauty, Love, and Joy. How much will that be?

MADAME: Fifty dollars.

> *Music.*

MADAME: And here are—

> *An area is lighted upstage and we see within it in decent circular dance, hands entwined or on each others shoulders, always two facing, always one turned away, are Flora, Dora, and Bella. They are not nude, only seem so with their transparent gowns flowing about them.*

MADAME: —are our three graces.

CAPTAIN: Charming!

MADAME: The three aspects of Venus unfold in Amor—Pulchritude—Voluptuousness *(As they dance.)* Pulchritude, or Beauty, calls forth the divine energy of Amor, or Love, which is then manifest as Joy, or Voluptas.

> *The graces dance.*

CAPTAIN: Which one is Voluptas?

MADAME: Only you can tell us that. *(Politely indicating offstage with her hand.)* The cashier. *(He goes off in that direction. Lights fade on the graces. Music rises. She affirms to herself)* It *is* worth it! Yes! Yes!

Before The Unamerican Committee

BY ERIC BENTLEY

(Investigator, Chairman, and another Witness)

INVESTIGATOR: Will you spell that please?

JESUS: J, E, S, U, S.

INVESTIGATOR: Permanent address?

JESUS: None.

INVESTIGATOR: None?

JESUS: The foxes have holes and the birds of the air have nests, but the son of man hath not where to lay his head.

CHAIRMAN: Hey, what kinda language is that?

INVESTIGATOR: We'll get back to who you're the son of in a minute, but as to your domicile I don't get it.

CHAIRMAN: You mean you move around? Generally stay with friends?

JESUS: I accept the hospitality of well-wishers.

INVESTIGATOR: Shall I put down *bum*, Mr. Chairman?

CHAIRMAN: Put down *vagrant*, Mr. Investigator.

INVESTIGATOR: Right: vagrancy is a misdemeanor here in Washington. Did you know that, Witness?

JESUS: Washington was made for man, not man for Washington.

CHAIRMAN, *dryly:* The devil can quote scripture to his purpose! Proceed, Mr. Investigator!

INVESTIGATOR: Where are you presently employed, Mister Jesus?

JESUS: I am not employed.

CHAIRMAN, seeing that Investigator is "thrown": *Un*employed then. Put down unemployed. Can't you see it just to look at him? *(The Investigator and Jesus stare at each other.)*

INVESTIGATOR: The Chairman doesn't mean your face, Mister

Jesus. He means the bare feet, the rags, the beads, the beard, and the long hair.

CHAIRMAN: Though nowadays it's not just the unemployed that use this get-up!

INVESTIGATOR: But it *is* just the malcontents. The FBI file on you, Mister Jesus, is more than eighteen inches thick. I'm not even going to question you on most of it. It's established beyond all question. The rabble-rousing on Union Square. The unremitting propaganda for alien ideas. The proselytizing everywhere—and not one of you registering as agents of a foreign power. Unauthorized mass meetings and parades, including that so-called triumphal procession not long ago— ticker tape through the Wall Street section—use of a live donkey without police permit. The phony miracles. The hate campaigns, not only against our American way, but against our allies in Rome and elsewhere.

CHAIRMAN: Yeah, for Unamerican Activities, Mister Jesus, you sure beat the band!

INVESTIGATOR. But we have subpoenaed you to pursue one line of enquiry only. We got a report that you *are* presently employed, Mister Jesus.

CHAIRMAN: Read it. There are press and media people out front.

INVESTIGATOR: A new electronic device which the FBI has been trying out on Mister Jesus during the past few months picked up this remark of his towards the end of a telephone conversation. "OK, but I must be about my father's business." By the way, what business is your father in Mister Jesus?

JESUS: Hm? *(Smiling)* I think you would call it government.

CHAIRMAN, *with a start:* He's in the government? *Our* government? *(The Chairman seems likely to look under the table for him.)*

INVESTIGATOR: *(Cool.)* Just which government would that be, Mister Jesus?

JESUS, *still with a slight smile:* My father never had less than the peoples of the entire world in view, Mr. Investigator.

CHAIRMAN, *directly at the press out front:* Hear that? Out of his own mouth! And this Committee has been damned up and down for even suggesting the existence of a world conspiracy!

INVESTIGATOR: While we're on the subject of the "Father's" schemes of world conquest, let me add that we also have a report on the Son's expectations in this regard. His followers have a song—and I can play this back to you on tape, if you wish, Mr. Chairman—THE WHOLE WIDE WORLD FOR JESUS.

CHAIRMAN: How about that, Witness?

JESUS, *just returns his gaze.*

INVESTIGATOR, *still silent, like one who is just waiting for others to stop playing games.*

CHAIRMAN: That would be contempt of Congress! You go to jail for it!

INVESTIGATOR: He's been in jail so often that isn't much of a threat any more.

CHAIRMAN, *to the press:* Another fifth amendment communist! *(To the Investigator)* Make him say who his father *is.*

INVESTIGATOR: Precisely. That is our Number One question this morning. Mister Jesus, who *is* your father?

CHAIRMAN, *not giving him time to speak:* Refusing to answer that one too?

JESUS: My whole life has been an answer to that one.

CHAIRMAN: Are you fencing with me? Direct the witness to answer the question.

INVESTIGATOR: Who is your father?

JESUS: My father is God.

CHAIRMAN: What?! Hey now, there *are* limits!

INVESTIGATOR: Let's see if he will repeat that under oath. Witness, do you swear that this is the truth, the whole—

JESUS: I do not take oaths.

CHAIRMAN: What?

JESUS: I just refrain from lying, it's simpler.

CHAIRMAN: We'll get back to your refusal to be sworn. Another jail sentence by the way. Just answer that question.

INVESTIGATOR: Do you really claim to be God's son?

JESUS: Don't *you?*

INVESTIGATOR, *losing his cool for the first time:* The man is laughing at us!

CHAIRMAN: Witness, you will be cited for contempt three times over!

JESUS: Contempt—to call you my brothers?

CHAIRMAN: You want your communistic delusions to rub off on us! It's blasphemy, anyway, this hairbrained notion of yours! Remember—we have good religious people on this Committee, Protestants, Catholics!

JESUS: I am a good religious Jew.

CHAIRMAN, *changing tone:* Yeah, well, we're not anti-Semitic, but we sure don't want this nation any more mongrelized than it already is. You weren't born in this country, were you?

JESUS: I was born in Bethlehem.

CHAIRMAN, *to Investigator:* Pennsylvania?

INVESTIGATOR, *whispering back:* Israel.

CHAIRMAN, *still to Investigator only:* What did I tell you? Always these New York Jews. *(Aloud.)* Continue the questioning.

INVESTIGATOR: Witness, we have reason to question whether the man planning this world conquest is your father. He certainly isn't *God* the Father. And anyway, you are an atheist, are you not?

JESUS, *again looks silently back at his interlocutor: this is what he always does when he feels words are not called for.*

INVESTIGATOR: The Committee—yes, and the Press—will take note that the witness is again relying on his so-called rights under the 5th Amendment. But we know he doesn't believe in any God because he has said the following and said it often: The Kingdom of God is within you—for this man, God's not in his heaven, and all's wrong with the world!

CHAIRMAN, *expansively, for the press:* Which will explain to you the company he keeps—bums, hippies, whores, alcoholics and other Jewish intellectuals . . .

INVESTIGATOR: The familiar outward vestments of the world-wide Communist conspiracy! But with all the talk of kingdoms not of this world and God and all, he has been able to get away with it! However, we have news for you today *(he faces the press),* gentlemen! And, Mister Chairman, I come to you with an item of news which I have held back even from you till the proper moment: this moment. We have been aware for some time that this man's God-talk is code. Code. And what do you do with a code? You crack it. The FBI employs the greatest cryptographers in the world. And they have at long last cracked even this man's code. That is why I asked the Chairman to subpoena him. That is why he is here today. And that is why I can now present you, Mr. Chairman, with a coup dear to your old anti-red heart. *(He pauses for effect.)*

CHAIRMAN: Go on, go on.

INVESTIGATOR: Like all the great codes, its greatness lies in its simplicity. Dope fiends will call their "connection" Mother. The agents of communism are the dope fiends of politics. Who then does this man call Father?

CHAIRMAN, *helpfully:* Kosygin!

INVESTIGATOR, *irritated:* Wrong. Mao Tse Tung! Mr. Hoover always thought it was Ho Chi Minh. But he was definitely an Uncle. Mao Tse Tung! Who has said of Jesus: "This is my beloved son in whom I am well pleased." And of whom Jesus has said: "Thy will, not mine, be done."

CHAIRMAN: My, you are a sly one, preparing this surprise for me. But what a surprise! This is the biggest thing in spy hunts for the past fifty years! So now we must do something to this guy—well, more than we did to these other itsy-bitsy little commies—I mean, just cutting off their source of income, spoiling their reputation, sticking them in the clink, . . . how about the electric chair?

INVESTIGATOR: The Rosenbergs got the electric chair.

CHAIRMAN: Oh yeah. Damn. *(Silence)* Something more unusual. But at the same time kinda spectacular. *(Pause)* I know: crucify him!

Four Plays From
The Little Theatre of
The Green Goose

KONSTANTY ILDEFONS GAŁCZYŃSKI
TRANSLATED BY DAN AND ELEANOR GEROULD

The Little Theatre of The Green Goose
Has the Honor of Presenting

RAIN

CHORUS OF PEOPLE WAITING FOR THE BUS: Oh, how
boring it is to wait for the bus.
RAIN *begins to pour.*
CHORUS OF PEOPLE WAITING FOR THE BUS:
Screw this rain.
Screw this waiting.
Screw that bus.
A MAN DRIVING BY IN HIS CAR, *gets out of his car in front
of the line of people waiting.* My car's very tiny. My car won't
hold all of you. But there's one simple thing I can do: I can
get out of my car, I can stand in line, I can wait and get
soaked with you. *(Stands last in line.)*
Curtain
1949

The Little Theatre of The Green Goose
Has the Honor of Presenting

THE BURIAL OF A WAR CRIMINAL

In which appear:
THE FUNERAL DIRECTOR
THE GRAVEDIGGERS
and THE PUBLIC

THE FUNERAL DIRECTOR: Ladies and Gentlemen. In a moment War Criminal No. 8 will be buried. Quiet, please.
THE PUBLIC: Bravo!
THE GRAVEDIGGERS *lower the corpse.*
THE PUBLIC: Encore!
THE GRAVEDIGGERS *raise the corpse up and let it down again.*
THE PUBLIC: Encore!!
THE GRAVEDIGGERS, *as above.*
THE PUBLIC, *completely carried away:* Encore!!!
THE GRAVEDIGGERS *keep giving encores without stopping.*
THE PUBLIC, *delighted to have disposed of the war problem, demand further encores.*
Curtain
1946

The Little Theatre of The Green Goose
Has the Honor of Presenting

THE SEVEN SLEEPING BROTHERS

FIRST BROTHER: *(Snores.)*
SECOND BROTHER: *(Snores.)*
THIRD BROTHER: *(Snores.)*
FOURTH BROTHER: *(Snores.)*
FIFTH BROTHER: *(Snores.)*
SIXTH BROTHER: *(Snores.)*
SEVENTH BROTHER: *(Snores horribly.)*
Curtain
1946

The Little Theatre of The Green Goose
Has the Honor of Presenting
Its author wielding a terrible pen

THE TRAGIC END OF MYTHOLOGY

Characters:

LEDA, the lawful wife of Tyndareus
JOVE, a noted sex fiend
and A FRYING PAN

LEDA: Jove! Ah!

JOVE, *grim, with a frying pan hidden in the folds of his chlamys:* What now?

LEDA: Jove, oh, how handsome you were as a swan! How you kissed me! How you kissed me!

JOVE: Well, what of it? That's enough rhapsodizing. What I'd like to know is where are the eggs and how many are there?

LEDA: Here they are, darling. Here. Three. Written out, T-H-R-E-E. Just the way it is in all the handbooks on classical mythology. And the sequence of events is the same. First you changed into a swan. Then that night in Acapulco. And in just a minute now our three mythological children: Castor, Pollux, and Helen, will be hatched from the three mythological eggs.

JOVE, *very grim, nervously handling the frying pan hidden in the folds of his chlamys:* That's enough! *(Pulls out the frying pan from under his arm, turns on the electric stove and using the three mythological eggs whips up some realistic scrambled eggs with chives.)*

LEDA: What have you done, miserable wretch?

JOVE: What the conscience of my Jovian stomach dictated. You're an idiot, Leda. But maybe you'll understand this: we can't expect anything worthwhile from Castor and Pollux, and as for Helen, everybody knows the consequences: the Trojan war. And we've certainly had enough wars. *(Digs into the scrambled eggs.)*

The curtain falls

1949

A Theatre of Iconography

JOHN LION

A new form of theatre is rising in America. Nurtured by the Off-Off Broadway movement of the 1960's which developed the short incisive play form dealing with the subject matters of a cult-oriented underground, the new theatre has become by 1971 a nationwide phenomenon.

Ironically, rather than representing a cohesive whole, the new "underground" theatres have fostered a type of regionalism based on the particularities of various areas. With the "spell" of New York theatre broken, groups tend to stay together longer and to develop common sets of values based on living in heterogeneous sets of circumstances.

In the case of The Magic Theatre of Berkeley, about 80% of the membership have been working together since the inception of the theatre in 1967. About half have experienced the entire whirligig of events in Berkeley since the free-speech movement in 1964.

This configuration is bound to, and in fact, does affect the entire outlook of the group. The tremendous diversity of living conditions in America creates recurring, yet individualistic environmental images that form the visual leitmotifs of our day-to-day existences. It is not enough to call those images *types* or *archetypes;* rather, they are *icons.* By this, I mean highly evolved visual pictures which strike us with a familiar yet complex jolt of emotion and understanding. The rapid juxtaposition of these pictures in a theatrical situation, such as the Magic Theatre's productions of Michael McClure's *Gargoyle Cartoons,* or the group-evolved *Sheriff Bill,* generate a sort of dramatic shorthand.

Decidedly, this method is heavily indebted to filmic montage techniques and to the visuals of "the new comix" as represented by R. Crumb. *Sheriff Bill* is, in fact, a satire on the standard image of the American Western, complete with all the standard types; however, the situations themselves are examined in the light of modern American power politics. No scene in *Sheriff Bill* lasts more than five minutes. Each scene was approached from the point of view of production similar to creating an effective pop music number. Changes in locale were indicated by slides. Costuming and posturing tended toward the flat effect of the comic strip. The satire on current political issues owed as much to the juxtaposition of the scenes as the scenes themselves.

By way of contrast, McClure's *Gargoyle Cartoons* (Delacorte Press, 1971) are relatively static cartoon settings peopled by ogres, trolls, worms, giant snails, and meatballs. Again the plays gain meaning through iconographic juxtaposition as the static settings become plastic. Beds that suddenly come to life and display anthropomorphic dispositions, cherubs talking through holes in cartoon clouds, and giant snakes using party favors as forked tongues are a few characteristics that display the fluidity of the animated cartoon.

It is, of course, impossible to relate the new style of "The theatre of Iconography" wholly to the specifics of the experience of living in Berkeley, yet it is perhaps inevitable that such a style would grow out of an area steeped in the proliferation of new ideas, and the Kaleidoscopic image clusters evolving from the abrupt confrontations of the new politics.

The Playwright's Search

In European and American theatre today, the director rules. Often, with the help of colleagues, he creates his own plays through documentary or chance methods or by new "versions" of the classics. The result is often unsatisfactory because of the lack of depth that comes from patchwork, egotistical collaborations. When the director does present a new play, the playwright is often an honorary appendage invited, perhaps, to attend rehearsals as a guest, but not really as a participant. Even in the case of a famous playwright, his guest role is rarely crucial to the important production decisions that the director makes. Theatre breeds a curious paranoia. Frequently, the director fails to conceal his resentment at "the word" which is invading the sanctity of his physical, theatrical domain. Or the playwright, secure in the isolation of his vision, rages at cuts and seemingly arbitrary interpretations of his characters. Caught in the midst of this dilemma, the actors begin to rebel and mutter their discontent. Debris litters rehearsals from countless cups of coffee, cigarette stubs, bits of food. Edwin Honig, the poet, playwright, and critic, has caught perfectly the savage spirit that lies beneath these rehearsals:

> The director fidgets and trembles coughing his words out like indigestible bits of cookies. He can't stomach his own thoughts but the words don't say this. He wants in a way to slaughter the actors, then the playwright, but first he means to

make them do a perfect job. Actually he is deranged enough to think that he must slaughter me, his critical audience.

Why do you have to sit there and say nothing, except to look more and more distant?

I want to kill you! This is in the play . . .

His perfect actors, his perfect playwright, are in his head, so he will never kill them—they'll be let go every night after the performance with a little pat on the shoulder, tit, or rump—whichever part of them did best that night.

But, since I am his perfect audience and always hostile, I must watch out. I am out there—and not in his head. And after each performance I must slink out fast, go home through dark alleys, avoid being tracked down by him, killed.

Come now, I tell myself, will he really kill you? Will he kill playwright, actors, dream audience? Because if he did, he'd have no audience he'd really care about, and so he'd have to commit suicide.

This enigma of savagery has its glory as well as its defilement. The clash of wills, if the wills are powerful and contain a mutual respect and blessing, may serve to create a stronger, more durable work. Theatre is a collaborative vision much like a ship sailing to an unknown destination. If the director masquerades as captain, there are mysterious mates, crewmen, and passengers aboard whom the director must serve.

An obvious panacea for the problem of the playwright is to incorporate him more directly into the theatre as in the companies of Shakespeare and Moliere. This has never really happened in the United States, although there have been a few brief, happy, accidental flowerings like that of Clifford Odets in the Group Theatre in the 1930s. What would happen if every theatre supported its own playwright-in-residence, including college and community theatres as well as professional, regional companies? The playwrights would become less literary and more flexible in terms of theatrical demands. The kind of working playwright that I describe in "Proposals for a New Playwright" might develop. Meanwhile, it is essential to look closely at the nature of the playwright and try to understand his needs and the sources of his unique isolation in the United States.

Eugene O'Neill: The Isolation And Endurance Of An American Playwright

In England, a playwright tends to be a little less isolated than in the United States. An obvious reason is the relative smallness of the country; also a greater, central tradition of theatre. Yet there is another reason, the greater influence of socialism in England, the idea of a benevolent community as opposed to individual, financial success, an idea to which George Bernard Shaw contributed so greatly, as much through his mastery of comic style as through his Fabian ideas. In the United States, the splintering of liberalism has given a nostalgic, disillusioned flavor—the sense of a promise destroyed, a wistful, backward look at the roots of disaster—to such social playwrights as Clifford Odets, even to Arthur Miller. Other important American playwrights, like Williams and Albee, tend to stress the neurotic individual or family situation behind which the shadow of a cruel, materialistic society is always felt. Among young American playwrights, the tone is likely to be bitter, farcical, stemming from absurdist techniques, or defiantly satirical. Usually, the feeling is defensive and isolated, as contrasted to the excitement and wonder of a large segment of scientific inquiry— whatever doubts the scientists may have about technology. Somehow the isolation is best represented in an event that failed to cause much concern in America—the fact that Eugene O'Neill, when he died, left the first performing rights to his new plays to a Swedish theatre in Stockholm. This disgrace created only a few, minor ripples of protest in the United States. Yet the isolation of even a famous playwright from ideal theatrical opportunities became suddenly an agonizing question to anyone who cared about theatre.

Consequently, it is important to consider the late years of Eugene O'Neill if one is to understand the risks, dangers, and achievements that are an inherent part of theatre in American society. Toward the end of 1936, O'Neill and his wife, Carlotta, left their home in Georgia and traveled west to Seattle. The damp climate in the northwest did not suit O'Neill's precarious health. In 1937 they moved to the San Francisco Bay Area. After living for a short time in Lafayette, in the East Bay, they planned and built a house near Danville, facing Mount Diablo. They called it Tao House, after the Chinese *Tao* meaning *the right way of life*, which the O'Neills had inscribed in Chinese characters on the gate. Disillusioned with the crass materialism of Western civilization, O'Neill had become more and more interested in Oriental culture. The beautiful house that he and his wife built embodied the sympathy that they felt for the traditions of the Far East. In this house he wrote all of his last and best plays, including *Long Day's Journey Into Night*.

Several years ago I visited Tao House. It was then called Corduroy Hills Ranch. In homage to O'Neill the new owners had kept in the name of their ranch some of the playwright's feeling for the landscape. O'Neill had spoken to them of the "corduroy quality of these hills."

Although the exterior was designed in the familiar California-Spanish style, the roof tiles were shaped to resemble oriental tiles. Behind the house O'Neill had constructed a twisting, curved walk in the spirit of the Chinese proverb that evil travels only in a straight line. The interior revealed the strongest Chinese influence. During the O'Neills' occupancy, the house was decorated mostly with Chinese furnishings. In his bedroom O'Neill slept in a high Chinese opium bed. Downstairs the walls were painted white to contrast with brilliant blue ceilings. Stone tiles in the front hall led to wooden floors painted black in imitation of teakwood. Two old Chinese dragons carved in teakwood guarded the foot of the staircase leading to the second floor.

In his comfortable, panelled study on the second floor, O'Neill began to write his final series of plays in a swivel chair at a high desk, facing a window through which he could see the towering shape of Mount Diablo. The irony at the end of his career was that all of his last plays were written in a house decorated with images of the Chinese search for tranquility, but staring at a mountain haunted by Spanish-American legends of his early Catholic faith, a mountain called *Diablo.*

The Chinese influence in O'Neill's last plays has been almost ignored by the critics. Many writers have pointed out the central theme in the late plays, the contrast between reality and fantasy, the idea that man through his "pipedreams" of fantasy creates an imaginary world that enables him to endure the tragedies of existence.

The view, of most O'Neill criticism, is that although the late plays are his best work, they represent a philosophical nihilism that rejects the Christian sources of Western civilization. Many critics add their belief that the slow failure of O'Neill's health was the major cause of the nihilism in these final plays. The truth is more complex.

In Tao House, O'Neill hoped that he had created a sanctuary where his new blending of eastern and western thought would enable him to create his most important work. The tension was too great. The advent of World War II and his increasingly poor health shattered his struggle to unify his sympathy towards Taoism with the conflicts of American society. Yet in this impossible struggle for a synthesis of eastern and western thought, O'Neill achieved a new dimension in his plays. This new dimension is the sense of learning to balance good and evil, to endure the raging polarities of existence, to reconcile pipe dream and reality. If the surface theme in these plays always seems to be the gap between pipe dream and reality, the deeper theme is always the necessity of reconciling them. Erie Smith, the small-time gambler in O'Neill's last, brilliant one-act play, *Hughie,* written in Tao House in 1941, describes the peace that he found with the dead night clerk:

> Yeah, Hughie lapped up my stories like they was duck soup, or a beakful of heroin. I sure took him around with me in tales and showed him one hell of a time. And, d'you know, it done me good, too, in a way. Sure, I'd get to seein' myself like he seen me. Some nights I'd come back here without a buck,

feeling lower than a snake's belly, and first thing you know I'd be lousy with jack, bettin' a grand a race. Oh, I was wise I was kiddin' myself. I ain't a sap. But what the hell, Hughie loved it, and it didn't cost nobody nothin', and if every guy along Broadway who kids himself was to drop dead there wouldn't be nobody left. Ain't it the truth, Charlie?

Behind the uneasy, western conscience of the characters who still cry for individual salvation, lies a world where the conflict between reality and fantasy can be resolved only if selfishness and worldly power are suppressed in favor of a simpler, more objective, Taoist way of life. It is no accident that most of the characters in the late plays live in a relatively timeless world of desire and imagination. They are cut off from the world of time by their inability or their unwillingness to fit into the practical materialistic nature of American society. One of the stages of Taoism is to find the source of power which reconciles a man with the Tao, the universal energy which unites the opposites and permits one to escape the earthly limitations of time and environment.

Consequently, the major characters in the late plays turn away from the practical demands of time, but they are unable to fit into the timeless world of spiritual values because they are still part of a dissolving western society rooted in the search for material possessions and a self-centered salvation. I do not mean to imply that the Chinese Taoist influence is dominant in the last plays, merely that it is strongly there. It is mixed particularly with the sense of "fate," which O'Neill derived from Greek tragedy, and with the sense of "pity," which came from his Catholic background. The striking interest of O'Neill's final plays is their widening out beyond national barriers into an area where various religions and philosophies flow together.

The true condition of O'Neill's health while he wrote these late plays in Tao House has never been told, but it needs to be known to appreciate the remarkable courage and dedication with which these plays were written. The stress commonly given to the pessimism and nihilism of the late plays ignores the extraordinary courage and determined work schedule that he could not have maintained without his new philosophical perspective.

His drinking resulted finally in continuous liver attacks symptomized by a toxic feeling, yellow eyes and depression. By 1943 these attacks were coming every two or three weeks. He also suffered at times from bladder irritation. His weight in 1943 was down to 138 pounds—this for a man who was five feet eleven inches tall. The tremor in his hands, which he had suffered for many years, had grown increasingly severe. This affliction bothered him most of all because it interfered with his writing. For many years it was called a "Parkinsonian tremor," or "a sign of Parkinson's Disease," although his doctors decided finally that it was not Parkinson's but a rare, similar disease.

In 1943 O'Neill's doctor was the highly regarded Oakland physician, Dr. Fletcher Taylor. Dr. Taylor, who became a friend of O'Neill's and admired him greatly, did everything possible to ease the playwright's suffering so that he could work. At night O'Neill had to take sedatives constantly. He still had trouble sleeping. Often he would wake early in the morning, depressed. His wife would make coffee for him. Mrs. O'Neill has been criticized for keeping O'Neill in extreme seclusion during these years. The fact remains that she served as a devoted nurse, performing many unpleasant tasks for a sick man who required isolation if he was to manage any work. In 1943, the last, real year of O'Neill's career, he was still writing determinedly three to three and a half hours every morning. His handwriting had grown smaller and smaller in a vain attempt to control the tremor, but his great courage kept him at his desk.

Already by 1939 he was afraid of a complete collapse and wrote to his friend, Clayton Hamilton: "I felt a sudden necessity to write plays I'd wanted to write for a long time and that I knew could be finished." These plays were *The Iceman Cometh* (1939); *Long Day's Journey Into Night* (1941); *Hughie* (1941), the only one-act play he finished from a contemplated group of one-act plays to be called *By Way of Obit;* and *A Moon for the Misbegotten* (1943). These final plays have their own cyclical unity. Discarding the impossible task of creating an American epic by tracing the tangled history of one family, O'Neill took his own family and wrote the stories of their misfortunes. The result is a far more moving and valid representation of American destiny than he could ever have accomplished in his projected cycle. Some day it would be revealing for an American theatre to produce five of the last plays in the following sequence: *A Touch of the Poet, More Stately Mansions, The Iceman Cometh, Long Day's Journey Into Night,* and *A Moon for the Misbegotten. A Touch of the Poet* and *More Stately Mansions,* written in 1936 and 1938-39, are the only two plays left from the projected long cycle, *A Tale of Possessors Self-Possessed.* The other three plays follow naturally because of the family theme. Such a sequence progresses from a more objective, historical view of the nature of the American family to a subjective, contemporary view of family ties and illusions. In *A Touch of the Poet* and *More Stately Mansions,* the European tradition of class differences creates an agonizing conflict in early Nineteenth Century America between the public dream of democratic equality and the private desire of materialistic wealth and power. The other three reveal the contemporary collapse of the family, its retreat into the pipe dreams of security that make the members of a family cling together despite their increasing separation from any essential connections with society. Together all of these plays are a powerful indictment of American family life presented with mature insight and a rare compassion.

Driving today to Danville, the new six-lane, divided freeway stretches like a giant, moving chain-belt through new, hastily built communities. Everywhere real estate is the dominant force, selling and shaping the land to the illusion of materialistic security against which O'Neill warned. Where are the roots in these tract homes, the traditions that make a real family life possible? In this rapidly changing area everything seems restless, temporary, exposed to the family pipe dreams which O'Neill examined so thoroughly in his last plays written here. From the rooftops countless television antennae proclaim a new kind of "show-shop." Visiting the lost sanctuary that O'Neill hoped he and his wife had created in Tao

House, a sanctuary that vanished under the pressure of ill-health and war, I felt a new understanding of O'Neill's attempts to come to terms with the American past and the family pipe dreams of our society. In an ideal home, at the peak of his career, he hoped that he had found the peace of maturity that would enable him to write the American epic, to reconcile the diffuse, contradicting strands of American experience. This proved to be impossible, but what he did accomplish was to find the extraordinary compassion of his last plays which enabled him to write about the disasters of his own family with such forgiveness, a forgiveness for his own guilt as much as for the guilt of his family. These Christian ideals, forgiveness and pity, combined, as I have tried to point out, with an eastern acceptance of the Taoist balance of good and evil to create his last and greatest plays.

As I left O'Neill's lost home, I thought that every American playwright today must still measure himself against the depth and ambition of O'Neill. All of the recent, familiar critical warnings about O'Neill's limitations are of little consequence. Ponderous, sentimental at times, an awkward prose writer who tended to bathos rather than the incisive metaphorical insight that marks the great writer—these faults cannot disguise the achievement. Driving away from Tao House, I thought it is relatively easy to be clever and entertaining on the television screen or stage, to decorate surface feelings, but who is willing to make the sacrifices that O'Neill made to bring a sense of grandeur to the American theatre? What playwright, or artist in any field, has the will to ignore commercial pressures and carry out a continuous series of experiments come what may over a period of many years? To be sure O'Neill was fortunate in winning financial success early in his career so that he had time to work freely and ignore commercial projects. Nevertheless, he was able to survive financial success and to continue with his experiments, good and bad. His work remains with all of its flaws and merits to remind every young, ambitious American artist of the essential ideals and perils of ambition.

As O'Neill said: "It is the Furies within that seek to destroy us."

What redeemed him in his last plays, is the rare quality of

compassion that he developed. If we admire in O'Neill his unique, final explorations of family pipe dreams, we honor in him also his contempt for the cynical, degraded standards of the "show-shop," his respect for the art of theatre that can transform and exalt man.

Proposals For A New Playwright

It is not enough to create new opportunities in the barren theatrical landscape, as I have urged throughout this book, opportunities to work as a resident member with regional companies and with college theatres. The problem is deeper, a social cancer, as evidenced increasingly by a generally cynical, ironic tone, an inability to confront problems and people directly, humanely. Compassion is absent, experience suffers from strange, hastily assumed masks that cover a national naivete with the nationalistic masks of power. In a time when our country has tremendous international power and a domestic crisis of spirit, what might constitute an ideal training for a playwright? At night, my dreams wander wildly:

Assume a sensitive, perceptive man or woman around twenty-five years of age, well-read with an open mind and a broad range of interests. Already he or she has written a good deal and has that primary, stubborn dedication to the extraordinary wonders that occur when language pours forth from its physical sources. Now begins an unusual, creative five-year effort.

1) *The First Year*—One year's travel around the world. All of the great theatres of the world will be visited for a study of the real meaning of style, valid as opposed to meaningless experimentation, true as opposed to false traditions (the criterion being which tradition continues to have vitality and growth as opposed to the tradition that is merely being enforced). In this first year of travel, any student who spends too much of his time in theatres will be considered a dubious prospect. The power of real theatre lies in its integral connections with humanity. The really promising playwright will be the one who seeks out all kinds of experiences as he travels around the world, who seeks to understand the nature and

tone of different societies, their political and economic systems, their customs, the sound of their languages, and, most important of all, the mysterious quality of dignity that is crucial to each way of life. If, after this preliminary year of travel and study, the student shows a rare understanding of these singular forces, he is ready for the next phase of study.

2) *The Second Year*—This year will feature studies of scientific history, natural history, and the problems of urban and country environments. The most important relationship in playwriting is between the character and the action, between the character and the nature of his environment. Frequently, young playwrights have little sense of this relationship. They look too easily, too cynically, at the nature of science which has been the most influential, creative force of the twentieth century. The studies in science, nature, and environment will focus on the lives of scientists, natural historians, etc. in relationship to their discoveries. In this way, the playwright will really begin to discover the roots of character and how character relates to action. He will perceive the curious way in which character dominates at times, action at other times. Part of each day during this second year, the playwright will spend with a small company of actors—say five or so. He will work mostly on short plays for this group. He will explore the new material that he is learning about science, natural history, and the environment. In addition to his own plays, he will help to act and perform other short plays by famous playwrights. In no case, will he permit himself to be hypnotized by the learning of theatrical techniques. The acquisition of theatrical techniques is a natural process and must be permitted to grow naturally out of organic experiences.

3) *The Third Year*—Again this year will be spent in a different environment (ideally the best college and regional theatres would collaborate in exchanging these playwrights), in a deeper experience with a resident company. The playwright's primary task would be to challenge constantly the frenzied activities of the theatre as they prepare for production after production—often functioning out of the weariest impulses. *Why are you running around like a chicken with his head cut off? What is the purpose of*

this continuous frenzy? Cannot you have a quiet frenzy? What are you doing and where are you going? This kind of impossible questioning of stereotyped activities will serve to establish once again the idea of a playwright as astonishing gad-fly, solemn Dostoyevskian idiot, conscience-stinger, prophet of integrity rather than assistant hack. As part of the company's training sessions, the playwright would have the task of writing a short play, often a monologue, for each member of the company with whom he would work out the performance. Once again the playwright would learn a great deal about character and action as he gets to know the capacities of each actor more intimately. These short plays, which would usually be for one character as indicated, but might include two or three characters, would be performed in a variety of places—schools, hospitals, parks, libraries, homes for the aged, etc., to test their humanity and to expand the humanity of the playwright and the function of theatre in society.

4) *The Fourth Year*—A meditative year again in different environments, half of the year in a foreign country, half in America in a small town or in the country. The playwright should avoid living in large cities that have a pretense to culture. The point is the discipline of isolation. During this year, he will be expected to write at least three full-length plays. The search is for deeply humane sensitivity and wide-ranging perceptions, not for over-polished articulation. No attempt at production will be made during this year. A year of solitary confinement and test of his inner power. If the playwright can grow in this isolation without becoming restless and cynical, if his vision and compassion can expand, then he has a chance.

5) *The Fifth Year*—In another different environment, the playwright will again be part of a large, dedicated company, either in a regional theatre or university situation. He will get a chance to have one of his full-length plays produced under ideal conditions. Ideal conditions mean not only good actors who can verify the physical integrity of the play, but also a director and designer who will continually force the playwright to justify himself. During this year, the playwright will also create an entirely different kind of

play with the company. This will be based on documentary, ritualistic, or mythological material which the playwright with the director will assemble, and to which the entire company will contribute. A re-examination of the values of commedia dell' arte styles is the aim. It will be the playwright's function to act as scribe, to transcend and unify the conflicting ideas and suggestions, yet not to impose his own ego. If the playwright reveals a true gift for relating to and helping to unify the company and play, he is successful in this phase of his work.

No graduation ceremony is held, no degree awarded, not even a promise of a position, although, hopefully by this time, theatres will have begun to hire playwrights as important members of their companies. After these five years of study, work, and writing, a blessing rather than a meaningless degree would be conferred, an invocation with the whispered, magical letters—P . . . P—Possible Playwright—may he possess the spirit of endurance and discover the right opportunities.

THE HAPPENING

MARTIN ESSLIN

In Xanadu did Kubla Khan
A stately pleasure dome decree
. . . .
So twice five miles of fertile ground
With walls and towers were girdled round;
And here were gardens bright with sinuous rills
Where blossomed many an incense-bearing tree;
And here were forests ancient as the hills,
Enfolding sunny spots of greenery.
But oh! that deep romantic chasm which slanted
Down the green hill athwart a cedarn cover!
A savage place!

Coleridge's pleasure dome anticipated those reformers of the theatre who compose new and magical environments, the creators of "Happenings." Wandering through those forests and gardens, where sunny spots of greenery dramatically gave way to savage chasms, while "ancestral voices prophesying war" were heard from the distance, visitors to Kubla Khan's pleasure dome enjoyed what the audiences at some of the best Happenings were to experience, albeit perhaps on a less grand and less satisfying scale: a *real* adventure, magical and poetical enough to alter their perception of everyday reality, a poetic vision lived through in three-dimensional space and biological time—"Poetry which has been torn away from the cemetery of the printed page; painting liberated from its daubed and commercialized canvas; psychodrama removed from the brainwashing factories," to quote Jean-Jacques Lebel, the Franco-American painter and one of the leaders of the Happenings movement.

In the era of the mass media the theatre has entered an age of transition. Many of the time-honored assumptions about its function and its aesthetic structure will have to be re-examined, radically thought out anew and some, perhaps, completely discarded.

The theatre had its origin in ritual, religious and secular. In this ritual, whether it was a war dance or a hunting dance or a fertility rite or a human sacrifice designed to placate the angry gods, the whole tribe participated. Men, women, and children danced and sang and there was no separation into performers and spectators. It was only later that the secular spectacle was divorced from the religious ritual and the performer from the audience.

The idea of theatre bequeathed to our generation by the nineteenth century—of the stage as a segment of real life watched, as it were, through a pane of glass like the antics of animals in a zoo or fish in an aquarium—is a very special and untypical form of theatre. This "Theatre of Illusion" is now radically threatened by the mass media. In the cinema and on the television screen the illusion is much stronger, much more convincing, because there we watch segments of photographed reality; they *are* magic windows into the lives of other people. Confronted with such overwhelming competition, the live theatre must seek to establish areas of experience its audience cannot get in the mechanical, photographic mass media. And these areas of experience *must* lie in the region suggested by the adjective "live."

Since the First World War the theatre has been struggling to free itself from the shackles of illusion. The expressionists and Brecht re-established the idea that the stage was not for the slavish reproduction of real life, but was a platform for the direct revelation of human emotion from actor to audience. It could be a lecture hall for the teaching of socially useful knowledge or a laboratory for the discussion of ideas and experimentation with actual human behavior.

The Theatre of the Absurd used the stage to represent a reality outside the scope of the photographic process, which, after all, can only mirror the surface of life. It peopled the stage with images of an inner reality of subconscious dream images. In doing so, the dramatists of the absurd used theatrical forms of the era before the illusionist stage became predominant: circus and music-hall clown-ing, *commedia dell' arte* types, mime and burlesque.

Another movement concentrated on the element of spontanc-ity—improvisation and direct audience participation. Solo per-formers like the ad-libbing satirists of the Lenny Bruce and Mort Sahl school and groups like The Second City belong in this cate-gory.

What have all these movements in common?

They concentrate on abolishing the idea that what happens on the stage is an illusion of real life. They no longer try to hypnotize their audience into thinking that the actor playing Lear really *is* Lear. By letting the audience into the secret that the actor playing Lear is, in reality, Joe Snooks, they are confronting the audience with *more* reality than before, for Joe Snooks is more real, more flesh and blood, than Lear.

The audience at one of the absurdist plays is also, albeit in a quite different way, more deeply and more really involved than the audience at an illusionist play. It is confronted with a spectacle that, in itself, could not be a reproduction of surface reality but that is all the more obviously the expression of the actual anguish of its author. The audience is taken right inside the mind of a Beckett or Ionesco and therefore put into the most intimate con-tact with a very frightening reality, a reality made up of symbols and images which each member of the audience must interpret and work out for himself. In that sense the play invades the spectator's mind, his subconscious.

The alienation effect, both in the theatre of Brecht and in the Theatre of the Absurd, therefore postulates an active involvement of the audience at a deeper level than the mere identification process in the Illusionist theatre.

This is the point from which the avant garde of today starts out: How can the spectator be even *more* actively involved? How can his experience become even more direct, even more real? Clearly it can happen only if the barriers between spectator and performer are broken down even more completely. The spectator must be drawn right inside the dramatic experience (whether this is still to be described as a play or not). He must become part of a new reality, at least as real as, and perhaps *more* real than, the ordinary workaday world he inhabits.

Antonin Artaud spoke as early as the mid-1930s of the need to tear down the barriers between actor and audience. Various movements for the reform of stage design have tried to solve this problem by arena stages or theatre in the round. These have drawn the audience more deeply into the play by placing it nearer to the actors, and also by drawing the audience into the decor, as it were. From every angle in theatre in the round, the audience forms the background to the actors, and it is often more fascinating to study the faces of the spectators opposite than to watch the actors themselves. Yet, ultimately, this is not a change of fundamentals. The play remains the play, the actors remain actors, and the audience remains an audience.

One of the most fascinating young experimental directors in Europe, the Pole, Jerzy Grotowski, directs the Theatre of Thirteen Rows on the top floor of an ancient reconstructed building on the market place of the city of Wroclaw. His novel solution to the problem is to design a fresh *space* for the audience in each production so that it becomes part of the action. A play that takes place in a prison, for example, is performed in a network of cells enclosed by wire mesh. The audience is led into these cells and watches the action of the play taking place in another cell, centrally placed so that it can be seen from the others.

For a production of Marlowe's *Doctor Faustus* Grotowski filled his theatre with a long horseshoe-shaped medieval dining table. As the audience came into the theatre they were led to seats at this table, at which Faustus was already seated, praying. Grotowski had reshaped the text in such a manner that the play became a flashback inside Faustus' last great monologue. The spectators thus became the dinner guests at Faustus' last supper (and the religious analogy was certainly intentional).

The play opened at the point when Faustus began his last

speech, and the flashback action took place on the table at which the audience sat.

But even here, although the spectator is drawn so closely into the action that the impact becomes frighteningly intense and intimate, there still is a *play,* a preordained sequence of events with a beginning and a foreseeable, and foreseen, outcome. And this still is a diminution of the reality of the experience the spectators undergo.

The next step is the Happening.

What is a Happening? How can it be defined?

So far as can be ascertained, the term was coined and first used in 1959 by Allen Kaprow. Born in 1927 in Atlantic City, he is a painter by profession and at the time was teaching art history at Rutgers University. In the literary review, THE ANTHOLOGIST, published by Rutgers, there appeared an article by Kaprow proclaiming the need for a really new art. This was followed by a text, which at first glance could have been taken for a poem. It was headed *Something to Take Place: A Happening,* and was, in fact, the blueprint for a kind of theatrical performance.

It called, for example, for an area with groups of chairs placed at random, and went on: "People will sit in the chairs whose arrangement causes them to face in different directions. Some are dressed in winter coats—others nude—others quite everydayish (visitors will be given numbers of seats where they will go upon entry—they will find themselves seated next to nudes, coats and bums, who will be placed amongst the seats). . . ."

Later the same year, in October 1959, Kaprow produced his *18 Happenings in 6 Parts* at the Reuben Gallery in New York City, and so the term "Happening" entered the language. Other artists working on similar lines had tried to find other names for the new form, but Happening stuck to them all in the end, whether their creators agreed with the term or not. Hence it does not describe a narrowly definable art form, but rather a spectrum of different creations ranging from a static, three-dimensional image—sometimes called an "environment"—to fairly elaborate performances that are almost, if not quite, plays. What all these events have in common is that the rigid time structure of a play, which follows a meticulously prescribed course, is abandoned; that much more is left to chance and improvisation; that boundaries between stage and auditorium, between illusion and reality, are far less clearly defined. The Happening is an open-ended image with which the spectator has to come to terms by himself.

Indeed, in doing so, he ceases to be a mere spectator, he becomes part and parcel of the image. He is sucked into it, as though it were possible, in walking through an art gallery, to be sucked right into a painting by Breughel or Bosch. Thus, in Kaprow's *Eat* (1964), the participants were introduced into a network of caves (once occupied by a brewery) and confronted with a variety of situations in which food was dangled before them in bizarre circumstances. In Claes Oldenburg's *Injun* (1962), the participants were led through a group of derelict buildings filled with strange things and even stranger human beings. And at the famous Happening at the Edinburgh international drama conference of 1963, devised by Ken Dewey, the staid proceedings of one of the conventional international conferences suddenly dissolved into a sequence of mad but highly significant events: a nude girl passing across the back of the platform; a famous film star suddenly darting from the platform into the audience, jumping across the rows of seats to fall into the arms of a bearded man in the back row; a bagpiper in Highland dress parading around the gallery, and the recorded voices of speakers at previous days of the conference echoing from all sides in snippets of cliché.

Each of these examples is very different in its own way. In the first, the participant was taken into a new environment, to which he had to adjust. In the second, he was led through an adventure. In the third, the familiar environment and context were suddenly undermined, crumbling away into grotesque distortions of themselves. But in each of these instances (chosen very much at random) the onus lay on the spectator-participant (or however he should be correctly described) to adapt himself to a new environmental situation of peculiar significance and psychological relevance to himself. He was no longer in the position of a mere voyeur who watches a play and decides for himself to what extent he can get himself involved from his safe distance. In these Happenings, the spectator experiences something himself, whether he likes it or not—and many of the good people of Edinburgh at that Happening did not like their experience in the least!

They had been drawn into the Happening against their will, unaware at first that they were faced with a planned artifact rather than with reality. For a moment they must have felt that they had gone mad, that their innermost secret wishes (yearnings for a nude girl) or their secretly voiced and repressed feelings about the drama conference ("All this stuff is really nonsense!") had suddenly materialized in the form of hallucinations. To them it was as though the solid ground of predictable reality were dissolving beneath their feet. No wonder many of them were deeply outraged; no wonder the organizers of the conference were sued in the Scottish courts for causing a public outrage (they were acquitted).

Such an experience is very different from that of the spectator of a play who, however deeply he may feel involved with the fate of the characters on the stage, always remains aware that those events are an illusion.

Happenings are written, composed, and planned as plays are written, or ballets sketched out on paper by the choreographer. Some are very rigidly worked out in advance; in others, a considerable latitude is given for change and improvisation. As Allen Kaprow has said: "I try to plan for different degrees of flexibility within parameters of an otherwise strictly controlled imagery. For example, a part may consist of sweeping thirty square yards of paper in a 'slow, unhurried way.' One could sweep it this way or that way, with a brown broom or a pink broom—in any fashion that one wishes, if it is generally done in that slow, ritualized way. Or: a riot is called for. Everybody exchanges clothes; a complete orgy is taking place. Who exchanges clothes with whom makes no difference at that point as long as one just keeps exchanging clothes. In these cases I will permit almost any flexibility. But there are other stricter limits of variability. . . . "

So Happenings can be staged more than once, following an identical pattern and yet each performance differing in numerous details from its predecessors. The degree of involvement of the audience also varies. Some authors of Happenings will prescribe certain actions to the participants, giving them an active role; others will merely let them watch the events that take place around them and might engulf them at any moment without ever actually doing so.

Happenings, three-dimensional poetic images that envelop the participants, are therefore anti-literary theatre of the most extreme kind—if they are theatre at all. In this respect they are a direct continuation of the tendency already manifested in the Theatre of the Absurd, which diminished the importance of the narrative line, character, plot, and dialogue in favor of the presentation of concretized poetical imagery. Put the spectator right inside such a poetic image and you have a Happening. The importance of the image is thus immensely enhanced. Indeed, the Happening owes a great deal to and is a direct continuation of similar tendencies in modern painting and sculpture.

In action painting, for example, the *action* of painting became almost as important as the image it produced. Action painters gave *performances,* and thus there came a point at which theatre and painting met. In collage and modern sculpture using *objets trouvés* (found and ready-made objects), the real world and painting intersect. A lavatory bowl or an old bicycle pump may assume a new and poetical significance if incorporated into a work of painting or sculpture. Pop painters like Robert Rauschenberg go further— their paintings tend to reach out into three-dimensional space. The Happening, as a three-dimensional environment in which people are introduced as an additional element of ready-made reality, is merely a logical continuation of this process. Indeed, many of the best practitioners of the Happening, like Lebel and Kaprow, are painters who have taken this logical step forward.

But composers and dancers have also contributed. John Cage, the avant-garde composer and musical director of the Merce Cunningham Dance Company, is rightly regarded as a founding father of Happenings. Cage is deeply concerned with the entire world of sound and considers any kind of noise as a form of music. He would even consider an occasion at which the orchestra sat silently on the platform as a concert. In the context of a concert, with the audience straining to hear something, chance noises from the outside, or the slight rustle of programs or shuffling of feet in the auditorium would *become* music—and at the same time theatre. For Cage defines theatre simply as "something which engages both the eye and the ear."

Seen from this angle, "one could view everyday life itself as theatre." This sounds paradoxical, but is anything but nonsensical.

What Cage is saying is that the attitude of the perceiver is the essential element. To a creative imagination, which looks at the world with the awareness of an artist or mystic, every incident of life, even the most insignificant, carries the impact of poetry—the buzzing of a bee, the way an old man crosses the road.

What the fully structured and organized theatre does is to bring this home to an audience whose senses in everyday life have become blunted. They are made to feel sentimental by a sunset evoked on a backdrop by spotlights with red filters—yet they fail to notice the real sunset outside their windows. What Cage and his followers are saying is: Let's put a frame around reality. Let people come and look through it at reality *with a sense of occasion* and they will suddenly see reality as they have never seen it before—which, after all, is the true function of art.

The German Pop artist and Happenings practitioner, Wolf Vostell, arranged a Happening for the citizens of the town of Ulm in 1964 which consisted in their being taken in buses to see the airfield, a car-washing plant, a garage, a swimming pool, a refuse dump, an abattoir, and a number of other everyday sights which, however, were somewhat heightened by strange announcements coming over the buses' intercom systems and by unforeseen details, such as the fact that the car-washing plant was decorated with a curtain of raw meat and that, in the swimming pool, the water suddenly started to go up in flames. The tour lasted some six strenuous hours, and the participants certainly learned to see their own home town with new eyes.

There can be no doubt that such Happenings, whether they confront their participants with artificially enhanced or actual chunks of reality, produce the effects usually postulated from an artistic experience—they make us see the world more intensely, with more emotion and insight. They provide us with a life-enhancing adventure. But the question arises: Is that still theatre?

My own opinion is that this is really a somewhat futile exercise in semantics. It all depends on one's definition of theatre, which, let us remember, arose from ritual—another way of presenting reality in an enhanced context. The ritualistic element in Happenings must not be underestimated.

The history of theatre is rich in examples of events that were theatrical but nearer to the present-day Happening than to our conventional idea of drama. There were the medieval mystery plays, performed on a number of simultaneous mansion stages, and the *triomfi* of the Renaissance, sumptuous processions with elaborate floats. In modern times there are the three-ring circus, the carnival parade, the Haunted House at Coney Island, the roller coaster that produces violent emotions of fear and relief as it hurtles over its steep course and makes the girl grip her boy friend tightly. All these are examples of a reality situation poetically enhanced and structured after the manner of the Happening.

Even the restaurant with a Venetian or Spanish decor, the Playboy Club with its Bunnies, or the movie house built like a Chinese pagoda make use of the same procedures, at however attenuated and vulgarized a level. They attempt to introduce poetry into our everyday life by artistic means, by putting us into an environment that is both real *and* artistically structured and enhanced.

And what of political rallies and conventions, bullfights, baseball games, heavyweight prize fights, military parades, and presidential inaugurations? Here, too, artifice and chance event are mingled in a new poetically structured reality that essentially serves the purpose of providing the audience with an enhanced experience of life through elements of ritual *and* theatre—costume, decor, music, lighting, and so on.

In other words, much of our life *is* theatrical—and by no means the least significant or enjoyable part. The dividing lines between fiction, artificially enhanced reality, and ordinary reality are extremely tenuous and exceedingly difficult to define. The part played by truly religious ritual in our world is diminishing, and it is only natural that the perpetual human hunger for significant occasions should be met in new and different ways.

A good many Happenings have been primitive and inexpert. Others have produced poetic images of great power and have enhanced the lives of those who took part in them. I have little doubt that the potentialities of this form of art—call it theatre or not—are immense. We are moving into a period of automation and undreamed-of amounts of leisure time for human beings in the industrialized societies of the world. The era of the Pleasure Domes is therefore bound to come. And Happenings are the modest germs of deeply felt, frightening or pleasurable experiences as yet unimagined: total theatre, concretized poetry, magically structured human experience.

Towards a Sense
of History:
Some Model Productions

If new plays tend to create their own style with relative ease because there is no handicap of preceding styles, the problem with the classics is always how to make the past live. One school of production insists that the past must always be re-created "on its own terms." The opposite school insists, "Each production must renew the past, adapt, re-shape if necessary to make the past alive in contemporary terms." Usually, the model production whose influence is lasting tends to be somewhere in between. These productions reveal both a sense of history and a sense of the new; they unite the images and sounds of the past with the images and sounds of the present. The following notes on several model productions seek to examine how this rare unity is sometimes achieved in occasional, magical performances. If we lose the sense of the model production, we have no way of using the past to help us create the present.

Eastern Influences

In the First Manifesto of his Theatre of Cruelty, Artaud wrote:

By an altogether Oriental means of expression, this objective and concrete language of the theatre can fascinate and ensnare the organs. It flows into the sensibility. Abandoning Occidental usages of speech, it turns words into incantations.

It extends the voice. It utilizes the vibrations and qualities of the voice. It wildly tramples rhythms underfoot. It pile-drives sounds. It seeks to exalt, to benumb, to charm, to arrest the sensibility. It liberates a new lyricism of gesture which, by its precipitation or its amplitude in the air, ends by surpassing the lyricism of words. It ultimately breaks away from the intellectual subjugation of the language . . .

Is this really true in Oriental theatre or is Artaud merely using his small experience with eastern dramatic styles to justify his attack on western theatre? This was a question that I began to answer for myself when a special Japanese Kabuki troupe with three of the foremost classical Japanese actors visited the Opera House in San Francisco in July, 1960. I wrote in a notebook:

This opening night in America many Japanese and many Nisei, whom we forced from their homes into camps so recently during World War II, are in the audience, proud of their dramatic heritage. Where is our dramatic tradition? How can Americans like myself, without lack of theatrical roots, appreciate a great Oriental theatre? The foremost problem is the voices. Even the simplest statement, "We are at the barrier," is spoken with a high-pitched, wavering, operatic quality. To an American ear, all of the voices are forced, unnatural, exactly the opposite of our voice-training dicta. Behind me in the audience several Americans laugh uncontrollably at the peculiar sounds. Only after several minutes do they quiet down. As the performance progresses, some merit in the seemingly unnatural vocal techniques becomes evident. Western actors concentrate too much on a natural, low-key speaking of the lines. This works sometimes with simple prose rhythms and they are congratulated for their "natural way of speaking." But more complex prose rhythms and verse drama demand the ability to phrase the line properly as a singer does. This is one reason why Shakespeare and other great verse dramatists of the past are so often poorly performed. The actors plod dully through the lines and the heightened quality that is gained by a knowledge of the *singing phrase* is lost. Western actors should study songs more; they have lost the

strong connections between music and language that contributed so much to Greek and Elizabethan society.

The first lesson for the Westerner, then, in seeing Kabuki is a
sudden knowledge of what the voice can do dramatically when the
level of speech is pushed into dimensions of chanting, wailing,
song. It must be added that, to the Western ear, the vocal effects
are sometimes overdone in Kabuki. The sense of measure fails.
Simplicity is occasionally lost when even the simplest direction is
delivered as an aria.

The second and major lesson for the Western theatregoer is the
art of gesture. Without adequate gesture, there can be no unified
pace, no fluid rhythm, no concept of motion. In American theatre
motions tend to be fast and jerky. The faster a motion the less
graceful it becomes usually. In a theatre that emphasizes colloquial
speech and movement little need for grace is felt with the result
that our performances of the classics suffer greatly. In Kabuki the
motion is studied, fluid, and vividly detailed. Again, to a Westerner, the motion seems often for the art of gesture rather than for
the meaning of the play. However, it is also true in American
theatre that the motion is often for the sake of "pace" rather than
for any real function in the play.

The third important lesson for the Westerner in Kabuki is a
vision of what can be achieved in theatre in a society where the
arts function together instead of separately. While certain great
Western theatres, such as the Greek and Elizabethan, were able to
unify the arts, our modern theatres still tend to think of stage
decor, music, and acting as separate arts that should be used to
enhance each other rather than as a unified sense of dramatic
action. In Kabuki, the presence of musicians and chorus on stage,
the way they function as intrinsic parts of the dramatic action, is
superbly exciting. The colorful make-up and costumes are part of
the style. They do not seem merely precious or effeminate as
exaggerated make-ups often do in stylized Western productions.
Also, one is struck by the fact that in a Kabuki classic like *Chushingura* there is a strong emphasis on the imaginative power of

poetry as a unifying force in society. The quarrel between Moronao and Hangan begins when Moronao reads a poem rejecting his
advances from Hangan's wife. Also Moronao says several times
during the play, "I have been a devotee of poetry." Imagine this in
an American play! It is a measure of what we have missed in the
American theatre. When Yuranosuki (played by the great actor
Shoroku) looks back at the gate of Hangan's mansion which he
will never see again, he takes an incredibly long pause, an expressive silence rarely seen in Western theatre. Suddenly Shoruku's
control and mastery, his stance, his presence, his facial expressions,
reveal his deepest sense of loyalty, faith, loneliness, death, tragedy.
I was moved as one can only rarely be moved by great art.

After this transcendant moment, Shoruku turns to farce to show
his versatility as an actor. He plays in another part of the program
an ugly, nagging shrew who gets revenge on her husband for his
night out. A fascinating aspect of Oriental theatre is the fact that
men who play women's roles have no homosexual connotation at
all as do female impersonators in this country. Some of this is
because the stylized gestures are designed to be the essence of
femininity rather than to *be* feminine. Also the voice makes no
attempt at exact illusion. The Japanese theatrical tradition wisely
does not separate sharply masculine and feminine traits. In the
United States a false image of masculinity has been established
which often creates an aggressive anti-feminine tone that conceals
a latent homosexuality. It is impossible for me to imagine, without
writhing, an American actor able to play both masculine and
feminine roles.

During the intermission I ran into a Japanese acquaintance who
has lived in the United States for many years and makes his living
as a gardener. A simple man, he said proudly that all of the Nisei
had turned out "to see their people." Particularly, he said that he
wanted to see *Chushingura*. This was a real lesson in the meaning
of tradition, a work that endures and spreads such deep roots that
it always creates new audiences. Furthermore, he was delighted by
the hanamichi, the passage-way from the stage through the audience, and the trap-door, and scornful that these worked so haphaz-

ardly in the cavernous space of the San Francisco Opera House. The theatre design for Kabuki meant a greal deal to him and I began to wonder how American audiences would change if their theatres were as exciting and intimate architecturally as the Japanese Kabuki theatres.

Ten years later in 1970, after more if still inadequate exposure to eastern theatrical traditions, I saw a performance by a traveling Indonesian Budaya troupe in Rhode Island and came to some additional conclusions about how eastern theatre can influence the west. Everywhere in theatre today we hear the call for magic and ritual, but these cannot merely be summoned in a room or on a stage. They come from the deep historical, religious roots of society. As I watched an excerpt from wayang kulit, the Javanese shadow puppet play, I began to realize physically that the history of music, theatre and dance in Indonesia goes back thousands of years. Even in the 4th century, when the Hindus arrived from India, they found dances accompanied by wooden and metal instruments performed in worship of ancestors and of local deities residing in trees, forests, mountains, lakes, and in the sea. It is said that a Javanese gamelan orchestra sounds like water and moonlight. Each gamelan tends to have its own name; for example one brought to the United States is called *The Venerable Dark Cloud.* Wayang kulit performances in Java with gamelan are usually organized by special committees on an occasion of public importance—a ceremony for the alleviation of drought, pestilence, epidemics, or natural disasters. Or performances may be presented purely as a public service in the conviction that the community witnessing the play may receive spiritual benefits. Such a performance lasts from 8 PM to 6 AM and is divided into three time sequences representing three phases of a spiritual journey—8 PM to midnight, midnight to 3 AM, and 3 AM to 6 AM. As in other eastern theatres, whole families attend; they bring floormats, sit, eat, and drink tea as they watch. They experience a voyage through time, an ordeal, a risk, an exposure to dangerous as well as beneficial forces, not a brief entertainment.

If Artaud in his famous essay on "Balinese Theatre" did not

understand the complex, historical ritual of Balinese dance-drama, he sensed its value to the interior world. That is why he called for a theatre with "the truthful precipitate of dreams." The key factor that we can learn from eastern theatre is *mystery*. In his recent experiments in England with *The Tempest,* Peter Brook proved this point when he used a Japanese actor along with his British actors. As Brook said, "We don't know how to bring magic into the theatre." To the Japanese actor "the way was quite clear."

This sense of mystery is not merely the sudden encounter with foreign traditions, the puzzle of different languages, gestures, rhythms, it is also a deeper matter of style, the recognition and celebration of gods, ancestors, spirits, nature. Such recognition takes different forms, depending on the particular country, religion, government, and customs practiced, but the kind of ritualistic voyage that occurs in far eastern theatres is difficult to achieve in western cultures that have become primarily materialistic. Particularly, eastern theatre enlightens us with discoveries about the nature of time. Our western sense of time is often too brief, too restless, too forced. In *Silence,* John Cage, whose seminal ideas in modern music and theatre have been influenced greatly by eastern concepts, tells the following Zen Story about time and enlightenment:

> A young man in Japan arranged his circumstances so that he was able to travel to a distant island to study Zen with a certain Master for a three-year period. At the end of the three years, feeling no sense of accomplishment, he presented himself to the Master and announced his departure. The Master said, "You've been here three years. Why don't you stay three months more?" The student agreed, but at the end of the three months he still felt that he had made no advance. When he told the Master again that he was leaving, the Master said, "Look now, you've been here three years and three months. Stay three weeks longer." The student did, but with no success. When he told the Master that absolutely nothing had happened, the Master said, "You've been here three years, three months, and three weeks. Stay three more days, and if at

the end of that time, you have not attained enlightenment, commit suicide. Towards the end of the second day, the student was enlightened.

Peter Brook's Midsummer Night's Dream

In the program for his 1971 New York production of *A Midsummer Night's Dream,* Peter Brook quotes from his book *The Empty Space:* "Once, the theatre could begin as magic: magic at the sacred festival or magic as the footlights came up. Today, it is the other way round. . . . We must open our empty hands and show that really there is nothing up our sleeves. Only then can we begin." If Brook begins freshly, eagerly, working toward a new synthesis in this production, his hands are far from empty.

What is this *white Midsummer Night's Dream?* It is a theatrical, white dream to see black, a conjuror's vision. Like a true magician, it borrows from everyone to create new magic. It takes from Brecht—a brightly lit stage so that nothing will be disguised. Everything in the open so we will watch carefully and see that there is nothing up the actors' sleeves. It takes from Meyerhold's bio-mechanical experiments dealing with love scenes on swings. It takes from the Commedia dell' Arte in a Puck dressed like a mischievous Harlequin. It takes from Oriental theatre in the frank manipulations of the stagehands and the open musical creation of sound effects. Yet the synthesis is magical; we realize that, paradoxically, a true synthesis can sometimes be the greatest originality.

No curtain is used. In dazzling white light, we see a towering, white-walled, cube-like geometrical space. An open gallery runs around the top of the walls on which the actors sit or stand to watch the action below. Two doors in the walls at the rear of the stage serve as formal entrances for the display of theatricalism. At the start of the play, the cast bursts exuberantly through these doors as actors in their cloaks and costumes to signify that this production will be the actors' magical dream. Later in the play, the actors who play Theseus and Hippolyta will exit through the doors, remain in full view of the audience as they become Oberon and Titania, and enter again in their new roles which emphasize the magical connection between the world of reality and the world of dream. Ladders in the side walls enable the actors to climb up to the ramparts where the high, manipulating acts of mystery always seem to watch and guide the mortal performers below. Brook uses the immense sense of height majestically and dangerously. Oberon and Puck fly through the air on trapezes; Titania floats in space on a scarlet ostrich feather bed; a silver plate representing the magical love-juice that Oberon commands Puck to use is flung down from the gallery and Puck catches it on the point of his wand, a feat of dexterity. Yet the mood is deeper than a display of aerial magic; the action becomes dark and sexual too. The play is presented in two parts and the climax of the first part is a cruel, ironic wedding celebration when Titania, caught in the web of Oberon's magic, falls in love with Bottom transformed into an ass. The accustomed sentimentality of Mendelsohn's "Wedding March" blasts out with an ironic flare, a phallic joke is played by one of the fairy attendants to emphasize Brook's view of the play as "a story about love and illusion, love and role playing, love and all the different aspects of making love, including the most extraordinary demonic notion of Oberon having his Queen fornicate with a physically repellant object—the Ass." Sex and weddings are demonic as well as blessed and the first part ends with an insane comic furore as paper plates and colored streamers swirl and clutter up the stage. Then the fairies, played as calm, energetic, manipulative, contemporary stagehands, come on during the intermission to clean up the party's devastating mess.

Part II takes a decided risk in de-emphasizing the traditional climax of the play presented by Bottom and his amateur company. The play about the "Most Cruel Death of Pyramus and Thisby" is a natural satire of crudely presented, affected comedy at which the aristocrats of Theuseus's court can laugh indulgently. In the glare of the modern world, the economic and racial struggle to eradicate class systems, Brook emphasizes the humanity of the mechanicals, their essential restraint and dignity in the face of their limitations.

The final scene becomes a ceremony of actors sympathetically watching actors play actors. The rhythm moves steadily, quietly, to a sense of peaceful watching. If this loses some of the comic tension of the play within a play, it permits the actors at the end to advance off the stage into the audience, shaking hands as friends with the spectators. Although this has been done many times, the spirit of friendship is contagious, a true celebration of theatre and a festival spirit of communion.

Amazingly, Brook does not tamper with the music of the text. The young actors of the Royal Shakespeare Company speak in a cleanly articulated, soft-spoken, natural way. The verse becomes the music of colloquial statement, not operatic arias to accompany Mendelssohn as I have seen it done by the Old Vic and other companies. In this way, Brook revives the language physically. No longer is poetry the mere surface of the action; it is now the action itself as language should be used in the theatre. In other productions, following the paths of Artaud and Grotowski, Brook subdues or reduces language to its barest roots as in his experimental stripping of *The Tempest.* However, to reduce, to change language in Shakespeare, particularly for an English director indebted to Elizabethan tradition, is usually an inadequate solution. Instead, the treatment of language in *A Midsummer Night's Dream* is a revelation, poetry treated as theatre first, poetry as action.

In an age of ironic questioning, when theatre has come to an impasse, the great distinction of Brook as a master synthesizer is that he begins with the basic questions as does Grotowski. What is theatre, what use is theatre in a time of technological warfare, how can theatre affect the audience, where is the lost magic of theatre? In his important book, *The Empty Space,* Brook divides theatre into four categories, Deadly, Holy, Rough, and Immediate. Deadly is the bad theatre that prevails everywhere. The Holy Theatre is a place "where the invisible can appear." The Rough Theatre, the popular theatre, is what saves us always because it presents the urgent, basic roughness, the necessary if not the polished performance. As for the Immediate Theatre, it is the autobiographical experiments of each contemporary, theatrical spirit, in this case

Brook's own spirit with his wide range of experimentation. It is to this generous, wide-ranging spirit that the modern theatre owes such a debt. Such a spirit must always search, renew traditions, establish new standards. As Brook said in an interview with Margaret Croyden: "I have always searched for new things. Nothing of mine is ever complete. Each thing has been leading to a passageway toward what a twelfth-century Noh actor called the 'flower.' The 'flower' is that rare moment when an actor and audience experience a real-life flow—like an act of creation—when, out of nothing, something is created and is complete." A 'flower' was created in *A Midsummer Night's Dream*.

from Theatre Journal 1969

DAN GEROULD

I. Two Cities: Paris and Prague

In June, 1968, I was invited to Paris to see a production of my play *Candaules, Commissioner* by L'Aquarium, the student theatre at the Ecole Normale Supérieure. I arrived in Paris just in time to see the last performance and three days before the general election between Poher and Pompidou to choose De Gaulle's successor. Remembering the nearly successful revolution of May 1968, when students and workers took to the streets and battled the police at the barricades, the government was taking no chances of a repeat performance and this time staged a show of its own—whether farce or melodrama was not yet clear. You might have thought a state of siege existed in Paris. . . .

Traditionally, the Ecole Normale Supérieure is a center of radical political activity. At the branch of the school in Saint-Cloud where I stayed, the walls, both inside and out, were covered with revolutionary slogans ("Vote red"; "Support the Viet-Cong") and sayings by Mao about the necessity of war to win the people's struggle against imperialism. In the improvised theatre dressing room, members of the company had written on a blackboard: "Continue the class war until the end."

In this highly-charged political atmosphere, played by students whose theatrical orientation came from the street barricades of May, 1968, *Candaules, Commissioner* took on new dimensions and resonances. It became transformed into a revolutionary drama, full of topical allusions, and turned into a source of controversy among members of the company as to the correct ideological interpretation.

The play itself is based on a legend in Herodotus' *History of the Persian Wars* about a king of ancient Lydia who insisted on showing his beautiful wife Nyssia stark naked to his bodyguard Gyges, and then lost his life and his empire when the queen, who discovered the shameful viewing, offered Gyges the choice of being killed or killing the king and becoming her husband. *Candaules, Commissioner* was written in 1965 under the joint impress of the war in Vietnam and my own experiences in a colonial army of occupation in Okinawa during the Korean War. I transposed the myth to an unspecified small Asian country racked by civil war and made Candaules the High Commissioner for Economic Assistance from a friendly occidental power and Gyges his native chauffeur. . . .

In America, *Candaules* was considered an anti-war play by almost everyone, and various peace groups and theatres became attracted to it as anti-Vietnam propaganda. The French students, however, were not interested in peace, but in the triumph of their cause, through violence and bloodshed when necessary. The production of *Candaules, Commissioner* at L'Aquarium was not anti-war, but pro-revolution. . . .

In the production at L'Aquarium, Gyges was in the driver's seat figuratively, as well as literally. He was played as the hero of the play—a guerrilla fighter who awaits the right moment to arouse the people to open revolt against imperialism. He cunningly flatters Candaules in order to force him to show his wife naked and trigger the revolution. . . .

To stress the revolutionary logic of this sequence of events, the production by L'Aquarium embodied the oppressed people in a chorus of four Lydians who chanted pro-Viet Cong slogans, as well as threatening Candaules at the end of Scene 1 and attacking Nyssia at the end of Scene 3. The name of the Trotskyite candidate for president—Krivine—was painted on the back of Gyges' old clothes. And in the final scene of the play Gyges gleefully douses his master with gasoline and invites the audience to enjoy the lighting of the matches. Triumphant, he strides off into the streets, with his gun drawn, ready to lead the revolution.

The audience, composed mainly of young students, actively supported Gyges and relished the destruction of Candaules and

Nyssia and the world they represented. It was a prophecy of what they felt or hoped would soon come true.

From Paris I went to Czechoslovakia, where the expectations and longings—especially among students—were of a different order. In Prague, there was a shortage of policemen. Since August, 1968, there has been little enthusiasm to join the Czech police force. The few policemen that were in evidence patrolled the streets unobtrusively, often paired with a young soldier used to fill the gap. Everything was orderly and peaceful, with no sense of ferment or visible signs of past unrest, except for a few effaced slogans which once told the occupiers to go home. No one talked of revolution.

Anger and resentment were now vented obliquely in jokes and in occasional stunts or improvised street spectacles. On Václaské Náměstí, Prague's main thoroughfare, a goose was set free with a sign on its back: "He's not mine." Husak is the Czech word for gander. It took several hours before the goose could be caught.[1]

More than anywhere else, suppressed feelings found an outlet in the theatre, which can become a place of high excitement in the eastern European world when other means of expression are denied. Beyond the quiet surface of the streets, the sense of hurt and outrage was forcefully voiced at the Balustrade Theatre (Divaldo na Zábradlí) where Shakespeare's *Timon of Athens* was played as a bitter, grotesque tragedy of betrayed friendship.

Famous for Grossman's version of Kafka's *The Trial* and the first Czech performances of the theatre of the absurd in the midsixties, the Balustrade is a small avant-garde theatre which has produced the plays of the best contemporary Czech playwrights, Vraclav Havel and Miron Kundera. Kundera's new comedy, *Ptákovina* (a made-up word suggesting something like "cockbrain"), a disabused and cynical satire on sex and politics, was playing in repertory at the same time as *Timon.*

As often happens in eastern European struggles over national independence, the Balustrade turned to Shakepeare for a text that

[1] Husak was a Czeck leader who collaborated with the Russian invaders.

would deal allusively with the present. The brutal discarding of all Timon's illusions at the discovery of the treachery of his friends was stressed by a rhymed couplet added to Shakespeare's text at the end of III, i, in order to sharpen the play's topical meaning:

> Those that have power to hurt and smother
> Will heap one injury upon another.

Conceived as a tragedy of betrayed friendship, *Timon* at the Balustrade showed the disastrous fate of trust in a world that is utterly corrupt. Jaroslav Gillar, who directed the production at the Balustrade, has gone to Timon's embittered ravings in the second half of the text and imposed this deranged vision on the entire world of the tragedy, theatrically embodying the moral depravity around Timon by means of the sexual images in his speeches in Act IV.

The corruption of Athens is shown by perverse sexuality and transvestitism. The poet and the jeweller, one of the senators, several of the flattering lords, and some of Timon's servants were played by actresses. These changes of sex in casting (besides providing more roles for women in a play with a large, overwhelmingly male cast) were not gratuitous; they served to suggest a slippery, decadent society where appearances are deceptive and everything is subject to betrayal. Perversion of natural function and affection became the production's prime metaphor for a world that is rotten and treacherous.

Alcibiades' two whores (indicated in the text in only one scene in Act IV) are present throughout most of the play, a silent chorus of perversion and venality in garish costumes: dyed hair and wigs in red and blue, bikinis and pink brassieres with edges in black and large black dots over the nipples, their bodies covered with coarse fishnetting. They fondle each other lasciviously and offer themselves in any combination or pairing—heterosexual, lesbian, or bisexual.

Perverted love becomes a surrogate of betrayed friendship; the production works by a whole series of substitutions. Food and eating—in the text associated with Timon's magnanimity—are replaced by erotic physical movements. The flatterers' gluttony is changed to lust. The two key banquet scenes, which reveal first Timon's generosity, then his recognition of betrayal, turn into wild sex orgies.

The pageantry and pomp in *Timon* (hardly possible in the narrow confines of the Balustrade) find their equivalent in an acrobatic, sensual use of the human body, whereby the physical dimensions of the small stage are utilized to the full; the actors tumble and roll about the floor, exploiting and consuming the space. Every aspect of the text was given a physical, sensory image.

The second banquet scene turned into a whirlwind of motion as Timon knocks the flatterers off the table where they have climbed, throws the furniture about the stage, and finally demolishes the table. The flatterers do cartwheels as they are scattered about the room, then return to push the table up again. Timon lets the table fall, flattening them all, as he prepares to leave Athens forever, to the accompaniment of a brief drum beat, torn apart, never to be the same again.

The audience was stunned at this point of high tension and, as the lights came on, could hardly realize that the first half of the play was already over. The first three acts of *Timon* were played in exactly one hour, at a tremendous pace, rushing forward to Timon's dropping the table—the violent crash of all his illusions. . . .

The second half of the performance opens with a drum roll, as Timon appears at the rear entrance and comes forward with a roar, his back to the audience. The gate falls, cutting him off from the city forever. After delivering his curse to the walls of Athens, Timon turns around for the first time. His hair and beard are now white; he has the fierce, insane stare of a soul in torment. When he throws off his black cape and robe, he has nothing on underneath but a hermit's penitent robe of gray sackcloth; a black and white panel in the setting is lowered behind him. Timon now has mythic stature. His eyes only black holes in his ravaged face, he appears as a saint in the desert, a venerable mystic sufferer of all human misfortunes. Chains draped over his shoulders and wrists, his elbows raised high in anguished poses, or his arms hanging down limply, Timon is a puppet, a martyr, a tortured, broken wreck.

At the Balustrade, Timon's death—which in Shakespeare takes place off-stage and comes as a strange anti-climax when reported by a nameless soldier—becomes a long workless scene, a grotesque, erotic dance of death. A voluptuous young girl (already introduced as one of the Amazons in the masque during the first banquet scene) appears as the allegorical figure of death. She dances for him, ghastly and sensual. Timon on his knees rubs his head against her stomach and sex organs. As his hands go convulsively from her breasts to her face, Death kisses him on the lips, reveals the death's head beneath her mask, and drapes a robe over Timon's head.

The drum beats, Timon's corpse is covered, and the panels shift for the last time. The Fool appears; he is wearing Timon's black cape and holds Timon's chains in his arms.

II. Poland

THE GREEN GOOSE: "The Smallest Theatre in the World"

The grotesque and absurd theatre is already classic in Poland, with a continuous native tradition extending from Witkiewicz and Gombrowicz in the period between the wars to contemporary Polish drama of the late fifties and sixties. The poet Konstanty Ildefons Gałczyński (pronounced Gow-chin-ski, with the accent on the second syllable) is an important link in this chain. An admirer and disciple of Stanisław Ignacy Witkiewicz (the great precursor of the modern Polish avant-garde who committed suicide in 1939) and a direct influence on Mrożek and Różewicz, Gałczyński (1905-1953) bridges the pre-war and post-war periods and unites the different generations. Immediately after the war, he was the first Polish writer to develop a new theatre built on nonsensical fantasy, absurd humor, and parody of serious forms of drama and solemn habits of thought.

As a poet, Gałczyński was able to combine wit, lyricism, satire, and surrealist imagination and yet remain intelligible and widely popular. Already famous for his poetry in the 1930's, he spent the war years in a German prison camp, and after a year of wandering in western Europe, returned to Poland in 1946 to resume his literary career in a country that had been shattered by the war and was in the throes of social changes, the results of which were by no means clear. At this uncertain moment in Polish history, with the old world destroyed and a new one not yet built, Gałczyński began his work as a playwright, contributing a new installment of *The Green Goose* each week to *Przekrój* ("Profile"), the Cracow literary magazine for which he wrote several hundred short plays in the next four years.

Originally intended for reading and journalistic in its setting, *The Green Goose* became the most celebrated and controversial work of this period—eagerly awaited, laughed over, attacked, and denounced. In it Gałczyński mocked everything, but especially the past and various national follies and intellectual pretensions. By demolishing stereotypes, *The Green Goose* shocked and made enemies; Gałczyński was called a clown abusing his talents for unworthy ends and came under fire from both the right and the left, in the Catholic press and in communist publications.

Called by its author "the smallest theatre in the world," the plays in *The Green Goose* range in length from three lines to a few pages. They have all the paraphernalia of the theatre—titles, subtitles, stage directions, a curtain—including, in many cases, a recurring cast of characters: a commedia dell'arte animal family—a pig, a dog, an ass, and the green goose herself, as well as a professor of angelology and a young hero named Aloysius Ptarmigan—all of whom became popular favorites, as in a comic strip. These characters sometimes appear as themselves and sometimes make guest appearances and star in different roles. In addition, other characters, real and imaginary, from past history, literature, and contemporary life, come on stage under unexpected circumstances; among the dramatis personae we meet Hamlet, Dante, various Poles ancient and modern, ranging from the 17th-century king, Jan Sobieski, to Paderewski and Gałczyński himself, and including even the prompter.

The great majority of plays deal with national and topical themes and ridicule what is sacred and overblown in Polish history and culture, but other forms of sanctified tradition also come in for abuse, namely, the Bible, Greek mythology, and above all else, throughout *The Green Goose,* the theatre and its accepted conventions. Theatrical form is used to undermine theatrical form: *The Green Goose* parodies the serious rituals of the theatre and calls into question their sanctity.

Different genres—society drama, romantic melodrama, opera, ballet—are presented in caricature. Characters are reduced to marionettes (an evening of *The Green Goose* was later staged by the Grotesque Puppet Theatre in Cracow). And titles, settings, and stage directions are turned into an element of absurd humor as important as the dialogue itself. By treating the conventions of his theatre over-literally, Gałczyński points out their preposterousness; he invites the audience to enjoy not what the theatre can show, but what it cannot.

In his mockery of stage tradition, the author of *The Green Goose* assigns an important role to the curtain. The curtain becomes an indispensable actor, sometimes listed in the cast of characters, who must be able to fall expressively and even speak lines when the need arises. In different plays, the curtain is required to fall "discreetly," "majestically," "eagerly," "jauntily," and "pedagogically." Several times it falls by mistake, occasionally rectifying the error by going up again. Once it falls "forever," and another time it falls and kills itself on the spot. Or it may sink with an ominous swish or moan, or come crashing down. Once it is lowered by an anteater, and once it gets caught on a palm tree. At the conclusion of a play called *The End of the World,* it falls "optimistically."

Based on the subversion of all conventionality, *The Green Goose* may at first seem impossible to stage; by all normal laws of the theatre it is. In fact, it was not until after the October revolution of 1956, which brought liberalization to Poland and the end of socialist realism, that *The Green Goose* became a part of the theatre and a force in the creation of the new Polish drama. As long as the Stalinists reigned, with their fabrication of new mythologies and sacred dogmas, there was little chance for a mocker of angelology; by 1950 Gałczyński had been forced to curb his high spirits and eventually "close" his theatre.

Since 1956 the plays have been an invitation to imaginative directors to look at the world of stage convention afresh and find their own ways of revealing its absurdity in the theatre. Gałczyński translated *Midsummer Night's Dream* and undoubtedly was an admirer of the artistic ingenuity and skill of Bottom and his company. And the pedagogic aim of *The Green Goose* is to debunk rigid ways of thinking and teach people to develop a taste for the unexpected and surprising.

Gałczyński became an influence on the student theatres and cabarets that flourished in Poland after the liberalization, and he anticipated the irreverent humor and skepticism of the young generation. His use of parody, fantasy, and bizarre juxtapositions forecasts the grotesque works of Mrożek and Różewicz.

The similarities between *The Green Goose* and the theatre of the absurd in the West are also marked and can be seen not only in form and technique, but also in theme. Frustration and defeat threaten man's feeble striving. Nothing works out as planned by the characters; they are thwarted and crushed by forces outside their control. But here a major difference from the Western absurd occurs. The plays in *The Green Goose* are not negative and pessimistic, but most often dramatized fables that teach a moral lesson.

Drawing on an anti-intellectual, practical belief in life and common sense, Gałczyński represents the didactic absurd, the fantastic tale with a rational basis and an instructive goal.

In "The Flood That Failed," Noah, his family, and animals cannot leave on the ark since it is winter and the waters have frozen over. But as often happens in *The Green Goose* when everything seems impossible, the characters are able to exert ingenuity and find another, surprising way out of the dilemma; Noah turns the ark into a sleigh and they all ride off on a sleigh ride to

Mount Ararat. The romantic and tragic view is constantly ridiculed, and the myths leading to defeat, disaster, and war are exploded. The last word is given to everyday human things. Jove scrambles and eats the egg that would have hatched Helen and the Trojan War.

WARSAW THEATRE FESTIVAL 1969

Since it was first organized in 1965, there has been a theatre festival in Warsaw every year sometime in November or December, at which the best half-dozen or so productions from theatres in the provinces are presented for Warsaw audiences. In 1969 the two most interesting productions were remarkable stagings of two contemporary Polish plays: Ernest Bryll's *November Theme* and Tadeusz Różewicz's *The Old Woman Hatches.*

Written by well-known poets, the two plays have this much in common: with little or no plot and characterization and loose thematic structures, they leave a great deal to the imagination and talents of the director and scene designer. They are ideal scenarios for the modern theatre. They are also both about war and its devastation—Bryll's play about the effects of the second world war, Różewicz's about those of the third. And both productions create catastrophic visions which are intelligible and communicative to anyone and which, perhaps, even improve upon the original literary texts.

Józef Szajna (pronounced Shina, rhyming with China,) who produced Bryll's *November Theme* for the Wyspiański Silesian Theatre in Katowice (a city of about 300,000 in the south of Poland), transposed scenes, gave one character's speeches to another, and so reshuffled and transformed the play as to make it his own. Bryll's original poetic drama became simply the pretext and occasion for Szajna's total theatrical reconception. Szajna's radical transformations of the literary texts he produces make him one of the most exciting theatre artists in Poland today and have led to coining the words "Szajnaize" and Szajnaization."

Born in 1922, Szajna spent the war years in the death camps at

Auschwitz and Buchenwald and miraculously survived. After the war, he studied painting at the Cracow School of Fine Arts, from which he graduated in 1953 as a painter and scene designer. All his work for the theatre is shaped by a terrifying yet moving vision of the horror of the extermination camps, expressed in powerful visual images.

For Szajna, painting and directing are closely related activities. The performance is only loosely based on the theme of a given play; the story and its literary significance is reduced as the elements of the production become integrated.

> Stage sets disappear, and what we see is the representation of images composed and directed with the use of objects which participate in the action and even interfere with it. This kind of staging loses the characteristics of mere decor, of an architectural fragment, and becomes the matter of the theatrical process. It becomes independent of the author's stage directions, and gains autonomous value, becomes "the space of expression." It does not describe the place and time of action, but uses concrete, often ready-made objects which participate in the theatrical action. The action takes place in empty spaces, or in open, deserted places, sometimes on "location" universally broadened, extending beyond the box set, often including the audience.[2]

In the production of Wyspiański's *Akropolis* which Szajna created with Grotowski for the Polish Lab Theatre in 1962, a turn-of-the-century symbolic drama becomes a parable of modern times about human suffering in the concentration camps. Objects, like wheelbarrows take on a value higher than man, who becomes subordinate to them. Szajna goes one step further in showing the dehumanizing machinery of war in his production of Witold Wandurski's proletarian minstrel-morality show *Death on a Pear Tree* in 1964. There is a war scene without the participation of actors:

> The action is created by metal wheels of various sizes rushing at each other from different directions and lit up by crossed

[2] This quotation and the following one are taken from an interview with Szajna in *The Theatre in Poland*, 5-6, 1968.

spotlights. Sometimes they pass by each other; now and then, though, they collide and with a great deal of noise, collapse on the stage. As a result of this "fight," they form a shapeless heap of hardware.

Bryll's *November Theme* opens in a cemetery in Warsaw on All Soul's Day when Poles mourn their dead. For Szajna, this image leads back to the war, the occupation, and the camps. In the production corpses are the magical objects that carry forward the action: human bodies with amputated limbs, dead mannikins, riddled and mutilated dummies, children's torsos, legs and arms and pieces of people pulled out of the sewer.

Szajna himself designs both the dummies and human fragments and also the stage space in which the objects and images become dramatic action. The stage is open at all times, both before the play begins and during the intermission; it consists of five massive gray walls, two on each side and one to the rear. On each side there stands out a large flat silhouette of a human head and shoulders, and on the back wall there are drawn the outlines of many smaller heads and shoulders. The legs and broken mannikins of women and children are stuck against all the walls, and automobile tires are scattered on the canvas-covered floor. The entire space is lighted by a small electric lamp, fastened to a cross bar, hanging in the middle of the stage. . . .

In the course of the play itself, those who were shot in the prologue come back to life; the dead celebrate their own All Soul's Day and take part in the affairs of the living. They become the guests at a wedding and dance the hully-gully—but in a dance of death, with the puppets and dummies taken from the walls as partners. Two corpses—one male, one female—are lowered at an angle, like figureheads on a ship, from either side of the stage, and a huge bandaged body, with wheels attached to its mangled torso, hangs head-down above the stage.

At the end of Szajna's *November Theme,* there is a ceremony of purification. After the living slowly pile up the dummies and cover them with a white cloth, the back wall lifts up and reveals a tall forest of burning candles, in tiered rows mounting higher and higher. The platform with the candles moves forward to the middle of the stage; each of the living takes a smaller candle and joins the circle of the dead.

Szajna's version of *November Theme* is "a play with corpses," to use the formulation of Witkiewicz, a playwright particularly important to Szajna. As scene designer or director, Szajna has staged four of Witkiewicz's plays; in them he found a precedent for the mingling of the living and the dead, the return of the dead to life, and the use of mannikins and dummies as partners for the living, as well as the catastrophic vision that gives these devices meaning. In August, 1939, Witkiewicz told a friend, "What awaits us is one gigantic concentration camp."

Jerzy Jarocki's production of Różewicz's *The Old Woman Hatches* for the Wrocław Contemporary Theatre did not radically transform the text and use it only as an occasion for a new spectacle, but was rather an act of collaboration which Różewicz himself invited. The author's stage directions, which constitute over a third of the printed play, are not descriptive or prescriptive, but offer the director suggestions and ideas which he is free to carry out as he wishes. Różewicz deliberately does not tell the director how to produce *The Old Woman Hatches*, but once having posed the problems, leaves his play partly unfinished and open to different kinds of solutions.

The Old Woman Hatches is a series of variations on the theme of rubbish. As its all-inclusive metaphor, it portrays the contemporary world as a giant trash heap and graveyard—a cosmic garbage can for all culture and civilization. Amidst the refuse, in a cafe-necropolis, a grotesque old woman, wearing multiple layers of discarded clothing, imagines that she is giving birth to new life. She celebrates the stomach: digestion and gestation. Throughout the play she is hatching something in all the pollution and filth:

> One ought to give birth, whoever can ought to give birth . . .
> They all ought to bear children. Greta Garbo and Sartre—and
> Bertrand Russell—and Cardinal Ottaviani and Salvador

Dali—and Picasso—and General De Gaulle—and Mao ...
All ... All of them without exception for age, rank, sex, or
politics.³

As the first scene ends, she calls for water and sheets. The
curtain falls; it is a huge, white, blood-stained sheet.
Like Gałczyński before him, Różewicz uses both the curtain and
the stage directions to comment on the play itself and on the
nature of drama, challenging and pushing beyond normal limits
the conventions and resources of the stage. In the second scene,
the war has taken place and now trash, particularly paper, engulfs
the entire world. There is no ground, no water, no air—nothing but
garbage:

A rubbish dump like the sea from shore to shore. A rubbish
dump right up to the horizon.... Perhaps a battlefield. A
colossal rubbish dump. A polygon. A necropolis. And yet a
beach.

In his production for the Wroclaw Contemporary Theatre, Jarocki took advantage of the leeway Różewicz offers and treated the
text freely as a score that lends itself to improvisation. In the first
place, he divided the performance into two contrasting parts much
more sharply than the author had his play. In the first scene,
Jarocki kept the stage relatively bare and empty of junk to
heighten the effect of scene two where the world in ruins is inun-
dated with its own refuse. The first scene was played on the front
of the stage against a wall cutting off the rest of the playing area,
and the tone was kept comic and light, as in a cabaret skit or
cartoon. Following Różewicz's suggestion about the use of random
comments, the young waiter makes a series of exclamations in
French during the old woman's long monologue on the stomach as
man's vulnerable and glorious organ, and he speaks aloud some of
the long stage directions on the nature of the theatre and technique

³ This and other quotations from *The Old Woman Hatches* are from the translation by Adam Czerniawski which is published in the special English-language
number of *Dialog*, the Polish drama magazine in which Różewicz's original text
appeared in 1968.

of the play. And there is an itching and scratching sequence in which all the characters are bothered by lice that could have come from a silent film comedy of the twenties.

Three different actresses play the part of the old woman, a radical innovation of Jarocki's which removes any monotony from the role of the protagonist and permits different, contrasting embodiments of her hatching spirit (as well as the simultaneous appearance of all three on stage at the end of the performance.) The third and youngest actress gives an acrobatic version of the old woman, delivering the long speech on the theme, "Everything is open to love," as she swings back and forth across the stage on the chandelier.

The second scene of the world as a rubbish heap is a masterpiece of complex, yet controlled staging. The entire stage is covered with a grey, paper-like refuse that does not remind us of real trash, but is its theatrical equivalent; a rubbish ditch runs through this wasteland, and all forms of life and death tumble in and out of this trench. The entire pattern of the second scene is built up of repeated actions involving the three sunbathing fates, the two roadsweepers, and the blind man.

Over and over again, as he talks about trees, the blind man falls off a rubbish cliff into the rubbish ditch, then is swept up by the roadsweepers and is dropped from their cart—along with arms and legs, dummies, and real bodies—back into the ditch. A female corpse, wrapped in bandages from head to foot but with bared breasts, a soldier, the young waiter—all are shovelled into the ditch, where a fight takes place between the dummies and the live corpses in which they seem to dance, make love, struggle, and throttle one another.

A strange hum is heard in the air. As the three fates, stretched out in the form of a star, wave their legs in the air, one of the waiters reads letters to the editor about breast sizes and breast care, the gentleman fondles the leg of the beauty parlor operator through the window of a basket chair, and the fighters writhe in the ditch. The gentleman and the blind man read old newspapers that are in shreds, as the road-sweepers shovel trash over them.

The fates trample on the corpses in the trench-grave. There is a tremendous explosion, and after the flower child drives off the policeman, the blind man leads him by the hand and gives him directions. The strange sound is heard again, and as the lights fade, the blind man and the flower child are on the very edge of the cliff, about to fall into the ditch.

Jarocki achieves the sharp effect of a total cut-off at the end of the play which Rózewicz indicated in his stage directions, but by totally different means. The spectators remain threatened by this suspended vision of devastation. When the lights come on again, the stage is empty of human actors. Only the vast sea of rubbish remains, which the audience is left to applaud.

Warsaw
January, 1970

Towards Ritual in Black Theatre

Notes on Black Theatre—On Theatre That Is Black

MICHAEL S. HARPER

For any black expression in America there are certain givens: that the system of white supremacy, though a closed, one-dimensional form by definition, does not define the character and imagination, and *being* of black people, and that the necessity of creating a vision commensurate with the complexities of human, black experience is *open-ended; that the black man is the universal man,* particularly in western culture, because of the conditions that brought him into its context, and which black people have internalized and *must* express imaginatively; that questions about oppression by oppressors always assault the victims because their rhetoric holds in their expression the answers to those questions; that the pursuit of excellence, through the regimen of personality and resilience of black people, allows an acceptance of traditions of the western world as vehicle to the artist with a black perspective as he demonstrates with subtlety, grace and in multi-dimension, the reality of the black community in its diversity and complexity.

Black people are not white people with black skins. Miscegenation, integration, freedom, equality, are words that veil the pervasiveness of oppression. Distinctions between the history of the

United States and the mythology of white supremacy will not make this country a white country, a white reality. Money, property, any translations thereof, are not humanly negotiable. A Man is not equivocably both subject and object; he is a Man.

The black artist cannot separate his art from his people; his aims are in keeping with the unity of black artist and black community in all its diversity. The assumptions of that art are: that man is in essence spiritual; that he has a modal perception of reality; that his concept of the universe is holistic. The black artist is concerned with life force; his art will be testamental—witness to the spirit and power of the universe; his art will be moral, and that morality will be defined man to man—it will be humane, its basis through contact, man to man, and not through objects. The black artist's responsibility is to create archetypal symbols and images that relate to original paradigms, original patterns, and connect with the African continuum. His concern will be with the folk experience of his people, and with ritual as it emanates from black institutions; his dramaturgy will consist of utilizing the dramatic forms implicit in the black community, in its ceremonies, public and private, in its styles, in its language, and in the modality of these ritual patterns, the black church, and the varieties in black idioms and rhythms. These will be defined by experiences which have projected themselves in diverse artistic forms: *power/tenderness/will*, art which can renew us all—like those blues and jazz artists who embodied the art forms they were, and who rejuvenated and renewed us as their vision and profundity demanded, the promise and profundity of the human heart. That art, that drama, will be dedicated to the energy and vitality, and survival, of the group, and because the artists are themselves.

GAMES:
A One-Act Play

GEORGE HOUSTON BASS

Characters: The Gang—BOB, FRANK, JOE, SUE, SALLY, ANNA, JANE, The Victim, CHARLOTTE. Place: *A Playground, an open field*

> *Members of The Gang enter playing individual games—jump rope, walking on cracks, etc. Bob enters playing a game of chase with Sally. Charlotte enters dragging a box containing a doll. She begins playing alone. The Gang stops playing and watches Charlotte. She ignores them. Bob begins group activity.*

BOB: Hide spy, mickey-moe-rye, snatch a victim from the sky. Fly to the east. Fly to the west. Trap the victim in her nest.

JANE: Honey-hiney-bee-ball, I can't see y'all. All my black sheep hid?

SALLY: All around my base is spy. All in the house is spy.

FRANK: Here I come with my eyes wide open.

SUE: Ready or not, you shall be caught.

JOE: Hide spy.

BOB: You better be hid by twelve o'clock.

ANNA: Ready or not you shall be caught.

JANE: Hide spy, mickey-moe-rye.

SALLY: All ain't hid just holler I.

BOB: Honey-hiney-bee-ball, I can't see y'all. All my black sheep hid?

JOE: Fly to the east.

ANNA: Fly to the west.

SUE: Trap the victim in her nest.

JANE: One, two, three for Johnny.

Timon of Athens, directed by Jaroslav Giller at The Theatre on the Balustrade (Prague). "Jaroslav Giller . . . has gone to Timon's embittered ravings in the second half of the text and imposed this deranged vision on the entire world of the tragedy, theatrically embodying the moral depravity around Timon by means of the sexual images in his speeches in Act IV." (Dan Gerould, 225) Photo by Pavel Jasansky.

Tadeusz Rózewicz's *The Old Woman Hatches,* directed by Jerzy Jarocki and designed by Wojciech Krakowski for The Wroclaw Contemporary Theatre (Warsaw Theatre Festival, 196). *"The Old Woman Hatches* is a series of variations on the theme of rubbish. As its all-inclusive metaphor, it portrays the contemporary world as a giant trash heap and graveyard—a cosmic garbage can for all culture and civilization. Amidst the refuse, in a cafe-necropolis, a grotesque old woman, wearing multiple layers of discarded clothing, imagines that she is giving birth to new life." (Dan Gerould, 234) Jarocki's production divided the old woman's role among three actresses, who appear on stage together at the end of the play. The sunbathers in the forground are the play's three Fates.
Photo by Grazyna Wyszomirska.

Ernest Bryll's *November Theme,* directed and designed by Józef
Szajna for The Wyspianski Silesian Theatre (Warsaw Theatre
Festival, 1969). "Bryll's *November Theme* opens in a cemetery
in Warsaw on All Soul's Day when Poles mourn their dead. For
Szajna, this image leads back to the war, the occupation, and the
camps. In the production corpses are the magical objects that carry
forward the action: human bodies, with amputated limbs, dead
mannikins, riddled and mutilated dummies, children's torsos, legs
and arms and pieces of people pulled out of the sewer." (Dan
Gerould, 233)
Photo by Zbigniew Lagocki.

Ritual to Regain Our Strength and Reclaim Our Power, The National Black Theatre at The Rhode Island Festival.
Photo by H. Theo. Ehrhardt.

George Houston Bass's *Black Masque, a ritual for the theatre,*
directed by George Houston Bass with mural and sculpture by
John Torres. Presented by Rites and Reason at Brown University
in 1971. "[The Black artist's] concern will be with folk experience
of his people, and with ritual as it emanates from black institutions;
his dramaturgy will consist of using the dramatic forms implicit in
the black community, in its ceremonies, public and private, in its
styles, in its languages, and in the modality of these ritual patterns,
the black church, and the varieties in black idioms and rhythms."
(Michael S. Harper, 239)

James Schevill's *The Pilots* directed by John Emigh with musical conception by Gerald Shapiro. "Actors in yellow slickers and hats were stationed around the room playing conch shells with different pitches and ringing bells that merged with the fog machines. I wasn't trying to create so much a realistic sea atmosphere but a sea mystery. The fact that I, the composer, also acted the part of the Pilot, who is assassinated in the play, enabled me also to function as a sort of mysterious conductor." (Gerald Shapiro, 272) Photo by Michael St. A. Boyer.

John Emigh's environmental production of *Marat/Sade* at Brown University's Robinson Hall. "Whenever posible I like to set up a dialectic between a place's ordinary appearance and use and its theatrical appearance and use — between the everyday space and the special event — between the present and history. I especially like the irony of performing *Marat/Sade* in the Economics department . . ." (John Emigh, 261)

SALLY: Home free!

FRANK: Home free!

BOB: One, two, three for Mary.

SUE: All behind my base is spy.

ANNA: Home free!

JOE: Home free!

SALLY: One, two, three for Kootie.

SUE: Hide spy, mickey-moe-rye.

FRANK: Home free!

JANE: Home free!

BOB: I caught you.

SUE: One, two, three.

JOE: Home free!

FRANK: Home free!

ANNA: Home free!

GANG: Home free!

BOB: Home free!

SALLY: Home free!

GANG: Ho-ooo-oo-ome Fre-eee-ee-ee!

BOB: Honey-hiney-bee-ball, I can't see y'all.

SUE: All hi-iii-ii-id.

> *Members of The Gang all run to home base and pile on top of each other, laughing, clowning, tickling each other, engaging in horseplay. Charlotte watches, eager to participate.*

GANG: Oh, here we go loop-de-loo. Here we go loop-de-la. Here we go loop-de-loo, all on a Saturday night. I put my right foot in, I take my right foot out. I give my right foot a shake, shake, shake, and turn myself about. Oh, here we go loop-de-loo. Here we go loop-de-la. Here we go loop-de-loo, all on a Saturday night.

JANE: Ring around the roses. Pocket full of poses.

SALLY: Ring around the roses. Pocket full of poses.

BOB: Leap frog!

FRANK: Leap frog!

BOB: Leap frog!

FRANK: Leap!
SUE: One, two, three, red light.
JOE: One, two, three, red light.
BOB: Leap frog!
FRANK: Leap!
JOE: One, two, three, red light.
SUE: One, two, three, red light.
ANNA: Here we go loop-de-loo.
JANE: Ring around the roses.
SALLY: Pocket full of poses.
JANE: Ashes.
SALLY: Ashes.
BOB and FRANK: All fall down.
BOB: Last one in the field is an old rotten egg.
ANNA: Here we go loop-de-loo.

> *The Gang exits; Anna, left behind, discovers herself alone and follows others. Charlotte, left alone with her own world, plays with her doll.*

CHARLOTTE: One, two, buckle my shoe. Three, four, knock at the door. Five, six, pick up sticks. Seven, eight, lay them straight. Nine, ten, start again. One potato, two potato, three potato, four. Five potato, six potato, seven potato more. Out goes the rat. Out goes the cat. Out goes the lady with the seesaw hat. I went to the river and I couldn't get across. I paid five dollars for an old blind horse. The horse wouldn't pull, I swapped it for a bull. The bull wouldn't holler, I swapped it for a dollar. The dollar wouldn't pass, I threw it in the grass. The grass wouldn't grow, I chopped it with a hoe. The hoe wouldn't chop, I put it in the shop. The shop wouldn't fix it, and so I had to nix it. Wish I had my money back.

> *Charlotte begins singing to her doll. The Gang returns, playing statue. Bob starts the game, and each member of The Gang freezes in the position he finds himself. They form a circle around Charlotte as if preparing to attack. Charlotte seems not to be aware of them.*

CHARLOTTE: Oh, Mary Mack, Mack, Mack all dressed in black,

black, black with three gold buttons, buttons, buttons up and down her back, back, back. She asked her mother, mother, mother for fifteen cents, cents, cents to see the elephant, elephant, elephant jump the fence, fence, fence. He jumped so high, high, high that he touched the sky, sky, sky and he never got back, back, back until the Fourth of July, lie, lie. Milk in the pitcher, pitcher, pitcher and butter in the bowl, bowl, bowl. She can't find a sweetheart, sweetheart, sweetheart for to save her soul, soul, soul. She feels very blue, blue, blue but there's nothing she can do, do, do except sit and sigh, sigh, sigh until the day she will die, die, die.

BOB: You moved. You moved. I saw you move.

SUE: I didn't.

BOB: You have now.

> *Sue covers her eyes and counts while members of The Gang assume new poses.*

SUE: On your toes, change your pose. One, two, three, four, freeze.

> *Sue looks the statues over and tries to make them break. Charlotte becomes interested and moves near.*

BOB, *to Charlotte:* Scram! *(Pause, then to The Gang)* Raccoon up the 'simmon tree, possum on the ground. Raccoon shakes the 'simmons down, possum pass them round. Little fishes in the brook; Willie catch them with a hook. Mama fry them in a pan and daddy eat them like a man. Now ain't I right?

GANG: Yeah!

BOB: Ain't I right?

GANG: Yeah! Yeah!

BOB: Ain't I right?

GANG: Yeah! Yeah! Yeah!

BOB: I told you so. I'm right.

FRANK: Old cow died in Tennessee. Sent her jawbone back to me. Jawbone walked. Jawbone talked. Jawbone ate with knife and fork. Now ain't I right?

GANG: Yeah!

FRANK: Now ain't I right?

GANG: Yeah! Yeah!

FRANK: Now ain't I right?

GANG: Yeah! Yeah! Yeah!

FRANK: I told you so. I'm right.

SUE: Too late. Too late. The door is locked and you're too late.

GANG, *except Frank:* Too late. Too late. The door is locked and you're too late.

FRANK: Whip! Whip!

JANE: Whip! Whip!

SALLY: Whip!

JOE: Whip!

GANG: Whi-iii-ii-ii-ip!

BOB: Whip! Whip!

SUE: Whip! Whip!

GANG: Whi-iii-iii-ii-ii-ip! . . . Oh, this is the way you willow-bee, willow-bee, willow-bee. This is the way you willow-bee, all night long. Step back Sally, Sally, Sally. Step back Sally, all night long. Strolling down the alley, the alley, the alley. Strolling down the alley, all night long. This is the way you willow-bee, willow-bee, willow-bee. This is the way you willow-bee, all night long. Step back Sally, Sally, Sally—

CHARLOTTE: Can I play? Can I play?

SUE: Can't you read? Are you blind? Don't you see you aren't our kind?

BOB: Stink fink not worth a wink, go jump in the lake and sink, sink, sink.

SALLY: Stink fink not worth a wink, go jump in a lake and sink, sink, sink.

GANG: Stink fink not worth a wink, go jump in a lake and sink, sink, sink.

CHARLOTTE: Stink fink not worth a wink, go jump in a lake and sink, sink, sink.

JANE: Monkey see, monkey do, monkey spelled Y-O-U.

BOB: Y-O-U spells O-U-T.

ANNA: O-U-T spells out.

CHARLOTTE: Sticks and stones may break my bones, but words will never hurt me.

BOB: Rain, rain go away. Little Mary wants to play.

GANG: Rain, rain go away. Little Mary wants to play.

CHARLOTTE: You're not bad, you just smell bad.

BOB: Eeny-meany-miny-moe.

SUE: Catch a *victim* by the toe.

FRANK: If she hollers let her go.

ANNA: But what if she won't holler?

BOB: Stamp her!

FRANK: Squeeze her!

SALLY: Squash her!

SUE: Bleed her!

BOB: Stamp her!

JOE: Squeeze her!

JANE: Squash her!

BOB: Bleed her!

> *The Gang forms a line and grabs hold of elbows to become a train, then moves about chanting and making train sounds.*

GANG: Stamp her! Squeeze her! Squash her! Bleed her! Stamp her! Squeeze her! Squash her! Bleed her! Stamp her! Squeeze her! Squash her! Bleed her! Stamp her! Squeeze her! Squash her! Bleed her! Stamp her!

> *Charlotte joins the train and begins playing, too. Bob sees her.*

BOB: Freeze!

> *All action stops. Bob leads The Gang in forming a circle around Charlotte. Sue confronts Charlotte.*

SUE: Put your foot on my foot. *(Charlotte remains still.)* If you don't I'll knock you down.

> *Charlotte puts her foot on Sue's foot. Sue knocks her down. The Gang laughs and makes faces at Charlotte.*

BOB: Last one in the field got two left feet.

> *Charlotte is left sprawled on the ground. She gets up finally, then returns to play with her doll.*

CHARLOTTE: Aunt Dinah's dead. How'd she die? Oh, she died like this and she died like that. She died like this and she died like that. She died like this and she died like that . . . all night long. Hide spy, mickey-moe-rye, snatch a victim from the sky. Fly to the east. Fly to the west. Trap the victim in her nest. Ready or not you shall be caught. Here I come with my eyes wide open. Too late. Too late. The door is locked and you're too late. Stamp her! Squeeze her! Squash her! Bleed her! Stamp her! Squeeze her! Squash her! Bleed her! This is the way you willow-bee, willow-bee, willow-bee. This is the way you willow-bee, all night long. Stamp her! Squeeze her! Squash her! Bleed her! Stamp her! Squeeze her! . . . Stink fink not worth a wink, go jump in a lake and sink, sink, sink.

> *The Gang returns playing follow the leader. Bob leads as if they were airplanes. The Gang makes proper sounds for the game. They move all about the play area making various patterns. Then Bob suddenly breaks away from The Gang, snatches Charlotte's doll from her, and begins a game of catch with the doll. Charlotte runs around trying to get her doll. Finally she attacks one of the members of The Gang. The entire Gang runs into her and knocks her down. The Gang moves away from Charlotte, leaving her on the ground. They join hands and form a circle about Charlotte.*

CHARLOTTE: My bread is burning.

GANG: You can't get out.

CHARLOTTE: My stove is burning.

GANG: You can't get out

CHARLOTTE: My house is burning.

GANG: You can't get out.

CHARLOTTE: My baby's in it.

GANG: You can't get out.

CHARLOTTE: She's all alone.

GANG: You can't get out.

CHARLOTTE: She's all alone.

GANG: You can't get out.

CHARLOTTE: She's all alone.
GANG: You can't get out. You can't get out. You can't get out. You can't get out.
CHARLOTTE: Button, button, who's got the button?
GANG: You can't get out. You can't get out.
CHARLOTTE: Eeny-meany-miny-moe.
GANG: You can't get out. You can't get out.
CHARLOTTE: Eeny-meany-miny-moe. Catch a—
BOB: Victim by the toe.
GANG: You can't get out. You can't get out. You can't get out. You can't get out. *(The Gang exits, one by one, in different directions, leaving Charlotte alone.)* You can't get out. You can't get out. You can't get out. You can't get out.
> *Charlotte is left alone. Shes goes to her doll, holds it close to her, and cries.*
CHARLOTTE: I can't get out. I can't get out. I can't get out.
Curtain

Dirty Hearts

SONIA SANCHEZ

PERSONS:
FIRST MAN, SECOND MAN, SHIGEKO, CARL, THE POET.
Two men are sitting at a table playing cards. They are neither young nor old. There are three empty chairs around the table. The lighting is dim.

FIRST MAN, *throwing the cards across the table petulantly:* I don't like it. let's wait for them. i don't like to play cards with one person; everything is known then. i like the suspense of crowds when i play. where are they today? i don't like to be kept waiting. *(Rises and lights a cigarette.)* that was one of the irritating qualities Helen had—always late *(laughs)*—even in sex. the night i decided to leave, she had a hysterical orgasm— the first one we had ever had together; if you'll excuse the fabricated ones she had before we were married. years togetha and she never once enjoyed touching my body swollen with love.

SECOND MAN, *still holding his cards but concentrating on the room:* today—have you noticed that today is quiet. extraordinarily quiet. listen. there's no noise coming from the streets. there's something different, i don't exactly know. like a yellow contagion left over from the nite. a quarantine of kind. some permanent isolation invading our world. don't you feel it?

FIRST MAN, *looking scornfully at second man:* sometimes i think i am a fool to live with you, a fool in search of perpetual frolic. i did not leave my wife, i did not walk out of that nest of congruity—from that female institute of intuition—yes, one wife and three gangling girls—to listen to this drivel that leaks from your conscience. *(Walks to the window.)* it is only cloudy today. i would say that it's cloudy on the average of once a week, and this week is no different from any other.

A girl enters the room. She wears a print dress and a beach hat that covers most of her face. She sits in a chair, her back to the audience.

FIRST MAN: hello, Shigeko. you're first. everyone is late. did you have much to do today? is she working you very hard?

SHIGEKO, *speaking English slowly and hesitantly:* no, your wife had no need of me today. she said she wanted to be alone. i left the house early—i wanted to walk, i wanted to feel this city, the pavement pressed by thousands of people, under my feet. i felt very sad; i felt as if i had forgotten something, but i did not know what it was; so i had no place to go. i miss perhaps my beautiful, leveled country.

SECOND MAN, *jokingly:* walking among these leisured ruins is not protocol for a young girl, Shigeko.

FIRST MAN, *looking meaningfully at second man while moving toward Shigeko:* i know exactly what you mean, Shigeko. you are lonely, but listen to it while it lasts. loneliness selects the sensitive people, the people who care and feel all the stupid faces of the world staring . . . if your work is too tiring, i'll find you another position, something easier since you are now in school.

SHIGEKO, *apologetically:* everything is fine, everything is all right, everything. all has been reduced to its simplest terms for me. you are a kind man. america is kind, it's merely that today, something about this day *(hands move nervously)* that makes me want to keep moving—to run and talk to strangers.

SECOND MAN, *sitting forward:* you feel it also, this blanket covering the day? is there noise outside? isn't there an active quiet about us, an isolated virus where you have been?

FIRST MAN: will you please shut the hell up or get out. *(Turns to Shigeko.)* take off that hat, you don't need it here. let's start our game.

Shigeko rises—removes her hat and takes a chair facing

*the audience. Her face is heavily made-up—but from the
nose downwards the face is disfigured.*
i am tired of waiting for the others.

SECOND MAN, *picking up cards and beginning to shuffle; repeating softly:* where you have been ... where you have been
... *(Looks at Shigeko.)*
i have been amid organized death that hurried
i have been at

SHIGEKO, *softly:* sea among charitable waves
i have been forgotten by those who once knew me
i have been alone.

i have been under bleached skies that dropped silver
i have been open flesh replaced by commemorative crusts
i have been taped.

i have been specific among generalities
i have been fed residual death in a bottle
i have been mourning for sterile faces
i have been obliged.

FIRST MAN: if you two have ceased your negative reminiscences,
perhaps we can begin.

SHIGEKO, *quietly:* i feel no bitterness, you know. i said those
words an evening long ago when i was still sensitive about
people staring. when i saw you looking, i had been remembering the past, when i used to run on my own hill in my
country—i was racing the skies and singing to the blossoms
that blessed our war-torn land; and my face tingled with the
day's color and my blood young and life. i was angry because
you made me remember. i am not bitter now. you did not
know what would happen—you didn't do it—it was someone
else who made the decisions—removed from you. i am grateful to be alive.

> *The doors open and a Black man enters. He carries a
> briefcase, bulging with papers. Cool drops of sweat pour
> from his head as he falls into the chair—his back is to the
> audience.*

FIRST MAN: well Carl, it's about time. you will have to delegate some of your responsibilities. this is the second time this week you've been late. but now, we can start the game.

> *A game begins. It is called Dirty Hearts. All of the cards are dealt out. Each person plays his cards slowly and as the cards diminish a slight tension develops among the players until each one separately looks at Carl. Then the first man slaps a card on the table triumphantly.*

CARL: why me again, today? i received the queen of spades yesterday. i don't deserve it. you had a chance to give it to both of them—but you waited like the controlled . . . *(Pause.)* i am finished. i don't want to play this childish game. i have too many important things to think about. *(Rises.)*

FIRST MAN: well—then perhaps we will discontinue playing your childish game of "who am i today?"

CARL, *turning excitedly:* what do you mean? everyone here knows who, what i am. i am a blk/capitalist. i am the president of Lanson and Company. i am in control of a company. i worked my way up from a stock clerk, yes a stock clerk to the top. i am the american way of life; i am the american dream. *(Picks up his briefcase.)* you see these papers—contracts, decisions to be made—people to meet and persuade to deal with me—trips to be made—schedules to follow. all of this i am—powerful, by hard work, constant ambition, constant awareness that the company needed me and *(sits down)* wanted me. *(Pause.)* where are the refreshments today? i think we need a drink. *(Moves over to bar and fixes a drink.)* this day is strange. i've had the feeling today that if i screamed no one would hear me, not that i entertained any such nonsense, but it is as if we are playing records and no music is heard.

SECOND MAN, *almost to himself:* yes, i know. i feel it and i haven't been outside, in fact, not since the last time. but, it is here again. three months ago it was like this also. what will save us today?

CARL, *glass in hand; sitting down to face the audience:* i had a dream last night. the first dream i have ever had or remembered. i was in a strange place—a southern town and i was picked up for vagrancy by the police. they took me to their country club for questioning. then i was released and escorted to a dining room. two waiters brought food and when i asked for silverware they laughed and the lights grew dim. they repeated this many times until the policemen came and took me to a hotel. there i filled out a card and gave it to a clerk who looked at me and threw the card away saying "it says where do you come from boy. write the truth." i repeated i am from N.Y. City. this continued until the discarded cards began to circle the room, drawing near me, suffocatingly. i screamed you dirty crackers—all of you—*(Rises.)* you dirty crackers, listen and laugh. *(Pause.)*

i come from white shadows that hide my indigence
i come from walking streets that are detoured
i come from pushing wagons that do not turn
i come from indifference.
i come from uncut cloth that patterns me
i come from vague violets, gift-wrapped by slum-parked
    thoughts
i come from hate.
i come from men who assume no responsibilities
i come from their wives who claw in the darkness
i come from white spit foaming with militant bubbles
i come from hell.

then they came toward me and beat me over and over, and over. and i laughed until my body began to shake with the knowledge that they couldn't hurt me and i laughed & rolled on the floor until it divided, was separated. and the cuts began to heal miraculously. and still i laughed. each day i looked at them from my side and laughed until i was a boy again. *(Sits down and begins to laugh softly.)*

   The first man rises, genuinely moved, and pats Carl on the
   back.

FIRST MAN, *meditatively:* yes we all dream for our analysts. i dreamed last night that i had a villa in italy. i was waiting for someone. and ten years passed. the servants were eunuchs;

and one remained with me at all times. i had peace, quiet, and protection anyone would envy. one night she came. she wore a blue chiffon gown that smelled of garden flowers. we loved the night into day. when i awoke she was gone and i cried in rage as i saw the young leaves falling from the trees. *(Pause.)* it is funny—i remember the servants were smiling and their smiling faces grew larger & larger each year.

> *During the above, the Poet enters the room and listens. He leans against the door.*

POET: if we lived our feelings we would not have to dream among cloistered rooms *(smiles)* although i live a constant dream, but poets are always alone, or lonely, while they put life at rhythmic ease. *(Pause.)* however i came to say that i cannot stay. i am at work on a poem concerning the aegean sea.

SECOND MAN: you write of seas, pianos and paintings that have had their say. i remember you used to write about life and people and flowers bent against the sky. are we so horrible now that you turn to dead things?

POET: i write about old things, past things, perhaps dead things because i am dead and at ease with my contemporaries. i no longer write about you—or Shigeko or Carl. you are the world's painful propanganda. my legends are tried and true. do u know i have discovered a new myth. her name is Masturbas. i have an outline for a long poem. i can make her beauty from the past. the one true beauty. i see her face as i tour my rooms. i touch her face as we kiss & we are one. happy. i return to this world breathing the past's ancient fumes. then i can sleep. *(Pause.)* i must go. but before i go, since we are reflecting today, i will tell u where i am going in young words. in words i said once long ago. *(Laughs.)* remember, i was drunk one nite. bloody drunk. i had just returned from jail. and we were celebrating my triumphant display of humanity over the bestiality of our society. suddenly i was tired and attempted to leave and when i was asked where i was going, *(laughs)* especially since there was no place for me to go to, i turned and said archly

i am going among neutral clouds unpunctured
i am going among men unpolished
i am going to museums unadorned
i am going home.
i am going to change congenital poverty
i am going to hold young heads in my hands and turn them
    slowly
i am going to cry.
i am going amid striped weaves forever winding
i am going unstyled into a cave
i am going in the blue rain that drowns green crystals
i am going to die.
(Pauses.) well enough of me and young dreams. i shall return
tomorrow when the nites suspend their images and the day
falls like a copper penny on my old face. for the days bring
reality of friends, hellos, eating & digesting food, while the
nites receive the tears of disillusioned old men who have lost
themselves among unseeing sights. *(Exits.)*

FIRST MAN: well he had another good load on. i wonder who
has recently rejected his plea of love. come let's play another
hand. we have time *(Shuffles the cards and the game begins.)*
    *The game proceeds as the other. There is little excitement
    in the beginning but when the cards diminish the first man
    gives the queen of spades to Carl.*
    *Carl looks. Then he begins to laugh. He picks up his cards.
    Looks and laughs again. He rises and falls on the floor
    laughing.*

FIRST MAN: come Carl. can't you take a joke? i knew you didn't
expect it again today and i couldn't resist the temptation. you
should have seen the look on your face. why . . .
    Carl continues to laugh.

SHIGEKO: please Carl. stop. we'll play bridge. i know how u like
to play. we'll be partners again & bid seven no trump. *(Pause.)*
please stop your laughter, it doesn't help. we'll play bridge and
beat them unmercifully. please Carl—
    Carl continues to laugh.

FIRST MAN, turning to second man: well say something. u are always talking. do something. he's hysterical. maybe a dunk or a slap. . . .

SECOND MAN, *holding his cards, singing:*
sometimes i feel like a motherless child
sometimes i feel like a motherless child
sometimes i feel like a motherless child
a long way from home sweet home
a long way from home. *(Continues to hum softly.)*
> *First man rises and bends to pick up Carl. Carl pulls away, still slightly laughing. He turns around and picks up his briefcase, moves toward the door. He turns reeling.*

CARL: listen u dirty crackers, all of you, u dirty crackers. listen and laugh. you hear me. listen & laugh. i am an ex-social worker. now i own a furniture store. a goddamn ordinary furniture store and nothing else. *(Exits.)*
> *A loud shriek is heard from the streets. It is Carl. Then other noises appear and his scream is dissolved by the everyday noises now entering the room. The room light ens.*

SECOND MAN, *softly:* and we offer human employment to those who have known so little humanity. *(Turns to Shigeko.)* what will u become Shigeko? a doctor, or a tender nurse in white?

SHIGEKO, *softly:* i think i shall become a nurse and treat new wounds already closing. i will give the medication of blue winds that stir dead tissues. i will bring love to man & spread its carriage over the universe until we forget the clouds & taste the sweet rain.

SECOND MAN, *softly:* we will not know u when you come.

FIRST MAN: ignore him Shigeko. imagine that from Carl. *(Pause.)* & all because of a little joke. well i have an appointment with a beautiful lady. i'll see u home Shigeko. *(Rises and begins to ready himself. Turns to second man.)* I won't come in tonight. we will talk tomorrow. & stop looking your excess of pity and sorrow. we did not make the world & her numerous problems. Carl is weak. i can't tolerate weak people. they make me nauseous. one of the most irritating qualities Helen had was her ability to feel sorry for people & to blame herself constantly for their predicaments. *(Has completed his grooming.)* let's go Shigeko.

SHIGEKO, *putting on her hat; turning to second man:* i'll see u saturday. maybe saturday will not bring the drumming of negligence. perhaps i will bring a funny story that will pierce these rooms. goodbye. *(Exits.)*

SECOND MAN, *sitting and listening:* no. it is not today. perhaps tomorrow. we will feel completely this conquering order. not today. the screams of the earth were once constant. what happened? now no one screams. hardly ever. will there be someone tomorrow to break the quiet? who is left now? *(Pause.)* who is left now besides the egoists? who is left now besides the breathers of forward lives who leave the noise of mankind bottled on a distant shore? who is left now besides the sitters? *(Rises. Goes to the window. Turns toward chair. Then suddenly exits.)*

> *Nine people pass on the stage in rows of threes. Three are ≅ to Shigeko, three to Carl, three to the Poet. They circle the stage, turn and look at the audience, and exit.*
>
> *Two men enter the room. They are neither young nor old.*

A Sense of Environment:
Director, Designer, Composer

Interview With John Emigh:
A Director's Sense of Environment

QUESTION: Could you describe Robinson Hall, the Economics
building at Brown University, that you used as an environmental setting for *Marat/Sade*?

EMIGH: It's a New England Gothic horror; beautiful and ugly.
All gray stone on the outside and chipped green plaster on the
inside. Very institutional: it was a library before it became the
Economics building. It even has white porcelain fountains.
I'm told that there is no wood in the building: nothing organic. It's all stone, procelain, and plaster—supposedly the
first fireproof building in America. Most important for us,
access to all rooms in the building is channeled through a
large central rotunda with a marble floor, an iron dome, and
two iron-railed octagonal balconies sandwiched in between.
Narrow iron stairways connect the three visible levels and
another stairway leads off the rotunda to a basement.

QUESTION: How did you use this space in staging the play?

EMIGH: Most of the action took place on the marble floor of the
central rotunda. As the audience entered, patients were being
brought out, exercised, given rub-downs. Sade's dais was set
up in one corner of a maroon square on the floor and Marat's

tub in the opposite corner. Once the rub-down benches were cleared out of the central square, the area created looked a little like a boxing ring. The audience occupied the balconies. They were ushered in through iron gates, past the gathering patients, up the stairs, and to their seats by those attendants who weren't busy giving rub-downs or preparing for de Sade's play. Then they watched the play—or most of it—from the top.

QUESTION: The audience arrangement sounds somewhat similar to the one Grotowski used in his production of *The Constant Prince*. The effect he achieved has been likened to that of medical students watching an operation. Were you after a similar effect?

EMIGH: Something like that. Actually, I hadn't seen any of Grotowski's work at the time. I finally got to see *The Constant Prince* at the Shiraz Festival in Persia last summer, and when I saw it, I realized that there were some important differences. In *Marat/Sade*—particularly as we staged it—the audience members are not only witnesses, they're important participants. Weiss casts the audience members as invited guests to de Sade's play—a role, perhaps the only role, that they can play with a minimum of self-consciousness. De Sade's play has to be thought of as a very special event at the Charenton Asylum and the treatment of the audience is the key to creating the specialness. Coulmier is excited and solicitous. De Sade knows who his audience is, where they are, and how they're responding to his play at every moment. The patients recognize the audience members as participants, too. They stare and point at them, talk to them or touch them as they are ushered through the rotunda. Like medical students, the audience members are ushered to a safe, isolated position; but their safety and isolation are imperfect and can be challenged at any moment. The challenges came with increasing force. Coulmier sat in a special section of the second balcony with his family and guests and had to make occasional descents onto the ground floor, excusing himself as he hurried past the audience members. Attendants patrolled all the areas and moved freely from level to level. The orchestra was set off in an area on the first balcony. The four singers—all trusties—ranged the balconies during their songs. At intermission, the audience was encouraged by Coulmier and the attendants to have lemonade and cookies below and to meet some of the more trusted and docile patients. The less trustworthy, more violent patients were locked up during this time. A complex set of disciplinary rules was established. Any patient caught begging a cookie or glass of lemonade from an audience member for example was himself locked up. Finally, at the time of the riot, the audience's isolation, the feeling of safety as spectators, was challenged. Some patients rushed the stairs and had to be beaten back by attendants. One patient, an acrobat, scaled the balconies, walked around on the railings and was chased by the attendants, while other attendants hastily lowered rope ladders to reach and subdue the rioting patients below.

QUESTION: Were the sections in which the actors dealt directly with the audience improvised?

EMIGH: They had to be improvised, but definite patterns emerged based on the characters developed. Many of the patients said nothing at all. One cast member, for example, was playing a former priest who had been seized in a mass lynching. The rope had broken, he had survived, but he thought that he was dead and was waiting for his fate to declare itself. Perhaps he was in hell, purgatory, even heaven? In any case, it wasn't for him to speak. Another patient, who had wanted to be cast as Simonne Evrard, was furnished a crude miniature bathtub and a cloth doll and spent her time wordlessly playing with the doll, or punishing it, or protecting it from audience members. Some patients, of course, were more vocal. Cucurucu kept seeking praise for his singing. Another patient developed a penchant for touching the guests' eyelashes and saying "good-girl," "good-girl," "good-girl," whenever reproached. The attendants had their rules to enforce, Coulmier was busy introducing people and being charming, and de Sade was interested in people's reactions to his play. The audience was a good bit less predictable. Some of their reactions were startling, in at least one instance even frightening. Some people would get very upset that the actors wouldn't break character during intermission. One night, an audience member started filling his mouth with lemonade and squirting it at the patients behind bars. Twice, audience members started attacking attendants during the riot and had to be calmed by Coulmier. The frightening thing happened when someone in the audience got carried away and tried to push the acrobat off the iron railing of the second balcony. I didn't hear about that until after the show had closed, and it still scares me to think about it.

QUESTION: Schechner says the opposite of total transformation of space is found space. Were you dealing only with found space in Robinson Hall? Or did you try to transform the space in any way?

EMIGH: There were some changes made. All the corridors off the ground floor rotunda were turned into barred and padded cells. Pine-Sol was used to mop down the floors, leaving its familiar antiseptic stench. It took over twenty gym mats and 200 yards of flannel bunting to damp an eight second echo. But reminders were also left of the building's usual use and appearance. The electric lights, steam radiators, and porcelain fountain were all used. The "Please Be Quiet" sign under the electric clock stayed up too. I don't think the anachronisms hurt; perhaps they helped. After all, the audience isn't going to come dressed in Napoleonic clothing, even if Coulmier and his family are. The name of the building was changed to Charenton Asylum; but names of Brown's economics professors stayed on the permanent directory, right under Coulmier's. Whenever possible, I like to set up a dialectic between a place's ordinary appearance and use and its theatrical appearance and use—between the everyday space and the special event—between the present and history. I especially liked the

irony of performing *Marat/Sade* in the Economics department, and I liked the idea that students would re-enter the
building for their classes with some new associations with the
place.

QUESTION: What about Churchill House, the space used for *The
Pilots?*

EMIGH: There again, there was a mixing of found and transformed spatial elements. Churchill House itself has about it
the sort of misplaced and faded elegance I associate with the
1920's luxury liners. As in *Marat/Sade,* the found and transformed elements in the space were used to mix the present
with the past, the everyday with the special event. The transformations were much more playful, though, and much less
illusionistic. The audience was cast as ripples in San Francisco
Bay, or perhaps they were bits of historical litter, corpses half-
perceived through an orange-scented fog that was dispensed
by a wandering prop man dressed in a black slicker. Yellow-
slickered musicians were stationed with conch shells and
ship's bells among the audience, and pictures of American
style heroism circled around and above the fog, projected
from the ship's balcony and passing over the pilot's boat:
George Washington, Columbus, Chief Joseph, William Henry
Harrison, the Marlboro Man, and many others, along with
visions of Viking ships, clipper ships, and modern battleships.
I wanted to reproduce the script's blend of mockery, nostal-
gia, and that peculiar passion for strange, real information as
it approaches the heroic myths of the American past.

QUESTION: Do you find proscenium and thrust stage arrangements completely outdated?

EMIGH: Not necessarily. What is outdated for me is the concept
of theatre as an illustrative art: as a series of moving pictures
set off on a stage to illustrate an author's words. Theatre is a
spatial art as well as a temporal one and the only rule is to use
the space and time as imaginatively and communicatively as
possible—and that includes the space where the audience sits
or stands or lies ... once—a way of giving actions new em-

phasis. The trouble is it worked too well; it, too, became commonplace and conventional; it got to be a bore—one thing that theatre should never be. Perhaps now that the proscenium stage is no longer a given condition for theatrical creation, we can begin to find, or re-find, its present usefulness. Ironically, what was invented as an aid to achieving stunning effects of illusion in the theatre now seems to work best for alienated or abstracted dramatic forms—melodrama, farce, Brechtian history plays—where the tired conventions can be confronted and, in the confrontation, given life again.
. . .

QUESTION: Two completely opposing tendencies seem to be inherent in today's theatre—the nihilistic or anarchistic production where anything goes and, at the other extreme, the highly disciplined productions of Grotowski with their quest for aesthetic perfection. How do you view these tendencies?

EMIGH: I'm not so sure the terms you use have to describe opposing tendencies; insofar as they do describe opposing tendencies, I think that it's unfortunate—perhaps especially so in American theatre. I admire Grotowski's work greatly, but his theatrical style and form just don't fit our special needs, myths, or even what's best in our theatrical traditions. The joyless dialectic of Catholicism and Communism simply doesn't apply. Anyone wanting to set down guide lines for theatrical impulses still viable in America should remember the Marx Brothers along with Artaud. After all, we're a whole nation of runaway slaves, and we seem to be at our best when we remember that. Harpo Marx may be an anarchist, but I wouldn't call him a nihilist, and he is certainly not without discipline. It's not an easy balance to hit. Barrault's *Rabelais* came off as precious, sterile, oddly lifeless in this country. On the other hand, much of the recent work in New York— O'Horgan's, for example, or the Ridiculous Theatre Company's, does come across as slop—for all the startling visual effects, adolescent and decadent at the same time; peculiarly narcissistic. Maybe that's inevitable. Perhaps our society, finding its long-prized virginity lost, has entered a long delayed adolescent stage. Still, the Open Theatre has impressed me consistently with its capacity to combine discipline with a sense of anarchistic play.

QUESTION: What about the problem of audience participation?

EMIGH: The problem is both formal and ethical. It's easy to either insult the audience by throwing in token bits of manipulated "participation" or to make formal promises of free response that can't be fulfilled. In *Paradise Now*, the Living Theatre built up an illusion of freedom which they couldn't support within the forms they had devised. One of the most exciting things about *Dionysus*—at least on the night that I saw it—was the way in which the audience was made secure as to when the form allowed participation and when it made participation inappropriate.

QUESTION: Can you remember some of the guerrilla theatre events you helped to formulate in the "strike" events in Providence following the Cambodian invasion in 1970?

EMIGH: Most of the activity was downtown, at the Westminster shopping mall. The attempts there ranged a good bit in intent, effectiveness, and degree of self-indulgence. At first, we tried some of the traditional shock-theatre techniques: soldiers tying up young people and shooting them, etc. I had staged Bob Head's *Kill Viet Cong* in New Orleans in 1965, but techniques that had seemed helpful then seemed at best self-indulgent at a time of psychological crisis when people's stock patterns of thought had already been jarred by history. So we (myself, Bob Bailey, Andy Arnault, Ray Mostel, Billy Siegenfeld, and many others) decided to drop all pretense of being anything but actors and started appearing at odd hours with huge puppet masks of Nixon and Agnew that a student named John Beatty had built. The masks drew a crowd very quickly. Most of the time we mimed articles read from the morning newspaper—reports of Spiro Agnew's speech at the confederate monument, for example. On the best day, we followed up on one of Agnew's own suggestions and brought a Roman

Catholic priest with us to read from *Jeremiah*. The material usually proved very provocative. Hecklers would soon start in and the focus would shift away from the performed actions and onto the issues. Sometimes, people would continue talking and arguing in small groups for up to a half hour. It was a very primitive form of theatre. The whole point was to grab attention and focus that attention on the forces at work in the nation, including the forces at work in our own minds and in the minds of the audience members. When it worked, people were sometimes surprised by their own thoughts and arguments. It was hard to jettison 90% of one's craft, but it seemed to be what history was demanding.

Other events took place—mostly symbolic gestures. Along the route of the march to the state house that followed the Kent State killings, about ten sets of actors held friezes based on the famous newspaper picture with the girl screaming. There was a gory funeral procession on campus after the Jackson State and Augusta killings in an effort to drive home the racist implications of the student reaction to Kent State. At the graduation procession a group of students set up grave markers for Schwerner, Goodman and Cheney, Fred Hampton, the murdered students of Kent and Jackson State, the Vietnam war dead, and others, and played an alternate cadence to the traditional graduation march. The puppet heads of Nixon and Agnew were worn on a balcony overlooking the graduation ceremonies and students and professors held up bananas when, in the tradition of university neutrality, the Ambassador to Guatemala was awarded an honorary degree. We didn't come up with any images as appropriate or effective as Christ's miracles, or the Boston Tea Party, or the Indians' burial of Plymouth Rock this past Thanksgiving Day, but it seemed necessary to try.

By graduation time, the heckling downtown had begun to abate; the crisis mentality had faded. People had gone back to their own patterns of thought or maybe some had found new ones, but in any case we had become superfluous. A few of us went down to New York to see if anyone had any better ideas as to how to continue, but the same thing had happened there. *Life* had gotten a few pictures, history had moved on; we had been a small part of it, and God knows if we had helped its course.

QUESTION: What are the possibilities and disadvantages of playing outdoors?

EMIGH: I like the open feeling in the audience, the use of natural settings, the bringing of theatre out of its guarded official boxes. I'd like to stage some small events outside. This spring, I'll be staging *The Serpent* in an open patio and next year, perhaps, Edwin Honig's adaptation of *Life Is A Dream* in an accidental amphitheatre that was formed when a new graduate center was built at Brown a couple of years ago. There is a huge market square in the old section of Marrakech where snake charmers, cyclists, acrobatic dancers, and story tellers all compete for attention as rings of people form around the various performers. In Persia, the most exciting theatre I saw was an ancient Muslim miracle play, still performed occasionally in the village bazaars. We've lost that sense of theatrical interpenetration with life while trying to turn theatre into a commodity. A lot of people are now trying to regain it.

Slave Ship: Notes and Design

EUGENE LEE

(Slave Ship by Leroi Jones, directed by Gilbert Moses, design by Eugene Lee at the Chelsea Theater Center, at the Brooklyn Academy of Music, Robert Kalfin, Artistic Director, Michael David, Executive Director.)

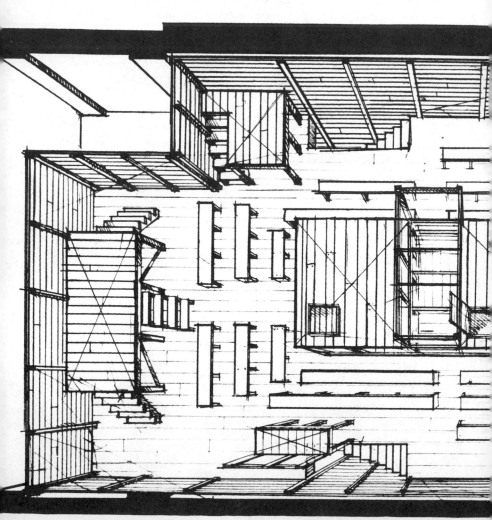

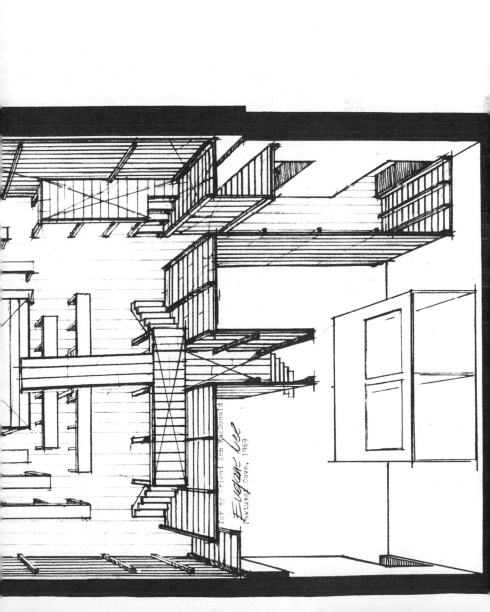

for my friend Ann MacDonald

Eugene Lee
Pawtuxet Cove, 1969

Ugly, ri-dic-u-lous theaters are being built throughout the land. ELECTRONIC lighting control boards, and other USELESS HARDWARE, spreads like the plague. Every city must have its own "Lincoln Center" type theatre. THIS MUST STOP.

I picked up the Jones script in Brooklyn, and had read it ALL by the time I reached Grand Central on the IRT.

I had to rip up the seats, and level the floor of the Chelsea Theater Center. In the center a large platform was constructed on rockers. The audience peers into the narrow space below, to observe the tortured slave cargo; frightened, screaming, vomiting, crying, giving birth. Jones' "Ship" is a metaphor, a symbol, connecting the memory of African roots, with the vicious containment of the present. The ship is the fulcrum from which the play moves both backward and forward in time. Gill Moses staged the piece in a very free form theatrical style, action occurred throughout the room. Smells, . . . incense . . . squeaking, sea smells, urine, dirt/filth smells/bodies . . . EXCREMENT, DEATH . . . LIFE, groovy . . .

Interview with the Composer, Gerald Shapiro

QUESTION: Although you're the director of the MacColl Studio for Electronic Music at Brown University, your major interest seems to be in a kind of live, theatrical music that involves the audience.

SHAPIRO: I don't much want to do tape pieces or incidental music any more. The participation piece (even though that description sounds inadequate) is what I do well and where I think I have something to say. It feels like a necessary thing to be done. The audience must be excited again, involved. I don't think we need albums of electronic music, just as we don't need one more symphony orchestra. What is needed is to heal the split between performer and audience. We're in danger of becoming a nation of watchers, whether it's television, sports, or movies. It's hard to stop watching. It's too easy to accept the fact that someone who has "studied" or is "good" can entertain you better. We find it difficult to realize that the simplest thing you do can become important. We can transform any sound or any action into meaning.

QUESTION: What about the technical limitations of an audience?

SHAPIRO: That's a problem, of course, but somehow perceived sound becomes meaningful. There is much more natural creativity and spontaneity in people, particularly Americans, than they permit themselves to express. If experience and meaning are satisfied, virtuosity is unimportant. Various folk and religious songs are exquisitely composed because they get into your life and don't fool you. I have to care for sound. If you are conscious for sound, you can get really good stuff from a lot of people. When you see the Musica Electronica Viva bringing in sticks and branches to use in one of their pieces, it's beautiful visually. It's a real theatrical event, but then they don't do anything with the potential of sound. There is no real loud or soft, no significant range of dynamics. You can't just give people instruments and ask them to play. I have to invent a musical and theatrical activity that is likely to be turned into meaning. The composer has to break through the barrier of irony and trust himself in relationship to the audience he wants to reach. The process is one of seduction. That's my task.

QUESTION: Do you find the age of audiences a problem? For example, most concert audiences seem to be relatively middle-aged.

SHAPIRO: No, I think a tremendous variety of audiences is still possible, although not, of course, in the usual commercial situations. No one is still fighting a battle against older generations. There is no more Debussy or Satie in music. The concern for a particular, individual, virtuoso style is not what excites me. Of course there are still individual virtuoso composers. My friend, David Rosenbloom, with whom I toured in the summer of 1970, is still involved with virtuosity. His infatuation with Indian music, for example, stems from the fact that their standards of technical excellence are so high. I believe that with theatrical participation pieces, there are things to do that are just right both for performers and audience. Virtuosity is not necessarily essential.

QUESTION: How do you feel about chance, improvisation, in music and theatre?

SHAPIRO: John Cage is germinal to everything, his writing as much as his music. Cage is very charismatic. For everything I say, I probably found the general idea in Cage. His idea of non-involvement, to clean out the ego so you stay smooth inside and don't muck things up with your ego, is terribly important to the arts in this self-pitying, confessional society. Chance and improvising techniques are not just imported haphazardly into my work. They happen as they do in life, but they're not an element with which I'm strongly concerned. If pitches are unimportant, then they can be left up to chance, but not otherwise. Cage is a precise person. Really what he is saying is that a lot of conventional concerns are not central to the essence of music.

QUESTION: Isn't the physical presence of the musician in effect a kind of acting presence? How can you replace this presence with a loud-speaker, a machine, without becoming more mechanical, more impersonal, more abstract?

SHAPIRO: You have to create a rich situation so people will turn things into meanings. At its best certainly electronic music is full of startling, human-connected sounds. Just because the sounds are not instrumental in the traditional performing way doesn't mean that the sounds are necessarily impersonal or abstract. However, for me there is a problem in the absence of the performer and the absence of participation. I've never made taped pieces; the only kind of tape music I've written has been incidental music for plays and theatre pieces. Electronic music is often well-suited for those purposes. Still I prefer the actual participation-piece where a wide range of immediate, personal reactions can be experienced. The best I can do in this regard is make pieces for the little gang of people like me.

QUESTION: In theatre and music today, there seems to be a movement away from tight, controlled rhythms to a much looser, indefinite, prolonged sense of time. In *Silence* John Cage writes: "In Zen they say: If something is boring after two minutes, try it for four. If still boring, try it for eight, sixteen, thirty-two, and so on. Eventually one discovers that it's not boring at all but very interesting." How do you feel about this conception of time?

SHAPIRO: When I'm listening correctly, any sound will do. Again it's a question of participation, of not being passive. Every sound can be interesting, but you have to listen to enjoy the distinction and variety of sounds. It's a great mistake to make the false idea of "Good Music," that seduction, an end in itself. My best experiences in music have come in performing, not listening.

QUESTION: In *Silence,* Cage talks about "the organization of sound" as being more meaningful than the term music. How do you feel about this?

SHAPIRO: It's the organization of sound that the *listener* does that is important. This refers to theatre too. The viewer has to organize space himself. I'm a bad audience member. I fall asleep at concerts. I wish I was performing, not listening. For me the most important part of music making is *doing*. In school I got a charge out of making music, not preparing for a concert. So I grew increasingly interested in participation pieces. Let me say there are lots of fake participation pieces, pieces that are merely indulgent, but I became serious about the possibilities of this kind of work.

QUESTION: Will you describe your participation piece *From the Yellow Castle* that has been widely performed, most recently in New York on your program at Automation House?

SHAPIRO: The work has a very simple structure. The instructions are the score to the piece and read simply as follow:

> Close your eyes.
> Don't initiate any movement; don't hinder any movement.
> Don't imagine any sound; don't ignore any sound.
> When you are finished, help someone else to begin.
> Leave when you like.

From the Yellow Castle may be performed by itself as an evening's entertainment or it may be presented as the last event in a concert. In either case, copies of the score must be printed and circulated among the audience prior to the performance.

There are three smooth, white cylinders, each approximately five feet long by eight inches in diameter. These tubes are equipped to transmit information by radio about their attitude (angles of rotation and inclination). This information is used to control the auditory environment in the performance area.

Six to eight performers manipulate each tube according to the score printed above. A technician controls the amplitude of the various sounds in the room. To begin the piece, the three groups of performers take positions around the performance area. They must have a large flat space as accessible to the audience as possible. Each group gathers around its cylinder, holding it vertically about six inches off the ground. As the technician allows the sound to be heard in the room, the performers close their eyes and begin the piece.

When the piece is fully under way the performers may step away from the cylinders, one at a time, open their eyes, and invite members of the audience to participate in the piece. When an audience member agrees to participate, the performer asks him to close his eyes and slowly and gently leads him by the hand to one of the cylinders. During this time the performer may repeat a few phrases from the score.

After he has replaced himself, each performer has a special responsibility to see that the piece continues to move smoothly. He may continue to bring new audience members up, especially if the audience members forget to replace themselves as they leave the cylinders. He may attach himself to any cylinder which does not seem to be moving well and even repeat pertinent phrases from the score in a soft voice if necessary. Finally, as members of the audience begin to leave, a few performers should stand by the exits and say goodnight, thanking the audience for attending.

The piece continues until all members of the audience who want to participate have had the opportunity to do so.

QUESTION: Have you ever done this piece on a stage?

SHAPIRO: At the University of Illinois, it was done on stage with stage lights of different colors, but I won't do it that way again. It made it too easy for people to watch. People sat in their seats and said "Oh, that's a beautiful piece," which spoiled the whole concept of individual movement and discovery that can illuminate the mind and body.

QUESTION: Please discuss your unusual concept for an environmental score for *The Pilots*.

SHAPIRO: My original idea, which I couldn't quite carry out the way I wanted to, was that the instruments to be performed would actually be the entire set. In other words you would build a set that would be the instruments to portray the environment of the play, the fog, sea, bells, etc. No instrumental music would be played. The whole superstructure representing the ship would be resonant. This idea would extend even to the actors. The floor they walk on might be a giant sheet of metal and every step they took would be music. The sound would grow out of what the performers were doing. Then I encountered the same problem that I've faced working with the technological theatre group in Cambridge, *Zone*, namely that technological devices are often not organically related to people. Apparatus flashes, projections, spinning discs, etc. are often startling when performers move through them, but they're not enough. The effect is often not even as good as people sitting on a classical set. Finally, in *The Pilots* I had to abandon the effects I intended and work in a simpler way.

QUESTION: Your final scheme in *The Pilots* was striking even if not your original conception. Can you describe it?

SHAPIRO: Actors in yellow slickers and hats were stationed around the room playing conch shells with different pitches and ringing bells that merged with the fog machines. I wasn't trying to create so much a realistic sea atmosphere but a sea mystery. The fact that I, the composer, also acted the part of the Pilot who is assassinated in the play, enabled me also to function as a sort of mysterious conductor. This enhanced the visual imagery, the theme of the play about the strange succession of "pilots" that have governed American history and experience. During the course of rehearsals, I gave up the familiar theatrical attempt to make the sounds move to a climax. The interesting thing is that sounds just keep going on. Maybe this is what we're learning from other cultures, particularly eastern cultures, that will help us to relax, forget about the ideas of tension and conflict that have dominated our society.

QUESTION: In your 1971 program at Automation House in New York, you premiered a fascinating new piece. Please describe this.

SHAPIRO: Again it begins with a score of instructions. In New

York, after equipping the participants, a guide led each participant into the dark performance room. As the guide led the participant very slowly into the room, he told him the instructions. It's called *The Second Piece: The One About Finding Your Way In The Dark:*

SCORE

Close your eyes and leave them closed.
Each participant is a sound source.
Each sound source is different.
You are free to move toward or away from any other participant.
You are free to touch any other participant.
Take your time; listen; find your own way.
Signal when you are finished.

Each participant is equipped with a headset and the necessary electronic apparatus for the piece which together form a kind of helmet. Each helmet contains circuitry which transmits a unique, complex, low frequency audio signal by modulating an invisible, infra-red light beam. Other circuitry detects those signals and routes them to the headset. Because of the highly directional, short range characteristics of this type of transmission, each participant will be able to "look" around the performance space and understand the placement and distance of the other participants. The auditory results of this scanning procedure will be a continuous but constantly shifting soundfield as the participant faces in different directions and the other participants move in and out of range. It is also possible for two participants to move toward one another and stop within touching distance of each other relying solely on auditory cues from their headsets. These two actions, scanning and coming together form the first phase of the piece and lead to the second.

The helmets contain, in addition to the circuitry mentioned before, a high frequency (approx. 2 MHz) oscillator whose output makes a direct electrical connection to the skin of the participant and to one imput of a beat frequency detector.

Phase two begins when two, or more, participants touch. At that moment, all transmission and detection of light beam carried signal is turned off for the participants involved and they hear instead a sound whose frequency represents the difference between their individual high frequency oscillators. It is possible to slightly alter this sound by touching more or less firmly. A different sound will result for each pair, or group, of participants touching one another due to differences in skin characteristics and different oscillator frequencies. Participants are free to move at will between phase one and phase two as often as they like.

Finally, each participant is equipped with a device for signaling to the Guides operating the piece when he is finished and wishes to leave.

A performance of THE SECOND PIECE begins with a group of participants being given the helmets and initiated into the possible actions of the piece by means of the score. They are then escorted into the darkened performance space and left to explore the permutations of listening and interaction inherent in the piece. When any participant is finished, he signals to the Guides, and is escorted out of the performance space and replaced by a new participant.

Another aspect of THE SECOND PIECE involves continuous monitoring by several video cameras equipped to detect the infra-red light beams used in transmission. This information is fed to T.V. screens in a space near the performance space to allow participants to see what they are about to experience, or have just come from experiencing in auditory and tactile realms.

QUESTION: Somehow your work seems to create a synthesis of the arts again, yet the concept of a passive audience has disappeared. A piece of yours is extremely theatrical in effect, yet its source is musical.

SHAPIRO: I no longer believe that the sound is the music because there is sound all around us, all the time, and any of it, at any time, may become music. The sound is always there, but we have music only when we listen, only when we listen with that particular kind of listening which we call music. Sound is not an abstraction. It is real, concrete stuff, energy transmitted in the form of vibrations in the air and palpable—at least to the ear. But I believe we share a common experience. By some metaphysical transformation, those vibrations, simple, measurable patterns of acoustic energy, become meaning. We create that transformation. That's where it relates to theatrical transformation. We do it when we listen and move with such total involvement that everything disappears except the listening. It seems to me very beautiful that moment in our lives when sound becomes everything. Then the sound disappears and we have music.

Some of us seem to be able to make music with only a limited variety of sounds. Symphony orchestra conductors are an example. Some people manage it only a few times in their lives. A lucky few seem to be doing it almost all the time. I have done it once with a Bach Prelude and Fugue on earphones in the Sibley Library, once with the cries of gulls and the sounds of wind, water, and bell buoys on Narraganset Bay near my home, once with a performance of Alvin Lucier's *Vespers*. There are others, of course. Together they form the body of experience which led me to become a musician in the first place, and sustains me now.

Grotowski:
The Purest Theatre

Towards a Poor Theatre

JERZY GROTOWSKI

I am a bit impatient when asked, "What is the origin of your experimental theatre productions?" The assumption seems to be that "experimental" work is tangential (toying with some "new" technique each time) and tributary. The result is supposed to be a contribution to modern staging—scenography using current sculptural or electronic ideas, contemporary music, actors independently projecting clownish or cabaret stereotypes. I know that scene: I used to be part of it. Our Theatre Laboratory productions are going in another direction. In the first place, we are trying to avoid eclecticism, trying to resist thinking of theatre as a composite of disciplines. We are seeking to define what is distinctively theatre, what separates this activity from other categories of performance and spectacle. Secondly, our productions are detailed investigations of the actor-audience relationship. That is, *we consider the personal and scenic technique of the actor as the core of theatre art.*

It is difficult to locate the exact sources of this approach, but I can speak of its tradition. I was brought up on Stanislavski; his persistent study, his systematic renewal of the methods of observation, and his dialectical relationship to his own earlier work make him my personal ideal. Stanislavski asked the key methodological questions. Our solutions, however, differ widely from his—sometimes we reach opposite conclusions.

I have studied all the major actor-training methods of Europe and beyond. Most important for my purposes are: Dullin's rhythm exercises, Delsarte's investigations of extroversive and introversive reactions, Stanislavski's work on "physical actions", Meyerhold's bio-mechanical training, Vakhtanghov's synthesis. Also particularly stimulating to me are the training techniques of oriental theatre—specifically the Peking Opera, Indian Kathakali, and Japanese Noh theatre. I could cite other theatrical systems, but the method which we are developing is not a combination of techniques borrowed from these sources (although we sometimes adapt elements for our use). We do not want to teach the actor a predetermined set of skills or give him a "bag of tricks." Ours is not a deductive method of collecting skills. Here everything is concentrated on the "ripening" of the actor which is expressed by a tension towards the extreme, by a complete stripping down, by the laying bare of one's own intimity—all this without the least trace of egotism or self-enjoyment. The actor makes a total gift of himself. This is a technique of the "trance" and of the integration of all the actor's psychic and bodily powers which emerge from the most intimate layers of his being and his instinct, springing forth in a sort of "translumination."

The education of an actor in our theatre is not a matter of teaching him something; we attempt to eliminate his organism's resistance to this psychic process. The result is freedom from the time-lapse between inner impulse and outer reaction in such a way that the impulse is already an outer reaction. Impulse and action are concurrent: the body vanishes, burns, and the spectator sees only a series of visible impulses.

Ours then is a *via negativa*—not a collection of skills but an eradication of blocks.

Years of work and of specially composed exercises (which, by means of physical, plastic and vocal training, attempt to guide the actor towards the right kind of concentration) sometimes permit the discovery of the beginning of this road. Then it is possible to carefully cultivate what has been awakened. The process itself, though to some extent dependent upon concentration, confidence, exposure, and almost disappearance into the acting craft, is not voluntary. The requisite state of mind is a passive readiness to realize an active role, a state in which one does not *"want to do that"* but rather *"resigns from not doing it."*

Most of the actors at the Theatre Laboratory are just beginning to work toward the possibility of making such a process visible. In their daily work they do not concentrate on the spiritual technique but on the composition of the role, on the construction of form, on the expression of signs—i.e., on artifice. There is no contradiction between inner technique and artifice (articulation of a role by signs). We believe that a personal process which is not supported and expressed by a formal articulation and disciplined structuring of the role is not a release and will collapse in shapelessness.

We find that artificial composition not only does not limit the spiritual but actually leads to it. (The tropistic tension between the inner process and the form strengthens both. The form is like a baited trap, to which the spiritual process responds spontaneously and against which it struggles.) The forms of common "natural" behavior obscure the truth; we compose a role as a system of signs which demonstrate what is behind the mask of common vision: the dialectics of human behavior. At a moment of psychic shock, a moment of terror, a mortal danger or tremendous joy, a man does not behave "naturally." A man in an elevated spiritual state uses rhythmically articulated signs, begins to dance, to sing. A *sign*, not a common gesture, is the elementary integer of expression for us.

In terms of formal technique, we do not work by proliferation of signs, or by accumulation of signs (as in the formal repetitions of oriental theatre). Rather, we subtract, seeking *distillation* of signs by eliminating those elements of "natural" behavior which obscure pure impulse. Another technique which illuminates the hidden structure of signs is *contradiction* (between gesture and voice, voice and word, word and thought, will and action, etc.)—here, too, we take the *via negativa*.

It is difficult to say precisely what elements in our productions result from a consciously formulated program and what derive from the structure of our imagination. I am frequently asked whether certain "medieval" effects indicate an intentional return to "ritual roots." There is no single answer. At our present point of artistic awareness, the problem of mythic "roots," of the elementary human situation, has definite meaning. However, this is not a product of a "philosophy of art" but comes from the practical discovery and use of the rules of theatre. That is, the productions do not spring from *a priori* aesthetic postulates; rather, as Sartre has said: "Each technique leads to metaphysics."

For several years, I vacillated between practice-born impulses and the application of *a priori* principles, without seeing the contradiction. My friend and colleague, Ludwik Flaszen, was the first to point out this confusion in my work: the material and techniques which came spontaneously in preparing the production, from the very nature of the work, were revealing and promising; but what I had taken to be applications of theoretical assumptions were actually more functions of my personality than of my intellect. I realized that the production led to awareness rather than being the product of awareness. Since 1960, my emphasis has been on methodology. Through practical experimentation I sought to answer the questions with which I had begun: What is the theatre? What is unique about it? What can it do that film and television cannot? Two concrete conceptions crystallized: the poor theatre, and performance as an act of transgression.

By gradually eliminating whatever proved superfluous, we found that theatre can exist without make-up, without autonomic costume and scenography, without a separate performance area (stage), without lighting and sound effects, etc. It cannot exist without the actor-spectator relationship of perceptual, direct, "live" communion. This is an ancient theoretical truth, of course, but when rigorously tested in practice it undermines most of our usual ideas about theatre. It challenges the notion of theatre as a synthesis of disparate creative disciplines—literature, sculpture, painting, architecture, lighting, acting (under the direction of a *metteur-en-scene*). This "synthetic theatre" is the contemporary theatre, which we readily call the "Rich Theatre"—rich in flaws.

The Rich Theatre depends on artistic kleptomania, drawing from other disciplines, constructing hybrid-spectacles, conglomerates without backbone or integrity, yet presented as an organic artwork. By multiplying assimilated elements, the Rich Theatre tries to escape the impasse presented by movies and television. Since film and TV excel in the area of mechanical functions (montage, instantaneous change of place, etc.), the Rich Theatre countered with a blatantly compensatory call for "total theatre." The integration of borrowed mechanisms (movie screens onstage, for example) means a sophisticated technical plant, permitting great mobility and dynamism. And if the stage and/or auditorium were mobile, constantly changing perspective would be possible. This is all nonsense.

No matter how much theatre expands and exploits its mechanical resources, it will remain technologically inferior to film and television. Consequently, I propose poverty in theatre. We have resigned from the stage-and-auditorium plant: for each production, a new space is designed for the actors and spectators. Thus, infinite variation of performer-audience relationships is possible. The actors can play among the spectators, directly contacting the audience and giving it a passive role in the drama (e.g. our productions of Byron's *Cain* and Kalidasa's *Shakuntala*). Or the actors may build structures among the spectators and thus include them in the architecture of action, subjecting them to a sense of the pressure and congestion and limitation of space (Wyspianski's *Akropolis*). Or the actors may play among the spectators and ignore them, looking through them. The spectators may be separated from the actors—for example, by a high fence, over which only their heads protrude (*The Constant Prince*, from Calderon); from this radically slanted perspective, they look down on the actors as if watching animals in a ring, or like medical students watching an operation (also, this detached, downward viewing gives the action a sense of moral transgression). Or the entire hall is used as a concrete place: Faustus' "last supper" in a monastery refectory, where Faustus entertains the spectators, who are guests at a baroque feast served on huge tables, offering episodes from his life. The elimination of stage-auditorium dichotomy is not the important thing—that simply creates a bare laboratory situation, an appropriate area for investigation. The essential concern is finding the proper spectator-actor relationship for each type of performance and embodying the decision in physical arrangements.

We forsook lighting effects, and this revealed a wide range of possibilities for the actor's use of stationary light-sources by deliberate work with shadows, bright spots, etc. It is particularly significant that once a spectator is placed in an illuminated zone, or in other words becomes visible, he too begins to play a part in the performance. It also became evident that the actors, like figures in El Greco's paintings, can "illuminate" through personal technique, becoming a source of "spiritual light."

We abandoned make-up, fake noses, pillow-stuffed bellies—everything that the actor puts on in the dressing room before performance. We found that it was consummately theatrical for the actor to transform from type to type, character to character, silhouette to silhouette—while the audience watched—in a *poor* manner, using only his own body and craft. The composition of a fixed facial expression by using the actor's own muscles and inner impulses achieves the effect of a strikingly theatrical transubstantiation, while the mask prepared by a make-up artist is only a trick.

Similarly, a costume with no autonomous value, existing only in connection with a particular character and his activities, can be transformed before the audience, contrasted with the actor's functions, etc. Elimination of plastic elements which have a life of their own (i.e., represent something independent of the actor's activities) led to the creation by the actor of the most elementary and obvious objects. By his controlled use of gesture the actor transforms the floor into a sea, a table into a confessional, a piece of iron into an animate partner, etc. Elimination of music (live or recorded) not produced by the actors enables the performance itself to become music through the orchestration of voices and clashing objects. We know that the text *per se* is not theatre, that it becomes theatre only through the actors' use of it—that is to say, thanks to intonations, to the association of sounds, to the musicality of the language.

The acceptance of poverty in theatre, stripped of all that is not essential to it, revealed to us not only the backbone of the medium, but also the deep riches which lie in the very nature of the art-form.

Why are we concerned with art? To cross our frontiers, exceed our limitations, fill our emptiness—fulfil ourselves. This is not a condition but a process in which what is dark in us slowly becomes transparent. In this struggle with one's own truth, this effort to peel off the life-mask, the theatre, with its full-fleshed perceptivity, has always seemed to me a place of provocation. It is capable of challenging itself and its audience by violating accepted stereotypes of vision, feeling, and judgment—more jarring because it is imaged in the human organism's breath, body, and inner impulses. This defiance of taboo, this transgression, provides the shock which rips off the mask, enabling us to give ourselves nakedly to something which is impossible to define but which contains Eros and Caritas.

In my work as a producer, I have therefore been tempted to make use of archaic situations sanctified by tradition, situations (within the realms of religion and tradition) which are taboo. I felt a need to confront myself with these values. They fascinated me, filling me with a sense of interior restlessness, while at the same time I was obeying a temptation to blaspheme: I wanted to attack them, go beyond them, or rather confront them with my own experience which is itself determined by the collective experience of our time. This element of our productions has been variously called "collision with the roots," "the dialectics of mockery and apotheosis," or even "religion expressed through blasphemy; love speaking out through hate."

As soon as my practical awareness became conscious and when experiment led to a method, I was compelled to take a fresh look at the history of theatre in relation to other branches of knowledge, especially psychology and cultural anthropology. A rational review of the problem of myth was called for. Then I clearly saw that myth was both a primeval situation, and a complex model with an independent existence in the psychology of social groups, inspiring group behavior and tendencies.

The theatre, when it was still part of religion, was already theatre: it liberated the spiritual energy of the congregation or tribe by incorporating myth and profaning or rather transcending it. The spectator thus had a renewed awareness of his personal truth in the truth of the myth, and through fright and a sense of the sacred he came to catharsis. It was not by chance that the Middle Ages produced the idea of "sacral parody."

But today's situation is much different. As social groupings are less and less defined by religion, traditional mythic forms are in flux, disappearing and being reincarnated. The spectators are more and more individuated in their relation to the myth as corporate truth or group model, and belief is often a matter of intellectual conviction. This means that it is much more difficult to elicit the sort of shock needed to get at those psychic layers behind the life-mask. Group identification with myth—the equation of personal, individual truth with universal truth—is virtually impossible today.

What is possible? First, *confrontation* with myth rather than identification. In other words, while retaining our private experiences, we can attempt to incarnate myth, putting on its ill-fitting skin to perceive the relativity of our problems, their connection to the "roots," and the relativity of the "roots" in the light of today's experience. If the situation is brutal, if we strip ourselves and touch an extraordinarily intimate layer, exposing it, the life-mask cracks and falls away.

Secondly, even with the loss of a "common sky" of belief and the loss of impregnable boundaries, the perceptivity of the human organism remains. Only myth—incarnate in the fact of the actor, in his living organism—can function as a taboo. The violation of the living organism, the exposure carried to outrageous excess, returns us to a concrete mythical situation, an experience of common human truth.

Again, the rational sources of our terminology cannot be cited precisely. I am often asked about Artaud when I speak of "cruelty," although his formulations were based on different premises and took a different tack. Artaud was an extraordinary visionary, but his writings have little methodological meaning because they are not the product of long-term practical investigations. They are an astounding prophecy, not a program. When I speak of "roots" or "mythical soul," I am asked about Nietzsche; if I call it "group imagination," Durkheim comes up; if I call it "archetypes," Jung. But my formulations are not derived from humanistic disciplines, though I may use them for analysis. When I speak of the actor's expression of signs, I am asked about oriental theatre, particularly classical Chinese theatre (especially when it is known that I studied there). But the hieroglyphic signs of the oriental theatre are inflexible, like an alphabet, whereas the signs we use are the skeletal forms of human action, a crystallization of a role, an articulation of the particular psycho-physiology of the actor.

I do not claim that everything we do is entirely new. We are bound, consciously or unconsciously, to be influenced by the traditions, science and art, even by the superstitions and presentiments peculiar to the civilisation which has moulded us, just as we breathe the air of the particular continent which has given us life. All this influences our undertaking, though sometimes we may deny it. Even when we arrive at certain theoretic formulas and compare our ideas with those of our predecessors which I have already mentioned, we are forced to resort to certain retrospective corrections which themselves enable us to see more clearly the possibilities opened up before us.

When we confront the general tradition of the Great Reform of the theatre from Stanislavski to Dullin and from Meyerhold to Artaud, we realize that we have not started from scratch but are operating in a defined and special atmosphere. When our investigation reveals and confirms someone else's flash of intuition, we are filled with humility. We realize that theatre has certain objective laws and that fulfillment is possible only within them, or, as Thomas Mann said, through a kind of "higher obedience," to which we give our "dignified attention."

I hold a peculiar position of leadership in the Polish Theatre Laboratory. I am not simply the director or producer or "spiritual instructor." In the first place, my relation to the work is certainly not one-way or didactic. If my suggestions are reflected in the spatial compositions of our architect Gurawski, it must be understood that my vision has been formed by years of collaboration with him.

There is something incomparably intimate and productive in the work with the actor entrusted to me. He must be attentive and confident and free, for our labor is to explore his possibilities to the utmost. His growth is attended by observation, astonishment, and desire to help; my growth is projected onto him, or, rather, is *found in him*-and our common growth becomes revelation. This is not instruction of a pupil but utter opening to another person, in which the phenomenon of "shared or double birth" becomes possible. The actor is reborn—not only as an actor but as a man—and with him, I am reborn. It is a clumsy way of expressing it, but what is achieved is a total acceptance of one human being by another.

Dear Grotowski: An Open Letter

ERIC BENTLEY

I won't say I know exactly what theatre is but I know that it is a something in the whole community's network of communications. What is *your* theatre? How does it relate to your environment, the Poland of 1969? There is little of Karl Marx in your theatre, but then there isn't all that much Karl Marx in your Communist Party, is there? So is your theatre a retreat to old Catholic Poland? Your published disclaimer of belief in God doesn't prove it isn't. The Church exists for you, whether God does or not, and the Church has reality for you, whether God does or not; a disproportionate degree of reality, even. Your slogan as a director would seem to be: when in doubt, fall back on ritual. And even the Church never went so far as to believe that in ritual there was salvation.

I am saying that what comes through from your theatre to a radical spectator—and in America very many of your spectators will be radicals—is a certain conservatism. Conversely, it will be our conservative press that will most readily call you avant-garde. Are you a reactionary? And, if not, does your work lend itself to reactionary interpretation and use? What attracted you to Calderon's play, "The Constant Prince"? The tacit assumption that Spain is entitled to a chunk of Africa because its princes are such devout Catholics? A nice retort to Peter Weiss's "Song of the Lusitanian Bogey"!

I'm kidding, but only just. Christianity without belief has a tradition, but an ugly one, one that, for my generation, recalls certain Frenchmen who supported Hitler. Even when not fascistic, that kind of Christianity was snobbish. T. S. Eliot, for example, whom you draw upon, sometimes seemed to suppose that Christianity was beyond the reach of common folk, was a religion for cultivated, superior chaps only. For Pharisees, not for publicans, whores and sinners, let alone fishermen. And such was the spirit breathed by your "Constant Prince," I thought. Not by Calderon's, though judged in our unhistorical way, he was an imperialist. For Calderon believed in a Jesus who, though divine, was no superior chap. Your Constant Prince might equally be called the Good Boy with a Slight Case of Masochism.

Conservatism in art, as is well known, often brings a certain formalism in its train. Your version of Auschwitz in "Acropolis" is over-esthetic and therefore distressingly abstract. Mythological analogies indeed! When the curtain goes up on Peter Weiss's "The Investigation," we see young Auschwitz guards dressed up, as by that time they were in real life, in senility and business suits. For dramatic truth and expressivity, that moment is worth any 15 minutes of your "Acropolis." And in it we forget Peter Weiss as we seldom, if ever, forget you in "Acropolis." Which means that in that moment "The Investigation" is art and not cult of personality. Those who disliked Weiss's show complained that its subject was too unpleasant. Those who liked yours praised various technical devices. In New York, thousands of whose families lost relatives in the extermination camps, you show us an Auschwitz that is of technical interest to theatre students! If that isn't an example of a deplorable formalism, what would be?

Am I too ideological? Very well, let's just speak of your tone, the tone of your book, *Towards a Poor Theatre*, the tone of your program notes, and the tone, apparently taken from you, of all other persons connected with your shows, right down (or up) to the ushers. Not that the ushers are all of one kind. They are of two kinds. Only one is hostile, snippety, peremptory, quasi-military. The other is a little unctuous, mealy-mouthed, and very reverential. Why the absence of humor? Why can no one relax? You have been a traumatic experience for New York and while this might do New York a lot of good, it would certainly seem that our city had a lot to put up with. Have you any idea how many people have suffered rebuff, if not insult, in their attempts to see the Polish Laboratory Theatre? I seem to have spent most of October and November visiting the wounded. Their cries still ring in my ears.

Church doors have not suffered such blows since Martin Luther drove great nails into them—rumor has it that Theodore Mann, for one, went on pounding on yours all through the night and never did get in—though he had tickets. Other luminaries of our benighted American theatre (no irony) got in and roundly declared your theatre was no good anyway. They were so miffed.

And so on. And so forth. A book could be written, and probably will be, on the mess *around* your performances. May it be a better one than yours! Do you realize that the Anglo-American version of your book isn't even in good English? And this was what, for many of us, heralded your visit. Mind you, we could have penetrated bad prose, if that was the only problem, but this, surely, must be a bad book in any language. If there *is* a new theatre, it deserves a properly articulated description, if not a grandly conceived theory. You have made the mistake of publishing a bundle of scraps and *pretending* that it is a worthy manifesto. A book that oscillates between the trivial and the grandiose.

In short, for many of us, your work got the worst conceivable send-off, and don't reply that so many have swooned over you, fawned on you, etc. etc., because we know that is true, and it only made the whole thing all the harder to take. It was not till the evening of your third show that I recovered from the trauma. During this show, "Apocalypsis," something happened to me. I put it this personally because it was something very personal that happened. About half way through the play I had a quite specific illumination. A message came to me—from nowhere, as they say— about my private life and self. This message must stay private, to be true to itself, but the fact that it arrived has public relevance, I think, and I should publicly add that I don't recall this sort of thing happening to me in the theatre before—or even in revivalist meetings, though maybe I haven't attended enough of the latter.

Do I digress? Say so at your peril, for your theatre is redeemed, it seems to me, by just this peculiar intimacy. Peculiar: not the "intimacy" of our own Off Off (off, off, off . . .) Broadway efforts, one part ineffectual goodwill, two parts clumsy aggression. A man shows you his penis, a woman clouts you over the ear, while the whole acting company shouts four-letter denunciations at you—that's our intimacy, our charming "audience involvement." When I see your theatre, and now that I've even got to the detraumatized point where I *can* see it, I note that your work, in this respect as in others, is a corrective to everything that happens here in your name. Any rudeness stops in the lobby. In your theatre a spectator is a person and is allowed to keep his dignity, i.e. his individual separateness. Sometimes your actors come within inches of us, but they never lay hands on us, nor whisper in an individual ear. In the space our body occupies, we are inviolate. Now if the closeness to the actor brings us something extra, the fact that it is not a complete merger like sexual intercourse seems to me equally important, embodying a dialectical law of art according to which, if there is closeness, it must be balanced and, as it were, canceled by distance.

Dignity is involved too. In your conservatism, you aren't afraid of being considered bourgeois when what is bourgeois is rather nice. Chairs are rather nice. The floor is, well, rather uncomfortable and, in New York, extremely dirty. The bourgeoisie's case against discomfort and dirt is definitive. Besides, a third of the American people have bad backs: they need a chair to prop them up. Although you sometimes use uncomfortable benches, I noticed that you had chairs for spectators right next to the ovens of Auschwitz at "Acropolis." Actually, one could have wished they were less near, for it was too comical to see a moustachioed man in mod clothes leaning against a gas oven. That is where I am even more conservative than you, and want my spectators "off stage." But I'm glad you sometimes hold on to chairs: make your American disciples buy some.

"Apocalypsis" is a very beautiful thing. It vindicates your idea of a theatre, and since only 39 other readers of The Times (or some small multiple of 40) will have seen it, I should perhaps tell what it is about: Jesus. Who else? He's your man, if not your Man, and this time you were, in his phrase, a fisher of men and caught him in your net. Him or someone else by the same name. Yes, there was a slight feeling of *déja-vu*, and your program notes spelled out for us the word "Dostoevsky." Who was it said you are antiliterary? You are too literary by half. You have read all European literature, and haven't forgotten nearly enough of it. But, literary though it is in inspiration, your image of Jesus becomes theatrical in its incarnation. That's how it becomes yours and, through the performance, ours.

Yours is a Jesus *sui generis,* a small young Pole, wearing an unbuttoned raincoat over just a pair of black shorts, and carrying a white stick. His eyes protrude. His mouth tends to hang open. He tends to run, to be "on the run." He has a strange, loping way of running, and when other characters stand in his way so he will collide with them, he is as much confused as frightened. Now possibly, as far as this description goes, there is nothing that could not be projected, say, by Marcel Marceau from the stage of a very large theatre. You insist on a very small theatre. Correction. You insist on *no* theatre. What you insisted on in New York was the Washington Square Methodist Church. And when I saw "Apocalypsis" I saw, too, *why* you had been so fussy. Fussiness is the name given to perfectionism by those who see no need of perfectionism. You needed it because, in addition to clear outline, you wished your image to have many delicate, shifting details which would get lost in a larger place. Your non-theatre is so small, it has many of the advantages of movie close-ups. One watches the play of wrinkle and muscle on your actors' bodies.

Here's an aspect of your conservatism that I'd call positive: you have created the conditions in which you can achieve a theatrical equivalent of modern poetry. I call this conservative because the kind of modern poetry your work evokes, and was suggested by, is that of the great, and now long past, generations, the poetry of the Symbolists and (again the name!) T. S. Eliot. Perhaps one would have the right perspective if one were sweepingly to say that the theatre tends to be out of date and that at last, with you, it arrives where poetry was some 50 years ago.

There is a question in my mind whether your work is dramatic. It's certainly lyric. You're a poet. And, as I say, it's theatrical. So it's poetry of the theatre. Drama comes about as a culmination, a kind of grand synthesis, late in any historical sequence (5th-century Athens, Elizabethan England). You, it seems to me, are going back to the beginning, scraping back, as Stark Young once put it (he was a painter), to the design. Stark Young was speaking of Martha Graham, for in America this return to the beginning, the rock bottom, of theatre has chiefly been undertaken by dancers. But you, too, are a choreographer.

"Apocalypsis" presents Jesus and his disciples *by the means of choreography*, and, looking back, I now see much more clearly than I did at the time how "The Constant Prince" and "Acropolis" were put together and how they present themselves to us. I would call your Poor Theatre *elemental theatre* to avoid those jokes about poor theatre at $200 a seat, which is what your tickets were selling for on the black market. Poor Theatre is theatre reduced to its elements, and this not as an economy in the money sense, but as an attempt to discover the necessary by removing anything that might prove superfluous.

In your notes on "The Constant Prince" you congratulate yourself on catching the "inner meaning of the play." Cool it. The inner meaning of a three-act masterpiece cannot be translated into any one-act dance drama. Its meaning is tied indissolubly to its three-act structure: otherwise Calderon himself would have reduced it to one act—he was a master of the one act. What you caught in "The Constant Prince" was the meaning, outer, inner, as you will, of another play, your own, which is vastly simpler and cruder than Calderon's and would probably bore his audience if it could return to life, but which for us is valid and therefore *not* boring. In retrospect, I very much admire the way in which each of your evenings was a *separate* exploration. I understand "environmental theatre" now, just as I now see what intimacy means. In "The Constant Prince," we were medical students looking down on an operating table or a bullfight crowd looking down on the fight. In "Acropolis," we were inside the world of the play and the players—within the electrified barbed wire of an extermination camp. In "Apocalypsis," we were a small group of onlookers, small enough to feel ourselves disciples of the disciples. The decision to limit the number of "customers" to 90 or 100 at the first two plays, and to 40 at the last, may be arbitrary, but, now that we know what you were after, we will grant, that *some* arbitrary figure must inevitably be named. These events are planned as a whole: such and such actors to be seen by so and so many spectators from such and such an angle at such and such a distance.

If I have indicated my initial revulsion from (some aspects of) the first two shows, I should add that I now think of them with much more satisfaction. Can an experience change after the fact? Clearly not, but one can realize after the fact that one had more fun than one has been admitting to. Irritation tends to make one forget, or disregard, non-irritating elements. And you came to us attended by more irritants than anyone in the whole history of the American theatre. The few of us who were lucky enough to see all of your work learned to be grateful for all three shows.

I do not withdraw the criticisms offered above. For one of my temperament and my views, those objections remain, but I can attest that the longer one stays with your work the more one finds to engage attention and even win admiration. More than that: one perceives, finally, that the irritating things (other than those for which you bear no responsibility) are the defects of a quality, the negative aspect of a fanaticism which is your main source of energy. "Fanaticism" is perhaps too strong an expression, but "enthusiasm" would be too weak a one. In uncharitable moments, one thinks of you as self-important. That is the note you sound in your published pronouncements, not least when you tell us you're not as important as all that: when you asked critics to pay attention to the rest of the company, it was as if you wouldn't settle for rave reviews for yourself, you would demand rave reviews for all your pals. But behind your self-importance is your importance.

If, on the one hand, you are conservative and at points even reactionary, you are, on the other, radical in the most radical sense of the word: you are digging for the roots, all the time for the roots of your art, and intermittently for the roots of the unprecedented sufferings of our time, man's unremitting inhumanity to man.

Politically, your theatre would help, I should think, to undermine a bad regime or to bolster a good one. Salud! Fraternally yours . . .

Grotowski in New York

(1)

Respect, tribute come first. Grotowski's Theatre Laboratory brings us a dedication and achievement almost unknown in American theatre. Art seems important again; it *can* change you. Tired of all the commerical intrigue, the false irony and cynicism that surround us, one sees a performance of depth and purity and achieves a new belief in the power of theatre. Another strange thing happens. Americans live from moment to moment, from one changing object to another, new gadgets, new masks to wear. Our sense of history is sentimental; we turn away from the dark roots. Grotowski makes us confront the mystery of the past as it clashes with the present. Seated very close to each other, we seem incredibly distant. Who would have thought that such powerful alienation could be achieved by intimacy. Each actor seems bent on a mysterious journey of exploration. He begins with the celebration of his own physical and mental capacities, but this is not merely an individual actor displaying his personality like the Broadway or Hollywood stereotype. The actor projects into those rare images that signify man's unity, man's hope, man's communion. Here is the true radiance of company—dedicated artists working together to achieve revelation.

(2)

The Poor Theatre. The acceptance of "poverty" in theatre, theatre "stripped of all that is not essential to it." Poor and poverty are suspicious words in a society that prides itself on its power and wealth. Elimination seems to be a key word to Grotowski. Eliminate lighting effects, make-up, costumes, scenery, music. Forget about the experimental American passion for Total Theatre. Return to the core of theatre art which Grotowski believes is the actor. It is easy to understand the necessity to simplify, to return to primal sources, particularly in a society that has suffered devastat-

ing wars and the final psychological and physical disaster of concentration camps. America is no longer exempt in this regard. We
have our own traumas; we profess liberty and independence and
deal with the shadows of militarism and the terrifying concept of
Strategic Hamlets. Still we are committed to technology, to its
beneficial and destructive aspects. We are split and we must deal
with the split in theatre. If we cannot escape from technological
images and subject matter, why should we eliminate all technology
in the theatre? Is it not possible to purify our attitudes about
technology, to use film, rock music, electronic music, lighting,
scenery that really reflect the problems of our existence? While the
advantages of simplifying are many, there is also the danger of
escape. The machines will not go away. Man will never give up the
advantages of technology even though he is faced with its perils.

(3)

Bentley speaks of the problems of Grotowski's conservatism and
over-aesthetic formalism. There is no room for the living playwright in Grotowski's theatre, a man who might give a more
contemporary perspective, yet is is significant that a very important role is played by his literary advisor, Ludwik Flaszen. This
implies a dialectical argument between physical movement and
verbal statement. Is that where theatre really is? Is it not possible
to have a truly revolutionary American company that can deal
with the experience of our country? The advantage of "poverty" is
tempting. Eliminate costs, union problems, even the physical theatre plant. Retire to the country, to houses, to barns. Do the
Grotowski thing. Study, meditate, exercise, rehearse without concern for economic restrictions. The commune as theatrical sanctuary. Little retreats of light all over the country creating civilization
anew.

Already Grotowski's chief disciple in the Pure Theatre, Eugenio
Barba has created an important "monastic outpost" in Holstebro,
Denmark. Grotowski has said of Barba, "He betrayed me, but he
betrayed me well." As Renée Saurel, the French critic, writes in an
article, "Scandinavian Seminary at Holstebro":

Grotowski and Barba share a philosophy of art even more than an aesthetic; they share an ethic founded on deep respect for the human being, which implies rejection of all artificiality and deception ... Like Grotowski's theatre, Odin-Teatret at Holstebro is a research laboratory open to the public. It is a sort of lay monastery located in the country, on a farm which must have been prosperous, to judge by the size ... Everything is marvelously simple, clean, functional; work is performed in a peace and quiet that are almost agonizing for someone fresh from London or Paris ... Like Grotowski, Barba (with the assistance of his literary adviser, Christian Ludwigsen) moves rigorously and scrupulously towards the regeneration of a prostituted art. At Odin-Teatret, research is conducted in an antiseptic milieu. Cupidity and exhibitionism, those wounds of the commercial theater, are unkown. One of the essential factors of this purity is that no theatrical problem is posed in terms of the marketplace. ..."

Despite its great merits, the danger of this purist approach is obvious. A retreat from urban reality, a possible aesthetic preciousness, and in America an anti-intellectual turning away from the great creativity of the sciences. It is amazing how the spreading influence of Grotowski in the United States can lead to evasions that deny Grotowski's great contributions.

(4)

Try to forget for a moment the Grotowski legends. What does one actually experience in New York? The commerical atmosphere that festers immediately around "aesthetically timely" artistic events is sickening. Tickets at ten dollars and rumors of favoritism to the theatrical elite, savage comments about the Grotowski cult, rumors of tickets selling on the black market for $200.00—the exact truth is fogged in by the haze of instant, incriminating publicity that goes with fame today.

Arriving at the theater, which is really the Washington Square Methodist Church, one is forced immediately into a different conception of time than the usual bustling theatre lobby. It is not just that an unpublicized sign announces a later curtain at 9 PM.

People are sitting, standing around the entrance to the church basement. As they wait, talk, and watch, they become a little familiar with each other. One woman is reading Arnheim's *Film As Art*, another the *Village Voice*. Only a hundred are permitted into this performance of *Akropolis* so the atmosphere is entirely different from a mass audience. There is a waiting list of names. A woman enters and asks, "Is this Grotowski?" and puts her name on the ominous waiting list. It is almost the middle of November, 1969, and Moratorium Day (November 15) and draft counseling signs are posted all over the walls. A man mutters, "Coming here to the gas chamber (*Akropolis* is set in Auschwitz) to celebrate Moratorium. It's ironic." A woman says wryly, "In *The Constant Prince* my chin and elbow got sore from leaning on the rail." Another tired woman complains, "I'd better take the pill before I go in. What a week." A man pokes his head through the doorway and asks, "Is this all the people waiting?" Someone smiles back at him, "What do you think this is, a mass theatre?"

Finally, when we are let into the church functioning as theatre, the reason why Grotowski refused to play in Brooklyn becomes clear. Not only the atmosphere of the church, but its height, the ceiling, the windows, the balcony around the stage tell us we are in an unusual place. This in not where we usually see theatre. Can it be that we have become bored with the image of conventional theatres? Space surrounds us, yet the hundred of us are cramped into a relatively tiny area. Everyone here has read or heard that the play is set in a concentration camp. That's too trite—there must be another reason for the confined playing area, the strange way we look at our neighbors from different angles throughout the rectangular stage space. The actors begin. Now it becomes clear. We don't belong to this secret camp world, but somehow we helped to shape it. As Camus wrote in *The Fall*, "A hundred and fifty years ago, people became sentimental about lakes and forests. Today we have the lyricism of the prison cell." Here we are, spectator-ghosts in the lyrical prison cells we have created. Around and through us, the actors drift in their asexual sack costumes and their wooden shoes. How strange that an actor a foot away from me is so distant. I am experiencing an agonizing truth about victim and executioner. The concentration camps were technological dream-models of our fantasies.

(5)

The prisoners are forced to work continuously. Is slave labor the perilous end of a technological dictatorship that is designed for profit and national glory? A heap of junk, dimly lit, is piled in the center of the stage. Rusty metal pipes, heating pipes. A wheelbarrow too. Mechanically, slowly, with a terrifying, condemned rhythm expressing the loss of will, the absence of individuality, the prisoners begin to erect the pipes throughout the audience. The designer, Jozef Szajna,* who spent five years in Auschwitz, invented these images and found these objects originally in junk shops. Invented is the wrong word because they came from his waking nightmares. The tendency to deify Grotowski must be avoided. This production is an extraordinary example of how dedicated theatre comes from collaboration, not from egotistical individuality. Suddenly I am looking at members of the audience and actors through and around an intricate tangle of pipes. Are they building a crematorium? Thank god, I don't know how to feel a crematorium; I can only feel they are building a nightmare. Are they giving the spectator "the association of fire" as Grotowski has said? I don't sense fire, I feel cold. They are building for me the frozen images of humanity. At Auschwitz prisoners of many different nations were brought together to freeze the myth of brotherhood. The original play, Wyspianski's *Akropolis*, describes how during the night of Christ's resurrection, the figures on the royal tapestries in the palace at Krakow come to life and enact key episodes in the history of Poland and western civilization. The play is called *Akropolis* because to Wyspianski the Royal Palace represents the ruined history of Poland, just as the Acropolis represents the ruined history of classical Greece. Auschwitz, now a museum too, is a ruin frozen in time, not only the cemetery of our civilization as Grotowski has said, but a heating pipe architecture of hell

* Cf. "Theatre Journal," pp. 231-237.

that works surrealistically to freeze all familiar human passions, love, freedom, and brotherhood. What is left is only the insane stomping rhythm of the prisoners' wooden shoes struggling to endure in this frozen hell of passion. The shoes, in Grotowski's words, become a paradoxical musical instrument. Occasionally a prisoner plays madly and ironically on a violin—it might be Chagall's fiddler on the roof trying to play a village to life or the devil strumming the violin in Stravinsky's *Histoire du Soldat*. But the shoes have taken the place of music, the shoes of slave labor pursuing their mad, clumping tasks. This rhythm can never be forgotten.

(6)

As in the original *Akropolis*, the prisoners begin to act out their mocking versions of western history. The incredible rhythm of this play is driving towards some Messianic act as in the classical Polish drama, that is clear, but one dreads this apocalyptic event. The prisoners dream of Biblical and Homeric heroes. These heroes who have created man's hopes, his legends of courage, no longer have a shred of free will with which to act. The struggle between Jacob and the Angel strikes me particularly hard. It is that dream fantasy we all have when a shadow figure emerges from our night minds and battles with our angelic concepts, as Rilke shows so powerfully in *The Duino Elegies*. In this camp world, the battle is between two prisoners separated by the wheelbarrow. Jacob, the kneeling prisoner, supports the wheelbarrow on his back, while the Angel lies in the wheelbarrow and tries to crush, to conquer Jacob. Neither can escape from the tool of their labor; the wheelbarrow somehow becomes far more sinister than a machine gun. The wheelbarrow is alive, traveling, working, carrying, and when it stops, men die. They struggle with it, hit it, wrestle with it; it continues on its way inexorably.

Here come the famous lovers, Paris and Helen. Helen is a man. In the institutional prison world, a mocking, sado-masochistic homosexuality takes the place of love. Public rape substitutes for private affection. Against this scene is juxtaposed the marriage of Jacob and Rachel. The bride is a pipe that the prisoner caresses as if it were a woman. A tragic, farcical wedding procession begins. Beneath it, however, is the memory of real marriage—Polish marriage songs are sung. The production is never superficial in its surface imagery. I become more aware of the danger of American irony that is often so purely defensive and remains on the surface.

Yet it is the culminating, tidal surge of the play that really shakes me. No intermission, of course, no time to relax. At last we face the Savior again in Auschwitz. He is the faceless, frozen corpse of our humanity. The prisoners follow a Singer who, like a Priest, leads a procession of death. A Christmas hymn is sung, torn by hysterical sounds of laughter and lamentation. This mad procession reveals the horror of ecstacy. We all want to be shaken out of our commonplace skins and sing transformed in ecstatic air. But ecstacy is intimate with horror as Christ is intimate with begging, flagellation, and crucifixion. At the climax of ecstasy, the Singer shrieks jubilantly, opens a hole in the box in the center of the stage, and drags the corpse of the Savior into it. The prisoners follow him, singing their frenzied, messianic discovery. The cover slams down. I have never heard a silence like this. Abruptly, quietly, a voice is heard. I don't understand it, but I learn later that the voice says simply, "They are gone and the smoke rises in spirals." This message I don't need to understand. I know now why there is a strange joy as well as terror in crematories, and I will never escape this revelation.

(7)

As a poet I have been deeply interested in sound poetry and performance poems—seeking the dramatic depth of sound beneath the conventional surface meaning of words. So I am better prepared than most for Grotowski's approach to language. I don't know Polish and accept, perhaps too easily, a kind of body language, grunts, chants, musical inflections, shrieks, groans. I detest American performances where actors without any sense of the physical nature of language indulge themselves in cynical, anti-verbal assaults without any depth. Depth is the key word. While I have no way of really knowing since I am unfamiliar with Grotowski's language, I feel a respect for the dedication of his approach to sound. Here is no longer a world where sound is specialized for particular purposes, politics, law, medicine, engineering, music, literature, worship. Everything is mixed together. Sound has become its own prison. The Tower of Babel has become a concentration camp of sound.

(8)

A final, indelible impression of space. I don't agree with Bentley that Grotowski shows us an "Auschwitz that is of technical interest to theater students." The aura of preciousness around the production created by the American appetite for instant fame has nothing to do with what I saw and felt in the actual production. The hidden, agonizing vision of Szajna's junk setting could only have been created by an Auschwitz inmate. As Grotowski says what is shown is "the rules of the game: in order not to be a victim one must make a victim of someone else." In playing according to these rules, the space has to be ordered in a way that would be impossible in a proscenium arch theatre. The setting of the church enhances the grotesque, religious images; it is as if Grotowski is saying through his choice of this environment that the church must share the blame for this vision of anti-Christ. I have a new vision now of what space can mean in a theatre. If this is truly a space age, we must stop thinking of theatre in terms of real estate, new plants, new centers. Nor does the concept of "flexible space and theatres" have much intrinsic meaning. Instead we must be far more radical. If every play has its own unique space, it is not enough to begin with the idea of a flexible theatre. What is more important is the vision of a company, uniting director, playwright, designers, and actors, creating their vision of space in each work. This will mean drastic changes at times, an ability and willingness to play in houses, churches, schools, outdoors, as well as conventional theatres. Grotowski shows us the possibilities of a company in a "Theatre Laboratory," a term which points to a potential, new unity of the arts and sciences. Even if a company plays only in its own theatre, it must find ways to abolish the idea of aesthetic, theatrical space and explore the transformations of dramatic space. This may mean not only the abolition of fixed seating and barriers of any kind between audience and actors, but also an architectural and psychological ability to transform the basic theatre into the ideal space for a particular production. After all Grotowski has had an architect connected with his company. The basic dilemma is clear. A theatre is a theatre. Grotowski's *Akropolis* benefits immeasurably from being performed in a church. Could one achieve the same effect in a theatre? I doubt it. Perhaps in 1970 our ideas that a flexible, theatrical space can represent anything are illusions. Perhaps we are too conditioned by the media to the terrible reality of exact environments. I believe we must explore these problems more deeply from the viewpoint of a united company working toward the unique space of each play in the setting or environment that is most appropriate.

(9)

Grotowski's Via Negativa, his methods of training actors and achieving theatre by constantly stripping away psychological and physical flaws—"an eradication of blocks" Grotowski calls it— helps to restore a sense of honor to a corrupt institution. It makes it possible to accept Grotowski's vision of the "holy" actor as one who climbs upon the stake and performs an act of self-sacrifice. This is another version of Artaud's concept of the theatre of cruelty, of an actor "signalling through the flames." Still Bentley seems correct to raise the sceptical issue of the formalistic danger of a ritual of self-sacrifice. American companies can too easily retire from the problems of our society and join the fervor of martyred, confessional, narcissistic searches. This is the risk of Grotowski transformed into American terms. We are likely to see hundreds of indulgent, self-pitying, "intimate" productions. Consider then some key sentences of Grotowski: "One cannot achieve spontaneity in art without the structuring of detail. Without this one searches but never finds because too much freedom is a lack of freedom. If we lack structured detail we are like someone who loves all humanity, and that means he loves no one." Perhaps there is a lesson here for us Americans, for our theatre. We have pretended to be a melting pot of love for all humanity. Does that mean we are in danger of loving no one? In the theatre it is only the vision of a dedicated company relating to each other and to society that can answer this question.

The Living Theatre:
Towards the Anarchist's Paradise

"Aggressive, not violent. We're never violent," Judith Malina has said. The difference may seem small to an audience at times. At the American premiere of *Paradise Now,* which I witnessed at Yale University in September, 1968, the performance started very casually twenty minutes late with actors approaching members of the audience throughout the old-fashioned, proscenium arch theatre. In obsessive, intense, trance-like voices, they stated accusingly:

"I am not permitted to travel without a passport."
"I don't know how to stop the wars."
"I cannot live without money."
"I am not allowed to smoke marijuana."
"I am not permitted to take off my clothes."

Julian Beck approached me in the balcony. An extraordinary figure—a bald monk's pate with a wild fringe of hair that gives him a medieval sorcerer's look, a thin, strong, middle-aged body with a superb carriage. No doubt that Beck is a leader, a zealot, a man with enormous inner resources, a Renaissance man with a wide variety of talents who has cast off his middle-class background for a prophet-like stance in the theatrical wilderness. A revolutionary? Is this anarchist, bohemian group of actors truly revolutionary? Mixed feelings. Yes and no. His eyes glaring wildly, Beck accuses: "I am not permitted to take off my clothes." Now it's going to happen of course. They're going to take off their clothes. Beck strips down to a loin cloth. The other actors take off their clothes and remain semi-naked the rest of the evening. In New York Richard Schechner will strip down to his mustache. By the time The Living Theatre reaches Berkeley, California, the front rows will be crowded with naked radicals shouting challenges of confrontation. Conservative critics will have charged them with "fakery," "boredom," and even a lack of "togetherness." Radical critics will have praised them with "the power to alter life."

Below me Judith Malina has also stripped down. Not particularly beautiful or even striking. Yet there's something powerful, honest, angry about her. Her near-nakedness seems to say, forget about your damn American glamour-fantasies. I know that world and here is what a woman's body is really like. Not an average woman certainly. An elemental Jewish power, a Jewish mother. No wonder it's so hard for many people to separate the aggressive anger of her performance from violence. Yet there is a strong difference. Aggressive celebration may be obnoxious to a lot of people because it involves the public display of emotional, egotistical power, but it also effects a curious release. One cannot remain passive. I discover in myself a paradox. I both resent and admire the aggression of these actors. Is this just because of my long involvement with theatre? No, maybe I'm too passive at times, too accustomed to the drift of things. The sudden difference between aggression and violence, so crucial to an understanding of the Living Theatre, becomes clear. Aggression can be self-defense, self-defiance, self-assertion. Aggression can also be obnoxious and ridiculous. But violence is merely blind rage, a compulsion for extinction.

In the end, after witnessing various Living Theatre productions, I come to believe what Joseph Chaikin has written so well about them and theatre in general:

> "The Living Theatre produced many works. Some fell apart. But it impressed me that the Becks were free of a certain business syndrome in which one says to oneself 'If I do this then I will get that.' They made their relationship to their

work and not to the praise or blame which it aroused. The trouble with most revolutionary thought is the lack of an alternative to the existing situation. Action is limited to dissent, and soon one feels the circular hopelessness of simply wishing against. Missing is the imagination to dream—to enter that area where dismay has not cancelled out the alternatives . . . The Becks demonstrate in their work and their activism that there are almost no boundaries, that no one need stay within the limitations which seem to be fixed. They represent a repudiation of the captive way of life. That is their spectacle."

"If I do this then I will get that." Surely Chaikin is right. That is the poison of ambition in the arts. The Becks know it as well as anyone. They have struggled for years to maintain their theatre. They want to do this to get that. But they also know that the pragmatic aim of cause and effect, while it may often work, can be deadly. Because it denies mystery, denies the sudden discovery, that is the nature of creativity. The effect of *Paradise Now* is curiously disturbing. I don't like a lot of it. Boredom sets in as four hours of agonizingly slow rhythms and haphazard summons and rejections of the audience pursue their tortuous track. Still, slowly, I admit that I am seeing something astonishing. This is a company, a way of life that's being asserted, not just a theatrical illusion. They perform with a brilliant, forceful sense of community and artistic dedication. With their stress on physical techniques in *Paradise Now*, they do far more astonishing physical things than they do verbal things. This is an indulgence reflecting a typical American split rather than a deep-rooted truth. To neglect the physical aspects of the word, as they seem to do in all of their recent productions, is to fail to unite "the body with the mind" which Beck has claimed as the goal of the "Theatre of the Revolution." Often the language that they evoke from themselves and the audience with their concept of a theatre of mass involvement in *Paradise Now* is banal indeed, but this too may be part of their mysterious purpose—to reveal the banality of the society that they are attacking. "To be free is a great responsibility," one actor

shouts out and an antagonistic member of the audience replies bitterly, "To be free is to be free of tickets"—since the five dollar admission price points undeniably to the capitalistic economic system that the Living Theatre claims to resist. Money is burned on stage and joyous, sarcastic rumors spread immediately that only one dollar bills were burned and others spared. Yet amidst the antagonistic turmoil and the conflicting opinions, a remarkable journey is taking place.

The journey of *Paradise Now*, as The Living Theatre describes it, is a tri-partite voyage—"a Rite, a Vision, and an Action, which lead to the fulfillment of an aspect of the revolution. The rites and visions are performed primarily by the actors. The actions are introduced by the actors and performed by the spectators with the help of the actors." About two-thirds of the play are known and, as Julian Beck has said, "one-third is unnoted and unknown. Unrehearsed." There is something exciting and stimulating in this idea of a map, a chart of a voyage of discovery where a large part of the territory, the unknown geography, has to be discovered anew every performance. Of course one can say that as the number of performances increases, the possibilities of discovery lessen. The geography is being mapped and the risks of the terrain are reduced. Nevertheless, this kind of structured map, proceeding from the known and pointing into the unknown, is a totally new kind of challenge to the relationship between audience and actors. How can a play become a map? I end up taking the map, the chart, the program home with me and putting it on the wall of my study. *The play as map*—something to remember. Every voyage must have its own structure. If the structure is too rigid, too definitive, it can only restrict and squeeze out suggestive meaning. One thing the Living Theatre does is suggest directions for playwrights.

Startling images of the Rites and Visions remain. The totem poles formed by the actors in tiers in the vision of the fate of American Indians, or the extraordinary flying sequences, the space fantasies, where bodies fly through the air ecstatically and land in the extended arms of aisles of performers. Even the physical spellings, the somewhat coy work-games, when the actors spell out with

their bodies ANARCHISM and PARADISE NOW are remarkably done. As Judith Malina has said, "The company is very good
on physical things. . . . We work from the cumulative knowledge of
the people in the company." Here is another illumination: only a
company working harmoniously can create real physical actions. A
director saying do this or do that, or a teacher instructing a class in
movement, achieve very little really. Organic movements become
startling actions only through group efforts where every actor
contributes his own resources toward the achievement of a particular goal.

   Why then be disturbed by the ultimate failure of *Paradise Now?*
Are we not sick to death with productions that are so accurately
mapped that they risk nothing? I am disturbed by the failure of
Paradise Now for me because I am so shaken by its possibilities.
Its structure seems to disintegrate into chaos; and paradise, not
chaos; is its aim. Its confessional aspect leads to indulgence, not
revelation. The lack of comic exploration is crucial. One gets the
sense of half-minds, not whole-minds—half-bodies exploring superbly, but never reaching whole-bodies. Julian Beck says that "I
don't think we came to a breakthrough in the theatre until we
became frankly political." But this American version of anarchism
doesn't seem political. It seems more related to the current confessional tendencies in our arts where the dangerous confusion is that
individual freedom necessarily leads to social freedom.

   Frankenstein is for me their most successful spectacle. *Spectacle*
is another unique form of which only a company seems capable.
When spectacle is attempted by Hollywood, the effect may be
lavish and temporarily sensational, but it has no lasting depth.
Spectacle to Julian Beck and Judith Malina is another matter.
Scope, sensation, stimulus—their concept of spectacle works more
in these directions. Particularly to Beck, a superb designer, space is
essential for large-scale effects. His set for *Frankenstein* is an
extraordinary three-tiered construction scaffolding that serves as a
laboratory for the creation of the mechanical man (he is far more

than a monster in the play), an immense head with its profile indicated by neon lights, and, finally, fifteen prison cells from which the actors stage a last revolt. After the failure of the revolt, the entire company creates at the end an image of the mechanical man who has now become a monstrous, enormous, technological image to haunt the world. In an incredible gymnastic feat, the actors form the legs, body, arms (two actors swing out from the shoulders and hang head-down to form the arms), and head (with flashlights for the two eyes shining into the audience through the darkness). This image of the technological robot that has come to haunt mankind looms approximately twenty feet tall and its bulky, massive, human trembling with its sense of devouring many lives remains indelibly in my mind.

Frankenstein has a curiously conventional three-act structure. Act I begins with a meditation "the purpose of which is to lead to levitation." After the inevitable failure of the levitation, a "victimization" occurs. The classical means of execution and cruel punishment—electrocution, gassing, guillotining, racking, hanging, garroting, beheading, shooting, and crucifixion—are enacted. From the dead, Dr. Frankenstein takes "the heart of the Victim" and begins his ironic resurrection. While social issues are fought out between the militarists, the Marxists, the Capitalists, and the technological voice advocating "Automation," Dr. Frankenstein labors over "the Body on the Laboratory table" in this grotesque science-fiction vision. "Paracelsus appears and directs the graft of the third eye. Freud appears and orders the sexual graft. Norbert Wiener appears and advises the use of electrodes. The electrodes are attached. The Creature moves." Here is where the literary and theatrical conceptions split apart. The audience is never aware of individual characters except for the Doctor and his Creature. Is this because The Living Theatre, working in Europe, exaggerates the visual spectacle to overcome language barriers? Why does there seem to be a strange split between their literary, mythological, Artaud-like vision of theatrical spectacle, which tends to eliminate personality, and their anarchistic, non-violent, individualistic personalities and beliefs?

Act II takes place inside "the Creature's head." As he comes to life he "translates into the mythological theatre of prototype." The classical myths of Daedalus, Icarus, Europa, Pasiphae, and others are enacted. Again an uninstructed audience has difficulty in differentiating these legendary events. A dream-world of physical events is the primary impression. Eventually, "the Body Vanishes," "The Word is born," and "The Creature narrates his story." Steven Ben Israel, a remarkably dynamic, physically astonishing performer who seemingly cares little about vocal projection, narrates a long section from Mary Shelley's novel about the Creature's despair at the contradictions between man's power and his viciousness. Does the Living Theatre really believe in the separation between action and language or do they merely reflect the peculiarly American split that exists?

Act III is extremely powerful in its visual incarceration of prisoners as they occupy their cells on the high levels and improvise the agonies of their cruel solitary confinement. However, the lengthy, interminable sequence of arrests that take place throughout the audience seem ultimately ineffective. They are only a monotonous, fake ritual of arrest, nothing like the carefully planned, actual staging of mass arrests that one witnesses in demonstrations. Still, perhaps, the Living Theatre means to show the monotonous indifference of both spectators and police to arrests? If so, their purpose is never clear because the actors have never worked out the sequence and remain merely individual performers, personalities, not actors. After all the police are *impressive;* if the Living Theatre does not believe in theatrical representations of police, why attempt to portray the ritual imagery of arrests? This is why ritual is so difficult, if not impossible, in theatre. Ritual is involved with the deep-rooted beliefs of a society and cannot merely be imitated. If the belief is missing, the ritual is missing— that is the basic problem of inept imitations of rituals.

The end of *Frankenstein,* the mass escape and death scene where the bodies of the prisoners are transformed into the final image of the Creature, arms outstretched in his grotesque crucifixion, is strongly related to Artaud's "The Plague" which the Living

Theatre dramatizes as their final event in *Mysteries and Smaller Pieces*. Through sacrifice, through disease, we discover the depth of action, in theatre and in life. It is up to our natures, audience and performers alike, how far we carry this discovery in theatre. The great merit of the Living Theatre is that they make you feel and think that the theatre can enter this world of discovery. In *Frankenstein* they turn the craftsmanship of technology into art; they reveal technology as the Creature. If this changes often the poetic, individual nature of the myths and legends that they illustrate throughout the play, this is what technology does—it conceals the individual in the mass. Consequently, the confusion in the Living Theatre between poetic, verbal concepts and physical actions is an all too familiar social confusion. Despite its jagged disunity, *Frankenstein* remains the most significant of recent Living Theatre productions because of its singular unifying image: the creation of the Creature, Technology, who is man's hope and fear.

"Why lie, why try to place on a literary level a thing which is the very cry of life? Why give an appearance of fiction to what is made up of the ineradicable substance of the soul, to what is the wail of reality?" In their book, *We, The Living Theatre*, created with Aldo Rostagno, Julian Beck and Judith Malina use this quote from Artaud's letter to Riviére in May, 1924, to introduce the section on *Mysteries and Smaller Pieces*. The quote illustrates the basic conflict in The Living Theatre. When I first saw their work in New York, they were involved with fostering American poetic drama whether written in prose or poetry. Poets themselves, they seemed to seek theatrical equivalents of the word. There is no such thing. When dramatic poetry is successful there is no separation between word and physical action; they are one. As a great poet, Artaud began to despair of the artificiality of language and thought he found in Balinese theatre and dance a style that pierced "the wall of reality." Perhaps because he did not understand the language he failed to see the physical word, the formal meanings and symbols implicit and explicit in Balinese performances. Perhaps, as in the

case of many western culture-heroes, Artaud was merely disillusioned with the brittle, trivial, ironic verbal surfaces of western
culture in the twentieth century. The Living Theatre represents the
same kind of reaction; they seek to make a poetry of the theatre
out of anti-verbal concepts. At the same time, their detailed, verbal, poetic concepts are there, the result of countless discussions
and rehearsals. Their revulsion against the "literary level" is in the
end a false understanding of literature. In the Soviet Union, for
example, it would be hard to deny in Solzhenitsyn's novels a
physical understanding of life. The suffering of his body is written
into his work. It is a peculiar characteristic of American culture
with its advertising distortions that so many theatre groups are
driven to distinguishing between mind and body, word and action,
as if these natural forces can be separated. What saves The Living
Theatre is the inherent love for poetry that they manifest, even if
their recent productions are basically anti-verbal.

Mysteries and Smaller Pieces is a good example of the problem.
It shows the physical qualities of the company superbly. It is truly
pieces for performance without any attempt at a unified concept.
"The Brig Dollar" at the beginning, derived from their earlier
production of Kenneth Brown's play about the tyrannical rigor of
a Marine Corps prison, is an excruciating portrayal of a military
society with its insane marching and incessant cleaning to no
purpose. However, when the actors stationed along the walls of the
theatre begin to read aloud all of the words printed on a dollar bill,
the verbal attempt to relate money and war simply does not work.
The same ineffective split between words and action is evident in
"Street Songs" where Julian Beck sits cross-legged on the stage and
starts to intone "current revolutionary slogans—Abolish money,
Abolish police, Change the world, Fuck for peace, Free all men,
etc." As the actors around the theatre begin to repeat the slogans,
members of the audience join in. Depending on the nature of the
audience, the joining-in process can be satirical, celebratory, or
both. The result is superficial because it has nothing to do with
revolution. Lenin had a far more theatrical sense of the physical
effect of words. Fortunately, The Living Theatre is extremely

effective and moving in other sections of *Mysteries,* particularly in "Tableaux Vivants," a satirical version of the kind of living pictures that one sees annually at festivals in Southern California. Within a framework of four wooden boxes whose open sides face the audience, six groups of four actors each improvise stances and expressions. Every few seconds the lights are turned on and off in a rhythmical sequence. When the lights are off the new group of actors comes on. The effect is ingenious, an instant transformation of poses and attitudes. The form permits humor and gayety, something rare in recent Living Theatre performances which tend to be severely solemn. A crazy Mack Sennett-like rhythm is achieved; also the poses have a wide range of mood that give the technique contrast and depth.

The end of *Mysteries* is a dramatization of Artaud's famous essay, "The Plague." In dim light, an apocalyptic vision of a society's death themes is presented. Bodies begin to collapse all over the theatre among the spectators. In Artaud's vivid description, "The body fluids, furrowed like the earth struck by lightning, like lava kneaded by subterranean forces, search for an outlet." Members of the audience react in disgust, in alarm, in sympathy. The disease grows inexorably. With their extraodinary breathing techniques, the basis of the physical style that they have developed, the actors die and become rigid. The rigor of death—their physical dedication is extraordinarily powerful in this case. Finally, the rigid bodies are carried on stage and piled up like logs. A pyramid of corpses. The Living Theatre describes this piece "as an attempt to make us aware of the state of emergency we have reached." All they make me aware of (and it is a good deal I admit) is the extraordinary and moving way in which they portray death. As social revolutionaries, since that is what they pretend to be, they are failures. They lack the Brechtian sense of truth being concrete. They present images rather than characters and actions. And characters and actions are the basis of revolution. In place of character, The Living Theatre gives us the illusion of a life-style, anarchistic and confessional in nature. It is not enough.

Yet the undeniably powerful image of company remains. If one is disturbed by some irresponsible statements of the Becks in regard to politics and drugs, if one feels a failure in their aim to relate theatre and politics, one still admires finally their dedication and exploration of group techniques. Particularly impressive is their ability to attract a new, young audience by re-creating a feeling of mystery. By researching western and eastern techniques, especially breathing techniques, they create often an electric vibrancy and exciting movement. Too many American actors merely stand, sit, and walk around as naturalistically as possible, reflecting an uneasy, isolated identity in the personality system of our culture and a resultant inability to reach for the source of mystery. One cannot be mysterious by oneself. Even the greatest, most isolated metaphysical poet is the one who is linked most strongly with God and the universe. This the Living Theatre knows instinctively. Even though their actors are often terribly self-centered, too absorbed in their own personalities and a boring, confessional approach to their problems, they create rare images and actions that are impossible outside of a company.

At the root of what a company can achieve is the mysterious nature of rhythm. American theatrical rhythms are often hyperintense, supposedly suited to the swift pace of a mechanical society. The Living Theatre deals with time as if chronology was an academic invention of pedantic scholars. They circle back and forth into history, religion, mythology, politics, treating time as secondary to the obsessive, dramatic images that control man's destiny. This treatment of time often gives their work a slow pace which can be maddening. Then one begins to wonder about the nature of pace, of rhythm. Why should everything be intense, tight, swift—all of the terms applied to "well-constructed" plays? Does every play have a distinct, inner rhythm? Yes, but The Living Theatre makes you feel that rhythm is far more complex, not only part of the play, but also part of the changing environment, part of the hidden relationship between actors and audience. Rhythm has strong social roots. If we are contemplative, nature-loving people, we may tend to like slower, metaphysical rhythms; if we are committed city and machine lovers we may prefer a swifter, tenser pace. Opposing rhythmical instincts may be present in an audience at the same time. America is an urban nation split by a nostalgic, agricultural tradition. Consequently, a production finds it difficult to establish its own inevitable rhythm. The challenge of The Living Theatre is that it breaks down rhythmical stereotypes. It can reveal breakneck physical speeds as in insane, military drills and then it can suddenly halt to let the audience develop its own sporadic responses, its own disparate rhythms. While their handling of rhythm is by no means completely successful, their experimentation with a wide variety of rhythms is perhaps the most challenging that theatre has seen in recent years.

After their American tour ended in 1969, The Living Theatre returned to Europe and decided to split up into different groups. Despite the shattering of the company, it is clear they will be heard from again. Perhaps this time the Becks will attempt more of a synthesis of their many verbal and physical experiments. Above all they have demonstrated that only in a dedicated, idealistic company can actors, playwrights, and designers be free of the devastating syndrome of "If I do this, then I will get that."

The Third Theatre Revisited

ROBERT BRUSTEIN

In the middle Sixties I wrote an essay saluting a new theatre that was just beginning to evolve in opposition to the existing theatre on Broadway and in the culture centers. At the time, the "third theatre" as I called it, was a fringe movement whose continued survival was as problematical as its anti-war position was unpopular, so it was with considerable surprise that I watched it, soon after, begin to take a position of power in the theatre. This development paralleled a failure of nerve among the middle classes, as the forces of conventional culture seemed to grow guilty and weak before the culture of the young, and the American avant-garde, for the first time in its history, became the glass of fashion and the mold of form. What was once considered special and arcane—the exclusive concern of an alienated, argumentative, intensely serious elite—was now accessible, through television and the popular magazines; vogues in women's fashions followed hard upon, and sometimes even influenced, vogues in modern painting; underground movies became box office bonanzas, and Andy Warhol's factory was making him a millionaire.

The narrowing of the traditional distance between serious and mass-middle culture was accompanied, in the "third theatre," by a growing callowness, sloppiness, and arrogance which made me suspicious of it. Indeed I developed much the same ambivalence toward the anti-war and black power movements as they have changed from noble acts of non-violent resistance by highly serious individuals to disruptive and histrionic acts by infantile "revolutionaries." For just as the frustrations over the endless conflict in Vietnam and the unresolved dilemmas of the black people have given a vaguely totalitarian coloration to certain cadres of the Left, so the success of the third theatre, which reflects these frustrations, has tended to sanctify its failings and conventionalize its virtues. What once seemed daring and original now often seems tiresome and familiar; stereotyped political assertions, encouraged by their easy acceptance, have replaced instinctive, individual dissent; and the complex moral and metaphysical issues of great art are being obliterated by a simple-minded nihilism.

Does this suggest that I am ready to repudiate my earlier assumptions? Only in so far as I must repudiate all theatre movements that begin to take an ideological direction. While the new theatre as a whole has taken a wrong turn, however, there are still many young American playwrights with the gifts to blast this theatre out of its formulas. Jean-Claude van Itallie, Sam Shepard, Charles Dizenzo, Ronald Ribman, Leo Rutman are a few of them. Similarly, while I overvalued Viet Rock in my relief to discover a play that mentioned the Vietnam war at all, I still regard *America Hurrah, Dynamite Tonite,* and *Macbird!* as works of real imagination and originality, and will continue to defend these plays against hostile critics who attack what is genuine in the new theatre movement along with what is spurious. On the other hand, it is becoming increasingly clear, now that the new theatre has begun to rigidify, that it may be as great a danger to dramatic art as the old theater. It already embodies similar defects. Its anti-intellectualism, its sensationalism, its sexual obsessiveness, its massacre of language, its noisy attention-getting mechanisms, its indifference to artistry, craft, or skill, its violence, and, above all, its mindless tributes to Love and Togetherness (now in the form of "group gropes" and "love zaps") are not adversary demands upon the American character but rather the very qualities that have continually degraded us, the very qualities that have kept us laggard and philistine in the theatre throughout the past three decades.

It is ironic that these qualities, already so conspicuous in the commercial theatre, should be offered as expressions of a new sensibility—even more ironic that one should find them in the work of the Living Theatre upon its return after an exile of four years. Initiating a tour designed to revolutionize not only the stage but the various university and civic centers that it visited, the

Living Theatre proved, upon its very first appearance, to have changed its style in a manner similar to the changes in the new theatre. Indeed, it soon became clear that it was the original source of many off-off-Broadway conventions. Having eked out a precarious existence for seventeen years as an embattled minority troupe dedicated to the great classic and contemporary European works as well as to the more experimental American plays, the Living Theatre returned to America with a fierce antagonism to all dramatic texts that could not somehow be translated into its special anarchistic program. The members of the company had developed an almost symbiotic unity in their years of traveling together over the European continent. The company had become a self-generating, self-perpetuating organism whose existence was more important than any work it performed; and it was inflamed with a sense of mission that was less theatrical or even political than religious and evangelical.

These changes were reflected physically as well. Julian Beck's features now contained an ascetic calm usually associated with Hindu gurus and Confucian monks, while his wife, Judith Malina, had taken on the look of an unprotected street urchin, her eyes sometimes ablaze with fervor, sometimes limpid with compassion for all martyrs, not excluding herself. The Becks—as well as the entire company—had developed an extraordinary physical integrity that gave at once the most immediate, and the most lasting impression one had of them. Dressed like gypsies, hippies, and nomads in clothing from every quarter of the earth, the men sometimes indistinguishable from the women, and even the children beaded, bangled, and longhaired, they moved with a beauty that testified to an inward grace, as well as to months of arduous training in breathing and the body.

Unfortunately, the Living Theatre had little of substance to contribute beyond its athleticism and its exotic style of life. Although two of the four works presented on this tour *(The Mysteries* and *Frankenstein)* showed original techniques, they did not fulfill their initial promise largely because they lacked a gifted playwright to conceive them intelligently. It was disconcerting to discover that the Becks no longer seemed interested in coherent theatrical productions. What obsessed them now was their missionary program; they were more eager to convert their audiences, through whatever means, to their special brand of revolutionary politics. In production after production, the company demonstrated its remarkable capacity to manipulate minds. Playing upon the general sense of emptiness in a world where even individual salvation seems far too complicated, the Living Theatre proselytized among the young in the manner of hip evangelists, encouraging each spectator to make his decision for love, freedom, and anarchy. The most depressing thing of all was how easily university students, and even some of their teachers, responded to the baldest of slogans and the most simplistic interpretations of reality.

After *The Mysteries*, a series of process exercises which for me was the most interesting and least pretentious of its offerings, the Living Theatre proceeded to demonstrate in *Antigone* (a version of the story which reduced it to a melodramatic confrontation between political evil and oppressed good), in *Frankenstein* (a Camp horror tale with Radio City Music Hall prestidigitation techniques about how civilization turns man into monster), and particularly in the audience-participation epic, *Paradise Now*, that it had virtually abandoned its interest in creating serious drama. It was now clear that the Becks' previous efforts to examine the boundaries separating art from life (in such pre-exile productions as *The Connection* and *Tonight We Improvise*) had been expanded into a full-scale assault upon any separation whatever between the spectator and the stage. Audiences were invited over the footlights to join some performers while other performers wandered through the house; actors whined plaintively about their inability to travel without a passport, live without money, smoke marijuana, or take their clothes off, after which they stripped to loin cloths and bikinis; students peeled down, upon this encouragement, to jockey shorts; mass love-zaps and petting parties were organized on stage among couples of various sexes and sexual dispositions; and after the endless, loveless, sexless groping was finally over, everyone was exhorted to leave the theatre and convert the police to anarchism, to storm the jails and free the prisoners, to stop the war and ban the bomb, to take over the streets in the name of the people—and, then, to disperse quietly lest any of this end (as it did one night in New Haven) with somebody in jail for disturbing the peace.

Needless to say, unfulfillable demands of this kind were extremely irresponsible, given the impressionable nature of young audiences; they were also extremely meretricious, since the Living Theatre invariably took refuge in its theatrical function whenever things threatened to get out of hand. For all its emphasis on reality, the company never quite managed to escape from its performances, for all its emphasis on spontaneity and accident, it still followed an almost fixed pattern which ended the same way every evening. To extend a theatrical action into the audience is not to annihilate the performance, it is to annihilate the audience—everyone becomes a performer, the seats become part of the stage. This paradox was not lost on Jean Genet, whose play, *The Balcony,* was based on his understanding that since revolution is dedicated to the destruction of artifice, its greatest enemy is playacting. But it was a paradox from which the Living Theatre was never able to escape. And when the Becks appeared recently on the Merv Griffin show, outlining their political theories between a series of nightclub acts, they only dramatized further their imprisonment in show biz in Genet's image, they were still in the brothel.

What was finally most disturbing about the Living Theatre was the content of the ideology it was marketing under the name of anarchism. In spite of all the invitations to participate in free theatre, it was constraint and control that remained most conspicuous: No spectator was ever allowed to violate the pattern of manipulated consent. At Yale, we saw a female student launch into a passionate denunciation of the Living Theatre, only to be hustled offstage by a group of performers who embraced her into silence— unbuttoning her blouse, feeling her legs, and shutting her mouth with kisses. Another student, beginning an impersonation of Ed Sullivan while navigating around the interlocked bodies on the stage, was prevented from introducing a note of satire into the evening by an actor who drowned him out with an imitation of the

Kennedy assassination. The company, particularly vulnerable to ridicule because of its lack of humor, allowed no alien laughter ever to penetrate its relentless solemnity, self-righteousness, and self-importance.

Love and brotherhood were continually on the lips of the actors, but no actors in my experience have bristled with so much aggression or more successfully galvanized the aggression of the spectator. As for love and brotherhood, all one saw was herd love and brotherhood among the anonymous. It was, finally, not a vision of human freedom that one took away from *Paradise Now* but vague, disturbing memories of the youth rallies in Hitler's Nuremberg. The return of the Living Theatre described a full circle in so far as the company had now taken on the very authoritarian qualities it had once denounced, the very repressiveness that had driven it from the country four years before.

The unprecedented success of the Living Theatre with the radical young—and with those who follow the radical young—was, however, of momentous significance because it indicated precisely what these audiences were now demanding of the stage. For those impatient generations, with their inability to sustain frustration for a moment, it was the opportunity for participation that proved most attractive. The passive role of spectator had become insufficient. Now theatrical production had to satisfy the thirst for an elusive, often spurious "relevance" and convince its audiences that they were helping to enact an episode in history. The Living Theatre promised the theatricalization of campus revolts, confrontations, and occupations—the theatricalization of those numerous quasi-revolutionary gestures by which students are persuading themselves today that they are having a significant impact on their times. That these gestures are aimed not against the Pentagon or the napalm-producing factories, but rather against the university itself (for all its faults, still one of the last outposts of civilization and humane values) only indicates that the desire for effectiveness *somewhere* far transcends the desire for effective change.[1] But it

---

[1] This is not to say that some of the more extreme revolutionists are not preparing, at least in their fantasies, for assaults on the Pentagon. My sixteen-year-old

also indicates that with the day of protest upon us, the conditions necessary for the creation of great art may very well be over, at least for a time. As one gifted acting student told me when he withdrew from Yale: "I don't give a shit about art. I want to create events."

For myself, I regard this development with mingled feelings, mostly sad ones. This extraordinary generation, upon whom so much praise and attention have been lavished, cannot help but inspire feelings of respect—but my respect is becoming mixed with great apprehension. At once so vital and idealistic, and so childish, irrational, and overindulged, the radical young are questioning the very roots of our civilization, but what they would substitute, apart from continuous improvisation and an ethics of expedience, is far from known. The silent and conservative students of the Fifties are no more, thank heavens; they have gone off to join the system and consolidate its errors. But some of the demonic students of the Sixties may very well, in their impatience for change, destroy what is valuable in our culture along with what is despicable—destroying even the valuable things their contemporaries have helped to create. While the theatre, along with popular music, has benefited enormously from an infusion of young energy that has transformed our way of seeing and hearing, the more radical theatre is less an advance than a throwback. With this theatre, we have returned to the Thirties, watching the same abuse of truths that do not serve political ends, the same contempt for writers who do not try to change their times, the same monolithic modes of thought, the same assaults on any expression that is not a form of consent. The "theatre of commitment," which had just begun to shake itself free from dependence on narrow ideology, is again becoming a theatre of naked slogans and raw emotionalism, and death knells are once more being heard for the works of Western civilization.

These works will, I hope, survive; they are certainly among the few things worth preserving. But they will survive only through renewed efforts at conservation, and this means renewed efforts of

---

stepson met a girl the other day who was practicing jujitsu in preparation for encounters with the US Army. "Can you throw a tank?" he asked.

intelligence and will. The threatening apocalypse is something for which many of us must share the blame: By radically questioning the prevailing humanism, we helped to start violent engines in motion which may end in pushing everything we value over the precipice. Secure in our powerlessness, and certain that thought would never lead to action, we let our minds play upon questionable possibilities, never suspecting that those possilities might soon be upon us, more swiftly and more irrevocably than we could dream. These were errors of judgment—but there were those who made less forgivable errors of power. Seeking a Mosaic role, they led these hungry generations to a violent view from Pisgah that could have no creative issue. Guilt-ridden, indecisive, flaccid, hating authority and enamored of influence, they surrendered principles they had once affirmed, accepting again what was so hateful in the past. In a time when intelligence is needed more than ever before, they encouraged a form of intellectual decomposition, becoming fellow travelers of a movement they could never hope to join, which would, in time, proceed to swallow them up.

We honor the young because without them there is no future. But there will surely be no future either unless the more extreme of our young can cease from trying to annihilate the past. With our civilization tottering, the tempation is strong to release our hold on reality and credit the most fantastic flights of absurdity simply because they signify change. But the more radical inventions of the new generation are nothing if they proceed from the same violent and mindless sources that originally brought our civilization to this terrifying juncture. We fail the future when we surrender what we know and value for the sake of fashion and influence, and we fail the theatre when we countenance the rejection of language, form, and accomplishment in favor of an easy culture. The third theatre I once described contains, in Synge's words, "reality and joy" which is to say it synthesizes the principle of work and of pleasure, discipline and imagination, form and process, reflection and improvisation, age and youth. It is a theatre that spans the generations—a theatre, in other words, that has yet to appear in this country of divided spirits.

Joan Littlewood:
Towards a Theatre of Ideal Comedians

A physical, plastic quality about Joan Littlewood's sense of theatre and film makes itself felt immediately, a feeling for line, motion, space relationships. What she calls "earthing the character" is her special ability, her way of helping the actor to give physical reality to the abstract character on the page. She hates abstractions and "allegory" is a pet peeve. When I first heard her speak to the Theatre Workshop company, she said that allegory is no longer necessary, although it may have been justified in historical, political crises when people had to state things indirectly.

She believes strongly in an actor-writer's theatre and said several times during our first meetings that this must come if theatre is to have any future. Her favorite playwrights belong to the great comic-satirical traditions. In the first meetings of the company, when we were reading and discussing various scripts, she mentioned constantly Aristophanes, Ben Jonson, and Moliére. She expressed a dislike for John Osborne's *Look Back in Anger* and for "Angry Young Men" plays in general. She felt that they were too allegorical in method, that their characters were not truly convincing.

As for American plays, she expressed great disapproval of Tennessee Williams' *The Glass Menagerie*. She spoke of this as possibly the key influence on all the plays dealing with "American mother problems," which she complained of receiving since her New York success with *The Hostage*. In regard to French plays,

322

she said that she didn't like Ionesco much (too much allegory and no real people), but that she did like Sartre.

Despite her aversions to allegory, she also spoke against naturalism, the plodding attempt merely to reproduce natural detail. What she wants chiefly is a theatre of realistic comedy, like Aristophanes and Jonson, open to wide-ranging theatrical techniques. Brendan Behan is the closest playwright in this vein whom she has discovered. Her problem is that the younger English playwrights are more inclined to a stylistic, poetic, symbolic handling of ideas, so she has made no effort to work with such playwrights as Pinter, Whiting, N.F. Simpson, or Arden. This is a shame for these are the writers with the verbal skills who would benefit most by her kind of "earthing the characters."

In rehearsal, she breaks a play down into small "units" and proceeds to cover each unit thoroughly like a conductor rehearsing a few bars of a symphonic movement. As these units are read through, motivations of the characters are discussed and improvisations develop. There has been a great deal of misunderstanding about these improvisations. Actually, in her long career, she has worked through many different styles from a strict stylization of the action to a much freer, improvisatory method concentrating on the actor's approach to the development of a new script. Let me try and give some impressions of rehearsal sessions in which she used the latter approach.

The week before Christmas, 1960, The Theatre Workshop company began to rehearse a new comedy at the Interval Club in Soho. This proved to be a quaint, theatrical boarding house with rehearsal rooms. The tiny, doll's house stage (which we didn't use—we rehearsed in a room) was set with imitation classical pillars as if demanding a return to the theatrical glory of the 19th century.

In the second week's rehearsal, Joan concentrated on shaping the rhythm of Act II. With the help of the company, she reduced the three acts of the rough script that we were working on to two acts. At this point she regarded the actors as rehearsing mainly to reveal the script's flaws. *True* was one of her favorite adjectives.

"That'll have to be extended and made *true*." Or, irritated as she constantly was by an excessively narrative, literary passage, she would say: "You don't have to explain everything in a narrative way in a play. There's too much narrative tense." The excessive narrative would go and the tense would change automatically from past to present.

Always, she encouraged and coaxed the actors, working for speed and lightness in the constant improvisations that she requested. "Come on, tosspots, Commedia dell'Artists!" No one could help responding to her enthusiasm. For her the actor is the theatre. In a theatrical age where the director is dominant, she has tried to restore the actor's importance while retaining the director's instinctive guidance of the actor's performance.

Occasionally, the young, inexperienced author who was unable to work in this process, would inject a wry remark such as "It's wonderful how you keep track of what's happening." Such a remark would occur in the wake of different improvisations and the development of new lines scribbled into the margins of the script. The author had difficulty in seeing that she was working for the rhythmic flow of the play, not merely for the words at this stage of rehearsals. "Don't produce it," she kept saying to the author. "That's deadly for actors." The author soon disappeared from rehearsals. She sensed that the only way to make this conventional TV script successful was to keep it light and quick and stylized like a Moliére farce, as she kept repeating. When things lagged, as they often did, she would exhort the actors ceaselessly: "Can you turn this into the going-mad mood of Act I?"

As rehearsals continued, she saw that the conventionality of the play could not take any serious or naturalistic weight in production. She began to stress: "There must be no heavy sex in the play—it must be all light sex." She worked more and more for what she called *physical objectives.* "Play the physical objective," she said to the actress who was playing the cleaning woman, Mrs. Batt. "Sweep her out of the room. Take over. That's your underlying objective." Every unit of the play began to assume a dynamic objective. To Klad's girl friend, entering the rooming house to visit

Klad, she said: "Your objective is to get up those stairs to Klad's room regardless of what happens." When too much theorizing interfered with these physical objectives she warned impatiently: "Let's not work with our heads. Let's see it." Always the sense of the unifying comic rhythm was in her mind: "Don't worry about details. Let's see about the sequence."

By the third week of rehearsals I began to feel that a major problem in her exciting improvising techniques was a tendency to forget about diction completely. There was something admirable and powerful in the way she brought language out of a physical situation in an attempt to counter-act what she felt to be the excessively mannered, rhetorical speaking habits of the British acting tradition. But I noticed that when diction was ignored completely for too long a time, the actors developed sloppy speaking habits.

Walking out with her after rehearsal one day, I saw in her hand a copy of a book about the Russian director, Vakhtangov. She admired his work very much. She felt that he had worked towards the same physical contact between actors that she desired. In many ways, she said, Vakhtangov's approach was superior to Stanislavsky, and it was a shame Vakhtangov died so young. Vakhtangov believed that the stage could not and should not try to reproduce life, but was a space through which the actor moved. The audience came to a theatrical event, and this fact should be accepted and used to advantage. The actor was always paramount, but this did not mean that he needed an unreal, virtuoso style. The great paradox and power of theatre, Vakhtangov recognized, was that the more realistic the actor became, the more attention given to details and subtleties of performance, the more theatrical power he commanded. In his famous production of *Turandot*, created just before his untimely death, he made no attempt at Chinese naturalism. He conceived the play as a legend told by actors. Four Commedia dell'Arte characters, Truffaldino, Brighella, Tartaglia, and Pantalone, represented the theatre. They spoke directly to the audience and commented on the action. The action of the play proceeded as the frank presentation of a fable, with immense attention to details, to the spontaneous handling of objects, to movements, to groupings. In addition there was a strong romantic element in Vakhtangov, a love of color and the reckless flare of personality. These elements seemed to me characteristic also of Joan Littlewood's direction. The major difference perhaps is that she is less inclined to "fix" actors in definite places with closely defined business. She is more convinced of the necessity for a constant change in the actor's approach to renew fluidity of movement and freshness of conception.

At the end of the week in our Chelsea rehearsal room there was a complete run-through of the first act. Before the run-through, Joan tried to work out various problems. She felt that she wasn't getting enough satirical tension from one actor, so she said to him: "Look, try to play this really as though you were in one of those Elia Kazan films," and she proceeded to give a marvelous demonstration of a "Method" Kazan actor slinking along frozen with tension and fear. One great advantage she has as a director, particularly of comedy, is her ability to demonstrate what she wants. Unlike other directors, she participated daily in the movement sessions she liked to hold whenever possible for her company.

Late that afternoon Joan worked on the first entrance of Mr. Dick, the funny little civil servant who was carrying on an affair in the boarding house with fluttery Mrs. Brent, the wife of the drunken, belligerent Irish handyman. "Let's just think a moment, darlings," she said to the actors. "If this were a Roman comedy, how would he appear?"

"There'd be a lot of near-miss meetings between Brent and Dick when Dick sneaks in," suggested one actor. Joan also mentioned Bocaccio—"The idea of a lover in the chest with the husband sitting on top"—or Moliére. The actor playing Dick began happily to improvise hiding himself behind a newspaper.

Joan continued to think: "It's still not right. The problem isn't so much where he comes from as the fact that he's always there. Try that. That might work."

"Like . . . ," the actors took up this idea enthusiastically, thinking of a would-be actor who was always hanging around the company. They began to tell stories about him. When the rehearsal started again the character of Mr. Dick took on a new satirical lightness.

By the fourth week of rehearsals, the actors' scripts were changed greatly, reproduced several times, but still in a tattered state with continuous, hastily added scribblings coming out of the new improvisations. At one point I saw several actors fumbling in the wastebasket for bits of script that seemed to be missing. In the last week of rehearsal at the Interval Club, Joan worked mostly on Act II. On Wednesday of that week a whole new ending was improvised out of the rehearsal. All the workers and hoarders in the house poured back on stage to haunt the owner, Gruchick. Pleased, Joan told the actors enthusiastically: "Acting is fun and alive if you always feel and play what the other actors give on the transitional units. Then the rhythm has pace."

On Thursday evening after the rehearsal we had a drink together and she said: "Sometimes there's a moment when you feel an actor is really communicating. The other day when John as Gruchick was complaining about his cold bath to Mrs. Wood, I went home to take a bath and remembered that line. That's what communion really means in religion. That's why the theatre can be a religion at times." She spoke of how she believed the old ballads like "Sir Patrick Spens" were greater than Shelley and all "the phoney poets of the 1930's." She spoke of Jean Vilar and how his Theatre National Populaire was subsidized; how she felt that she could achieve the same standard in England if she were subsidized. "Recently," she said, "I've been experimenting with a different kind of style where the acting is everything and nothing is fixed. Everything comes out of the director working very freely with the actor. Of course it's rough at times, but it also creates the greatest freedom and the most daring results at times. Still I've worked in lots of different ways as a director and just because I'm working this way at the moment it doesn't mean that I'll always work this way."

During the last day of rehearsal at the Interval Club we worked on sounds and music. First, Joan experimented with boiler noises.

"That boiler has to be human," she grinned. She tried a combination of one actor blowing into a tuba and another talking gibberish into a microphone. After a particularly successful mumble through the microphone she asked excitedly: "What were you saying there, Roy?" "My, my, my, my, my, it's chilly," he answered.

The music for the entrance of Mrs. Batt, the cleaning woman, was much too slow. "It needs to be twice as fast to create any character for her," Joan called impatiently and Mrs. Batt came bustling in. The sense of speed and timing so necessary to farce are an essential aspect of Joan's technique. That Thursday her musical, *Fings Ain't Wot They Used To Be*, won the Evening Standard Drama Award for the best musical in London in 1960. Joan pretended a great embarrassment and unbelief about this when it was mentioned to her. She said that "Fings" had deteriorated completely in performance. On the subject of tempo the judges of the award were quoted: Miss Elizabeth Jane Howard: "It had an astonishing tempo, almost like a film being run a little too fast." "Joan Littlewood could make 'The Merry Widow' look like that," agreed Philip Hope-Wallace. "Or even the Old Testament," added Milton Schulman.

As rehearsals progressed, it was increasingly apparent that Joan was working for a fresh kind of comic style based on expert timing closely related to the cutting of a film where the time sequence does not count as much as the impulse of intuitive, dramatic moments based on characters in different moods. This kind of style depended totally on the capacity of the actors to produce and invent a fresh approach to their parts. When one actor came down with the mumps, Joan said of the actor being considered as a replacement: "He's an awfully nice straightforward actor, but that's not style. Believe it or not, you have been creating a kind of style these last weeks and we can't have a straight, naturalistic actor."

Her sense of acting, she told me one evening after rehearsal, had been influenced greatly by Rudolph Laban. Particularly Laban had influenced her ideas of movement. She said it was a shame that Laban was so underrated compared to Stanislavsky. She told a story of how Laban had gone once to a Stanislavsky rehearsal. Entering the theatre he had seen two actors on a bench sitting back to back. The atmosphere was very solemn and the men sat motionless, saying only a few words. Laban began to get impatient. "Try it again," said Stanislavsky. "We are beginning to get something." And the two men repeated the sparse words over again sitting motionless back to back. At the end of the morning's rehearsal the actors were still sitting motionless on the bench. Furious at not seeing any movement, his passionate concern, Laban fled and never returned to a Stanislavsky rehearsal. Joan spoke of how Laban, as a young man, had reformed German opera by his movement techniques, and the difficult time he had in getting singers to act and move dramatically instead of merely singing.

Joan mentioned how Laban had been particularly interested in the relationship between words and dance and words and movement. "One of his last questions before he died," she said, was "I wonder if there is any such thing as pure, lyrical dance? It's that kind of integration between movement and words that interests me too. We've had too much of the kind of theatre that's all fancy language imposed on movement."

When he came to England after Hitler's rise to power, Joan said that Laban had never really been appreciated. He went to Manchester, feeling instinctively that London was not the place for his experimental work. In the last part of his life, Joan reflected, it was a little sad that he became so involved with the educationists and lost contact with the life of the theatre. Joan mentioned how the whole Theatre Workshop company had gone to serenade Laban at his Manchester home on one of his last birthdays and how touched he had been. "He was a rare man," she said. "At seventy he could still walk across a room and you could feel his dynamic presence. He was a kind of Leonardo in a way. His work in science on crystals was important. He had an extraordinary range of interest in the arts and sciences. It's too bad his books were rather badly put together in English and didn't have the impact they should have had."

During the last week of rehearsal on stage in the theatre, working on the fine set of John Bury, Joan worked frenziedly to achieve the comic style that she desired. Again there was a strong relationship in her approach to the pace of comic films. "Everybody play as if the camera's running too fast," she would cry out. Or again, "Keep it all like comic cuts and camera." More than any other director I have seen working in theatre, she saw that the physical presence of the actor on stage could be used for transitions in the same bold way that films are cut. The actor could not disappear as easily, of course, but even if he remained on stage a gesture or a change in style could be used to emphasize a change in mood or scene and maintain the kind of rapid time sequence that fits modern, urban life.

As might have been expected, this particular production was a failure when it opened. The script was too slight and all of the tinkering didn't help. While improvisations can help with characterization and can add important and original lines to a play, they cannot create an adequate play out of a bad play. Actors are not writers and the good reasons for Joan's desire of a theatre of actors and writers working together became more apparent. Above all one knew that in her dedication to actors and her constant encouragement "Come on Tosspots, Commedia dell' artists!" was the only kind of unity, the true creative spirit of *company* that is necessary for great theatre.

After Theatre Workshop collapsed in 1961, Joan Littlewood's company functioned only spasmodically during the 1960's, although in 1970 she resumed production at their intimate, pleasant, nineteenth century Victorian theatre at Stratford in London's East End. Her basic problems remain her inability to find a gifted nucleus of playwrights with whom she can work and her frustrating failure, due to insufficient subsidies, to maintain a permanent company with the ability to perform a wide range of classics and new plays.

Joan Littlewood herself remains a remarkable enigma. She sought in Theatre Workshop to create a "British People's Theatre," where "the art of theatre ... can and will be a necessary part of people's lives; that theatre should be grand, vulgar, simple, pathetic ... but not genteel, not poetical." She made her reputation with brilliant, modern productions of such classics as *Arden of Feversham*, Marlowe's *Edward II*, and, particularly, Jonson's *Volpone*, which was the hit of the International Theatre Festival in Paris in 1955. Robert Kemp wrote of this production in *Le Monde:*

> I swear that if Ben Jonson came back to life—dressed not in doublet and hose but in a black roll-necked sweater—he would not for a moment want to contest his fatherhood of this modern dress *Volpone*. He would not be more scandalized by the telephone or the perfume which Volpone uses than by the bicycle that the busy Mosca rides. And I'll bet that that wheelchair of the half-dead Corbaccio would not seem absurd to him. Perhaps he would frown at the stockings embroidered with stars which Celia wore, the sort you see on the pavements of the Boulevard Sebastopol around midnight; at the hideous tummy-dances of Volpone's hermaphrodite; at the almost obscene costume of Peregrine, dressed by Miss Littlewood as an American tourist. For the rest everything is perfect. I repeat atrociously perfect. Miss Littlewood knows every fraction of her metier. I owe her a night of nightmares.

After this period of modernizing the classics, she began to concentrate more on new plays and conquered the West End and Broadway with Shelagh Delaney's *A Taste of Honey* and the plays of Brendan Behan. Particularly, in Behan's first play, *The Quare Fellow*, the power and dedication of her improvisation techniques and her devotion to movement so influenced by Rudolf Laban began to be felt. This experience was described by members of the company in *Encore:*

> For the first week of rehearsals of *The Quare Fellow* we had no scripts. None of us had even read the play. We knew it was about prison life in Dublin, and that was enough for Joan. None of us had ever been in prison, and although we could all half-imagine what it was like, Joan set out to tell us more—the narrow world of steel and stone, high windows and clanging doors, the love-hate between warden and prisoner, the gossip,

the jealousy, and the tragedy—all the things that make up the fascination of dreariness. She took us up onto the roof of the Theatre Royal. All the grimy slate and stone made it easy to believe we were in a prison yard. We formed up in a circle, and imagined we were prisoners out on exercise. Round and round we trudged for what seemed like hours—breaking now and then for a quick smoke and furtive conversation. Although it was just a kind of game, the boredom and meanness of it all was brought home. Next, the "game" was extended— the whole dreary routine of washing out your cell, standing to attention, sucking up to the screws, trading tobacco, was improvised and developed. It began to seem less and less like a game, and more like real. By degrees the plot and the script were introduced, although some of us never knew which parts we were playing until halfway through the rehearsals. The interesting thing was that when she gave us the scripts we found that many of the situations we had improvised actually occurred in the play. All we had to do was learn the author's words.

In 1964 I saw Joan again when she brought her London success, *Oh What A Lovely War,* to Broadway. Despite the problems of a pick-up company which she deplored (she was able to offset this somewhat by using many actors with whom she had worked at Stratford), the quality of that success was evident. The simplicity of John Bury's stage set—two towers at stage right and left with a string of colored lights between like the facade of an amusement park—provided a perfect frame for the Pierrots in their costumes singing the songs of World War I. The remarkable, film-like pace of her comic style pierced the theatre. When I visited her, it was several days after the New York opening and, contrary to all Broadway rules, she was doggedly rehearsing her company every evening before curtain time to assure the proper style and rhythm of the production. Ushers and stage hands stood around watching happily. It was the first time I have seen the house personnel of a Broadway theatre look really animated and involved.

Much of Joan's energy during the 1960's was expended on a remarkable environmental project that she called *The Fun Palace.*

"All my life I've been trying to get such a place," she said once in an interview in her usual wry tone. "I'll need millions and it will run at a tremendous loss which must be paid by the government which wastes money on libraries and universities where people don't learn anything. It would be what the theatre should be." She described *The Fun Palace* as follows:

> In London we are going to create a university of the streets—not a 'gracious' park but a foretaste of the pleasures of 1984. It will be a laboratory of pleasure, providing room for many kinds of action.
>
> For example, the 'fun arcade' will be full of the games and tests that psychologists and electronics engineers now devise for the service of industry or war—knowledge that will be piped through jukeboxes. In the music area we shall have, by day, instruments available, free instruction, recordings for anyone, classical, folk, jazz, and pop disc libraries; by night, jam sessions, jazz festivals, poetry and dance—every sort of popular dancing, formal or spontaneous.
>
> There will be a 'science playground' where visitors can attend lecture-demonstrations supported by teaching films, closed-circuit television and working models; by night, the area will become an agora or *kaffee-klatsch* where the Socrates, the Abelards, the Mermaid poets, the wandering scholars of the future, the mystics, the sceptics, and the sophists can dispute till dawn. An acting area will afford the therapy of theatre for everyone: men and women from factories, shops, and offices, bored with their daily routine, will be able to re-enact incidents from their own experience in burlesque, mime, and gossip, so that they no longer accept passively whatever happens to them but wake to a critical awareness of reality, act out their subconscious fears and taboos, and perhaps are stimulated to social research.
>
> A plastic area will be a place for uninhibited dabbling in wood, metal, paint, clay, stone, or textiles, for the rediscovery of the childhood experience of touching and handling, for constructing anything (useless or useful, to taste) from a giant crane to a bird cage.
>
> But the essence of the place will be its informality: nothing

is obligatory, anything goes. There will be no permanent
structures. Nothing is to last for more than ten years, some
things not even ten days: no concrete stadia, stained and
cracking; no legacy of noble contemporary architecture,
quickly dating; no municipal geranium-beds or fixed teak
benches . . .

The curiosity that many people feel about their neighbors'
lives can be satisfied instructively, and with greater immediacy
than in any documentary film . . . and an occasion of major
popular interest—a Cup Final, happenings of international
interest, or a royal funeral—would be presented on screens of
maximum size. The visitor can enjoy a sense of identity with
the world about him.

Many who start by wandering half-attentively, or even
sceptically, through the complex will be drawn into these and
other elementary exercises in social observation. In what has
been called the acting area, for instance, there will be no rigid
division between performers and audience—a generalization
of the technique used in Theatre Workshop for many years . . .

If her mention of "the pleasures of 1984" sounds deliberately
satirical, there is no doubt that *The Fun Palace* is part of Joan
Littlewood's infectious sense of community. She feels that the
British and the Americans are too lonely and isolated. A new sense
of fun, a new sense of communion is necessary in an age where
seriousness is both pedantic and deadly. This communion is the
essence of a theatrical company and her whole plan bespeaks a
theatrical revolution that will use technology at last to benefit the
people. She is not afraid of the people's ability to use and enjoy
technology provided that they control the buttons and knobs and
the flow of images. Only if *The Fun Palace* became institutional,
she points out, would it become a bore. Instead, she insists it must
remain a place where we can enjoy, "Instant Cinema, Genius
Chat, Kunst-Dabbling, Fireworks, Clownery (she likes to call her
actors clowns), Adult Toys, Star Gazing, Science Gadgetry, Battles
of Flowers, Rallies, Concerts, Learning Machines, Gala Days and
Nights."

Theatre to Joan Littlewood is nothing less than a celebration of life. If she is wary of the danger of theatre becoming too serious, too aesthetically isolated, she calls us back to the spectacular, large-scale, joyous nature of theatre in the market place. It is hard to imagine her functioning in an experimental aesthetic, rigorous situation like Grotowski. "The hell with it," she would soon say. Her basic, fervent belief is in a people's theatre—a pride of company like a pride of lions—that will function as a center of life and entertainment in a community. Such a theatre composed of Ideal Comedians would reveal by the harmony of their efforts the pleasures and follies of their society. "Tosspots, Commedia dell'artists" in her affectionate words.

The Open Theatre:
The Thinking Actor and
the Working Playwright

The Open Theatre And *Terminal*

The qualities of self-discovery, the projection of astonishing, confessional images derived from the actor examining his own personality and characteristics, are common to many recent theatre companies with different styles. These confessional traits, so characteristic of the arts in the late 1960's, are evident in such varied groups as Strasberg's Actors' Studio, the Living Theatre, the Performance Group, and the Open Theatre. As Joseph Chaikin emphasizes (in his interview with Richard Schechner), a good director must often suppress his own perception until the actor has discovered the unique creativity of a scene. In a commercial, pick-up company meeting and rehearsing for a few weeks, a director often finds it difficult to relax and feels it necessary to dominate from the beginning because there is so little time. The four to six week rehearsal period becomes a curse because the actors have no chance to create an ensemble. As opposed to this pick-up method of rehearsing, the Open Theatre has done important, experimental work because of its ability to focus on rehearsals rather than performance, to relax and investigate more leisurely. Perhaps this is why Chaikin is considered a great teacher even more than an important director. As he says, only a dedicated company can proceed to accomplish the first essential purpose: "To be able to mark off the area of belief that the company is projecting into."

How many companies go into rehearsal without any "area of belief"; instead, they focus blindly on the play at hand as if the play will make them believe.

In The Open Theatre's powerful production of *Terminal*, the area of belief, as the title indicates, is nothing less than death. The actors are mainly young. They bring to the production their own naivete, their youthful innocence and ironic attitudes towards death. Yet these typical American attitudes become part of the strength of the production. Each actor projects a personal sense of death and, somehow, this creates a rare sense of unity.

Coincidentally, I saw *Terminal* in the same New York church where Grotowski's company performed. Again the setting—the high, rounded stained glass windows rising above the balcony— had a powerful effect on the central theme of the play that could not have been equalled in a theatre. *Terminal* is in three swift sections without intermission: 1) The Dance on the Graves of the Dead; 2) The Pregnant Dying; 3) The State of the Dying. There is no plot, no characters in the conventional sense of drama. Like the Living Theatre, themes, events, actions are meant to be experienced. But two elements are very different from recent Living Theatre productions. The rhythm is tenser, swifter, more rooted in American patterns of urban life as if testifying to the Open Theatre's New York background. Also, the Open Theatre's integration of writers into their productions is evident. The gifted young playwright, Susan Yankowitz's hand is strongly felt in this production, which manifests a concern for the unity of word and gesture that is rare in experimental theatre.

The stage is simply arranged. Clothes are hung on a rack at the left. Several metal stools with wooden seats are visible. An eerie touch is provided by several teeter-board structures with metal legs—slab-like is the morgue image that immediately strikes you. A few other theatrical props are apparent—a ladder, a typewriter on a stool, a drum, a microphone . . .

The production begins with a procession by the actors through the audience. Hardly a novel device, but always effective if done well. It is well done this time; the actors move under a red canopy playing harmonicas, a kazoo, a tambourine, and other instruments. They are dressed in white jackets, white tights, bare feet for this is a play in which movement is crucial. The visual effect is formal antiseptic, in keeping with America's decorous, official attitudes towards death. We tend to sentimentalize, to purify death out of sight. Death is dark. Treat it with whiteness that the final darkness may be conquered or eliminated.

A trumpet sounds. An actor announces, "The Dance on the Graves of the Dead." Anti-American really, a necessary lesson, Hasidic frenzy and exultation. Begin by celebrating death. None of your sentimental mourning. As the section named "The Calling" moves into "The Dance," words, the instinct to name things, give way to the last physical encounter with death, the body dancing against its approaching immobility. A powerful illustration of the mysterious relationship between language and gesture. Here is a real collaboration of writing and acting, an ability to take language far beyond specific, naturalistic details into high-pitched, deliberately garbled word-images that are a kind of sound poetry, sound music, as opposed to conventional dialogue. This is a new, possible direction for playwriting.

Dance and mime movements united with theatre. Chaikin has pioneered in this direction. His techniques are more formally sacramental, more akin to Grotowski's sacred thrust than to the anarchistic direction of the Living Theatre. As the program note to *Terminal* points out, "In a collective work there are stages equal in significance to the performance stage. When the Ensemble begins to prepare directly for the performance stage it relies entirely on the initial investigations." Well, this is pretty self-conscious. It seems a way of saying that the Open Theatre is experimenting with a collaborative method in which the various rehearsal stages are as decisive and exciting as the performance. In rehearsal, under the expert eye of Chaikin, the actor discovers his own creativity. The group accepts or rejects the actor's or writer's contribution by a kind of instant recognition—it fits or it doesn't fit. Obviously the success of this method depends on a dedicated, disciplined company. Particularly, an assertive, defensive ego can undermine this kind of group development of a play. Another major danger of the collaborative method is a diffusion of images. What unity of tone there is derives from the group's unity, not from the singular unity of vision that has been the playwright's traditional contribution.

Consequently, one remembers in *Terminal* the theme of American actors, directors, designers, and writers exploring the images of death. Above all one recalls the remarkable rhythms with which these images are often presented. In Part II—"The Pregnant Dying"—a sequence of rapid scenes covers those pregnant moments when we suddenly become aware of the imminence of death. A woman says to a man: "This is the last time you will see." He takes a last, breathtaking view of the desire of his fleshly world. Then he puts two patches over his eyes. The woman says, "This is the last time you can speak." Suddenly, the man sings a sharp, poignant, final, high note. He puts a patch over his mouth. Silence, a terrifying silence.

In Part III—"The Stage of Dying"—a basic, ironic image of "The Embalming as Required by Law" runs through this last section. The embalming procedure represents the formal, cruel, bureaucratic side of death that masquerades as a sentimental preparation for eternity. Mockingly, we struggle to restore and preserve that which we will not admit is dead. Through this bureaucratic procedure that turns death into cosmetics (I could not help remembering the death of one of my own relatives when I walked into the mortuary and the first thing I saw was a large sign, "MEMBER OF THE BETTER BUSINESS BUREAU, INC."), comes the struggle to resist and attain a new understanding of death. Various compulsive, agonizing images are presented under the title, "The Dead Come Through." A man is slapped and hit over the head in an initiation which becomes an interrogation. A man is executed and, eerily, the song of his death is heard. Most extraordinary of all these death images is that of "Marie Laveau and the Soldier." Death has made sex meaningless. Is the actor playing Marie Laveau and the actress playing the Soldier? Maybe. We can't be sure, nor does it make any difference. What counts is the jagged, frenzied rhythm of insanity, the actor chanting and screaming out lines such as "See my people smile and eat each other ... and my people live like slaves"; while the actress marching back and forth in mock military precision, saluting the air mechanically, shrieks compulsively mechanical lines such as "And dead because I said Yes ... and dead because you said Yes." The words are rattled out fortissimo, swiftly, in a chant-like rhythm to the exotic sound of tambourine and drum. Somehow the effect is both Eastern and Western, a truly original, powerful ritualistic effect.

At the end of *Terminal,* the Dying imagine their judgment. American pragmatic, didactic views break through the sacramental tone—"the judgment of your life is your life." The end of the play returns to the beginning. The actors pick up their instruments and play again under the red canopy. Abruptly they stop and stare out into the audience—"Presence and Absence." Death can be that swift. Death will claim us, but there is something about man's nature that is like the nature of theatre. Both assert their immortality in the repetition of action, the face of loss, the force of absence, the discovery that the presence of death can lead to the assertion of life.

The rare physical harmony, the power of the Open Theatre, is a lesson in training and production. I am impressed by the way they use playwrights to achieve a new physical dimension of the word that seems to fit Artaud's idea of "a kind of unique language halfway between gesture and thought." This kind of theatre, if it develops and is supported in the right way, may be the theatre of the future—small groups of actors, playwrights, and directors working together towards a common goal. Ideal theatrical communities striving together to reconstitute a theatre of depth. Yet some reservations remain—reflecting perhaps my bias as a playwright. Although *Terminal* presents a rhythmically powerful and unified sequence of compelling images, it presents no real characters. We do not feel people, but ideas and symbols. The Performance Group, The Living Theatre, The Open Theatre, and other important experimental groups, are all confessional in approach, tied emotionally to a time of personal, psychological breakthroughs. In Erik Erikson's term, they tend to portray "identity crises" without singular, individual identities. Wisely they retain in their techniques the theatricalism of the tribe, a theatricalism that tends to de-emphasize individuality. They claim the arts of dance, of mime, of chant, of song, as well as that of speech to break through the rigorous isolation of the lonely American personality cut off behind a shield of irony. It is no wonder that following tribal instincts they discard character. Still it does seem to me to raise a question. Essentially we are conflicting historical and contemporary natures compelled to live in certain situations. While the new theatre is quite correct to explore the revival of a physical stage that is centered around the actor and his place in a company of his peers, the danger is the lack of a wild, individual vision that the playwright provides. No matter how dedicated and original the group may be, the group process induces a certain amount of conformity. The group becomes the egotistical center of the work; actors are presented instead of real people in relation to society. The danger is a certain abstract, precious quality to the work.

Still the Open Theatre points to a possible solution. They have invited gifted playwrights to work with them, particularly Megan Terry, Jean Claude Van-Itallie, and Susan Yankowitz. In addition to their group works, they have produced important plays such as Megan Terry's *Keep Tightly Closed in a Cool Dry Place*. It may be the fault of we playwrights that we have not been dedicated enough to struggle to create our own companies. Instead we have hidden behind the word which betrays too easily when it is divorced from the body. Theatre is a unique phenomenon. It requires both communality and individuality. Alas, the playwright often stubbornly struts his individuality at the expense of the communal experience that is theatre. The Open Theatre, even though it is primarily an actors' theatre, points to a possible way out of this dilemma.

An Interview with Joseph Chaikin

RICHARD SCHECHNER

SCHECHNER: Would you agree that theatre, as R. D. Laing says, is a situation in which a person pretends to be himself, art pretending to be reality?

CHAIKIN: Yes, but you can control theatre in a way that you can't control occurrences as you walk down the street.

SCHECHNER: But what Laing is saying is that "elusion" is a sickness because it permits people to avoid making decisions. If you're "pretending to be yourself" then anything anybody says about you might be but it doesn't penetrate. In *The Cherry Orchard*, Ranevsky pretends to be a ruined aristocrat—which she really is. Whenever Lopahin says to her "You're a ruined aristocrat," she says "Of course," but underneath she is saying: "I'm going back to Paris," and "It's not really happening to me, it's happening to the person I'm pretending to be."

CHAIKIN: The connection between that and what theatre can investigate is that you can project a reality and be faithful to a reality which isn't one you live in.

SCHECHNER: But it is one you live in—just that you merely pretend to live in it. That's what is so interesting about Laing's idea. We could make this room into a theatre: I pretend I'm sitting in this chair talking to you. It's all "real"—the only difference is that in my head I'm pretending or playing talking to you. It is a theatrical reality simply because I feel I'm in control of what I'm doing. Some of the things you do at the Open Theatre seem along these lines. People say, "Well, they're not naturalistic." Of course not. But at the same time, your work is very "natural," from Laing's perspective.

CHAIKIN: The teacher of the actor is like the teacher of small children. He looks for the right steps for each student. And when the student is about to make his discovery, the teacher must disappear. If the teacher looks for his own satisfaction at the point of discovery, the student does not fully discover. When a child has a bunch of blocks and is about to make a particular shape, but can't find a way with the blocks—if the teacher guides him in making the shape the child wants to make, the teacher should disappear when the child is about to make the definitive step. By making this step himself, the child discovers his own thoughts. Take an actress doing Electra, she has this definitive moment when Orestes says, "the dogs on the stairs know me but not even my own sister." Then she says, "Ah, it's Orestes." The director can help the actress through the steps of having lost hope, of hatred and despair; at that moment when the actress is at the point of recognition, the director must not be present.

In Jean-Claude van Itallie's *The Serpent* there's a dialogue between Eve and the Serpent, who is played by five men. They are trying to talk her into eating the apple and she is explaining why she can't do it. They tell her that they want her to eat it not because that is such a good thing, but because they don't think she should stick to the limits she started out with, the rules her boyfriend told her about. They want her to go beyond; her actual eating of the apple they don't care about. They want to convert her. So they say, "Why do you think you shouldn't do what you are told not to do?" and she says, "Because I have this life"—in other words, I have this garden to live in and it will be taken from me if I don't cooperate, if I don't heed a certain kind of restraint. Then they say: "Maybe it's better somewhere else." They don't push her: "I can't guarantee it but you won't know until you eat the apple." The

Serpent's argument is that she should do what she wants to do. And she says: "What if what I want to do is listen to God and not to you?" But as soon as Eve says that, the Serpent has won the argument: she's doing what she wants to do; he doesn't really care whether she eats the apple or not and he says: "Then don't eat it." She answers: "I'll eat the apple because that's what I want to do."

After the apple-eating, the problem for the actress is to go on a trip of a person unlike herself. Underneath style and exterior everybody is extraordinarily shocked and shockable—we are astonished all the time and we develop methods that keep us from continuously experiencing our astonishment. Eve after the apple was to go inside this person who is astonished; she discovers everything: the room she's in, the fact that she's an actress, the other people on the stage. If I had said, "You go off the stage and look into people's eyes," I would have limited her even if she did it very well. Leading this actress to this life-and-death stage of her mythical character and having her see at all points that she wants the apple but that she musn't have it because death is a threat: that was my task. At the moment when she eats the apple I had to be absent so that she could see and discover for herself—the first few times anyway. Later I would control it, making it into a score with some open ends, but the actress had discovered what was then scored. She had a different relationship to it.

SCHECHNER: How do you suppress your own inventiveness at this moment? How can you stop from making suggestions precisely at the time when the actress must discover something for herself?

CHAIKIN: It's important that you have no rules for that. Each time you feel it out—empathy—and then you may be able to suggest something without destroying her involvement. While working on the garden sequence of *The Serpent* the premise was that everyone has his garden in the mind, this place that the world isn't, this utopia—where creatures are themselves. The creatures who live in this garden are compatible with each other. We went first of all toward breaking, destroying the false Garden pictures: the illustrated biblical ones, the modern Hollywood ones, those from *House and Garden*—all the commercials (riding and Marlboros). But we had to find a place where we could play out this garden. A place to rest, after getting rid of the false notions. Then an authentic image came; somebody got on that stage and introduced it. The stage is totally empty. The action is to appreciate its emptiness as much as possible, so as not to see the things that could be there but to imagine it as empty. And to then project on it the image of your garden. One actor will get up and do his garden and if another actor is sensitive to it, he will join him so that they make a little world. A third actor may or may not join—depending on whether this garden does or does not signal anybody, give them something they can identify with and understand. Then it's over and someone else tries it. Soon somebody will start a world with its own logic, its own rules, and its own sense of things. Then we have the garden. Ah, but it's so delicate, the process.

SCHECHNER: That is the garden, but it's not everybody's garden. In other words, some people may be in the medieval garden of the unicorn and some may be in the swimming pool. But they equal the same thing: the unicorn is to me what the swimming pool is to you. And as director, are you in the garden?

CHAIKIN: Sometimes. Sometimes everyone in the room is in it. But usually we circumscribe and limit the space, making a concentrated place for imagining.

SCHECHNER: How do you score this type of thing?

CHAIKIN: We are developing a vocabulary to refer to nameless things that happen. Sometimes when you give something a name, you change the thing named. But if the name doesn't interpret but only labels, it can be useful in scoring.

SCHECHNER: How do you know that my garden is equal to yours?

CHAIKIN: We only know by talking and doing. The talking is

very dangerous when you talk what you might be playing, but
talking can start an action as well as refine it. You have to feel
the right point to stop talking and start doing.
SCHECHNER: The man who played the Bird seemed to be a very
positive and negative force at the same time. Positive because
he was so articulate in his movements and negative because he
wasn't really in the community of the garden. He was like the
unicorn: trapped in the garden.
CHAIKIN: When we were researching we came across a piece in
the Talmud about a bird called the "Ziz," King of the Birds.
SCHECHNER: How conscious was the Ziz during the performance? He seemed aware of what he was doing, but also out
of it.
CHAIKIN: It was one of those cases where I found so few problems in his performance that I didn't go into it.
SCHECHNER: It occasionally happens—to be conscious the first
time and to maintain it. Why?
CHAIKIN: Well, I know sometimes when it doesn't happen—
when you communicate to the actor the importance of awareness you often paralyze him. In the case of the actor playing
Ziz, he is very responsive and sensitive, and the garden was
very clear to us all and particularly to him. It may have been a
sound that inspired his creature and in some cases it was
nothing that they did but a sense of the environment, the
brightness of the sun.
SCHECHNER: What about the sound, a repetitive sound which
was almost a punctuation, Adam's sound of the guilt.
CHAIKIN: One of the things I wanted to do—a far-fetched
idea—was to take all these creatures, as though they are
locked in our minds in some way, and to have each character
in a locked action, one phrase of action which is their synthesis. Where they are arrested in our minds, stuck in an action
even though another scene is being played out. Each actor
had to discover that single action; it was very difficult and in
some cases they didn't find the essence of the character. Adam
had one: "It wasn't me—it was her," he points to Eve, who
sighs "I want." Cain's could not have been clear. Its source
was an idea of a speech not in the play: "How can I live at all,
knowing I am going to die? How can I attach myself to
anything precious if I know it's going to perish?" The gesture

was a wavering and non-committing. The source was never clear, but I hope that the feeling was. The ultimate value of even a temporary community of people—that of the audience and actors—is to confront our own mortality.

SCHECHNER: The real heroism of the actor is to give himself to his role. The actor's flesh is exposed, he is going through something. He is responsible for his acts.

CHAIKIN: The only thing that makes theatre different from movies and TV is this encounter with mortality—your own and everyone else's. A man's mortality is his beingness, his appreciation of being. That it terminates. The sense of being alive now in this room, in this place. We are alive here. The Living Theatre is very successful in conveying this sense of now, which is a sense of community and mortality. A confirmation of the mutual mortality of the people in the room. If you go to a play you must participate in it, you may or may not like it.

I think one of my reasons for rejecting naturalism is because it corresponds to social order, certain kinds of emphasis, and certain kinds of repression. What you were saying the other day is what I think is pertinent to this situation: the mode of behavior which a theatre chooses to emphasize is a political choice, whatever the content. Naturalism corresponds to the programmed responses of our daily life—to a life style which is in accord with the political gestalt of the time. To accept naturalism is to collaborate, to accept society's limits. I've seen idealistic people turn to an austerity and a militancy which makes them no longer citizens of that world from which their idealism sprang.

SCHECHNER: The old revolutionary style and the new radical style. The Soviets are still jailing their artists. I would like to be a Marxist, a socialist, and it's a real dilemma. In Eastern Europe, socialism is crushed by monoliths who just can't abide breathing. If Russia hadn't crushed Czechoslovakia, the U.S. would have subverted her.

CHAIKIN: Humor is a good thing, and a certain kind of introspection obviates humor, conspiring toward an austerity that seems to me to be a dead end in terms of understanding. Action is what matters, not the good reasons.

Herbert Blau:
From the Impossible Theatre to the T'ai Chi

The great achievement of Herbert Blau has always been to attack the basic complacency, the conformity of the easy entertainment complex in this country. In his important book, *The Impossible Theatre*, he writes, "Little of what goes on in the American theatre, for all the occasional attention to Vital Issues, seems in touch with anything that really counts, and I don't mean didactically in touch, but rhythmically, viscerally, in the bone structure, where anxiety eats like strontium 90." As a co-founder and co-director with Jules Irving of The Actor's Workshop in San Francisco from 1952 to 1964, Blau helped to create a company that became renowned not only for its level of production standards but for its devotion to the *idea* of theatre. Not that the Workshop was perfect by any means. It was torn apart at times by internal dissension. Occasionally, as is the fate of all regional theatre, it compromised for the box office that determines endurance, since subsidies were infrequent. Nevertheless, in retrospect, the Workshop's achievements were striking. They presented the American premieres of such plays as Brecht's *Mother Courage* and Pinter's *The Birthday Party*. Their primary achievements were undoubtedly the important productions that Blau staged of Beckett's great plays, *Waiting for Godot* and *Endgame*; also Blau's production of *King Lear*. Blau and Irving formed a unique team that somehow managed to strike through the hazardous, commercial maze of regional theatre. Jules Irving, the managing director, provided the business acumen along with his experience as an actor and his talents as a director. Together with Alan Mandell, the dedicated right and left-handed Manager of all details, Irving proved extraordinarily tenacious in coping with the myriad of dragging details that keep a theatre going. This ability to cope enabled Irving to remain as head of the Lincoln Center Repertory Company in New York, although he has been unable there to foster the *idea* of theatre as he and Blau did in San Francisco. It is an old story. The Actor's Workshop was a young, eager company searching for standards. At the Vivian Beaumont Theatre, the home of the Lincoln Center Repertory Company, it takes thousands of dollars for security guards before the notion of theatre even begins. How can one create a unified, aspiring company in such an atmosphere? In New York an actor's struggle is a desperate, individual one for recognition and survival. When the houselights go off, is he going to participate joyously in an ensemble? Not in the present system. It is no wonder that Herbert Blau resigned after two years at Lincoln Center. The real dialogue in a company that keeps the vision, the forward thrust, the challenge, alive requires the presence of an imaginative and stubborn dialectician and Herbert Blau was that man—in the Actor's Workshop.

Blau's progress as a director is infuriating to many "professionals" in theatre. He began as an outsider, a Ph.D. in Literature yet, not even in Drama, an English and Comparative Literature Professor at San Francisco State College. Therefore it was easy for the antagonists he gathered to label him as "academic," particularly since he had no experience as an actor. How easily we like to pigeonhole talents and how self-destructive theatre likes to be in such cases. The facts of the matter are quite different, and my comments on Blau are from years of first-hand observation of his development with the company. Since he is a friend, this is naturally a partisan report, but often friendship is the only way that one can observe the real work of a man.

Blau brings to the theatre all of his weight of intellect, his knowledge of literature. As a distinguished teacher with many years of experience in a wide variety of classes, he creates often in rehearsals a wide standard of comparison. His rehearsals are likely to include all kinds of political, cultural and literary comments that seem pertinent to the play. He fails to see why an actor shouldn't think as well as feel. He senses deeply that the anti-intellectualism one often finds in American theatre is too often merely an excuse to cover up an inability or an unwillingness to probe deeply into the play at hand. Blau himself, at rehearsals, is an example of the ability of the intellect at its best to create exciting emotions; he makes one realize the fallacy of the argument that ideas and emotions have different sources and lead to different effects. In *The Impossible Theatre,* he clarifies the issue:

> At its profoundest, American art brings the fact into the service of the eternal. Melville, writing of Hawthorne, knew that greatness or genius does not exist without "the indispensable equipment of . . . a great, deep intellect which drops down into the mind like a plummet."
> Intellect. It has rarely been respected in the American theatre. But we must bolster our failing hearts by using our minds. . .

Blau knows that a risk of intellect is necessary to bolster the "failing heart" of American theatre. His constantly ironic jabs at the "soft hearts," the sentimentality of commercial and educational theatre, have earned him many attacks. These attacks focus on the accusation that he is arrogant, over-intellectual, and won't listen to criticism. Yet real talent, genuine idealism, always decide alone. No group decisions rule art or life. There are only individual viewpoints, individual styles, adjusted to the demands of the immediate situation. Blau's vewpoint comes out of a powerful fusion of experience, a slum childhood in the Jewish section of Brooklyn, a scientific, undergraduate education as a chemical engineer at New York University, wartime service as a paratrooper, years of graduate study in English at Stanford University, and twenty years of practical and theoretical work in the theatre.

In rehearsal he can be one of the most exciting directors I have ever seen. His physical energy, the complex intensity of his emotional and intellectual make-up, tend continually to shake the actors out of complacency. He expects a great deal from them. In *The Impossible Theatre*, he says:

> What I prize in an actor—beyond training, beyond talent, beyond brains, beyond the 'spine' of performance,—is mystery, the ability to bring out of nowhere an action that is incredibly strange and perfectly right, so that one feels, after it is performed, that he has witnessed an enchantment, and can only ask in admiration, "Where did that come from, it was so true?"

Although his demand for this final mystery of performance is great, and a tribute to the possibilities of acting, he has learned from experience the necessity of patience on the part of a director. Patience, at first, was not one of Blau's great gifts. Slowly he learned the first requisite of a good director, the ability to sit still, watch, and listen to the actor, to become the ideal audience. Always he had the physical ability to communicate a sense of movement. This came naturally to him. Despite his lack of experience as an actor, he has a gift for gesture and the suggestion of movement that is striking. When he was directing my short play, *The Master,* I remember vividly one moment when he was staging the final eagle dance. Suddenly, while pondering possible movements, he became the image of a fierce eagle. Another time, during a rehearsal of the swagger stick sequence in the same play, the situation called for the Candidate to imitate an illiterate, good-natured Schweik of an American revolutionary soldier. Abruptly, there was Blau marching along in a slump, the perfect image of an American Schweik. Together with this physical ability for movement, Blau's teaching background gives him an extraordinary verbal facility.

Indeed this verbal facility is a danger that Blau has had to learn to control. At times the actors in his productions have felt overwhelmed by the flood of his ideas and his enthusiastic quotations

from the history of literature. Yet, surely, it is better to have too
many ideas than too few. Blau has a gift for constant metaphorical
parallels that enable his acotrs to see their characters in a new way.
Once when Erica Speyer, the talented actress who was playing the
Candidate in my play, *The Master,* was having trouble with the
rapid, zany sequence of events, Blau suggested to her: "Think of
the woman as a diamond and the scenes as various facets of the
diamond. Not just cause and effect." And she stopped struggling
for a rational hold on the sequence and began to look for the
inherent rhythm.

Rhythm, the great puzzle and the great power of the theatre.
One of the most interesting things about Blau's productions has
always been his sense of pace, his ability to find a rhythm that
holds a play together. Pace is a concept about which little has been
written; it is the central mystery in drama, far more difficult to
realize than the rhythm in music which is notated more clearly and
therefore often more obvious. Blau writes about pace in *The Impossible Theatre:*

> The aesthetics of pace has never been sufficiently explored.
> What I have been trying to emphasize is that it has something
> to do with the mileage of moments—the degree of *illumina-
> tion* in each instant . . . Fast or slow, let me stress this: there is
> a difference between an enlightening succession of "events"
> and a lustreless sequence of "behavior." To those for whom
> the brilliance of the rational mind remains a supreme value,
> the catatonic naturalism of such a drama as *The Connection*
> may be momentarily engaging, but interest is bound to run
> out. . . .

Blau demands then, as Brecht does, that the audience participate;
they cannot sit back mindlessly for some superficial enjoyment.
What creates pace is understanding. A "lustreless sequence of
behavior" is mere existence, not drama. Color and excitement
come only from revelation, which Blau calls "the illumination of
each instant." Pace in a Blau production always has tension, a

reflection of his kinetic energy. But with his growing understanding of theatrical matters, his best productions have shown how pace is linked inextricably to the particular demands of each succeeding "event" in a play. The rhythm at this point, whether fast or slow, may be determined by one factor, a line, a gesture, a song, an action, a dance, or several factors together. To find the right rhythm Blau digs deeply into all of the elements of a situation. As he rehearses each scene, one feels and hears him holding in his mind the kind of rhythm that will clarify the whole structure with the right contrasts and connections to maintain the proper unity.

In Blau's productions of Beckett's two great plays, *Waiting for Godot* and *Endgame,* he was able to discover a style that made the fantasy of Beckett's situations terribly real and timely. It is not easy for an American audience to experience the disillusion of the "absurd." They are still mainly accustomed to rational hope. In *Waiting for Godot,* by using burlesque techniques, Blau was able to give the European character of the play an American tone that made it one of the most successful productions the Workshop presented. Blau explained his approach to *Waiting for Godot* in *The Impossible Theatre:*

> In discovering a style, the effort was to extend the natural into the unnatural, to create the reality of illusion and the illusion of reality, to make the theatrical real and the real theatrical, to test the very limits of style and stage. Thus, the actors, who might be going through the routine motions of anxiety, as natural as possible, would move, almost without transition, into the shoulder-to-shoulder, face-front attitude of burlesque comedians. Or Gogo, wandering about the stage in irritation, would suddenly strike the proscenium and cry: "I'm hungry!" The motive was personal, the extension theatrical, the biological urge becoming the aesthetic question.

In *Endgame* Blau created a slow, inexorable rhythm that was one of the most agonizing I have ever seen. *Endgame,* playing in the smaller of the two Workshop theatres, was a fascinating test for the audience. Finally, it seemed that only about thirty people a night were able to endure the test, a piddling failure by Broadway standards, yet those thirty people in the audience received an experience that affected their lives. At least they seemed to when I saw the play. Rarely have I sat through such tense silences. Blau has said of *Endgame:* "There was nothing more regenerative in our repertoire. . . . For it was with *Endgame* that the eye-opening Blitz of modern art came most stunningly into our theatre." Robert La Vigne created a ripped, dark painted sculpture of a cave-like room that brought the textural intensity of modern art to the stage. In the process La Vigne became legendary in the company for his prowling of the streets and his discovery of unusual "found" objects. No curtain was used. To illustrate the daring of Blau's rhythm, the opening mime, before the ritual unveiling of Hamm, took as long as fifteen minutes without a word being spoken and with hardly a sound. With two of the key actors in the company, Robert Symonds and Tom Rosqui, whose talents developed rapidly through the years as they played many different roles in repertory, Blau was able to create an ensemble that was incredible in its exploration of the physical meaning that lies behind Beckett's curt, connotative language. Suddenly, for the first time to me, Artaud's concept of the Theatre of Cruelty took on an American reality. Paradoxically, the experience was so excruciating that one did feel purged by it; one did feel the weight of grandeur. As Blau has written about *Endgame:* "What is amazing about the play is its magnitude. Haunting the limits of endurance, it finds grandeur amidst the trash, trivia, and excrement of living."

In addition to *King Lear* (a production modeled on the stark qualities of Beckett before Peter Brook tried the same approach in London), Blau's most original stagings included Genet's *The Balcony,* and Brecht's *Galileo.* All of these productions suffered from the technical inadequacies of the theatre in which the Workshop was forced to play. It was impossible to create the large-scale movements and the spatial dimensions required by many scenes in these plays on a stage as small as that of the Workshop's. Yet Blau achieved a great deal in these productions. For the first time, *King*

Lear proved that the Workshop could make a success of the classics in the same way that Peter Brook has rejuvenated Shakespeare in England. Blau said: "It was after producing *Godot* and *Endgame* that I began to see most luminously those great black scenes after the storm, when the play researches for truth in the waste-land." He built up his production on the subtext of "nothing," a key word repeated many times in the play. "We began, then, not with a Shakespeare, but with a certain kind of experience. 'Nothing will come with nothing ... All's cheerless, dark, and deadly.' " As in *Endgame*, the result was not depression, but a kind of illumination, a lesson in tragedy for Americans in order to come to terms with our own violent experiences.

Blau's production of Genet's *The Balcony* was especially daring in concept. He took Genet's powerful homosexual fantasy (Genet specified that all of the whores should be ugly grotesques) and used all of the sexually attractive and youthfully innocent actresses of the Workshop in the most provocative heterosexual way. While the result may not have been Genet's true intent, Blau made the play into a unique fantasy of sexual illusions that seemed all too relevant to American audiences. He staged most of the play before enormous mirrors. At the end he brought up the houselights to leave the audience gaping uncomfortably at their illusions, an act that cut off any curtain calls and left the audiences to straggle out uncomfortably with the final lines of Irma engraved in their minds: "You must now go home, where everything—you can be quite sure—will be even falser than here. . . ."

Galileo was another important step in Blau's search for a true unity of the arts. As in *Lear*, he commissioned Morton Subotnick to do an electronic score. However, this score did not seem to me as effective as in *Lear*, where the electronic music served as an eerie metaphor for the entire storm sequence of some thirty-five minutes. Also for *Galileo*, carrying out his visual aims which are part of his directorial gifts, Blau commissioned various artists to design the many props, even the impressive chess set that he used. The result was a visual grandeur that was truly impressive. The handsome front curtain flew up like a sail and the audience entered the play with a marvelous sense of historical voyage. Blau worked throughout the production to create the right tone for Brecht's rational comedy, an aim which Blau defined in *The Impossible Theatre:*

> One of the missions of Brecht's drama is to restore a comedy which is virile, critical, Rabelaisian, obscene, a mockery of what is worshipped, as in the satyr plays. (It is a kind of comedy to which our company has become most receptive and at which it has become increasingly adept.)

This comic sensitivity that Blau mentions is a clue to the Workshop's success as a regional theatre company. Unlike the ACT which has failed so far to strike any deep roots in the San Francisco bay area, the Actor's Workshop found a certain unity in a virile, ironic, mocking, yet socially involved stance. If the stance was Blau's, a theatrical company as I have said often derives its identity from a dialectician. Yet the Workshop took too from the atmosphere of the bay area—a time when important scientists, writers, and artists were at work, a time before Reagan, Rafferty, and Hayakawa had begun to affect the educational system drastically, a time when the war in the far east had not yet developed into a full-scale disaster, a time when the liberal thought behind the Workshop still seemed politically hopeful.

For an actor, the Workshop represented a challenge of artistic craft. Blau stressed always his belief that if an artist, a writer, a composer had to risk poverty in his work, why shouldn't an actor take the same risk to achieve high artistic standards? In time Robert Symonds exemplified the company's achievement. Often he rehearsed all day, performed at night, and then went to his job of hauling vegetables at a produce market. Soon it became apparent that he was the perfect example of a character actor who can best develop within a company situation by playing a variety of parts. His best roles revealed the mocking, ironic, liberal comic style that characterized the Workshop's best productions—Hamm, Gogo, Harpagon, Volpone, Sir Toby Belch, Goldberg in the American premiere of *The Birthday Party*, Archie Rice, Krapp, Undershaft, and many others. No wonder Symonds, by resisting commercial offers and remaining in San Francisco, came to represent the true achievement of a regional theatre actor.

The sad fact remains that the Workshop, like other regional theatres, was unable to find a place in American society. Blau has said, "More than any other form, it (the theatre) calls constantly for its own purification . . . Because it aspires to function, however marginally, at the dead center of community, the theatre is more subject to compromise and adjustment than other forms." There is a paradox here. If the ideal of a great theatre company, at the "dead center of community," calls constantly for the sacred act of purification and sacrifice, how can it also compromise and adjust? The perils of regional theatre have always been financial and the stress has been of necessity on "fund-drives." However necessary, the elements of a fund-drive in our materialistic society tend to resist the ideal of purification. Theatre is split apart constantly. Still Blau clings to his belief that "the theatre has greater possibilities than other forms because it takes greater risks with more vulnerable means." In a lecture in 1969 he criticized revolutionary theatre as not having "even the faintest claim to be overwhelming. It is cutting itself off from personal accord—a point Beckett always reminds me of . . . What I want is a theatre distinctive in its humaneness."

Humaneness, exaltation, these are words that Blau uses frequently, and they suggest the crucial problems of regional theatre. How can we be humane, how can we exalt, in a society whose major tone is technological, materialistic, ironic? Again and again, in his discussion of playwrights, Blau comes back to this necessity in *The Impossible Theatre:*

> Of Pinter: "And while he knows the cleansing action of the scourge, he does not—as Beckett does, as Artaud's Theatre of Cruelty portends—exalt."
> Of Genet: "The most degraded fantasy in Genet redeems itself by exaltation."

In his brief position as head of theatre at the California Institute of Arts, a new professional college of the arts, Blau had exciting ideas about training groups of actors as companies rather than merely instituting the usual, formal classes.[1]

During the past years he has been studying T'ai Chi. From this

[1]After this book was sent to the publisher, I learned that Blau had been fired from his position as Provost of the California Institute of the Arts and had resigned as Dean of the Theatre School after an ideological hassle with the Disneys and other trustees. As a result of widespread protests, he was invited back to run the theatre program, but refused finally because he feared a lack of artistic freedom. As he wrote to me, "Corrigan has been ordered to shape things up. I suspect the interference won't be direct, it rarely is. The money will tell that story." Since Blau's departure in 1972, Corrigan has been fired, despite his attempt to remain as President. The new theatre (see illustrations), designed by Blau and Fisher, remains unopened, an artistic and educational disaster. A highly promising, experimental college of the arts, dedicated to the highest standards, seems destined to drift into another conventional art school.

In the spring of 1972, with his usual spirit and tenacity, Blau took another important job as Director of the Inter-Arts Program at Oberlin College in Ohio. Several actors from his California training program went with him and established at Oberlin an exciting new theatrical company. With the help of the Rhode Island State Council on the Arts, in the summer of 1972 Blau brought his company to Roger Williams College in Bristol, Rhode Island, where I watched several rehearsals and lecture-demonstrations. This new group of Blau's is potentially one of the most exciting theatre companies in the country. Physically, they are already tremendously exciting to watch. In addition to the T'ai Chi, which has helped to give the group "the idea of moving meditation that is a performance" as Blau has said, they use many of the Grotowski exercises, and various new techniques that Blau and his actors have developed. Stylistically, no matter how arduous the physical demands, they can represent anything. Their problem, and it is the central problem in the new theatre, is to find a new, poetic relationship between language and action, word and body. Too often in rehearsal their physical prowess overpowered their verbal techniques. As Blau kept telling them "You must find the *precise* relationship between what you're doing vocally and physically." To conquer this problem, the company was working on material based on the concept of "The Enemy," hoping to develop a play through the process of collaboration that has become central to so many important contemporary productions. Watching this group convinced me more strongly than ever that the new playwright will be one who can unite physical and verbal techniques into a unified poetry of the theatre suited to the scientific and artistic problems of the twentieth century. Blau's Oberlin company is one of the few with the potential for transcendent experiences such as *ecstasy, wonder,* or *mystery* (a word that Blau uses frequently). These experiences contain a language of action almost totally absent from conventional American theatre. Blau's new company is one of the few deeply involved in uniting oriental and occidental techniques into a search for new theatrical dimensions.

ancient source, combined with his wide variety of experience, he hopes to develop new spiritual disciplines in theatre, the discipline combined with the freedom of inspiration that American theatre needs. The following short article by Blau, written in October, 1970, discusses his experiences with the T'ai Chi and the goals toward which he aspires.

Shadow Boxing: Reflections on the T'Ai Chi Chuan

HERBERT BLAU

We are rooted in a place; we are rooted in the absence of a place. Between the two is the breathing of a shadow. There, for me, T'ai Chi Chuan unfolds. Or so it does in my imaginings. In practice, I have only the mistiest intimations of where it might lead. The experience is too short. What drew me to it, however, was the commitment to evanescence. I responded to the lure of an exercise and a spiritual discipline that has the character of a performance. Actually, I was looking for the shaping energy behind the performance—"the force that through the green fuse drives the flower."

I came to the T'ai Chi through long questionings about the art of the theatre, where action passes through absence and the reverse. For years in the theatre I have wondered about the primal cue for action, the relation between motive and behavior, form and content, body and being, idea and incarnation. Which comes first, the doing or the conceiving? What is the connection between the source of energy and the dramatic use you make of it? The *yi* directs the *chi,* we're told; as I understand it, what occurs is very much like what happens to an actor when his technique is most accomplished. Craft passes into art when, surpassing function, it becomes gratuitous. Between the conception and the act is the barest shadow. The gestures are impossible unless you have the vision, the vision is impossible unless you do the gestures. Inadequate to begin with, they materialize with each other. The form is the actualization; to perceive the form is to want to do it.

What is attractive about the T'ai Chi in a period of loose improvisations is that it is exemplary because it is exacting. To see it is to want to do it right, to do it as it has been seen. In the T'ai Chi, as in the performances I admire most, precision is next to godliness. One realizes very shortly that what is being done has been done archaically and developed through long devotions. The forms are a repository of learning, an accretion, a body of lore and a lore of the body in its motions. One hesitates to violate the form, especially when it is discovered that the form, done strictly, solicits what is individual in the doer. The separate but inseparable forms are elusive and inexhaustible. In reality, how does one grasp a sparrow's tail?

Long before I studied the T'ai Chi, there were impulses in my work (if not entirely in my body) that resembled it. In a craft oriented toward production as the theater is, one of the chief problems is to discover how not to do the doing that must be done. What gets in the way of performance? Fear, distraction, vanity, anxiety, ego, narcissism, sentimentality, the obsession with results; dislocation, no center, lack of gravity. The cleansing action of a true craft is a "negative capability"—no irritable reaching toward an answer and an end but an attitude of reverence about the moment; letting it happen rather than making it happen, relinquishing oneself, getting out of one's own way. "Let be," says Hamlet, after all the desperate enterprise of his wild and whirling mind. With that "Let be" he came to the very center of indifference, the Void, where the great power of western thought, inevitably failing, touches upon the East. For that moment, the excruciating choice between to be and not to be disappeared into the abyss. Another sort of energy arose from quietude, the intrinsic strength of interior calm. For Hamlet, the desperation wasn't entirely over. Neither is it really, in this world, for most of us. But the qualities of calm, softness, slowness, flow, as well as the lost suppleness of the child are worth trying to retrieve from the surrounding derangements of a violent time.

To recover time itself from our collective urgencies is a consummation devoutly to be wished. The repose of being toward which the T'ai Chi moves is the basis of a substantially expanded consciousness in a period addicted to false mind-blowing and instant gratifications. The T'ai Chi requires time as the condition for forgetting it. Any craft of consequence does the same. As in the Creative hexagram of the *I Ching,* there is a furthering and a perseverance, the one depending on the other. Progress is a conservation, the moving forward is a going back. The mystery is in the repetitions. The T'ai Chi is an endless rehearsal, a perpetual present moment sowing the seeds of its returning future, like the theatre. One performs it, sentient among the successions, outside of time, with timeliness. The sequence, whether for exercise or meditation, has its proper duration. By a "commodius vicus of recirculation," as in Joyce's *Finnegan's Wake,* the end returns to its own beginnings. There, here, now, in the incessant and impeccable changes, is an imposing stillness. "Movement," according to *The Secret of the Golden Flower,"* is only another name for mastery." All is still at the still point of the turning wheel. The circular movement activates all the dark and light forces of human nature. Mutability and mortality. One hopes to understand them through the metamorphoses, the changing avatars and darkling embodiments, parting the wild horse's mane to perceive—what?

The vanishing is what the actor is after; it is what any man is after who contemplates his place in time, or the absence of a place. Like the *chi,* the reality we seek, or the mystery, is there and not-there. Shadow and breath are the declensions of the actor's art. Immaterially—diaphanous rather then immaterial—they constitute a definition of the actor's being. The dead in *Purgatory* knew that Dante was alive when his body cast a shadow on the ground, when the shadow moved. There is shadow within shadow, measuring time. There is a shadow in the eye of the beholder. Breath is the shadow of a shadow, yet the tensile strength and lifeline of being— a skeleton key. Radiance in the actor is the shadow's brightness, illumining a breath. I confirmed these fancies in other dimensions as I traced the lineaments of the T'ai Chi.

Performed in the sun, it is a corporeal reflection on shadow and breath. It stresses clarity in vacancy—movements which are exact, clean, and pure, even while inseparable and indecipherable. The circle is its secret. There is a mysterious lucidity in a circle which one can only approach with the imperfect calligraphy of the body. Yet one tries, as an act of faith and self-respect. I grow impatient with performance in or out of the theatre uncleansed of irregularities and carelessness, as if artlessness were a thing of the spirit. The T'ai Chi knows that the spirit is exact. Like thunder. Like gravity. Like grace.

Adrian Hall and the Trinity Square Repertory Company:
The Problems of Regional Theatre

I first met Adrian Hall when he directed a new production of Melville's *Billy Budd* during the 1968—1969 season. At first his intention was to do the familiar Coxe-Chapman version. Then, as he wrote in the program note: "I could not find in any existing play version the Promethean torment, the unresolved complexities that Melville suggests in his book. It is for this reason that we put together our own script . . . The Coxe and Chapman play is just as valid today as it was in 1949. It is we who have changed. If we cannot examine Shakespeare, Melville, and James Joyce with the sophisticated eyes that we have today, I am not interested in looking at them through a veil of the past (the box set and the 'good' story line)."

Hall asked me to sit in on rehearsals and to help make suggestions about material that could be adapted from Melville to dramatize the complexities of *Billy Budd*. Having worked in this way with Joan Littlewood in London, I was aware of the possibilities and problems of this approach and was glad to consent. Sitting there in the problematical space of the Rhode Island School of Design auditorium—a space that Hall called "the most lethal, killing thing that I have ever tried to conquer"—I observed how his company was beginning to achieve a new kind of American theatricalism. At first his techniques seemed influenced largely by some of Brecht's Epic Theatre ideas and by Grotowski's idea of confronting myth rather than merely identifying with it. Hall had

363

seen Grotowski's company in Edinburgh in 1968, when the Trinity company performed there. Although it was clear that Hall had been excited by Grotowski's methods, basic differences soon became apparent. Hall's theatricalism seemed to depend uniquely on three factors:

1) *Space*—Hall uses this word frequently. While it has become a little trite to say that someone from Texas has a particular sense of vast spaces, it is true of Hall. It is an inner space as much as an outer space, a feeling for the distance of loneliness, an awareness of racial isolation, an instinctive understanding of how far one man can exist away from another man even though they share the same background. Basically Hall is a lonely man. He makes it clear in his relationships that his dedication to theatre comes first. Trust, in his experience, is too often betrayed. It is an attitude characteristic of many sensitive people in theatre. Particularly in the commercial structure of the American stage, promises mean little. As a result of long years spent fighting chaotic theatrical battles, Hall has armored himself.

In the enormous space of the Rode Island School Of Design auditorium, it often seemed that Hall sensed Billy Budd not merely as a tiny figure in a cosmic design, but as some small particle of nature adrift in a world controlled by historical, elemental distances. The whole theatre, in Eugene Lee's brilliant design, became images of a ship sailing through history; not a conventional ship separated from the audience; a ship that represented images of war, cruelty, repression, revolution on which the audience was part of the crew. Hall has said about his changing concepts of space:

> As time went on and we began to experiment with certain things, people began to say things that interested me. Our stage designer, Eugene Lee, said to me one time in a moment of despair, "Adrian, men are on their way to the moon and we're still building flats out of canvas." And I thought about that ... I began to examine why we always think in such visual terms. And what is space. And why must space be divided in certain ways. I think back to many, many years ago when I saw a production of *Glass Menagerie* on Broadway

which was a horrendous production. The space used in this particular production was as if it were cast in iron. There was a house on one side of the stage and a house on the other side of the stage and there was a center section that could not be violated. We knew when the lights came up here we were in this house: we knew when the lights came up *here* we were in *this* house. And yet, that is not the way we think; that's not what happens in the mind. So why did an art experience have to have those kinds of rigid limitations?

2) *Characterization*—Like Brecht, Hall presents actors as actors—the pride of their theatrical abilities. No more "personality" types to dominate productions and interfere with the unity of the company. He wants actors with a variety of gifts, who can sing, dance, move, shift abruptly from one character to another. As he resents plays with every little movement indicated in the script, so he detests actors direct from a casting service stereotyped and pigeonholed as "romantic leads, lawyers, truck drivers, etc." He has concentrated for several years on building an extremely flexible company.

3) *Time-Rhythm*—Hall wrote in his program note to *Billy Budd:*

"The further we progressed the more sure I was that a direct story-telling line or plot-giving device or successfully building suspense (rising action it was called in the old days) was not what we wanted here. To read Melville's novel is to have a disturbing, fragmented look from many sides at the individual against the structure."

The significant words "a disturbing, fragmented look from many sides" describe well not only the unique, special angles of vision that Hall attempts to conceive, but also the interrupted, jagged rhythms, similar to films, similar to the daily disruptions of urban life, for which he strives. The rhythm of a Hall play is tight and forceful in the sense that it always has his fierce energy behind it. This kind of rhythm is impossible to structure classically or chronologically in time. Instead it builds on a fluid, shifting perception

of time past, time future haunting, influencing the theatrical time
that is always *now*. In *Billy Budd*, the rhythm was "fragmented"
like a dream, and the transitions served to accentuate the psychological and political pressures that led inexorably to Budd's hanging.

In the spring of 1969, Hall asked me to write a new play for his
company. Something on a large scale, with a wide variety of
characters, with rapid sequences of compelling color. I hit upon
the idea of *Lovecraft's Follies*. The idea of *follies* furnished me
with both a musical sequence capable of many changing scenes
and a form capable of portraying the central American conflicts of
our time. Living in Providence, Rhode Island, near the house
where H. P. Lovecraft, the horror fiction writer, lived, gave me an
idea for the way the play could move rapidly through fantastic
visions of reality. In my poetry I have always been intrigued by the
fantasies produced by the actual details of everyday life. I decided
to use Lovecraft as a narrator into the follies of our time. For the
central character of the play, I created a physicist, Stanley Millsage, who worked on the bomb at Los Alamos under Oppenheimer
and at the Marshall Space Center in Alabama under Wernher Von
Braun. As the play opens, Millsage has fled from the restrictive
security procedures at the Marshall Space Center and is living in
Rhode Island. He is building a statue of H. P. Lovecraft. In his
mind the statue comes to life and a sequence of folly-visions results
based on experiences from Millsage's life. In the first part of the
play, the visions proceed comically from a scene based on the
generation gap to the moon landing and a wild version of the white
man's approach to "primitive" cultures as exemplified in *Tarzan
and the Green Goddess*. The second part of the play deepens the
comic focus into a vision of Oppenheimer as an Indian shaman
trapped in the secret rituals of the new military-industrial state and
a final, ironic vision of key characters in American history contending in the Alabama state insane asylum where Millsage was
once confined. I hoped to use the popular, funny, agonizing images
of American life in a ritualistic, stylized manner to suit Hall's new

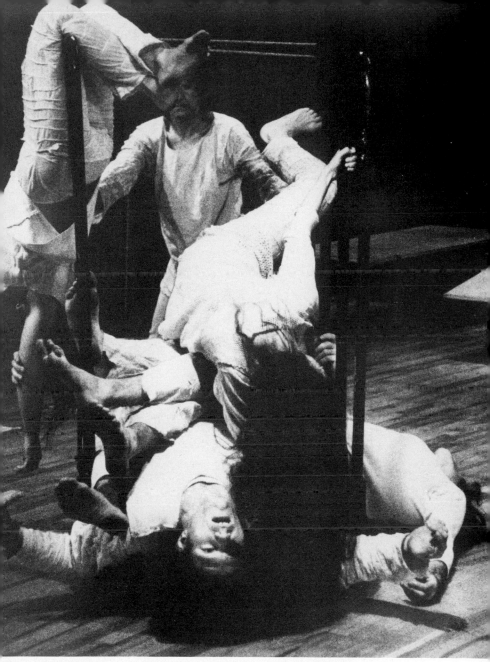

Terminal, The Open Theatre, directed by Joseph Chaiken. "A confirmation of the mutual mortality of the people in the room. If you go to a play you must participate in it, you may or may not like it." (Joseph Chaiken, 347)

Paradise Now, The Living Theatre, directed by Julian Beck and Judith Malina. "One cannot remain passive. I discover in myself a paradox. I both resent and admire the aggression of these actors." (303)
Photo by Gianfranco Mantegna

Alice in Wonderland, The Manhattan Project, directed by Andre Gregory. In Andre Gregory's production of *Alice in Wonderland,* the modern psychological distortions under the surface images is stressed. A vision of the relationship between adult and childhood fantasies emerges. The merely verbal images of fantasy are rooted theatrically in painful, physical reality. (J.S.)

Following two pages: Eugene Lee's institutional setting for *Son of Man,* The Trinity Square Repertory Company, directed by Adrian Hall. Lighting by Roger Morgan.

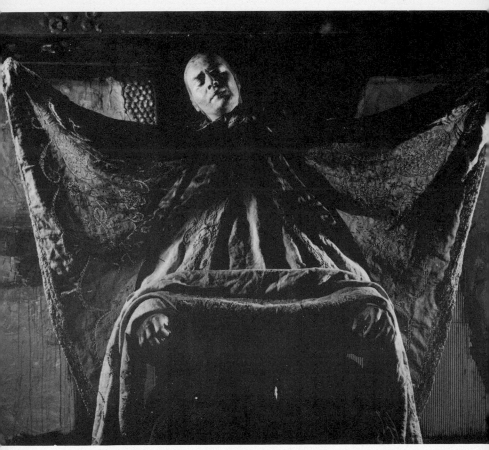

Endgame, The Actors' Workshop, directed by Herbert Blau with setting by Robert La Vigne. "To illustrate the daring of Blau's rhythm, the opening mime, before the ritual unveiling of Hamm, took as long as fifteen minutes without a word being spoken and with hardly a sound." (354)
Photo by Chic Lloyd.

The Balcony, The Actors' Workshop, directed by Herbert Blau.
Photo by Hank Kranzler.

Commune, The Performance Group, directed by Richard Schechner. *"Commune* is not something taken from the outside. It was made by us in our theatre." (Richard Schechner, 382)

theatricalism. Alternately, Adrian was excited, baffled, antagonistic, and enthusiastic about the vast problems this kind of style presented.

He spent the first week of rehearsal reading and casting the play, an extraordinarily long period of time to keep the actors off their feet. Much of the dramatic color, he saw, would come from the excitement of actors transforming themselves into many roles. For example, one actor played Hitler, then Cheetah, Tarzan's ape, then Oppenheimer as an Indian shaman. In the second week of rehearsal, Adrian showed his characteristic, intense preoccupation with the rhythmical flow of a play. He stressed to the actors: "If an event is just a *curiosity*, treat it just as a curiosity. Then we go on to the next event." Even in those frequent crises that mark an American company's perilous existence, he fought doggedly to stimulate the actors to his goals. Rarely angry, when a rehearsal goes badly, he gets fidgety, tense, and begins to speak even more rapidly than usual, spitting forth his impatience through the syllables "and so and so forth." Once, when he wasn't getting the concentration he desired, he stopped the rehearsal and addressed the entire company indignantly: "This is a god damn holy temple that we're in. If you don't continually come back with more love, then we'll cut you off, cut you off. I hope we don't walk into a trap, or a glass of warm milk, the way it sometimes happens when you talk this way."

During the five-week rehearsal period, Hugo Leckey, the writer and Executive Director of the Rhode Island State Council on the Arts, visited rehearsals and kept notes. Some of these notes reveal well how Hall works with his company:

> Adrian interrupts while Millsage is reading the Lovecraft speech: "How do we cope with the supernatural, how do we do that? We cope with it in symbols of reality. That's all we have. This is close to the center of the play—the Lovecraft speech. Terrifying visions of reality. I want to go for that reality. Play it. Do you remember when we were doing *Julius Caesar?* I wanted to bring in a dog or a goat and actually make you kill it. If I hadn't been such a snivelling coward I'd have done that. You sometimes won't extend yourselves to get

at the reality. . . ."

There's a frenetic sense of activity in the theatre today. When I arrive they're working on the scene based on a Lovecraft horror fiction story. A retrograde process is described showing a retreat to sub-human babbling. Millsage begins his speech and halfway through it is broken down into one-liners which the other actors deliver. The scene involves acting out aspects of horror—the ravaging by birds and animals of a girl, a cannibalistic, ritual sacrifice. There's a lot of motion and frenzy involved. Adrian swings around the stage, full steam, organizing movements. "I'm not trying to butter you up," he shouts to the actors. "This is really fun to play. I know it's a pain in the ass right now." As they begin the scene again, he interrupts. "We have to establish images we want to leave with the audience. If we could cause an uproar that reaches alarming proportions." Here he speaks to two actors who are moving down through the audience making animal sounds, and I gather, dragging something over the heads of the audience. "These images are important. Watch the accent. Science has gone too far—Accent. Rat. Accent. Old Ones. Accent. Ah ee ehmm. Accents." Jim Schevill leans over to me and says, "It's interesting how elements of sound poetry are beginning to filter in." The scene is a pretty hair-raising one even at this stage. When the lights come up, Adrian says suddenly, "Stop acting and walk off. Our craft has been exposed." I like the idea of creating a horrific scene, and then being discovered acting it. I've never seen Adrian do that before . . .

The Asylum-Folly Ship scene at the end of the play is denser and more moving now. Bill Cain as Millsage begins to be a dominating sensibility in this. There's an enormous moment created for the chorus of "Sail on oh Folly Ship." Adrian's redone it since I last saw it. The idea stems from the Fat Cat and Burner of Cities rowing against each other. Now the company forms two teams downstage rowing against each other. At the apex of a triangle from this line, two other groups sit waving tiny American flags, while around the stage, imitating the 'Spirit of 76,' a drummer, flagbearer, and a flutist march. It's blatant theatricalism and cheap in its utter uproarious emotionally tugging effect. Perfect. The irony and glory of the scene are absolutely captured. It reminds me somewhat of Balanchine's 'Stars and Stripes'—the tone and spirit. The crews collapse at the end of the scene and then act out the MIRV missiles. It's all vulgar beyond belief. I love it . . .

I remember noting a long time ago that Adrian didn't leave much movement to the actor's choice. He depends on fairly fixed blocking, being intent on creating a precise, choreographed action. In his kind of theatre, cutting across time and space on a non-realistic set, one can't expect an actor to dictate choices in movement—at least as opposed to the same actor sitting in a simulated drawing room. On the other hand, Adrian will accept ideas of action or movement from actors when they seem useful. An example in this show is the whitewashing the two space officials go through when they paint each other with huge brushes as they talk about the necessity to 'purify' the moon landing. The actors brought that in themselves and Adrian likes it. But since Adrian is usually extremely precise and detailed about the action that he wants, what happens is a two-fold thing. In his theatre, he takes on the position and importance we are accustomed to seeing a movie director have. And secondly, a new acting style is being developed. It's hard to define, especially now as it is in transition, developing rather than settled. But briefly: Rather than an actor working towards character, and then being placed in relation to other actors, and movements—the movements and group actions begin the work. Partly from this, and partly from his feelings towards the lines, character emerges. On the whole, character is subordinated to a larger effect. Part and parcel here is the type of play, script. An action not dependent on character and events to show development. But dependent on events containing character, which illustrate more general questions. In other words, we're getting away from the story of a man at the center of a drama—it's still partly there, but not as the main thrust. The actors move toward mime techniques, although it's not pure mime. It's still infiltrated with individualistic character work. One notices teamwork more than one to one confrontation. One sees events, large brimming events, events with social and political significance, rather than personal . . .

Perhaps the most difficult problem in theatre today is the relationship between audience and actors. The advent of film and television brought about a vast, eager public for the camera image, but also served to increase the passivity of audiences in general. An era of increasing fantasies and frustrations developed. The new theatre attempts desperately to break down the passive audience, to bring the hidden fantasies developed in the dark of film theatres into the open and confront them. If the audience is accosted directly, an artificial antagonism is likely to result. On the other hand, to cajole the audience into participation may turn embarrassingly into a brief encounter with an amateur therapy group. Determined to involve the audience, Hall has made many experiments in this regard. Indeed he has been accused by some indignant spectators and critics of firing cannons and creating general noisy alarms merely to attract attention. His awareness of the complex problems involved are revealed in a statement about his brilliant production of Robert Penn Warren's play, *Brother To Dragons*, adapted by Warren himself from his long poem:

> Warren's play was a very rewarding experience because we just began to—well we had to begin by eliminating a great many of the things that we had learned in the theatre. In that play, we found that it was possible for the audience to play games with us. That is, if the game was so set up on stage that the audience wasn't aware that they were being called upon to do something. Now then, one of the things we did was a crazy little experiment. The time of the piece was about 1812 with one of those early American socials which would have cornhusking or a square dance or apple-bobbing. The actors had great fun just by being challenged by the water and the tub and the apples and so forth. I was very confused how to bring the audience really into it, knowing if you confronted an audience directly with "We want you to participate in this game with us," etc., etc. . . . Immediately, eyes begin to look down and people begin to shift away and they hope their neighbors are going to be called on and they are not going to be called on. Actually what happened was that various actors began to throw apples into the water from various areas in the

audience. As that grew to a kind of excitement, as the actors picked up energy on stage and began to clap their hands a little faster and a little faster, a girl suddenly took two apples and ran into the audience, and said, "Hit the water—hit the water." And then ran right on. And sure enough, the audience threw their apples in the water. And the people around them were excited by their actually participating and so and so and so . . .

Brother To Dragons was performed in the superbly proportioned, intimate, small theatre of the company. Consequently the space lent itself more easily to an exciting involvement with the audience.

In the 1970-1971 season, Hall presented a controversial play, *Son of Man,* that he wrote with Timothy Taylor. Disturbing visions of the Manson family shifted, dream-like, as if in a drug-induced hallucination, through a fascinating, environmental space designed by Eugene Lee (see photo). Hung on steel rods from the ceiling down through the audience and over the stage were high metallic pathways suggesting institutional corridors. The grim effect of these corridors was enhanced by Roger Morgan's powerful lighting with huge, naked institutional lamps glaring down through the scaffolding. When the actors walked and ran on these pathways, they reverberated mechanically, as if reflecting the vain struggle of confined, regulated bodies to survive. Although the play somehow lost the institutional sense it set out to reflect, the concept was extremely effective.

In his second production, Hall set out grimly to confront the bugaboo of Shakespeare again. As Peter Brook writes in *The Empty Space:* "Nowhere does the Deadly Theatre install itself so securely, so comfortably, and so slyly as in the works of William Shakespeare. We see his plays done by good actors in what seems like the proper way—they look lively and colorful, there is music, and everyone is all dressed up, just as they are supposed to be in the best classical theatres. Yet secretly we find it excruciatingly boring—and in our hearts we either blame Shakespeare, or theatre as such, or even ourselves . . ." Since Hall's plays, whatever their faults, are never boring, his solution, again with Eugene Lee and his costume designer, John Lehmeyer, was a search for the modern, atmospheric equivalent of the Elizabethan theatre. He said: "With the Shakespearian plays we've done here, I would like the concepts and ideas *relative to the production* to be spoken about years from now, and not that they were productions *for* a particular time. Not the sort of productions one could say, 'This was done in 1957,' or when-have-you, but ones with a kind of timelessness. And most of all, that they are not being done in 'reverence.' So, for *The Taming of the Shrew,* we're going to try and create an atmosphere. The actors are going to be obviously actors, playing on high platforms, in the middle of the stage area. There's going to be milling around with the groundlings, and attempts at the actors moving about in the audience selling things, talking to people, singing. If we can get it the way we'd like it, it will be an attempt to touch on the essence and spirit of what the Elizabethan Theatre really must have been like."

What developed on a high platform in the middle of the theatre ringed around by the audience was an area in which student "groundlings" sat and stood while an enormous horse on wheels pushed around by several actors carried Petruchio on his journeys. The horse was so huge and tall that its every appearance was impressive, astonishing, and perilous to the actor, William Cain, who played Petruchio. He had to train rigorously at a gymnasium every day to keep in shape for the leap onto the horse. This concept was influenced by the production of *Orlando Furioso* in New York, with horses raging through the standing spectators and scattering them. Hall and Lee's adaptation of this device to a Shakespearian environment was a fascinating example of the way an authentically modern approach to an Elizabethan atmosphere can be established. Interestingly enough, in those performances where there were only a few student groundlings, the play sagged in pace and power. When there were a large number of groundlings, a fascinating exchange of movement and colorful action occurred between the actors and the spectators.

The advantages and agonies of a regional theatre company involve crucial issues that American cities and communities have not confronted. The advantages of continuity, variety of productions, roots, a life in a community, are obvious enough. The agonies need closer consideration. A regional company tends often to become provincial, cut-off from the life-stream of society. Even in England, after Glenda Jackson, the gifted, young actress, left the Royal Shakespeare Company, one of the two supreme, well-subsidized British theatres, she confessed: "I'm just not a good company member. In Stratford, we were isolated from the company of everyone but actors and I found the experience incredibly boring and debilitating. And internal politics inevitably arise there; they tend to forget in Stratford that there is a world outside."

Although Hall has struggled to create a link between his theatre and the surrounding community, like all regional theatre directors he has not been entirely successful. With the help of a federal grant, he has managed to create the most successful secondary school program that regional theatres have achieved. Thousands of students from all over Rhode Island are bussed to Trinity productions. Yet there has been a constant change in the administrative structure of the theatre that reflects the precarious, fringe place that theatre has in American society. The omnipresent, administrative financial problems make it difficult for Hall to concentrate on the artistic development of the company. There is no time or money for a training program. His worst problem is the lack of time and relaxation for really creative consultation and planning.

If Hall and his company are to grow and fulfil their unique promise, they will have to solve the two major dilemmas of regional theatre: they will have to create adequate planning time within the company instead of operating hand to mouth; and they will have to participate with all Americans in the re-shaping of our society to humane rather than materialistic, technological ends.

Hall hopes that the new theatre his company will occupy in 1973 in the center of Providence (see photos in final section) will be the start of a closer community relationship. As long as theatre is not at the center of society it will remain of secondary importance. Conversely, a society that ignores the central meaning of theatre to the just, imaginative life cannot for long claim to be anything but a crass, materialistic power.

Future Visions

Towards The Twenty-First Century

RICHARD SCHECHNER

It is 1971 and we haven't closed the books on the 19th century
yet. Read one of Eric Bentley's most recent anthologies, *The
Theory of the Modern Stage* (1968) and learn how much the 19th
century is with us. "At one extreme, we make stage space absolute,
the stage setting purely architectonic, and depend entirely on the
movements of actors, singly or in mass, to create the stage picture.
Light then acquires, in our eyes, a classic purity of definition. At
the other extreme the stage becomes murkily romantic and the
dynamics of light is used to create the illusion of an actual extension of the space played in. [. . .] The asethetics of modern stage
setting, like the aesthetics of modern art in general, accepts tactile
value as the supreme value and the basis of significant form." Thus
Lee Simonson in 1932 summarizing the Adolph Appia of 1895. Or
take Gordon Craig in 1905: "I am now going to tell out of what
material an artist of the theatre of the future will create his masterpieces. Out of ACTION, SCENE, and VOICE. Is it not very
simple? And when I say *action*, I mean both gesture and dancing,
the prose and poetry of action. When I say *scene*, I mean all of
which comes before the eye, such as the lighting, costume, as well
as the scenery. When I say *voice*, I mean the spoken word or the

375

word which is sung, in contradiction to the word which is read, for the word written to be spoken and the word written to be read are two entirely different things." Or Arthur Symons summarizing in 1907 what Wagner wrote nearly a half-century before: "Literary poetry still exists, even literary drama written, as Goethe wrote it, from outside, as by one playing on a lifeless instrument." Even men of the 20th century, like Artaud and Brecht, had their ideas shaped by WWI and the twenties. I will not summarize their ideas because they are so *current*. Enough to remember that Artaud wanted to "abolish the stage and auditorium and replace them by a single site, without partition or barrier of any kind." And Brecht saw the actor and the action as confronting each other in a way designed to encourage the spectator to judge both the skill of the actor and the meaning of the action.

When we think of modern theatre—or, worse, when we don't think of it but simply talk about it—we light on ideas and techniques that had their origins, definitions, and pioneer performances in the 19th and early 20th centuries. Grotowski synthesizes the tensions between Stanislavski and Meyerhold; Brook puts into play the ideas of Artaud. Theatre is still coping with the turmoil of the years from 1848 to 1918: the manifestation in practical politics of Marx's thought; the first seminal writings of Freud; the experiments of Planck. It would be stupid to proclaim the 21st century while practicing the 19th. We ought to start where we are, acknowledging that not much fundamentally has happened in theatre during 75 years. Or maybe the problems of the 19th century are so shattering and basic that we will be hassling them for a long while.

Understanding theatre means understanding four areas of conjecture and practice: architecture, characterization, theatric structure, an overview of modern theatre history. If we are clear about these, we would know where we are and where we might be going. The 19th century luminaries would arrange themselves into perspective, some coming forward to the first rank, others falling back. I want to go into these four areas and reveal my own feelings on each of them.

(1) ARCHITECTURE. This is decisive. A space can be used as found (a village square), found and renovated but keeping its original qualities (Avignon Festival, many off Broadway theatres), specially designed as a theatre (Broadway houses, most college theatres), or internally redesigned for each production (environmental theatre such as the Garage of The Performance Group). Also important is how the audience sees a show, and how they participate in it, if at all; what their spatial relationships are to each other and to the action; whether the performance is localized in one or several places or is generally distributed; whether the performers are very near the audience, at medium range, far away—or in a space that encourages swift changes of these distances. There are endless combinations or arrangements. This variety is what is modern: theatre architecture is no longer the variations of a single (proscenium) model.

It is shocking that most productions get up with little thought given to fundamental spatial relations. There was an excuse 75 years ago when only one kind of stage was available. Directors are rare who think through the plasticity of what they are doing, who cope with or transform the theatre space. Fixed seating (proscenium, thrust, or arena) is the enemy of architectural creativity in staging. Putting actors in among the audience is no solution. Only when the whole theatre is ready to be designed, can a performance possibly achieve itself. Maybe the proper solution for a particular production is a proscenium stage—but this solution must not be enforced *a priori*. So-called "multiple" stages—George Izenour's things, for example—are not the answer; these are cumbersome battleships, outmoded and rigid. The only creative solution is an empty space—rectangular, cubic, or spherical. Whatever needs to be built for each production can be built.

We have had good results with the empty space approach at the Performing Garage. For *Dionysus in 69, Makbeth,* and *Commune,* the interior of the 50 x 40 x 20 foot space was entirely redesigned. For *Makbeth* the loft over the theatre was used as well. Each use of the space had its own feel. In all cases, however, the audience was generally organized high along the outside with a central acting area. On very crowded nights for *Dionysus* there were as many as 100 people on the floor, and these were formed into islands around the two central towers. For *Commune* only 50 people were allowed on the terrain-floor each performance. These were used during the performance and their movements contributed to the weight and fluidity of the space. During several performances of *Makbeth* spectators were encouraged to follow the action around, under the platforms, to the banquet table, up the ramp. The Garage is not the perfect environmental theatre. It is part of the perfect theatre. I would like to have a truly cube theatre and a spherical one. I would alternate productions in each of these three basic indoor spaces. I would like to have money enough to build some structures out of transparent material so that I could have a massive structure in the center of the space and still know that the big thing is transparent. The tendency to keep much of the action in the center is because I want most of the audience to see most of what's going on. A whole aesthetic of degrees is developed in environmental theatre—distinctions between those actions which are "public" and those which are "private." The feel of having the audience in the same space as the performers is exalted; there is so much that can be done, so many nuances, and such a great range of movements and feelings.

Concerning theatre architecture there are two kinds of absolute alternatives: (1) between indoor, artificially lit performances and outdoor, sunlit performances; (2) between single-minded-space performances and divided-space performances. In sunlit performances the audience sees itself as well as the players. I have had a good deal of experience with this kind of performing. Most guerrilla street theatre is done outside during the day. And in 1961 I directed Sophocles' *Philoctetes* for a performance on the beach at Truro and in the center of Provincetown on the steps of the Chrysler Art Museum. Working in sunlight is giving up theatre's hocus-pocus. Every director and performer should do it once a year as a remedy. The only thing outdoors that can focus an action is the action itself; one is always contending with the surprises and glorious shows of the street, sky, sea, audience. You learn to absorb these into your production, or they kill you. For *Dionysus* and *Makbeth* we painted the walls of the Garage white so that we would have *less* control over the lighting. We wanted it to spill and approximate the feel of sunlight; we didn't want the audience blacked out. For *Commune* the walls are a light earth color; there is still a lot of bounce. Orthodox theatre black is an abomination.

Putting everyone together in one space is the architectural version of sunlight. It makes people share in the event; it makes them *responsible* for the event. Appia well knew what I'm talking about. "The antique stage was unlike ours, not a hole through which the public was shown in a constricted space the combined effect of an infinite variety of media. Antique drama was the event, the act itself, not a spectacle." Performing in divided spaces leads to illusionism; it brings forward the gimmickry of theatre. It's a cheat and, more often than not, a bore. Far from diminishing audience involvement, single space staging sharpens it by throwing each spectator on his own. There is no "best" seat, nor any single vantage point, or even any single line of events. A lot of what happens depends on where you are when it happens. You may be close or far; you may hear or not hear. And you are free to move closer to something that calls you, and further away from something that repulses you. All within the envelope of the single space which makes the experience more dangerous and more communal.

One of the paradoxes of single space staging is that by giving himself up to the action, adhering strictly to his score and letting his emotional impulses flow freely through the score, the performer shows more of himself than in any other kind of space. He is so close to his audience that he is driven to extemes. Either he will become tense and panic into self-indulgent over-acting or he will relax, grow open and vulnerable, and let the energies of the performance space flow through him. The shared sense of being part of a community evokes in the performer his highest responses of giving, taking, vulnerability, and openness. Audiences, too, become friendly, cooperative, and moving. They are really beautiful.

(2) CHARACTERIZATION. The orthodoxy says a character is a person and the actor's job is to "live the life of" or "become" the

character. We're going to have to drop all that. I want to retain the systematic elements of Stanislavski's work, and get rid of its programmatic goal of building a character."

Not playing a character is playing the actions, regardless of their consistency one to the next. It is not worrying about causal chains or story lines. It is denying that theatre is a "mirror" of anything and asserting that theatric structure is musical—that is, related only to itself. The performer builds his score not out of a sense of becoming someone else but by being precise, moment to moment, about what he is doing. There is no buffer of character either between him and the actions or between him and the audience. During rehearsals a complicated set of actions is made. The collection of these may seem to be a character to someone in the audience, but for the performer they belong entirely to himself and it is through them that his own feelings flow. Not self-indulgently (where the visible effect exceeds the invisible cause) but in ways that give depth and flow, and ways that concretely make him give, exchange, and share.

The performer does not play himself, he does not play a character, he plays the actions. The actions are objective. That is, they are part of *mise-en-scene*, and their function is to bring to the audience's attention what the director and performers decide to bring. The actions do not vary from performance to performance.[1] They are specific and concrete, like musical notes. But they have no intrinsic emotional value. This is the hardest for performers to learn. That is, Action A does not guarantee Feeling B. The feelings of the performers will vary from performance to performance, sometimes wildly. Action A guarantees Feeling X—and X *is unknown* until it happens. It can't be anticipated. The performer

---

[1] Improvisation is a tool in finding and making a *mise-en-scene* and a score. It can be deadly when you are trying to maintain a score during performances. For the performer to be truly free to let his feelings flow during a performance, he must know that for himself, and for his partners, each detail of the score will be strictly adhered to. He depends on these details to carry him along as the trapezist depends on his partners and his bars and ropes. When they are secure the performer can relax and let his feelings flow *through* these details. To be able to depend on the *mise-en-scene* and the score is to perform with trust. That is the only way.

prepares himself by relaxing, doing many exercises in self trust and group trust; he reviews his score, which is always physical and concrete, until it is second nature to him. What happens for the first time *each performance* (no illusion) are the feelings stimulated by the score. These are not those of a character, but of the performer. The unity of the performance is guaranteed by the *mise-en-scene*, and it may not be a unity of character or a story. The vitality of the performance is made possible by the evocation of the unanticipated feelings expressed by the performers. Let me be specific.

Commune was made by The Performance Group during May-December 1970—eight full months of painstaking composition. The text was assembled from newspapers, old American writings, Melville, Thoreau, Whitman, Shakespeare, Marlowe, the King James version of the Bible, and group improvisation. Improvisation took two forms. First, at the end of and blending from 30 to 45 minutes of psychophysical exercises[2], I would lead some or all of the Group into improvisations that used or needed the invention of texts. Sometimes these would be free verbal associations closely related to a specific psychophysical exercise. That's how we got the "Songs of First Encounter" and the "Death Raps." Sometimes they would be the acting out of stories and situations we knew from previous work, reading, or common knowledge. That's how we got parts of the first and second killing scenes. Sometimes they were infusions of specific texts or rhythms into exercises that were modified from other uses. That's how we got the "Slow Motion Race" and the "Recapitulation." Second, we were working on four scenes, three from Shakespeare (Gloucester jumping, Stephano &

[2] These exercises relate parts of the body-mind to each other, and contradict the apparent duality of systems. The exercises are a set of more than 20 dealing with the gut, backbone, face, head, neck, extremities, and torso; they are rolls, twists, bends, balances, throws, wiggles, shakes, jumps. The physical work encourages "associations," either of a direct, imagistic kind; or within parts of the body itself, such as feeling happy in your wrist. The exercises were taken from Grotowski, Yoga, The New Orleans Group (I was one of the founding directors); and I have developed them over the years. They are done in accord with improvisations and "on-the-spot" exercises that I invent as I go along.

Trinculo finding Caliban, Richard III courting Lady Anne) and one from Marlowe (Lightborn coming to kill Edward II). These scenes were picked by me in May as a means of helping individual performers face problems I noticed in their work. The scenes became part of *Commune* because they were the *work we were doing at the time.* I cannot over-emphasize the apparent gratuitousness of the choice of scenes; nor say strong enough how organic they are to *Commune* now. The struggle to understand, transform, and perform those four scenes is the struggle to make *Commune. Commune* is not something taken from the outside. It was made by us in our theatre. The four root scenes are gratuitous only from the point of view of drama. From the point of view of who and what the Group was in the spring of 1970, these scenes of love, rage, death, and rebirth are archetypal. They sank into *Commune* until they were embedded at the very base of its structure, its foundation. Along with slow motion running, an exercise in hearing sounds and moving-singing to the sounds heard, elements of the Manson-Tate murder case, and our relationships to each other, these four scenes are the *donées* of *Commune.*

We tape recorded each improvisation. During the summer we made the text *at the same time* as we were developing the *mise-en-scene* and beginning to work on individual scores. One portion of the work does not precede the others; all are incomplete until all are nearly finished. But they do not move in lock-step. The *mise-en-scene* comes first, and is like a rough sketch of the whole; next comes portions of the text; last are elements of the performers' scores. It will take years to complete all the scores. The text is finished, and the *mise-en-scene* nearly so. Each element feeds the others; and one that gets too far ahead waits for the others and is usually modified when they catch up. For example, the forging of a missing part of someone's score makes changes in the scores of others, probably modifies the *mise-en-scene,* and possibly leads to changes in the text.

None of this painstaking work is done on character. None is devoted to finding the "right emotions." All is spent on the text, mise-en-scene, and scores. In brief, it is all focused on doing things and the relationships among the things done. The performer makes his way through a performance by knowing what he is doing, where, and with whom. Nothing more, nothing less.

Most performers in *Commune* use names other than their own for two reasons. First, to isolate *for themselves* those parts of themselves that are used in the production. (Like athletes, performers develop whatever skills are needed for the tasks at hand. Only some of the performer's self is called on for each production; but whatever is used, is used to the utmost, and developed until it is whole.) Secondly, from the *audience's point of view* a whole person is seen during the performance. But this person is not a fiction. Aspects of the performer have been brought out, enlarged, focused.

Unity of performance is not unity of character. Often during a single performance performers will play contradictory actions; or actions that are not linked in a causal chain. Sometimes a performer will be at the center of an action, sometimes he will be chorus; and the two functions may have no narrative or character relation to each other. The only thing a performer does through the whole performance is to perform. This is the key to it all. The objective unity of the performance is the *mise-en-scene*. The inner unity is that the performer performs, just as the athlete plays his game. Joan MacIntosh is not pretending to be Clementine in *Commune*. Clementine is the name given to a set of actions and words that MacIntosh does. What makes her performance unified is that at each moment her actions are concrete; she is present in what she does; her feelings are free within the actions; she is open to her partners and to the audience; she knows her way around the space; she is making a score for herself. In other words, she performs. If I described what Tommy Agee does in center field and at bat for the Mets, I would have a list like MacIntosh's and I would end by saying, "In other words, he plays baseball."

To show the details of a score, and to demonstrate how it is a matter of fact and not feelings, here is an indication of part of MacIntosh's score during the first 15 minutes of *Commune*. This is only MacIntosh's work with Fearless Jim (Jim Griffiths); she has much work with others during this period, and some alone. And it is not a score proper. Scores are rarely written out. If they were, they would be many times longer than the text. A performer learns his score by doing and doing, selecting, adding, subtracting, inventing, and doing again. It is a tedious, creative business. And if a person doesn't like it, he should find something else to do with his life.

1. Looking for Jim while singing "Big Rock Candy Mountain."
2. Pig fuck.
3. Animal fight during Jim's "Song of First Encounter."
4. Jim holds me around my waist during my "Song of First Encounter."
5. We take each other in.
6. We have our picture taken together.
7. Jim looks at my body paint and then invites me to join him and Spalding horse riding.
8. I decline.
9. Jim dances by me and invites me to dance with him during the "Death Valley" dance.
10. I accept.
11. After the dance I sit with Jim and David Angel.
12. Jim and I go horse riding.
13. I rush to Jim after the gunfight and sing *Oleana* to him.
14. We walk to the name circle together and sit next to each other.

Each of these indications is the root of an exacting score. The "pig fuck," for example, has more than 15 specific moves of its own, each worked out in precise detail, beat by beat.

In some ways this work isn't different from what Stanislavski urged. Few are the theatres that have carried out his plans. But in a fundamental way we have shifted from building characters and coaxing feelings to planning actions and letting whatever feelings there may be flow freely. We have moved toward the extremes: a strong, autonomous *mise-en-scene;* precise and detailed actions through which the performer cannot help but express himself.

(3) THEATRIC STRUCTURE. I don't mean anything super dif-

ferent than Meyerhold's "theatricalism." Most common theory is
of *dramatic* structure—analysis of text and characterization. Naturally, if we're developing a theatre without characterization, dramatic structure will not answer our needs. The terms of dramatic
structure are 19th century adaptations of basic Aristotle. Phrases
like "rising and falling action," "conflict," "discovery," "reversal,"
and "climax" are all clichés. They are founded on the assumption
that theatre is an imitation, a mirror of experience. Stanislavski
wasn't immune to these clichés. Meyerhold, on the other hand,
insisted on an *autonomous* theatre related to other experiences
only by analogy. Both Artaud and Grotowski followed Meyerhold
strictly on this central point. Theatre cannot be understood by
appealing to things outside the theatre. But systematic theatre
theory is scarce. A whole way of thinking must be built nearly
from scratch.

If the relationship between theatre and non-theatre is analagous,
what are some of the better analogies? Aristotle's was natural
enough: theatre is like the lives of individuals; a plot is the arrangement of incidents that happen to the characters; the play is
like an organism whose destiny is fulfilled. Kubler suggests another
analogy, one better suited to our days. He thinks of theatric structure as electrical or nervous energy transmissions. The play on
stage is like a model of the brain, or a power grid. There are nodes
or synapses to and from which energy is always flowing. Some of
these store energy and then suddenly, explosively, discharge it;
others distribute energy evenly and steadily; others are circuit-
breakers. Some nodes are out of order and cause short-circuits.
Others are wired in series so that tripping one trips many.

Any given moment on stage many different connections are
being made. There is movement horizontally between different
points of one mode—say dialogue—and movement vertically or
diagonally between different points of different modes—say between some dialog and a gesture, or between a gesture and a
change in the lighting level. Kubler's model lets us take into account the text and other elements of the performance without
saying of any *a priori* that it is more important. In his model, at

any moment, a certain element may be the most important; and at the next moment, it can be another element. This is the kind of flexibility lacking in Aristotle's model.

During every moment many connections are being made, although perhaps only a few of these are noticed by the audience. Nevertheless, a seemingly minor connection may be of overriding importance. Othello's handkerchief has its counterparts in every corner of theatric structure. According to Kubler, every kind of theatrical exchange either transmits, interrupts, transforms, short-circuits, re-routes, absorbs, or gives off energy: dialog, gestures, movements, lighting, props, sounds, etc. The scheme is not of rising and falling action, but of connections, circuits, boosters, transformers, resistors, and so on. Kubler's model focuses us squarely on the stage and the interactions there. He leaves no room for idle psychologizing or the making of off stage biographies. For him, energy is either actual or virtual; when it is actual it is moving in some direction, at a given frequency, with a certain effect; when virtual, it can be made actual by the proper circumstances.

Kubler's analogy allows for sudden shifts in energy, concentration of focus followed immediately by diffuse or multi-focus. His idea does not discriminate against lights, props, sound, etc. Everything that goes on on stage is plugged into Kubler's circuitry; it remains for the analyst to chart the direction, amplitude, frequency, and pattern of the energy impulses.

I would want to make only one modification of Kubler's excellent scheme. I would like to speak of "bundles of relationships" rather than of electric circuitry.[3] The electric imagery is a little too non-human, and it suggests movement at the same speed, if at different frequencies. If you think of Kubler's nodes as bundles of relationships, and the many-strand lines connecting bundles as the flow of a performance, you will see the picture I'm drawing. What happens on stage is complicated, but it includes at least the following: (1) performers who relate to each other and the audience; (2) an "autonomous" structure, such as a story, a set of actions, a

[3] I take the phrase "bundles of relations" from Lévi-Strauss's discussion of myths. I use the phrase with different emphasis than Lévi-Strauss.

choreograph, a text, etc.; (3) "technical" effects, such as lights, sound, costumes, etc.; (4) over-all arrangement of space—how the audience is seated, or allowed to move, where the stage is, or the stages are, etc. Each of these four levels exist independent of the others; but they are always interacting. The exact structure of these interactions at any moment is *one* bundle of relationships. How one bundle ties into the others, and how they all relate to all the others, is the structure of the whole piece.

It is probably unnecessary to know the structure of a whole theatre piece. But a director may need to know for any problem what the bundles of relationships are at a certain moment. To apply Kubler's analogy, as I have modified it, will, I think, help resolve staging problems. It is important that we start to think of *theatric structure:* that we learn the theatre in its own terms.

(4) THEATRE HISTORY.[4] Orthodox histories are out of date. They still draw on the assumptions of the period just before ours, a period that ended *circa* 1950. This earlier, pre-modern period was dominated by playwrights, and their ideologies conditioned the approach of the historians. Thus, the text of a play was untouchable; the function of director and performers was to interpret the text; the nature of criticism was to analyze playtexts. Even the underlying politics of our theatre historians stems from the playwrights. Characterization was all important, thus grew up the myth of the identity between humanism and individualism; and the flourishing bourgeois theatre—except that it isn't flourishing anymore. There is a Marxist, as well as an individualist, humanism. Playwrights no longer dominate our theatre. Texts are taken apart and put back together with meaning for our days. Directors and performers are without doubt more creative than the current crop of playwrights. The times have changed. And now we need new histories written from the vantage of our predispositions. Enough of old prejudices, it is time for some new ones.

We need new histories on the following topics: (1) On the "underground" from the end of the 19th century to the 1950's

[4] I am indebted to conversations with Michael Kirby, Brooks McNamara and Darko Suvin for many of the ideas in this article.

when the underground emerged. This study would tie together the avantgardes of all the arts—theatre, dance, film, music, graphics. It would carefully follow the careers of leading futurists, formalists, surrealists, dadaists, Happeners, etc. We would see that this underground is long and strong, with many entries into the mainstream; we might even begin to wonder what the mainstream is, and what the underground is. (2) Studies *relating* the work of the major directors to each other. (3) Studies of the popular and vulgar arts of circus, vaudeville, travelling shows, magicians, sex shows, etc. (4) Studies of major productions not from the point of view of character but from that of theatric structure, as outlined in the previous section of this essay. (5) Marxist and other non-bourgeois studies of pre-modern drama and theatre.

If these projects were undertaken by young, forward-looking scholars, we would be confronted by some challenging discoveries and hypotheses. Each age buries itself in the assumptions of the previous age. Getting out from under is tough work. But it's the only way a people gets to know itself. What might we find were we to know ourselves?

From *I've Left*

BY BERN PORTER

Considering the vast array of problems that confronted me and those which I attacked because the odor of stagnation about them could hardly cause me to do otherwise, the theatre was by far the simplest to approach. I say the simplest because at the very outstart I had only to throw out everything that comprised it. And of everything that comprised it there was nothing more crust laden with dull tradition, artifice and plain rotting stupidity. By everything I mean the auditorium, the stage, the settings, the orchestra, the actors, the costumes, the dialogue, the lighting, the sounds, the ushers, the balconies, the tickets, the box office, the directors, the managers, the stage hands, the writers, the scripts, the curtains, the props, the stage effects, the backers, the angels, the producers, the entire everything in total, all there ever was. With the grand upheaval and discard went interpretations, themes, scores, criticisms, theories, definitions, concepts, ideas, texts and all other related matter. Thus completely liberated I was free to reconstruct the only plausible theatre, the one based on physics and called by me *scithe.*

On a flat, open space I inscribed a circle of sufficient diameter to accommodate twelve hundred swivel seats each capable of rotating a full 360 degrees and with sufficient space between each to allow occupants to rotate without touching one another, plus some additional footage to allow free and easy passage of all theatre goers and the performers or "feeders," as I now called them. These seats were mounted in the firmly packed yet resilient earth to form a huge spiral evoluting concentrically from the center of the circular space. These seats were both radiantly heated and lighted to temperatures and color ranges controlled from an unseen organ. These seats were in effect both stoves and lamps; any theatre goer so physically constituted as to resist the full emotional intensity of the spectacle to follow could be made to heat and light up like a glistening torch, while for the less inhibited viewers the swivel seats were but pulsators of ground level glows and light sequences of the upcoming spectacle. It was characteristic of the light emanating from the seats, or pipes as they more properly were, that they more than brightened and warmed but also angered, frightened, carressed, soothed and bolstered, the combination of heat and light having qualities and variations of tones, now felt, rather than heard or seen. Moreover the heat and light could be spread continuously, intermittantly; spread in waves, sheets, in torrents, in arrow-like advances, directed, piercing, streaking under, over and about the audience at the will of the organist playing from a composed score for each presentation.

Since no one could enter my theatre, which as you will note has no gates, aisles, doors, walls or stage for I have not mentioned them, without bringing with him his own mask and costume chosen by him to represent his particular mood and contribution to that particular evening, the seated audience before the performance began was a breathtaking spectacle to behold for now the theatre goers were themselves the set, the stage, the play about to begin. As the curtain rose, that is to say, when the heat and light came on sectionally, individually, alternately, completely and then not at all in continuing pulse, rhythm and movement throughout the circular space and light shafts and sound beams began to cut the air vertically and angularly as the organist covered his keys in modulated, now frenzied zest like any other concert pianist, the feeders appeared, that is to say the performers who were actors, musicians, dancers, magicians, directors, speakers, singers, all in one, appeared at the particular section of the great circle through which they moved as the participants of theatre goers rotated in their chairs to follow them.

The entire circle of people under the manipulation of the feeders became a stewing pot of emotional brew, sound pierced, light struck and heat riddled with dialogue replaced by gesture and thought, with music replaced by feeling and spirit, with props replaced by the very theatre goers themselves. As the surrounding air space became electrified in this highly charged manner, individ-

James Schevill's *Lovecraft's Follies,* The Trinity Square Repertory
Company, directed by Adrian Hall, designed by Eugene Lee. "One
notices teamwork more than one to one confrontation. One sees
events, large brimming events, events with social and political
significance, rather than personal. . . ." (Hugo Leckey, 369)
Photo by Michael St. A. Boyer.

Above: Another segment of Gerald Shapiro's program at Automation House.

Opposite page: Gerald Shapiro's *The Second Piece: The One About Finding Your Way in the Dark,* Automation House (New York). "Each helmet contains circuitry which transmits a unique, complex, low frequency audio signal by modulating an invisible, infra-red beam. Other circuitry detects those signals and routes them to the headset. . . . Scanning and coming together form the first phase of the piece and lead to the second." (Gerald Shapiro, 273)

Following two pages: Josef Svoboda's collage projection for *The Soldiers,* an opera by B. Zimmerman. "More than anyone else in ontemporary scenography . . . Svoboda embodies the fusion of rtist, scientist, and professional theatre worker." (Jarka M. Burian, 06)
hoto by Josef Svoboda, National Theatre Scenic Studios (Prague).

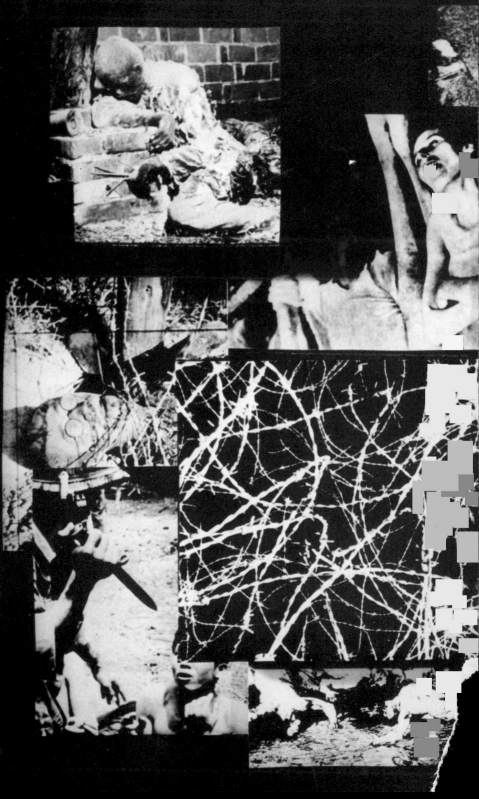

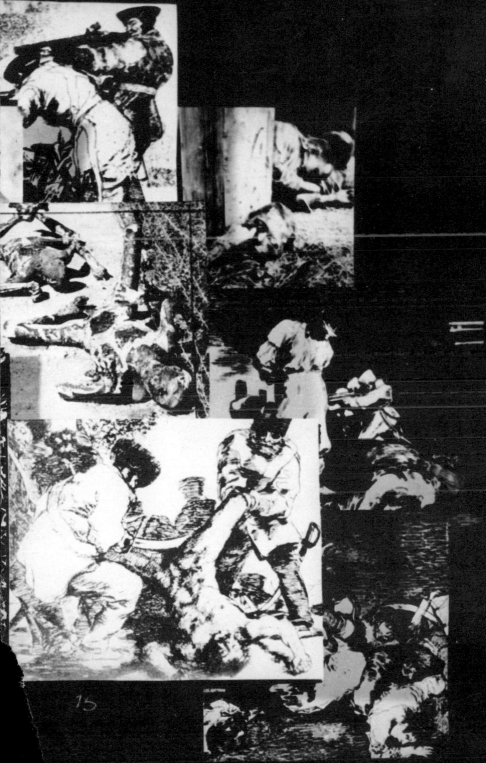

15

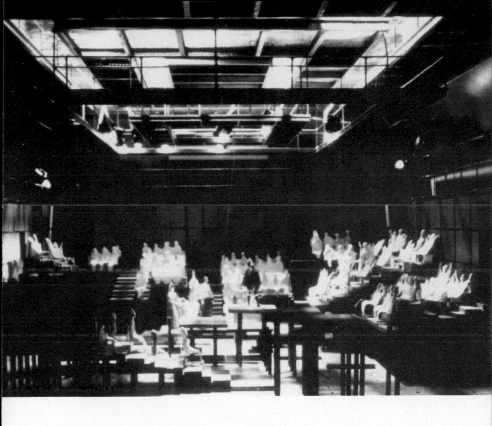

Three variants of The Modular Theatre, designed by Jules Fisher for the California Institute of the Arts. "To begin with, one likes to imagine a space with infinite possibilities that doesn't get in the way — that may even be invisible — but there to be seized upon when the spirit moves." (Herbert Blau, 407)

Marshall Ho'o instructing a class in T'ai Chi Ch'uan at the California Institute of the Arts.

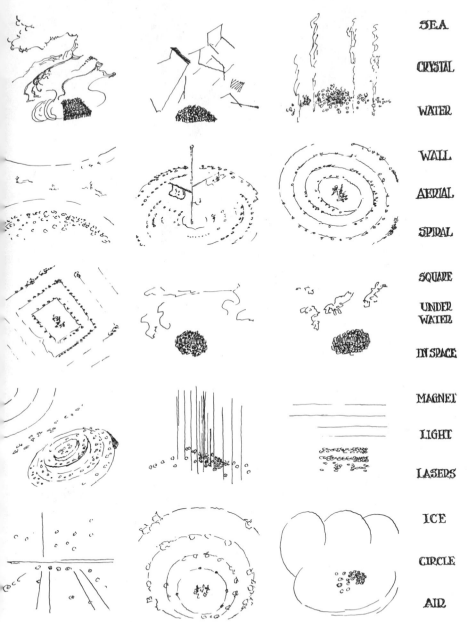

SEA
CRYSTAL
WATER
WALL
AERIAL
SPIRAL
SQUARE
UNDER WATER
IN SPACE
MAGNET
LIGHT
LASERS
ICE
CIRCLE
AIR

Aspects of New Theatre: Environmental conceptions of theatre in relation to nature and science, by Bern Porter.

uals here and there under the total impact and proximity of a feeder (actor) passing perhaps on adjustable stilts, broke out in solo chant, then in choral effects, with soloists cutting up under here and there and so subsiding only to break out in one whole group articulation much as the organist and feeder-actors desired in their prepared plan of the play in progress. Groans, shouts, cries, songs, belches, coughs, appeals arose from the stew causing further auto-suggestion, hypnotism, controlled violent response, shaking the participants, healing and releasing them as image after image in epic form is called up, put over and realized in this three dimensional theatre of idea, aspect, attitude, suggestion and the concrete wherein the extraordinary, the magic, spontaneous redirects ambitions, wills and urges; this spatial language which transforms the mind's version of happenings into events to be perceived, this world of absolute gesture free of written scripts, scored music, dated chorography, theatre noises and props which is the idea itself; this air of perspective in sound, color and movement undulating as a whole throughout the circle with meaning, content and validity.

Obviously this theatre of the spirit, for it was that and more, induced trances, orgiastic releases, mental flushings, emotional washing and other highly desirable internal cleansings which would clear men of hate, lust, greed and war if properly conducted throughout the world. On another level mental disorders of all kinds, physical, psychosomatic ailments were cured, making many forms of medicine and psychiatry unnecessary. Such reported and authenticated observations by competent observers made upon regular attendants to my theatre were of course outside my providence and indeed that of the theatre itself whose first and only objective was to bring people out of themselves and face to face with the reality which was and most certainly out of the stagnation and boredom that engulfed them, i.e., make pure theatre.

As I became more skilled in the composition of spatial scores I added occasional forms of hierographic import, tall masks of suggestion and designed statues which were really devices of hallucination, musical instruments and works or objects of tribal worship, gigantic fetishes and symbols of luck, taxation or death. These devices were employed only with great discretion as the magnitude of the productions enlarged to meet the public demands that eventually obliged me, among other things, to increase the size of the circle, though by preference I had held it to the less than twelve hundred seat capacity. Thus it was that I later succumbed to the repeated howls of the now defunct theatre industry and show business that certainly some kind of stage must evidently be had and so erected at the true center of the circle where the spiral began a small raised space from whose center rose a single mast supported by guys that held an upward rising spiral runway opened and spread out like a leaf at certain levels as it rose to permit the feeders better grip upon the moods of the spectators below and the better to carry the continuous flow of sound, movement and thought throughout the circle.

It was clearly evident to me, however, that the closely knit quality which I had initially desired to achieve was somewhat lost by this aerial quality of coordination, though it also had many features notable for further experiment and retention in part or in full as research continued. The latter work led me to devise a conical pit or inverted cone in the earth, terracing its walls but slightly for the swivel seats placed for passage and turning on all sides and rising spirally from the center from which also rose the supporting mast of the spirally rising and rotating feeder levels for thought transference and idea imparting. As a subsequent concession to the weather I allowed the single masthead to also support a conical roll of aluminum foil cut by plastic lightlocks and air-conditioning directors, until I subsequently eliminated these by manufacturing weather or more correctly making simulated atmospheres which also became part of the spectacle. Approaches to the theatre were marked by the dancing waters device of the German named Brzytawik, the light systems of the Viennese named Planer, the light organs of the Dane Wilfrid coupled with the creations of development found in *sciarch* of my own devisement. Indeed all of these eventually found use directly or in modified adaptation in researches that followed.

Josef Svoboda: Theatre Artist in an Age of Science

JARKA M. BURIAN

As he approaches his fiftieth birthday, Josef Svoboda is in mid-career and at the height of his powers as an architecturally trained stage designer.[1] Although he is without a doubt the most productive, celebrated, and sought after designer in Europe today, he is known in America primarily by vague reputation, which is rather ironic in view of the substantial element of modern technology that he employs in much of his work.[2] A consideration of the main features of his creativity and an account of a few of his most striking scenographic techniques may help to place in perspective the special combination of talents that identify him as a truly distinctive theatre artist in an age of science.

The sheer quantity of his productivity is in itself remarkable: in less than twenty-five years he has designed almost three hundred and fifty productions, roughly split between the operatic and dramatic repertoire, for most of the major theatres of Europe. During much of this same period he has been chief designer and technical director of the National Theatre in Prague, a repertory complex that produces between fifteen and twenty new productions annually and performs an average of thirty different productions monthly. Although he himself designs only three to five productions for the National Theatre annually, he is responsible for all technical and scenic elements on its three stages and supervises the

[1] Svoboda was born on May 10, 1920, in Cáslav, a small city about fifty miles from Prague. His liberal arts education was interrupted by the German occupation in 1939. After the war, he completed a five-year, university-level architectural study in Prague, while concurrently functioning as chief designer of the largest theatre in Prague, the Smetana.

[2] Svoboda has designed one production in the United States: Luigi Nonno's opera, Intoleranza, for the Opera Group of Boston (February 1965). Two other productions failed to materialize: Robert Graves' adaptation of the Iliad for Lincoln Center in 1967, and Strauss's Salomé for the Civic Opera in Chicago, 1968.

activity of the several hundred technical personnel of the theatre and its workshops.

He has, moreover, taught at various times, and is currently Professor of Architecture in the College of Fine and Applied Arts in Prague. Still another branch of his creativity is his exhibition work at major international expositions. At Brussels, in 1958, for example, he won three medals for his work displayed in the Czechoslovak pavilion, and his several kinetic and film projects were among the most popular attractions at Expo 67, Montreal. Other international honors have included the gold medal award of the Sao Paolo Biennale in international stage design (1961), an honorary doctorate from England's Royal College of Art (1969), and the Sikkens Prize of the Netherlands in architecture (1969), a previous winner of which was LeCorbusier.

Although Svoboda's name is chiefly associated with a full-scale exploitation for stage purposes of the latest mechanical, electronic, and optical devices (many of which he has developed himself), with the so-called kinetic stage, and with wide-ranging use of sophisticated lighting and projection techniques (including new theatrical forms uniting film and stage), the role of the technical in his scenography is slightly ambivalent and requires elucidation. It is true that he welcomes the contribution of the latest techniques and devices and is able to derive maximum benefit from them, but their use or non-use is really not essential. Underlying his scenography is a basic pragmatism:

> What is essential is the approach to the job: I would be delighted to create a setting of *cheese* if it best suited the play. You have to use expressive means that precisely fit the production concept. And that's where the true beauty of my work lies, for me.*

Nevertheless, forming the background of Svoboda's scenography, both at its boldest and its simplest, is his profound, scrupu-

* Mr. Burian's research included a number of tape-recorded interviews with Mr. Svoboda. This citation and those that follow marked with an asterisk (*) are taken from those interviews.

lous respect for the frequently painstaking technical experiment
and research that precede its ultimate appearance before the public. Many critics and artists sincerely believe that science, technology, and systemization are inherently hostile to art and creativity.
Svoboda is emphatically not of their number. He has, if anything,
a rage for order, for precision, for the laws that define his work
because, as he puts it, "it means that the given element has been
mastered and can be used as an instrument."* His feelings about
music are significant in this respect:

> I admire its order, its purity, its cleanness—this is what I
> would like to establish in scenography. I know it's impossible
> but at least I want to aim for it. I'd like to eliminate dilettan-
> tism and make theatre truly professional. I've been pursuing
> an ideal for twenty-five years: precision, systemization, perfec-
> tion, and control of the expressive means available to scenog-
> raphy, even the ordinary means. Why shouldn't this age make
> the most of its technical developments as previous eras did?
> that is, the machinery of the baroque era, the electric light at
> the turn of the century.*

Offsetting what may seem to be an excessive preoccupation with
the technical in such statements, especially when they are taken
out of context, is Svoboda's more characteristic observation that
the technical is solely a means: "My dream would be not to have it
there; but I have to use it now because certain things would not
otherwise be possible. In five years there may be other means and
other results."* Perhaps most directly to the point is Svoboda's
simplest assertion, "Knowledge of the technical makes creativity
possible."*

Trying to classify Svoboda's scenographic mode as primarily
symbolistic, constructivistic, expressionistic, or even illusionistic, is
ultimately a fruitless exercise. The fact is that his work exhibits
instances of each of these modes as well as combinations of them.
Svoboda's comment is characteristic: "Style is a matter of solving
each work by the given conditions, which means not only consideration of the specific author, but also the given director, the theatre
building itself, the main actor or actors: each element is unique,

and you have to consider the features special to each one. Theatre is a synthetic, componential phenomenon that ideally needs balancing—if it's short here, say in acting, you add there, in the scenography—or the opposite."* . . . Central to Svoboda's use of projection techniques in whatever form are his theatrically oriented concerns with space and synthesis: "We in theatre are constantly aware of space, and we can enhance it by many means, whereas film can only transcribe space. In fact, in theatre we can enhance space by the use of film; that's why theatre is the art of greatest synthesis."[3]

Of the two primary projection systems or forms devised by Svoboda, Laterna Magika and Polyekran, the latter is relatively simpler, and although its evolution is difficult to disentangle from that of Laterna Magika, it was Polyekran that contributed to the final form of Laterna Magika, rather than the other way round, according to both Svoboda and Alfred Radok, Svoboda's creative partner. For these reasons, Polyekran (literally, "multi-screen") will be described first.

Polyekran, one of Svoboda's contributions to the Brussels World's Fair of 1958, is fundamentally a pure projection form; it is not combined with live acting or scenic elements. Its origin was related to Svoboda's response to the development of various wide-screen techniques of the 1950's; in contrast to such techniques, all of which attempted to eliminate the impression of a screen and to give the spectator the sensation of being part of the picture, Polyekran deliberately emphasizes the presence of the screen, or, rather, screens. Its principle is a simultaneous and synchronous projection of slides and film on several screens during which the images on the individual screens are in dramatic interplay with each other in the creation of a total, organic composition. Svoboda adds:

> Polyekran offers the possibility of free composition, a free shaping and creation on several screens. Images of real objects

[3] Svoboda, quoted in "Entretien sur la Laterne Magique," *Théatre en Tchecoslovaquie,* ed. V. Jindra (Prague, 1962), p. 53f.

and people are projected, but the relationships among them are not realistic, but rather supra-realistic, perhaps surrealistic. Essentially, it's the principle of abstract and pure collage, which is an old and basic technique of theatre. "Op art" is perhaps simply a more recent name for it. In any case, the contrast of varied things on stage is basic to theatre; the objects thereby acquire new relationships and significance, a new and different reality.*

Technically, the elements of the Brussels productions consisted of seven screens of different size and shape suspended at different angles from horizontal steel wires in front of a black velvet backdrop. Eight automatic slide projectors and seven film projectors, synchronously controlled by electronic tape, threw images upon these screens. The visual collage was accompanied by stereophonic sound (also carried on the electronic tape), the total ten-minute performance being thematically unified by its depiction of the context of the annual Prague Spring Music Festival.

In describing the relation between Polyekran and Laterna Magika, Svoboda says:

> In comparison with Polyekran, which is totally a film spectacle and technically a concern of film, Laterna Magika is theatre with living actors, singers, dancers, musicians. . . . On the one hand we used familiar scenographic techniques such as slides and film projection. New expressive possibilities were added by panoramic film and projection with multi-exposure on several screens at once. A second feature is the use of mobile screens that are joined to the performance of a live actor.[4]

Commenting on the essential non-autonomy of each medium, film and living actor, in Laterna Magika, Svoboda added, "The play of the actors cannot exist without the film, and vice-versa— they become one thing, a synthesis and fusion of actors and projection. Moreover, the same actors appear on stage and screen, and interact with each other. The film has a dramatic function."*

⁴ Svoboda, quoted in "O světelném divadle," *Informační Zprávy Scenografické Laboratoře* (Sept. 1958), p. 5.

Laterna Magika becomes, in effect, a new, hybrid medium the potential force and expressiveness of which are perhaps suggested best in some remarks by Marshall McLuhan made without reference to Laterna Magika, when he spoke of "true hybrid energy": "The hybrid or the meeting of two media is a moment of truth and revelation from which new form is born.... The moment of the meeting of media is a moment of freedom and release from the ordinary trance and numbness imposed on them by our senses."[5]

Like Polyekran, Laterna Magika was devised for the Brussels Fair of 1958, where it enjoyed a spectacular success. It consisted of three film and two slide projectors, synchronously controlled, plus a device that enabled deflection of one projection beam to any desired spot, including a moving screen. In a stage space measuring approximately 50' x 24' x 20' were arranged eight mobile screens with special, highly directional reflecting surfaces; they could rise, fall, move to the side, fold up, rotate, appear and disappear in precise rhythm with the actors. The stage itself was provided with a moving belt and special scissor traps to accommodate the need for virtually instantaneous live action in response to the film. One of the screens, moveover, was equipped with a diaphragmatic framing curtain that could alter both the size and shape of the screen. And the total presentation was enhanced by multi-speaker stereophonic sound.

Jan Grossman, himself a theatre director as well as a critic in Prague, was involved with the theoretical groundwork of Laterna Magika; his remarks on the new form elaborate some of its potentials:

> Laterna Magika offered the dramatist, film scenarist, poet, and composer a new language: a language that is more intense, sharply contrasting, and rhythmic; one which can captivatingly project statistics as well as ballet, documents as well as lyric verse, and is therefore capable of absorbing and artis-

[5] McLuhan, *Understanding Media* (New York, 1966), p. 55.

tically working over the density and dynamics, the multiplicity and contrariety of the world in which we live."[6]

Alfred Radok, director of Laterna Magika, suggested its special quality in this way: "Above all, Laterna Magika has the capacity of seeing reality from several aspects. Of 'extracting' a situation or individual from the routine context of time and place and apprehending it in some other fashion, perhaps by confronting it with a chronologically distinct event."[7]

That Laterna Magika was not without its special problems, however, became evident even while it was experiencing its greatest success. For example, the filmed portions had to be prepared far in advance of their integration with the live performers, which meant that many artistic decisions had to be made and became binding long before there was any way of knowing how they might work out months later. A more profound problem was that the film virtually enslaved the live performer, whose margin of variability in performance approached zero because the film was a prefabricated element to which the performer must inflexibly adapt. Svoboda put it this way: "It means that Laterna Magika is to a certain extent deprived of that which is beautiful about theatre: that each performance can have a completely different rhythm, that the quality of a performance can be better or worse, that a production can expand its limits."[8]

Again, on a more fundamental level, Laterna Magika never experienced the ultimate test of presenting a work that was written especially for it; that is, a work other than revue or cabaret entertainment. In its original version, as an entertaining propaganda piece for Czechoslovakia, it was a success. Its original creators had hopes of eventually using the form for Shakespeare or explorations

[6] Grossman, "O kombinace divadla a filmu," *Laterna Magika,* ed. J. Hrbas (Prague, 1968), p. 76.

[7] Radok, quoted by Grossman, p. 77.

[8] Svoboda, "Problémy scény Laterny Magiky," *Laterna Magika,* p. 103. Svoboda managed to overcome this problem to some extent in a few subsequent productions by employing live TV transmission onto screens during the course of the performance: e.g., Nonno's *Intoleranza* (Boston, 1965) and Orff's *Prometheus* (Munich, 1968).

of challenging contemporary realities, for example the Eichmann case, but managerial and administrative elements viewed Laterna Magika in terms of economics and politics, as a source of profit and an instrument of propaganda, with the result that its subsequent artistic career was aborted; its several sequels rarely rose above tourist level entertainment.

One other noteworthy and recent variant of Svoboda's projection techniques is the Diapolyekran system, which had its first public exposure at the Montreal Expo '67 as a ten-minute feature entitled *The Creation of the World*. It, too, employs a multi-screen, multi-projection (only slides) technique reminiscent of Polyekran in its pure film, non-actor features, but in a tighter, shallower, and more stable form. As the illustration suggests, the projection screens form a wall composed of cubes, one hundred and twelve in all. Each cube has two automatic slide projectors mounted at its rear, capable of flashing five images per second, even though the actual rate was considerably slower; a total of thirty thousand slides were used, and the whole operation was computerized. Moreover, each cube was capable of sliding forward or backward approximately twelve inches, thus providing a surface in kinetic relief for the projections. The basic technique is of course a collage or montage that allows for a great range of visual effects: the entire wall of cubes may unite to present one total, conventionally coherent picture, or else literally disintegrate that picture into fragments, or, indeed, present a surrealistic collage of disparate images. And all of this occurs in a dynamic, rhythmic flow ideally suited to projecting *process* as well as startling, abrupt confrontation. The original presentation was an eloquent, sensitive expression of wonder at the miracle and mystery of creation, evolution, and civilization.

Within a year after the introduction of Laterna Magika and Polyekran at Brussels, Svoboda began to apply their techniques to conventional theatre production. Polyekran became the basic scenographic principle in the National Theatre's production of a new Czech play, Josef Topol's *Their Day* (October 1959). The play, a study of the aspirations and disenchantments of youth in the late 1950's, was notable for its impressionistic, episodic manner.

In Brussels, the Polyekran system was based on fixed, stable screens; in *Their Day*, Svoboda added a Laterna Magika technique: mobile screens that appear and disappear in rhythmic connection with the movement of other scenic elements; namely, three specially prepared stage wagons that transport scenic objects such as furniture and properties. The basic principle, however, remained that of Polyekran, this time nine screens distributed in space,in different planes, with two slide projectors covering each screen; three of the screens, moveover, had film projectors assigned to them; the result was a great flexibility in the choice and blending of pictures at will. Svoboda's subsequent remarks on the production point up its chief characteristics:

> Why Polyckran for this production? The play presents a mosaic of city life, a mosaic that evolves with the action of the play. We deliberately avoided a simultaneous scene because you can't get rid of its scenic elements when you don't want them, no matter how sharp the lighting. Besides, here we wanted changes in the dimensions of space as well as rapid shifts of scene. Because we could project various images at various angles, we could create space and spatial relations at will. My essential point in using projections is the creating of new stage space, not as a substitute for decor or establishing a locale. We could use all the screens or only one, not merely to describe a locale, but to establish different relations. The result is real psycho-plastic space created by transforming the dimensions of space in response to the nature of the scene. The basis is a confrontation of selected realities: actions, objects, people, plus the accenting of things. For example, an object or projection functions and then disappears, very much like the film techniques of cutting and transitional blending. The method is essentially more persuasive, because more theatrical, than all the painted sets and usual stage constructions. The larger point is the creation of a total instrument to be used on stage like a concert piano. I've been pursuing this goal for twenty years. Krejča [the director of *Their Day*] says that

so far it's an instrument that can only play a child's nursery tunes. But eventually it may be much more. I think, for example, that *The Last Ones* and *The Soldiers* show progress. We must keep on learning to play the instrument.*

The Last Ones, a dramatization of a Gorki novel produced by the National Theatre in Prague (September 1966) under the direction of Alfred Radok, gave particular satisfaction to Svoboda. It was the first work he had done with Radok in several years, and it featured, in Svoboda's words, "a revision, a refinement of Laterna Magika."

The Last Ones indicts a whole era and regime in depicting a family dominated by a tyrannical, insecure career officer. The deterioration of values, the shabbiness of life, the compromises and stupidities, the cruelties inflicted and endured, all of these social deformations are mirrored, with frequent irony, in the family's material and spiritual bankruptcy. The inherent duality of the subject, the family and its larger social frame, blended superbly with the modified Laterna Magika form, the very nature of which is rooted in a juxtaposition and interplay of elements: the dramatic integration or counterpoint of screened image and live actor, of the same character on film and on stage, and the powerful, implicitly ironic comment of the one on the other.

Svoboda's observations on the production suggest its significance for him:

> In effect, we rehabilitated the Laterna Magika principle after its discreditation by business interests. [Svoboda refers to its use in connection with commercial enterprises.] This production expressed our credo, an honest application of Laterna Magika, with certain changes and the addition of new techniques. Originally, Laterna Magika operated with a lateral format of images and stage action, but in *The Last Ones* we changed this to a depth principle in order to create a cumulative effect, to increase the impact rather than disperse it, to intensify. We stacked things, people, scenes behind each other; for example, action around the wheel-chair downstage, above that a girl in a tub being stroked by twigs, "in front" of

her a boy being flogged on the screen; then, suddenly, a drape covering part of the screen opens and we see a small, live orchestra playing a waltz, with pomp—an image of the regime. A space collage using a tryptich principle, truly a dramatic poem—what I want to do. A clear spatial aesthetic is formed by the contrast of stage action, flat projection, and live orchestra behind the screen on which the images are projected. It's all structured like music, and a law is present. Break it and a new one is set up. This is what attracts me— leitmotifs and repetitions, then sudden contrast; plus tempo indications. Themes disappear only to crop up again later. Radok is especially good at this. Why the crumpled projection screen? I wanted to prove that you *can* project on a relief surface with a depth of more than fifteen centimeters and create the effect of a smooth surface; and then, too, the surface at other times suggests the deteriorated conditions depicted by the play.*

The Soldiers, a contemporary German opera by Zimmermann that had its premiere in Munich (March 1969), is the latest product in the evolution of the Polyekran and Diapolyekran forms; it follows the latter more closely in that its screens are, with one dramatic exception, immobile and rather tightly clustered together in parallel planes. They depart from the Diapolyekran model, however, in being far fewer (thirteen), much larger (up to 18' × 12'), and in several planes. Another distinctive feature is the placement of two box-like spaces in the midst of the screens; spaces which may be used as interior acting areas or curtained off to form two screens. Rear projection is employed on all of the screens, and the two acting areas just mentioned have front projections as well. Black and white slides form the basis of projection, with film projection being available for three of the screens.

A striking example of the evolutionary process in Svoboda's creative work with a given form is the kinetic variant of the Diapolyekran principle employed at the climax of the opera: the total cluster of the screens literally disintegrates, the screens separating from one another and moving offstage. As they sink below stage level, rise up out of sight, or move off laterally, a huge, futuristic "war machine" grinds forward toward the footlights, accompanied by a pulsating, increasingly blinding light and ear shattering dissonant music:

> With the help of improved instruments and materials, and with new placement and composition of the screens, I was able to create a concentrated, massive visual impact, a collage of military life from Rome to the Franco-Prussian war in confrontation with World War II and Vietnam. Especially effective was the juxtaposition of Goya's etchings with photographs depicting intolerance and martyrdom today. The sheer size of the stage and auditorium [the Munich Staatsoper] was another factor: aiming at psycho-plastic space, I designed everything with the proportions of the theatre in mind.*

What is especially interesting is that Svoboda does not feel that he has yet found the right dramaturgic material for the Diapolyekran system: "The form has yet to be employed with a congenial artistic-poetic text, at least not in the same sense that other forms or devices reached full realization, for example the use of mirrors in *Insect Comedy*, or Laterna Magika in *The Last Ones*."*

Perhaps the most sophisticated use that Svoboda has made of the combination of stage and projected human image occurred in the Munich production of Carl Orff's opera, *Prometheus* (August 1968), for which Svoboda made striking employment of live, closed circuit television as a source of projection. Svoboda himself described the problem as he saw it, as well as part of his solution:

> The chief problem in any production of *Prometheus* is that the protagonist is immobilized for two and a half hours while discussion dominates action. There is real danger of boredom, even when, as in this case, fine music is involved; the problem is how to express the music. Orff's music conveyed an image of metal to me, resonant metal planes and angles. I recalled the principle of steps that I used in a production of *Oedipus* ... I adapted it here, covering the steps with a metallic surface. But I added a notch in the top of the stairs, and a diamond shaped, piston-like shaft, some fifty feet long, that

rested in the notch, the front surface of the shaft presenting a rock-like metal surface to which Prometheus is nailed. . . . I used projections on the stairs and the rock, the surface of which was rusted, oxidized, textured. But the main device was the use of live television to project an enlarged image of Prometheus' face onto the very surface of the rock to which he was nailed. In other words, we saw Prometheus "in" the image of his face, thereby providing tremendous emphasis to his torment. We used the technique at special moments only, for maximum impact.*

Common to all of the projection forms here briefly discussed, as well as to virtually all of Svoboda's work, is a vivid sense of separate elements imaginatively combined to express new insights into reality. It is a principle that may take a variety of forms, including, for example, cubism, especially as defined in the following remarks by Marshall McLuhan, remarks that suggest yet another aspect of Svoboda's work:

> Instead of the specialized illusion of the third dimension, cubism sets up an interplay of planes and contradictions or dramatic conflict of patterns, lights, textures . . . [It] drops the illusion of perspective in favor of instant awareness of the whole . . . Is it not evident that the moment that sequence yields to the simultaneous, one is in the world of the structure and of configuration?[9]

. . . Svoboda's scenography bears obvious kinship to that of such giants of modern theatre theory and practise as Appia, Craig, and Piscator, as well as the Soviet avant-garde of the twenties. Nevertheless, such comparison requires qualification in order to define the essential features of his talent. He is less of a theoretical visionary than either Appia or Craig but surpasses them in his mastery of sophisticated materials and techniques as well as in sheer practical experience. Although many of his productions recall the emphasis on scenic dynamics and stage-as-mechanism evident in the early post-revolutionary work of the Soviet theatri-

[9] McLuhan, p. 13.

calists, Meyerhold and Tairov, Svoboda's greater technical sophistication and more suggestive approach provide a richer, more emotive experience. Similarly, although some of his most audacious work in the fusion of film and stage relates to the earlier work of Piscator, he has carried the work to a much higher, more complex level that amounts to the creation of a new, hybrid medium combining actor and screened image.

More than anyone else in contemporary scenography (one is tempted to say, *uniquely*), Svoboda embodies a fusion of artist, scientist, and professional theatre worker. Technically a master of his complex medium, and thoroughly conversant with the realities of theatre production—the pressure of deadlines, budgets, personnel supervision, and inter-artistic cooperation—he is above all a superb theatre artist whose approach to each production challenge is that of a poet in its exercise of creative imagination applied to the fundamentals of space, light, and movement.

The Modular Theatre: A Premise

HERBERT BLAU

If you thrust a stage out at an audience or surround an audience by a stage, you are not automatically back in the Sacred Grove. Yet new stages *are* new ideas, and transformed space may, like painting or music, turn on an actor as a play itself really can't. It may even turn on a new play. A really new space will solicit the imagination to exceed itself. Something extraordinary happens in the theater when there is a mortal exchange between a play and a playing space, each testing the other's limits. But actually, it's space we're talking about and not a stage, since we've moved into an era of staging where the whole environment performs. To begin with, however, one likes to imagine a space with infinite possibilities that doesn't get in the way,—that may even be invisible but there to be seized when the spirit moves.

Some Random Notes on the Design of The Modular Theatre

JULES FISHER

I have designed a space that can be neutral. By this I mean as free of conventional forms as possible: blank wall, a blank floor. If you want a door on a wall, you can decide where it should be, not only left or right, but above the floor at any height. Most important is that this is a decision: to have a door or not to, and to start anew with the question, "What for?" In this neutral space, it may be easier to search for the invisible.

When you begin to design a space for a play in the Modular Theatre, you approach a neutral rectangular room, darkly colored, with a flat floor, a level balcony area that extends back from the top of the walls and a ceiling equipped for lighting and the flying of scenery. Within a fixed modular pattern, you may express designs upon this space in the following manner:

The floor is actually a grid pattern of four-foot squares, six-inch-high platforms finished in battleship linoleum. Any one, a combination of many, or all the platforms can be raised above the floor ("zero"). At any height, the platform can be considered a seating platform, an aisle, a stage or a piece of scenery. As a seating platform, a single unit of two seats is fastened to the platform, facing in one of four directions. In addition, the seats swivel freely for greater freedom of sightline orientation. It is possible to set up the seating in countless combinations with or without any degree of pitch or rake. Since everything sets up without tools, you have the freedom to change the format as often as you wish.

The walls on all four sides of the room consist of four-foot square doors hinged on one side and removable. The walls are five doors high and the room has a total of 320 doors. The doors are mounted on vertical columns eight feet apart so that a four-foot or an eight-foot opening can be created. By removing any two doors, one above the other, a doorway is created. This gives the designer/director/playwright the freedom to decide where an entrance shall be made, not only around the room, but vertically as well. If one chooses to have an actor enter from a 12′ height on the middle of the east wall, the appropriate two doors are removed, the platforms, with step units on top, are raised ten feet in front and behind the wall and the actor makes his appearance.

The balcony level, 20′ high, runs around the perimeter of the room. This can be used for lighting, scenery, and acting. Above the entire space is a gridiron ceiling with remotely operated, synchronous winches. A number of three-dimensional objects can be raised and lowered in the theatre at varying speeds simultaneously. Built into the grid is a pattern of catwalks designed for optimum lighting flexibility. Specific outlets and positions have been provided throughout the room for the use of projected scenery devices. Front and rear screen projections are possible anywhere in the theatre. Mounted on the underside of the catwalks are house-lights that can be circuited to conform to any seating pattern created on the floor below. Doors, lights, flying apparatus, levels: all conventional theatre elements, except they may be put together unconventionally.

This space is not to be a "Theatre Building." It is simply a room—a six sided space that is a "tinker-toy." The elements have been stripped of ornament, essential shapes to be put together to help express ideas. The reason for providing "given elements" at all is not to waste time in gathering the building blocks together to create the conditions one needs to make communication possible

I see the educational theatre today not only educating and training practitioners of an existing craft, but allowing the artist to discover the forms that will lift the art beyond today to something universal and ecstatic.

A Note On The Designs For The
New Trinity Square Reperatory Company

EUGENE LEE

I've designed a large space which is not sterile, with acoustical considerations—it will be a space-in-flux . . . One is bored with the constant limitation of five hundred seats screwed to the floor . . . In André Gergory's *Alice In Wonderland,* which my wife and I designed, you're engrossed in watching it. No matter where it was produced, it was designed to have an intimate focus, a sense of personal humor and madness . . . Modular, technological theatre is a mistake. You can fly anything any place. What a bore. Theatre doesn't want the machines of the Metropolitan Opera ("Send down for Scene 2") The most successful solutions are the simple solutions . . . I would like to do what Grotowski does on a big scale. Start with a specific space—if people want to sit, let them. There should be things for everyone, maybe different places to stand and sit when you feel like it . . . There are two general points of view about theatre. The technologists, like George Izenour, believe that you can change everything mechanically. The other point of view is that you start with a neutral space. The production should develop out of space. For example, Peter Brook liked the Chelsea Theatre Center in Brooklyn where I've designed a good deal because it's a kind of neutral space to begin with . . . When you start in a neutral space, the birth looks like something when it's born. Then you can start molding it . . . It's hard to talk about the space in Trinity Square's new theatre because we're trying to avoid the restrictions of a definite space. No extravagant money poured into expensive exteriors with a lack of interior space like many expensive modern theatres. Just an old American dream-film theatre, with its vast interior space re-arranged and available for two theatres. What we want is a theatre that when we know what the production is, we know how the space will work. . . .

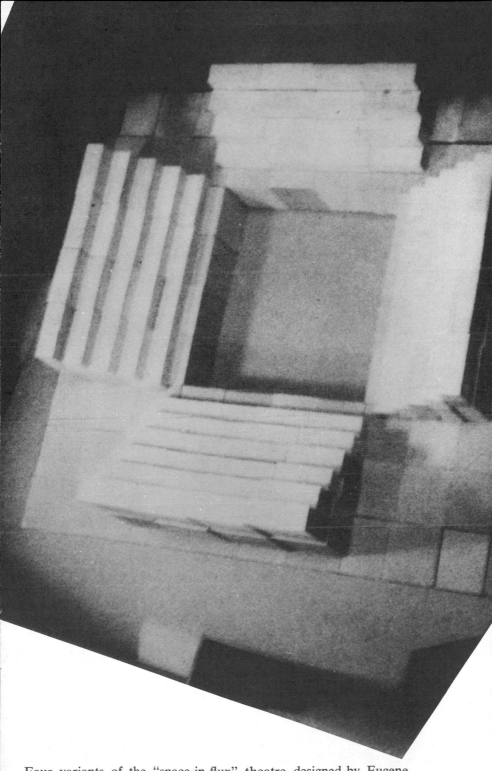

Four variants of the "space-in-flux" theatre designed by Eugene
Lee for the Trinity Square Repertory Company.

Acknowledgments

"At Night" copyright © 1968 by Boleslaw Taborski. From the book *Theatre Notebook* 1947-1967 by Jan Kott. Reprinted by permission of Doubleday & Company (New York) and The Methuen Company, Ltd. (London).

State Office Building Curse copyright © 1970 by Ed Bullins. First published in *The Drama Review*, Volume 14 no. 4 (September 1970). All rights reserved.

The Jig Is Up copyright © by Lawrence Ferlinghetti. From the book *Routines* by Lawrence Ferlinghetti. Reprinted by permission of New Directions Publishing Corporation.

"A Panel Discussion . . ." copyright © 1969 by The San Francisco Mime Troupe, Inc. Reprinted from the pamphlet *Radical Theatre Festival*.

"Street Scene" from *Brecht on Theatre*, edited and translated by John Willett. Copyright © 1957, 1963, 1964 by Suhrkamp Verlag (Frankfurt am Main). This translation and notes copyright © 1964 by John Willett. Reprinted by permission of Hill and Wang and The Methuen Company, Ltd.

The Red Morning copyright © by Jean-Pierre Bisson. First pub-